Franciscan Writings

Franciscan Writings

Hope amid Ecological Sin and Climate Emergency

Dawn M. Nothwehr

t&tclark

T&T CLARK
Bloomsbury Publishing Plc
50 Bedford Square, London, WC1B 3DP, UK
1385 Broadway, New York, NY 10018, USA
29 Earlsfort Terrace, Dublin 2, Ireland

BLOOMSBURY, T&T CLARK and the T&T Clark logo
are trademarks of Bloomsbury Publishing Plc

First published in Great Britain 2023

Copyright © Dawn M. Nothwehr, 2023

Dawn M. Nothwehr has asserted her right under the Copyright, Designs and Patents Act, 1988, to be identified as Author of this work.

Cover design: Tjasa Krivec
Cover photo: Used with permission, Mayo Foundation for Medical Education and Research, 2022. All rights reserved
Cover photographer: Matthew Meyer

All rights reserved. No part of this publication may be reproduced or transmitted in any form or by any means, electronic or mechanical, including photocopying, recording, or any information storage or retrieval system, without prior permission in writing from the publishers.

Bloomsbury Publishing Plc does not have any control over, or responsibility for, any third-party websites referred to or in this book. All internet addresses given in this book were correct at the time of going to press. The author and publisher regret any inconvenience caused if addresses have changed or sites have ceased to exist, but can accept no responsibility for any such changes.

A catalogue record for this book is available from the British Library.

A catalog record for this book is available from the Library of Congress.

ISBN: HB: 978-0-5676-9916-9
PB: 978-0-5676-9914-5
ePDF: 978-0-5676-9915-2
eBook: 978-0-5676-9917-6

Typeset by Integra Software Services Pvt. Ltd.

To find out more about our authors and books visit www.bloomsbury.com and sign up for our newsletters.

*With gratitude to the
Sisters of St. Francis,
Congregation of Our Lady of Lourdes
Rochester, Minnesota
especially
S. Ingrid J. Peterson, OSF
S. Ramona Miller, OSF
S. Margaret Pirkl, OSF
and
Friars of the Sacred Heart Province
and Colleagues
at
Catholic Theological Union, Chicago
Zachary Hayes, OFM
Thomas A. Nairn, OFM
Gilberto Cavazos-González, OFM*

Contents

Preface ix

Part I The Bible: Hope in Creation through the Word

Introduction: A Phenomenology of Hope— Abrahamic Religions in Harmony with Complexity Science 3

1 **Hopeful Hebrew Testament Stories of Original Creation and Covenants** 22

2 **Hopeful Christian Testament Stories of a New Creation and Covenant** 44

Part II St. Francis and St. Clare: Models of Faith and Sustainable Living

3 **St. Francis of Assisi—From Birdbath to Patron Saint to Papal Encyclical** 69

4 **Wisdom from St. Clare of Assisi for a "Climate Emergency"** 93

Part III From Vernacular Theology to Scholastic Theology

5 St. Bonaventure of Bagnoregio—Creator, Christ, Creatures, Cosmos 115

6 Bl. John Duns Scotus—Sacred Subtle Thoughts Concerning Creation 136

Part IV Ecological Vocation: What Is Ours to Do?

7 Anthropogenic Climate Change: A Leper Awaiting Our Embrace 159

8 Wholly of Water—Water and a Sacramental Universe 187

9 Eating Is a Moral Act—Access to Food and Food Security 214

10 Freedom from Fossil Fuels—Financing Family 251

Afterword: Franciscan Hope amid Ecological Sin and a "Climate Emergency" 281

Bibliography 284
Index 299

Preface

A Personal Note

It was a quiet late May evening in Windom—my small southwestern Minnesota hometown. Having finished planting our large vegetable garden, I sat with my mother on the back steps of our three-bedroom stucco house, sipping ice-cold lemonade. The newly planted garden was but a short distance away. The air was moist with the scent of the recently turned soil, seasoned with wisps of sweetness from the freshly mown grass and the piney scent from the tall spruce trees artfully placed about the yard.

Through the lacy pine branches, the late evening sky signaled the day's impending end with shades of pinkish red orange and contrasting shades of gray. A soft high-pitched insect chorus lulled us into restful meditation. Then, spontaneously harmonizing with that peaceful flow, came my mother's words: "Only God can make the garden grow." Those faith-filled words stirred up something deep within me, but my twelve-year-old self could not name it, so I just held them in silence for many years.

Indeed, my adolescent *persona* required a certain amount of rebellion at being "forced" to help weed, tend, and harvest the garden produce. Yet, secretly, I loved working in the garden. I was quite awestruck by the fact that you could put this hard, flat, little yellow thing in the ground and, weeks later, you could find a sweetcorn plant in its place! It was only some thirty years later that I would be able to name what had so deeply moved me that evening.

Years later, on my twenty-fifth jubilee as a Sister of St. Francis, I had the privilege of going on a pilgrimage to Assisi, Italy, and the region of Umbria, the "Franciscan Holy Land," where St. Francis and St. Clare lived. As we journeyed from place to place, no one could miss the lush verdancy of the fertile fields of sunflowers and the vineyards covering the rolling hills. Those striking vistas combined with St. Francis' *Canticle of the Creatures* reawakened my many "garden experiences" and the profound sense of awe and wonder I experienced that evening with my mother. Like me, but in their own time and place, St. Francis and St. Clare came to know well what

I had only tasted on that late May evening—the vestiges of an incarnate God cradling them in love and mercy in the miraculous, lush nest of creation!

For about thirty years I lived in Chicago. Though there are many conveniences to city life, I always had a real love–hate relationship with those environs. Everything is huge, impersonal, paved over, fast paced, human built, constantly in motion, competitive—often violent. For me, the "saving grace" was the park system that abuts Lake Michigan. There, some semblance of intimacy with the web of life pervaded amid trees, grass, flowers, open sky; people smiled and greeted one another; and Lake Michigan stretched out to the horizon, while the rhythm of the waves lapping against the sands of extensive beaches set the tone and pace of more peaceful living. The manifestations of the sacred there are quite distinct from those found in all the cavernous cathedrals that dot street corners of that sprawling metropolis. Yes, St. Francis was definitely "on to something!" The vestiges of the incarnate God can be seen all around us—if we not only look but open our eyes to see!

The Sacrament of Creation and Ecological Conversion

Franciscan scholar, Ingrid J. Peterson, OSF, noted that Franciscan spirituality "is sacramental in that all created things are also seen as signs pointing to God as Creator."[1] St. Francis knew this—as we can today—by observing the beauty and splendor of the natural world and through the loving ways we touch each other's lives. But Giovanni Francesco di Bernardone was not always so aware! In fact, in his youth he was a carousing, spoiled brat of an up-and-coming cloth merchant, who went off to war as a knight in the Crusades hoping to gain fame and fortune! He soon discovered, however, that none of that met his deepest heart's desire. It was only after he embraced a leper and did a 360 degree about-face on his life's journey that he found what he was looking for.

What he had been trashing in his early life was the reality that it is in truly caring for people and God's creation that there is potential to arrive where he most desired to go—to the very heart of God. Carousing, war-making, seeking fame and fortune, the use and abuse of people and creation were ultimately desperate diversions leading him away from his deepest longings for intimacy with God, people, and all creation. So it was, finally, through joining his intuition and his appreciation of the beauty of the Umbrian landscape with God's grace, that Giovanni Francesco di Bernardone became St. Francis of Assisi.

To Follow in the Footprints

Francis' deepest desire was to "follow in the footprints of Jesus." But why "in the footprints" (and not footsteps)? There is an intimacy to be found in attempting to place one's foot into the impression of another's footprint. In practical terms, a footprint leaves a barefooted, distinctive mark of a human person on some material object. Forensic scientists can learn a lot from studying footprints: a person's approximate height (a foot is about 15 percent the length of a person's height) or their weight—depending on the size and depth of the impression. Footprints have characteristics that are unique to each person: creases, flatness, horizontal or vertical ridges, or other deformities.

While Francis was no forensic scientist, he knew that footprints marked the physical presence of a person in a particular time and place. Attempting to place one's foot in the footprints of another requires careful attention to the original form, and thus one needs to learn something about the author of those impressions. Also, by following footprints, one most likely would eventually encounter the one who made them. For Francis, the "footprints of Jesus" symbolized the reality of the Incarnation—Jesus, the "Word made flesh"; the One who came to dwell among us, as one of us! It was that intuition that attracted Francis. Jesus is, indeed, the pattern and model for our life in God and with all others *in this world*. And because Jesus became part of this material world, everything and everyone is now deified, made whole, holy, and sacramental. Just as a painting or a sculpture reveals something of the artist who created it—so, too, everything in the cosmos speaks to us of God.

Therefore, to walk in his footprints is to touch something of Jesus, the human expression of God. Francis found the footprints of Jesus as the tiny feet of the Babe of Bethlehem—the Incarnation. He saw profound love through the prints of Christ's nail-pierced feet on the cross—the Redemption. In the Eucharistic bread and wine Francis recognized the footprints of Christ's earthly journey—life sifted, refined, and poured out for us, and desiring to remain intimately present to us and within us. And, most clearly in the Sacred Scriptures, the many footprints of Jesus the Word entice, inspire, instruct, console, and empower us, marking our pathway to rich and wholesome living.

Following in the footprints of Jesus requires that we be attentive and attuned to the world with all our senses, for they are our point of contact with reality. The best way we can keep in touch with the creative Word is to also remain in touch with this world—sights, sounds, smells, tastes, stories, symbols, concepts, encounters with the Sacraments, or human rituals. In these ways, humans come to recognize they are part of the created universe and continually renew and restore their relationships with each other, God, and the entire cosmos. Christ, as the firstborn of all creation, stands at the center of all of this (Col. 1: 15-20).

Incarnate Jesus and Cosmic Christ

Jesus is at the heart of history, but he is also the transcendent Christ who is divine and lives at the heart of the Trinity. He lives as the Cosmic Christ permeating the heart of the entire cosmos. In all these ways, footprints are left for us to see. We need only become attentive, opening all our senses to see, learn, and follow. If we are attentive to the footprints of the person of Jesus, we will come to know our truest possibilities and potentials.

St. Francis of Assisi: Exemplar

From the mid-twentieth century onwards, scientists and theologians have agreed that at the root of the ecological crisis is a more profound spiritual crisis.[2] Finally, in 2015 Pope Francis published *Laudato Si'—On the Care for Our Common Home* (*LS*).[3] *LS* is suffused with Franciscan influence, including that of Romano Guardini, a Third Order Secular Franciscan, the subject of the Holy Father's (unfinished) dissertation.[4] *LS* provides extensive treatment of the growing ecological crisis, including significant themes such as the human cause of the ecological degradation §s 23 and 53; burning fossil fuel as the climate change culprit (§s 26 and 165); the poor suffering most (§s 325); that poverty and inequality must be addressed (§s 49, 52, 175); the urgency to act falls on all humanity (§s 95, 202); it is a myth that humans can dominate the Earth without consequences (§67); the current level of inaction is indefensible (§s 54, 59); and there is hope (§s 165, 205)—and much more.

Pope Francis upheld St. Francis as "the example par excellence of care for the vulnerable and of an integral ecology lived out joyfully and authentically. He is the patron saint of all who study and work in the area of ecology, and he is also much loved by non-Christians."⁵ In St. Francis' terms, the "footprints of Christ have been covered over and forgotten."⁶ The sacred relationship between God, humans, otherkind, and the cosmos has given way to pillaging, plundering, raping, and otherwise exploiting our Sister, Mother Earth, and ultimately her children—especially the poor and vulnerable.

LS Five Years On: The State of the Planet and Journey

Canceling the COP26 on December 2, 2020, UN Secretary General António Guterres presented a grim report on the "The State of the Planet."⁷ Guterres continued: "We are facing a devastating pandemic, new heights of global heating, new lows of ecological degradation and new setbacks in our work towards global goals for more equitable, inclusive and sustainable development. To put it simply, the state of the planet is broken."⁸

People "awoke" anew to how we are surrounded with the fallout from people treating others as so much chemistry or mere resources to be exploited for selfish profit and gain and with impunity. By contrast, as Peterson reminds us, we must look at the world with the eyes of St. Francis and to see "the value of an object is never more important than the fact that it is a 'vestige' [footprint] of the divine, an object that enriches us spiritually by providing us with a contact with the presence of God."⁹ That is just what Pope Francis compelled all people of good will to do. In 2020 the Vatican's Interdicasterial Working Group of the Holy See on Integral Ecology published "Journeying towards Care for Our Common Home: Five Years after *Laudato Si'* Celebration."¹⁰ The document outlines a seven-year plan to be implemented worldwide by Catholics and all people of good will toward halting and reversing the "Climate Emergency."

Franciscan Creation Theology and Virtue Ethics

As St. Bonaventure pointed out, God loved every bit of creation into life, with a unique love, and for its own sake. The purpose of creation is not to satiate human desires but rather for each element to find its own unique way to fulfillment in loving, transforming union with God. Because of our distinct capacities as humans, people are to be the guardians, nurturers, and protectors of all sisters and brothers—human and otherkind.

Significantly for us, St. Francis also knew the value of penance. Today "following in the footprints of Jesus" also means confronting our personal role in "covering over and forgetting" the "vestiges of the Divine." Most sobering is to realize that our personal and communal ecological footprints result from what we take for granted and consume daily, and much of this activity is effectively causing genocide and ecocide! While this may be disheartening, I recommend that, before you read further, you measure your Ecological Footprint.[11]

Use of such tools (above) helps us learn what actions are needed so we can all begin living sustainably. Like St. Francis, conversion of heart and a change of habits must be only first steps toward following in the footprints of Jesus. Each day, we can grow in our capacity to grasp how all things are revelations of God and divine actions in the natural world. Coming to the truth of our individual and communal abuse of our sisters and brothers, human and otherkind, opens a hopeful moment of penance. We *can change and learn* to cherish hospitality and presence in contrast to the utilitarian objectification of people and other creatures.

St. Bonaventure, the major Franciscan theologian, held that all creation is theophanic—it reveals something of God. His scholarly writings about God as the Trinity reflect St. Francis' intuitive understanding that all creation is bound together in praise of God. St. Francis' *Canticle of the Creatures* is echoed in Bonaventure's metaphor of creation as song—all the parts create the whole work. The Trinity as communion of persons suggests understanding God as relationship. The divine persons are interdependent, and the relationship between the Godhead and creation is one of interdependence. We will see how Bonaventure's theology of Trinity is remarkably compatible with current scientific notions of the ecosystem; the emphasis on relationship between entities is fundamental to both. Briefly, our radically relational God created a cosmos that is related to its core—humankind included!

Some Key Terms

Several pivotal terms are used throughout this text: "sustainability," "Climate Emergency," and "ecological sin." A brief definition of each is in order here. The context for understanding "sustainability" is the Christian belief that the Earth is "the dwelling place of God." That belief supplies the content and motivation for Christian action for environmental justice. The Early Christian communities understood the world as *oikumēnē*—"the whole inhabited globe." The *oikonomia tou theo* was known as "the economy of God," and it was an ancient way of speaking about the redemptive transformation of the world, brought to us through Christ, Incarnate.

However, the 1987 UN-sponsored Brundtland Commission presumed that "sustainable development" meant raising productivity, the accumulation of goods, and technological innovations and profitmaking.[12] Brundtland failed to address key sources of poverty—the exploitation of workers and the pillaging of nature. This thinking has permeated the globalization of world markets for generations.

By contrast, "sustainability," as it is defined in biology and ecology, is "the trend of ecosystems toward equilibrium, sustained in the web of interdependencies and complementarities flourishing in ecosystems."[13] Genuine "sustainability" requires social and economic structures that support *social justice*—the right relationship between persons, roles, and institutions—and *ecological justice*, which is the right relationship with nature, sufficient access to resources, and the assurance of quality of life.[14]

A renewed vision of community is essential for interdependent sustainability.[15] That vision is found in Early Christian sources and was gleaned from the Greek root *oikos*. The habitability of the Earth is the central reality that links "economy, ecology, and ecumenicity." "Economy in its Greek root meaning, is the ordering of the household for the sustenance of its members."[16] Theologian Larry Rasmussen explained the importance of this:

> Economics is *eco* (habitat as the household) + *nomos* (the rules or law). Economics means knowing how things work and arranging these "home systems" (ecosystems) so that the material requirements of the household of life are met and sustained. The household is established as hospitable habitat. The basic task of any economy, then, is *the continuation of life*, though no economist has put it this way for ages. In fact, the kind of economics generating earth's present distress resulted from three decisive moves away from *oikos* economics ... to consider nature as interchangeable parts ... to develop the propensity of generating affluence by expanding to ever-new worlds ... and to shift economic attention from the household (sustainability) to the firm or corporation (profit making).[17]

The term "Climate Emergency" is defined as "a situation in which urgent action is required to reduce or halt climate change and avoid potentially irreversible environmental damage resulting from it."[18] The term reflects the reality, presented by the Intergovernmental Panel on Climate Change (IPCC) in October 2018, that the world has only twelve years' time to halve our greenhouse gas emissions to avoid the worst impacts of a climate crisis brought about by extensive warming of the Earth's climate.[19] Pope Francis used the term on September 1, 2019, when proclaiming the fifth commemoration of the Season of Creation: "egoism and self-interest" have created the "climate emergency" by turning creation, "a place of encounter and sharing," into "an arena of competition and conflict." He noted "urgent need for interventions that can no longer be postponed."[20]

"Ecological sin" is best defined in the Final Document of the 2019 Amazon Synod:

> 82. We propose to define ecological sin as an action or omission against God, against one's neighbour, the community and the environment. It is sin against future generations, and it is committed in acts and habits of pollution and destruction of the harmony of the environment. These are transgressions against the principles of interdependence, and they destroy networks of solidarity among creatures (cf. *Catechism of the Catholic Church*, 340-344) and violate the virtue of justice.[21]

One strong contextual influence in understanding ecological sin is the teaching of the Ecumenical Patriarch Bartholomew cited in *LS* (8 and 9).[22]

> 8. Patriarch Bartholomew has spoken in particular of the need for each of us to repent of the ways we have harmed the planet, for "inasmuch as we all generate small ecological damage", we are called to acknowledge "our contribution, smaller or greater, to the disfigurement and destruction of creation." He has repeatedly stated this firmly and persuasively, challenging us to acknowledge our sins against creation: "For human beings … to destroy the biological diversity of God's creation; for human beings to degrade the integrity of the earth by causing changes in its climate, by stripping the earth of its natural forests or destroying its wetlands; for human beings to contaminate the earth's waters, its land, its air, and its life—these are sins." For "to commit a crime against the natural world is a sin against ourselves and a sin against God."

This Book: Context and Outline of the Chapters

Earth is undergoing a "Climate Emergency" and the 2020s are crucial for sustaining life itself. Overall, this book unfolds a positive trajectory to learning the theological, ethical, spiritual, and practical knowledge and skills to resolve the emergency. I utilize key elements of Christian Franciscan theology, ethics, and spirituality and illustrate how they are relevant for ecotheological reflection and action in today's critical context.

In *Laudato Si'—On Care for Our Common Home* (May 24, 2015) Pope Francis called everyone to spiritual conversion and behavioral change toward renewing and healing a planet in crisis. He upheld St. Francis of Assisi, the Patron of Ecologists, as our exemplar.[23] St. Francis understood God and all creatures as sisters and brothers, interdependent for their total well-being. At the heart of *LS* stands the Franciscan theological, ethical, and spiritual tradition. This book explains key Franciscan values and a hope-filled vision of peace, justice, and sustainability, for all of creation. The Franciscan tradition is deeply compatible with the world's spiritual traditions and respectful of all life-giving ways. Topics of "ecological sin," environmental destruction, a positive Franciscan soteriological path forward, practical tools necessary for conversion, planet-healing actions, and life-sustaining changes are addressed.

Part I includes two chapters exposing (Hebrew Testament and Christian Scriptures) texts frequently utilized by St. Francis and St. Clare that uphold values essential for Franciscan ecotheology.

In Part II, in a chapter on St. Francis and another on St. Clare, the distinct major tenants of their vernacular theologies on creation care are outlined.

The two chapters of Part III expose the formal Franciscan theology and spirituality of St. Bonaventure of Bagnoregio and then the Christology and ethics of Bl. John Duns Scotus.

In four chapters, Part IV treats *LS*'s four ecological issues considering current science, Franciscan theology, ethics, spirituality, and praxis. I focus on climate change with attention to sustainable energy sources and fossil-fuel divestment; water as a human right and the heath of all bodies of water; biodiversity among plants and animals; and sustainable agriculture and food security. Each chapter includes discussion pertaining to dialogue, social and political strategies, called for in *LS*, Chapter 5 (§s 163–201) and practical resources, considering particularly *LS* Chapter 6 (§s 202–46). This section also sustains the discussion of ecological sinfulness and hope amid a "Climate Emergency."

Each chapter includes excerpts from original sources, suggestions for reflection and application, questions for discussion, ideas for action, and sources for further study.

Notes

1. Ingrid Peterson, "Franciscan Spirituality: The Footprints of Jesus in the Classroom and the Marketplace," in *As Leaven to the World: Catholic Perspectives on Faith, Vocation, and the Intellectual Life*, ed. Thomas M. Landy (Franklin, WI: Sheed & Ward, 2001), 291.
2. "The Joint Appeal in Religion and Science: Statement by Religious Leaders at the Summit on Environment," National Religious Partnership for the Environment, New York City, June 3, 1991 https://fore.yale.edu/sites/default/files/files/Joint%20Appeal.pdf.
3. Pope Francis, *Laudato Si'—On Care for Our Common Home*, http://www.vatican.va/content/francesco/en/encyclicals/documents/papa-francesco_20150524_enciclica-laudato-si.html.
4. Dawn M. Nothwehr, OSF, "The Brown Thread in *Laudato Si'*: Grounding Ecological Conversion and Theological Ethics Praxis," in *Integral Ecology for a More Sustainable World: Dialogues with Laudato Si'*, ed. Dennis O'Hara, Matthew Eaton, and Michael T. Ross (Lanham, MD: Lexington Books, 2020), 111–26.
5. *LS*, 10.
6. "The Tree of the Crucified Life of Jesus Book V [Excerpts] by Umbertino DaCasale (1305)," in FA:ED, Volume III—*The Prophet*, 148.
7. Brady Dennis and Chris Mooney, "Amid Pandemic, U.N. Cancels Global Climate Conference," https://www.washingtonpost.com/climate-environment/2020/04/01/un-climate-coronavirus-cop26/, April 1, 2020. "UN Secretary General António Guterres, The UN Secretary-General Speaks on the State of the Planet," https://www.un.org/en/climatechange/un-secretary-general-speaks-state-planet.
8. Ibid.
9. Peterson, "Franciscan Spirituality," 303. Pope Francis, *Fratelli Tutti: On Fraternity and Social Friendship*, http://www.vatican.va/content/francesco/en/encyclicals/documents/papa-francesco_20201003_enciclica-fratelli-tutti.html.
10. See The Diacastery for Promoting Integral Human Development, https://www.humandevelopment.va/en/news/2020/presentato-in-sala-stampa-il-documento-in-cammino-per-la-cura-de.html. Isabella Piro, "Vatican Document on Integral Ecology: Safeguarding Creation Is Everyone's Responsibility," June 18, 2020, https://www.vaticannews.va/en/vatican-city/news/2020-06/vatican-interdicastery-document-laudato-si-safeguarding-creation.html.
11. Global Footprint Network, https://www.footprintnetwork.org/our-work/earth-overshoot-day/. Scroll down the page to the links "Visit Overshoot Day Website" and "Calculate Your Footprint."

12. Cited in Leonardo Boff, *Cry of the Earth, Cry of the Poor* (Maryknoll: Orbis Books, 1997), 66. Daniel P. Castillo, *An Ecological Theology of Liberation: Salvation and Political Ecology* (Maryknoll: Orbis Books, 2019), 168–86.
13. Boff, *Cry of the Earth,* 66.
14. Ibid., 105.
15. WCC, *Accelerated Climate Change: Sign of Peril, Test of Faith* (Geneva: WCC Publications, 1994).
16. Ibid. Cited in Larry L. Rasmussen, *Earth Community Earth Ethics* (Maryknoll: Orbis Books, 1996), 144.
17. Ibid., 91–2.
18. Brandon Pytel, "'Climate Emergency' Is the 2019 Oxford Word of the Year," Earthday.Org, November 21, 2019, https://www.earthday.org/climate-emergency-is-2019-oxford-word-of-the-year/.
19. IPCC, *Global Warming of 1.5 ºC,* https://www.ipcc.ch/sr15/. William J Ripple, Christopher Wolf, Thomas M Newsome, Phoebe Barnard, and William R Moomaw, "World Scientists' Warning of a Climate Emergency," *BioScience* 70/1 (January 2020): 8–12, https://doi.org/10.1093/biosci/biz088.
20. Gerard O'Connell, "Pope Francis Issues New Call for World Leaders to Act on the Climate Emergency," https://www.americamagazine.org/faith/2019/09/01/pope-francis-issues-new-call-world-leaders-act-climate-emergency, September 01, 2019.
21. Synod of Bishops Special Assembly for the Pan-Amazonian Region, the Amazon: New Paths for the Church and for an Integral Ecology—Final Document, Vatican, October 26, 2019, http://www.vatican.va/roman_curia/synod/documents/rc_synod_doc_20191026_sinodo-amazzonia_en.html.
22. Pope Francis cited the Patriarch's work: *Message for the Day of Prayer for the Protection of Creation* (September 1, 2012) and *Address in Santa Barbara, California* (November 8, 1997); cf. John Chryssavgis, *On Earth as in Heaven: Ecological Vision and Initiatives of Ecumenical Patriarch Bartholomew* (Bronx, NY: Fordham University Press, 2012).
23. *LS,* §s 1–2, 10–12, 66, 87, 91, 125, 218, 221.

Part I

The Bible: Hope in Creation through the Word

Introduction: A Phenomenology of Hope— Abrahamic Religions in Harmony with Complexity Science

In this third decade of the twenty-first century, we live amid a burgeoning "Climate Emergency" that is an existential threat to the possibility of life—including human life—on Earth. The complex burning questions looming large over this situation concern the meaning and the possibility of any *hope* to reverse the threats soon and thoroughly enough to avoid the demise of human-sustaining life. What relevant meaning for the value and virtue of *hope* is offered in the sacred texts of three dominant world religions—Judaism, Christianity, and Islam? How—if at all—do those texts find common voice with *complexity science* to affect the necessary reversal of the current threats?[1]

Part I opens with an overview of the phenomenology of hope expressed in notions widely held in common by Judaism, Christianity, and Islam. First, the biblical and qur'anic moral imaginaries hold that life overcomes death. Second, understanding biblical hope entails three sets of elements: cosmological, epistemological, and ideological, and especially qur'anic hope balances hope with fear. Third, biblical and qur'anic hope is presented as a virtue that is similarly defined theoretically by nontheists, as *commanding hope* utilizing complexity science.

Particular attention is given to those biblical texts prominent in (Christian) Franciscan theology and ethics. Chapter 1 treats texts from the Hebrew Testament and Chapter 2 focuses on the Christian Scriptures. Throughout, current interpretation of the biblical texts is influenced by Pius XII's 1943 encyclical, *Divino Afflante Spiritu*[2] and *Dei Verbum*, the Dogmatic Constitution on Divine Revelation of the Second Vatican (1965),[3] as well as Christian feminist methods of reading of the texts.[4] These resources ground how Catholics understand Scripture in relation to the doctrines of creation and redemption and the current "Climate Emergency."

The Biblical and Qur'anic Moral Imagination: Life Overcomes Death

There is no absolute agreement among the Abrahamic religions concerning the more nuanced theological understanding of hope. Yet, in practice, hope inspires, motivates, and sustains Jews, Christians, and Muslims in supporting the planetary common good by caring for the life of all peoples, living creatures, and the major life-giving and life-sustaining planetary systems. Here I can only briefly address major concepts and themes common to the three great faiths, shaping the moral imagination and actions of believers. Put simply, believers of these great traditions hold that "life overcomes death." Insofar as these three traditions uphold scientifically supported basic requirements for a healthy human life, one that does not fatally disrupt vital planetary systems, these traditions also find some common ground with nontheistic philosophical and scientific notions, as well.

First, following Daniel C. Maguire, I outline some key concepts held in common among Jews and Christians, and then expose similar notions found within Islam, in ways that harmonize with Christian and Jewish positions. For a more exhaustive study readers are invited to pursue "Sources for Further Study" at the end of this part.

Biblical Hope: Three Sets of Elements

Life is not possible without the energy of hope. According to renowned ethicist Daniel C. Maguire, "hope lives on the brink of simpleminded optimism, naiveté, and unreality."[5] Indeed, it is that reality of apparent fragility which gives hope its unique vitality, inner dynamism, and potential. Hope, worthy of engaging, holds the potential for igniting an instantaneous, intense, concentrated outburst of energy or a more gradual outflow of power that is sustained over centuries. Hope's opposite dictates catatonia and paralysis rather than energy for life. In short, hope is the well-grounded religious and moral conviction that "reality is ultimately reliable; the possibilities of good outweigh the possibilities of evil, however formidable it may be."[6]

In Judaism and Christianity, hope is closely identified with the God of Israel (Jer. 14:8; Ps. 71:5; Rom. 15:13).[7] Israel's origins tell the story of an enterprise set on gaining good governance, which created and sustained freedom from oppression, plenty, good crops, and harmonious living rooted in a genuine justice that exceeded other nations (Mic. 4:1-4; Isa. 1:26, 28:6, 32:1). For Jews, the clear expression of hope is contained in the command for the celebration of Passover: "you and your children for all time" (Exod. 12:24). In a similar vein, Christians celebrate Easter annually.

Hope stirs even those of a secular orientation to move beyond the status quo. The strong want to sustain their privilege and luxury, while the weak want betterment. To some extent humans answer to hope at every moment of life—to sustain life or give it up, resurrection or death.

As Christian theologian John Macquarrie holds, the biblical imagination is grounded in a reality, namely "the implicit promise already present in the human vocation to personhood and community" (cf. 1 Jn 3:2).[8] The Jewish imagination links creation and human salvation in ways that exceeded the miraculous myths and accidental marginal experiences of creation of other peoples of the ancient near east.[9] Indeed participation in God's offer of life is regarded as the obvious preferred choice (cf. Deut. 30:11-14 and Deut. 30:19). Clearly, ignoring this option for life in God skews human choice toward arrogant, controlling, and pessimistic death-dealing behaviors. Yet when pessimism is confronted it is done so "with thunderous dissent and unleashing the possibility of progress."[10]

Cosmological—Fate, Tragedy, Suicidal Option

Hope elicits a cosmology in response to the universe into which humans are cast that deals with their fate, experience of tragedy, and that copes with the possibility of giving up on life—a suicidal option. As Maguire suggests, everyone must decide at least three things within the cosmological setting: fate, tragedy, and a suicidal option.[11]

Fate holds a stance toward life that "what is, is, and what will be, will be."[12] By contrast, hope claims that what is, is becoming—an evolutionary worldview—and that within limits, people can shape the future. The biblical view of history is linear. The early Christians rebelled against the Platonic theory of cycles (1 Jn 3:2). Created in the *imago Dei*, though limited, humans have potential to be the stewards, administrators, or curators within creation, participating in divine providence (1 Cor. 4:1).[13] The standard of measure for human efforts was to be none other than God. By contrast to God's ways, the rule of the Pharaoh was understood as always prone to myopia, rewarding immobility, preservation of hierarchical power, and was laced with ubiquitous fatalism.

Tragedy, Maguire asserts, is so real that it obfuscates the possibility that things might be otherwise. As Holocaust survivor Elie Wiesel profoundly claimed, not all evil has a human source.[14] Indeed, such theodicy disturbs us to the core; biblical hope of Christians and Jews is not romantic. Rather, as Maguire astutely puts it:

> Biblical morality responds to tragedy by first rushing to the aid of its victims. This is the heart of *sedaqah*. It knows that hope in this kind of world is precarious. Yet we struggle, with bloodied grip, "never to be dislodged from the hope" we have achieved (Col. 1:23). Rather, the goal is to fix our pained vision on the precariousness that coexists with tragedy and seems ultimately more real. This kind of hope does not descend into optimism, and it is compatible with turbulent streams of despair. This sturdy hope lives amid chaos and bears the wounds that are the insignia of that chaos. Ultimately, it is impressed with good more than evil, with what can be more than with what is not. It is convinced that whatever chaos is, it is not the name of God. It is not what is decisively and ultimately real. … This painfilled reality of ours is ambiguous to the core, but hope sees its enduring promise and stays stubbornly faithful to its possibilities. Bloodied by life, it reinvests in life. Such is hope.[15]

Suicidal option is most often not exercised as the direct, intentional termination of one's physical life. Rather, it languishes as human detachment from relationships—separation from God, humans, creation—coldness, insensitivity, inability to listen, to respond, or to create.[16] Amid often overwhelming conditions the fires of hope are quenched by an insidious "NO" to the deep moral beckoning of life for life. But "hope the struggler says yes."[17] As Thomas Aquinas holds, hope is the rejuvenator that renews the desire and joy for life.[18]

Epistemological—Truth, Fear, Magnanimity, Planning

Truth abounds in genuine goodness that originates in the unlimited goodness of God, not in political schemes or military alliances (Isa. 31:1-3; 36:4-9; Hos. 10:13). Not surprisingly, the Jewish and Christian Scriptures warn against false hope and press for attention to the truth. Genuine truth is made possible by a hopeful vision. Unsubstantiated or ungrounded claims to truth may elicit temporary hope, but "from falsehood, anything might follow."[19] As Aquinas noted, hope that is grounded in truth is "arduous but possible of attainment."[20]

Fear of the possible future that hope beckons us toward can cause us to sustain what is currently known—no matter the cost. People thus become antisocial, withdrawn, or hostile—indeed they often even turn to destructive defensiveness or militarism. Yet fear can be overcome.

Magnanimity, a virtue distinct from fear, which narrows one's horizons, signals "the aspiration and enlargement of the spirit to great things."[21] Together magnanimity, truth, and courage join to reach for new life and new horizons. From that position, it is possible for new life and renewed healthy ways of being to emerge. The restless human heart reaches out for something more that fear itself cannot satisfy. Hope blossoms into magnanimity.

Planning our actions helps to sustain their relevance and effectiveness. Thus, as with all worthy human activity, we do well to plan. Simply put, "hope without homework is sterile."[22] The connection to truth requires our consideration beyond blind impulses, simpleminded optimism, arrogance, or illusion.

Ideological—Cognitive, Emotive, Mythical, Habitual

Maguire defines ideology as "congeries of myths, emotions, and thought patterns through which we somewhat systematically organize our interpreting and thinking"—a mixture of cognitive, emotive, mythical, and habitual engagement.[23] Hope can be understood as an ideology. For example, Jesus taught that God provides sunshine and rain for the just and the unjust (Mt. 5:45; Lk. 6:35), signaling a hopeful ideology. This is an ethical cosmic generosity open to possible reform of criminals and outcasts and an openness to all in "love, supreme artistry, and gracious creativity."[24] Believers are called to do likewise—to see reality as promising and to work to enhance goodness. Maguire cautions that the symbols of hope can become reified. The symbols of hope are not hope itself. God did not "do" hope alone. Hope is an open system that lives with freedom, humility, inclusion, and participation as found in the biblical covenants between God, humans, and the entire cosmos. In short, concerning hope, Christians and Jews assert—"The *yes* is mightier than the *no*. Hope is at home in our universe."[25]

Qur'anic Hope: A Balance

Like Judaism and Christianity, in Islam, hope is ultimately rooted in having and sustaining faith in the One God. Generally, in the *Holy Qur'an*, the notion of hope can be understood using some form of three key words: *Raja*—aspiration or waiting for something that is loved (39:53); *Amal*—a desire that includes a long wait (18:46); and *Tamanna*—a request for something, with an appreciation of its essence (53:24).[26]

In practical terms, hope is grounded in three central beliefs held by Muslims. *Monotheism* is the belief in one God who is all merciful and who guards believers from despair or confusion in times of misery (13:28). *Prophecy* and its effects bolster monotheism, providing explanations, examples of fidelity and failure, assuring people that monotheism is a path to salvation (33:21; 54:31).[27] Belief in the *resurrection day* confirms that there is a life of total peace and security that awaits the faithful beyond earthly death, in which all their wishes will be fulfilled and where present miseries will be absent (50:39; 6:127).[28] Generally, Islam defines hope as a positive virtue of confidence and desire, a belief and expectation of pleasant outcomes in one's own life and in the world. Hope has personal and communal dimensions that are mutually reenforcing.

For individuals, remembering God (*zekr*), especially in prayer, is the starting point (2:152; 13:28). Such remembrance involves the language of the heart and mind.[29] Muslims believe that the connection between humans and God begins and lasts from such recollections. Indeed, there is no rest for the human soul until it reaches God (103:65). "Hope-bringing fear" presses against one committing sin and elicits the desire for truth and virtue (87:175). While people do sin, hopelessness can be avoided, and peace regained by seeking and responding to God's acceptance of repentance (13:27-28; 42:25). For those who worship late into the night, God provides true hope (39:9). True hope is also found in those involved in migrations or crusades for God's sake, while expecting mercy (2:218).

Social expressions of hope include nourishing (*Infagh*) in the form of donating something, such as property, to the poor.[30] Such actions can alleviate poverty and bring hope (9:103; 2:265). People can be hopeful when they expect God's mercy, believe divine promises, and practice benevolence (7:56). Forgiving and practicing generosity signal beneficence that promotes hope (5:23; 7:56) and can bring great peace to society. The fidelity of believers, living in anticipation of union with God and inheriting Heaven, extends hope to all who experience the ongoing goodness such a life exhibits in daily practices in community living.

Seeking the Balance: Fear, Hope, Hope and Fear

Qur'anic texts and especially medieval Islamic writings hold a variety of references to hope (*rajā*) and fear (*khawf*), as both separate and paired concepts.[31] The notions are presented as emotional, cognitive, and behavioral conceptual elements and are considered "praiseworthy" when associated with the one God, and held in equilibrium or balance, not exercised in any excessive way.[32] Any excess holds potential for disobedience to God (immorality). In the *Holy Qur'an* there is a remarkable holistic understanding of the human person as a thinking, feeling, willing being. Both fear and hope are known in various ways through all the human faculties.

Fear

"*Khawf*, the noun form of the Arabic root *khwf*, means something unpleasant based on a certain doubtful sign."[33] Most occurrences in the *Qur'ran* mark the relationship between God and humans that includes "restraining one's soul from surrendering to its lower desires and being heedless toward God that is most apparent in the verse 79:40."[34] The recognition of God as "Lord (*Rabb*)" views God as the one creator, but also the one who nourishes all of creation, completing and perfecting it. Human violation of this relationship invites God's wrath (*qadhab*). Such wrath awakens fear—the person's recognition of their moral violation of God and the option to seek repentance and God's mercy. Alternatively, self-conceit can move a person to pridefully rely on their own goodness (excessive hope) becoming heedless of God's commands and thus engage in sinfulness (7:97-99).[35] Hard heartedness results in neglecting God's commands and sinfulness, as well (2:74).

Hope

The word *rajā* (the noun form of the Arabic root "*rjw*") does not appear in the *Qur'an* but the concept of hope appears in verbal form.[36] Hope is closely attached to the notion of God's mercy (12:64). True hope must be part of acts of devoutness (2:218). Indeed, "[m]ercy encompasses all things and affairs in its *Qur'anic* concept (7:156) and hope in God's mercy connotes a promise for man to be in pursuit of this all-pervasive mercy."[37]

The opposite of *raja* is despair (*ya's*) and it results from disbelief in God's mercy and bounty. Despair is considered a major sin because it blocks repentance and leads to greater sinfulness.[38] A type of hopelessness is *qunūt*, a state "wherein the effects of despair appear in the deeds and sayings of man, and is a greater sin than *ya's*."[39] However, to despair of all creatures is considered a virtue, because it avoids hypocrisy and idolatry, which would replace hope in the One Creator, with hope in creatures.[40]

Hope and Fear

There are seven occurrences in the *Qur'an* of the paired concepts of "hope and fear." Two instances refer to the awesome, though mixed experience in nature, of crashing and glaring lightening along with refreshing rain. The other five instances refer to human feelings, especially during prayer. One reference (39:9) substitutes *hadhar* for *khawf*, introducing the notion of avoidance of something out of fear. *Tama'* replaces *raja*, the four other verses. Both of those indicate desire that results in action; however, the idea of desire is stronger in *tama'*.[41]

From texts such as these, Islamic scholars concluded that an ideal state of a person at prayer is that which balances, hope and fear concerning personal and social effects of service to God and neighbor, as well as acts of worship and prayer. This balance is achieved according to al-Ghazālī because "[k]nowledge is the cause for the feeling, and the feeling leads to the action." In this way, the emotions of fear and hope have an inseparable cognitive basis and inevitably lead to certain behaviors. Such implicit philosophical elements support an ethics of hope, grounded by Islamic philosophers in a theological scope, which regards hope or fear beneficial only when their object is God.[42]

Commanding Hope: Social and Complexity Sciences

For environmentalist and complexity theorist Thomas Homer-Dixon, considerations of "hope" began by confronting the reality that the world is facing a "Climate Emergency," and humans have less than two decades to make real and necessary changes to ensure planetary survival and life anywhere near what we have known.

"Climate Emergency"—Disparately Desperate Responses

People have dealt with this reality in ways involving varying degrees of hope. For example:

- At age fourteen, Greta Thunberg suffered "climate despair." Deeply depressed, she "stopped talking, eating … and in two months, lost 10 kilos."[43] In recovery, she became a passionate climate activist.
- "Climate nihilists" simply excise "the climate crisis" from their consciousness so that it does not affect their decision-making at all.
- Considering the dire implications of the climate crisis for the future, many young women have chosen to not have children.[44]
- "Techno-optimists" cite significant steady improvement in human development. However, climate change metrics overwhelm those benchmarks because most improvements are fossil-fuel dependent and not sustainable.

Thomas Homer-Dixon and Commanding Hope

Utilizing historical and scientific data about how hope works, in *Commanding Hope: The Power We Have to Renew a World in Peril*, Thomas Homer-Dixon provides a sober but invigorating analysis of the status of our planetary emergency, how we got here, and how we can get moving to its authentic resolution—beginning with the human mind.[45] He posits that *imagination* is key to solving this most pressing problem. Some compare Homer-Dixon's planetary version of hope to the "Stockdale Paradox." James Stockdale survived seven years of torture as a prisoner of war in Vietnam. He held that to retain hope: "You must never confuse faith that you will prevail in the end—which you can never afford to lose—with the discipline to confront the most brutal facts of your current reality."[46]

Homer-Dixon sees the central challenge to hope in resolving the "Climate Emergency" is human's inability to understand their own views, how and why they differ from those of others, and how they relate to institutions and technologies. Political polarization, related social disintegration, and "social earthquakes" are evident everywhere. Homer-Dixon developed a cognitive-affective mapping tool intended to help people better understand themselves, their adversaries, and the conflicts in which they are embroiled. He marshaled his vast background in complexity science to show the potential for the development of strategic intelligence.

Hope is summoned from within the human spirit, but empirically rooted in proven natural and social sciences. That understanding of hope is also highly compatible with major tenets of hope that shine forth from Judaism, Christianity, and Islam. For all three religions, hope is a cooperative affair between God and humans, not a magical, mythical, enterprise. To the contrary, human intelligence and all the senses and virtues need to be actively engaged, consistently and constantly.

In brief, Homer-Dixon holds there are three major changes people need to make to "avoid descending into savage violence."[47] Individuals need to understand why each sees the world different from others. Second, people need to actively create a shared story from their vast diversity, a "shared we" that can together address common problems and thrive. And third, people must fully mobilize human agency to produce the future. For Jews, Christians, and Muslims the common narrative of love of God, neighbor and care for creation opens pathways to these nonviolent ways.

Homer-Dixon's thesis is that humans must acquire and activate a "commanding hope" that is "grounded in historic and scientific knowledge of how hope works at every level" in individual lives and societies.[48] His initial distinction is to ascertain what changes are "enough" and necessary to accomplish halting catastrophic climate change and what is "feasible" given current social, political, economic, or technological roadblocks. Changes currently considered feasible are not likely enough. So Homer-Dixon asserts that fundamentally "the death of hope is not an option," but "commanding hope" is.[49]

Homer-Dixon first defines hope in psychological terms as "a state of mind; a person's desire or longing for an imagined set of circumstances that might occur in the future."[50] He warns that a loss of hope can become self-fulfilling by fatally weakening our sense of agency and the potential for making changes. By contrast a "commanding hope" is characterized by a shared vision among peoples; a radical advance in understanding each other's worldview; and being truly honest about the problem ("Climate Emergency") without destroying hope. This understanding and vision must be coupled with personal and communal motivation and capacity to act. He contrasts the kind of personal agency expressed in the passive expression, "I hope that" with the active, "I hope to." Where "hope that" communicates a whimsical wish, "hope to" boldly asserts a plan of action rooted in honest hope.[51]

"Hope to" engages "honest hope," a state of mind that faces up to real danger, never relying on selective or exaggerated evidence. Rather, it is grounded in acute moral clarity that readily exposes the folly of opposing views, while maintaining the opponent is well intentioned and good.[52] "Hope to" begins with an imagination of the future, anchored in clear-eyed vision. Everyone's personal agency is the source for "input to" and "output of" their hope. Memories of the past are the source and support for the strength or weakness of one's current sense of agency.[53] For Jews, Christians, and Muslims genuine hope and morality require active, life-giving engagement in personal and communal aspects of life in the world.

Homer-Dixon's "commanding hope" has three components: (1) "Honest hope" is "a *moral* attitude" that presumes the importance and a commitment to truth; (2) "Astute hope" is "an *epistemological* attitude" that is rooted in "deep knowledge of people's worldviews and motivations"; and (3) "Powerful hope" is "a *psychological* attitude" that stresses "a vision of a positive future and a clear roadmap of strategies of how to get there."[54] The three Abrahamic religions require the active engagement of believers morally/spiritually, intellectually, and psychosocially.

Honest hope provides the foundation for *commanding hope*. Here individuals inhabit a discernable reality where some claims are more accurate than others. People rely on the scientific method and make judgments on empirical evidence. Truth here means what is scientifically meaningful and defensible. Ultimately truth is tied to trust of both individuals and institutions. All three Abrahamic traditions have deep and long-standing engagement with education and civic institutions that consistently promoted research and acted on the implementation of that knowledge for the common good of humankind—and the wider world. Here an explicit moral stance is upheld, namely "trying to see the truth and accepting its full implications are morally good behaviors."[55] This stance is justified in that practically to do otherwise is "spectacularly counterproductive."[56] The price for dealing in "untruth" is planetary life itself. *Astute hope* recognizes that attaining what is hoped for is most likely if we can understand diverse mindsets and motivations. We take seriously how other people see us and how they think we see them. *Powerful hope* comes from a pragmatic vision of the future that is supported by clearly defined values, goals, and identities. Such a vision invigorates people with moral passion. It brings humanity together around a compelling common purpose—broadly construed principles that are the bedrock of healthy societies; e.g., opportunity, safety, justice, and a common feeling of "we-ness."[57] Homer-Dixon concludes that hope "is under our very direction and command."[58] We can assert our intelligence and imagination. Indeed, hope is compelling—it draws us in and commands our attention. The common tradition of the universal purpose of created things found in the Abrahamic religions gives support to Homer-Dixon's proposals.

Commanding hope grounds "tempered intelligence's pessimism" and the "will's optimism" in "resolute realism."[59] It also keeps realism from becoming resignation—balancing understanding the gravity of the emergency with simply giving up in defeat. It sees something larger, more beautiful, dignified, and necessary at stake. This leads to cold resolve and ardent tenacity. Homer-Dixon concludes, "Imagination creates the possibilities that act like oxygen for hope; and hope creates psychological space in which our imagination can thrive."[60]

Imagination and Possibilities—Entrees to Hope

It is fundamental discomfort with a current situation, which propels the human imagination forward and outward beyond the limits or edges of a given situation. Homer-Dixon names four such metaphysical edges: "what we know more or less, and what we don't really know at all; between the past, present, and future; between events inside our minds and outside; and between the impossible and the inevitable."[61] If we are to hope for something, we need to believe possibility lies between the present state and what we think is possible to attain.

Citing Thomas Aquinas, *Summa Theologica*, q.40.5.3, "[t]he object of hope is a future good, difficult but possible to attain," Homer-Dixon notes that fear arises at the edge of the known and unknown.[62] Overcoming fear requires engaging one's imagination, while also keeping reality in perspective, utilizing one's episodic memory—recalling images, sensations, and emotions. One then involves recursive thinking by selecting "chunks of past memory" and recombining them, creating images and notions for a possible future.[63] As the work of David Tracy brilliantly illustrates, the religious and moral imagination exemplifies a fertile field of positive experiences and knowledge for such activity.[64]

One's quest for "good data" to support honest hope does risk becoming overwhelmed by the preponderance of threatening factors that define the "Climate Emergency" and being thrust into a state of pathological denial. But Homer-Dixon offers ways to keep space open for *honest hope* to thrive. Pointing to complexity science he notes, while an honest assessment of our complex world does not allow us to *know positive* outcomes *will occur* in the future, simultaneously, neither does it permit us to *know* that *positive* outcomes *will not be possible*.[65] He proposes that people carefully weigh and measure what *can* be known and predict what we *can* or *cannot* change. Yet one needs to actively "push back" against what *seems* impossible and aggressively explore how things *could be* different. The time-tested narratives and covenantal promises upheld by the three religious traditions reinforce this proposition.

Wisdom and imagination play equally important roles in achieving *honest hope* and discerning what is open to positive transformation. "While wisdom can provide imagination with valuable letters for its alphabet, in the form of recognition patterns drawn from experience and a sense of balanced judgment of what is possible, it's imagination that uses the alphabet to tell stories that can be the basis for our honest hope."[66] Indeed, complexity itself expands the number and the variety of novel, unexpected combinations in the adjacent possible, the zone of the unknown beyond the edge of the known.[67] At any point in history, factors unknown to previous generations have emerged through a variety of changing elements, ranging from social composition, institutional and technological developments, and the nonlinearity of complex systems—small changes that produce major changes.[68]

Homer-Dixon and his University of Waterloo colleagues developed two tools using complexity science to uncover "what goes on in people's minds, specifically how the world works—their 'worldviews.'"[69] The first, "called the 'space-state method,' provides a way of identifying and analyzing key differences between worldviews. It builds on the concept of a *state space*, which is a picture, much like a three-dimensional map, of all the possible states of a given system…." The second tool is a "cognitive-affective map

(CAM)," "a way of diagraming people's mental networks of *emotionally charged concepts*. ... CAMs give us a detailed internal view of a single worldview as it looks and feels to the individual holding it."[70] When used together, the two tools allow a trained eye to discern the worldviews of individuals involved in bitter disagreements, chart them out in a visible manner that reveals hidden features of disputes, and then use them to suggest ways to bring disputing parties together.[71]

Homer-Dixon notes three ways the state-space and CAM can assist in creating real supporting data to ground a *commanding hope*. First is "to better identify potential allies and judge whether and how differences can be bridged. Second, they can ease our fear and anger when dealing with people who see the world differently from us. Finally, they can help us navigate more strategically through tomorrow's complex—and conflicting terrains."[72] All of this can work together to free up the human imagination, opening vast unexplored vistas wherein we will locate a new "rough-and-ready but shared global worldview that's generous, inclusive, trusting, compassionate—and that empowers us to live together more wisely on Earth."[73]

Harmonizing Hope: A Virtue Acceptable by Theists and Nontheists

Though expressed differently, there is considerable consensus and commonality among the three Abrahamic religions and complexity science concerning *hope* for the possibility of drawing down the effects of global warming and climate change, sustaining, and maintaining it.

All four approaches are committed to empirical science as a means for securing the truth about the reality that constitutes the current "Climate Emergency." All four require both personal and communal involvement by people of good will to restore past damage and prevent future harm to people and the planet.

The four approaches all claim that hope is not the whimsical optimism of one who sees the "glass half full," e.g., asserting that though climate change is destroying global habitats, eventually "they" will find a "fix," and all will be well. Nor is hope the mere presumption that one's own ends will be achieved in due course. Rather, hope is grounded in truth—empirically known and rooted in wisdom. Hope's enemy is fear that stymies progress. Magnanimity builds on the innermost desires (spiritual and psychological) of the human heart to move forward, amid difficulty, with truth and courage.

While the Abrahamic religions base their ultimate source of hope in the Divine, they acknowledge the legitimacy of empirical science that exposes an orderliness in the world that is knowable, though always evolving, as partial grounding for that hope. For complexity science, it is the time-tested honest assessment that while our complex world does not allow us to *know positive* outcomes *will occur* in the future, simultaneously, neither does it permit us to "*know* that *positive* outcomes *will not be possible.*"[74] For Jews, Christians, and Muslims there is a cosmic generosity that is accessible to humans—named "God."

The balance of hope and fear, most visible in Islam, is also essential in Judaism and Christianity as a profound reverence for God. It requires us to sustain a sober fidelity to the truth which the empirical data of complexity science provides. All systems require personal and communal forms of engagement, signaled by Homer-Dixon as "hope to"—active interaction with the complex issues of global climate change. Fear is existential, psychological, and empirically based for all four approaches. However, moral implications for the source and consequences of being fearful differ. In the Abrahamic religions fear is the awe-filled reverence for God as the place of ultimate concern but also as a source of hope-engendering mercy in the face of moral failure. Hope is found in mercy in this life and fulfillment for the faithful in the future. In complexity science hope is chosen by commanding it.

Commanding hope insists on the social dimension of human relationships and cooperation toward a common good rooted in what is scientifically meaningful and defensible. It is like the religions in noting that planetary life is at stake (though not considering life after death). It provides a strong pragmatic vision of a future supported by clearly defined values, goals, and identities. The human imagination is central insofar as it propels humans beyond the current uncomfortable situation to a possible future.

Notes

1. Thomas Homer-Dixon, *Commanding Hope: The Power We Have to Renew a World in Peril* (Toronto: Knopf Canada, 2020), 38. Complexity science aims to explain the inner workings of systems such as forest ecologies, Earth's climate, the human brain, human economies, and human societies.

2. Pius XII, *Divino Afflante Spiritu*, https://www.vatican.va/content/pius-xii/en/encyclicals/documents/hf_p-xii_enc_30091943_divino-afflante-spiritu.html.
3. *Dei Verbum*, "The Dogmatic Constitution on Divine Revelation," https://www.vatican.va/ archive/hist_councils/ii_vatican_council/documents/vat-ii_const_19651118_dei-verbum_en.html.
4. "*Wisdom Commentary Series* Interview with Barbara E. Reid, General Editor," https://www.youtube.com/watch?v=OoTmqgpY8uE. Also http://www.wisdomcommentary.org.
5. Daniel C. Maguire, *The Moral Core of Judaism and Christianity: Reclaiming the Revolution* (Minneapolis: Fortress Press, 1993), 194.
6. Ibid., 195.
7. All biblical references in Maguire's work are from *The New English Bible*, 1969, 1970 by the Delegates of the Oxford University Press and the Syndics of the Cambridge University Press.
8. John Macquarrie, *Christian Hope* (New York: Crossroad, 1978), 50 cited by Maguire, 197.
9. Gerhard von Rad, *Old Testament Theology*, 1 (Edinburgh: Oliver and Boyd, 1962), 136.
10. Maguire, *The Moral Core of Judaism and Christianity*, 198.
11. Ibid., 199.
12. Ibid.
13. Thomas Aquinas, *Summa Theologica*, 1–2, q.91, a.2, in corp., in *Saint Thomas Aquinas (1225–1274), Summa Theologiae*, trans. Fathers of the English Dominican Province, First Part Treatise on Man (Questions 75–102), https://www.logoslibrary.org/aquinas/summa/1091.html.
14. Elie Wiesel, *Night* (New York: Bantam Books, 1982), 31.
15. Maguire, *The Moral Core of Judaism and Christianity*, 201–2. The precarious hope Maguire speaks of is implicit in "IPCC Report: 'Code Red' for Human Driven Global Heating, Warns UN Chief," August 9, 2021, https://news.un.org/en/story/2021/08/1097362.
16. Ibid., 202.
17. Ibid., 202–3.
18. Ibid., 203. Maguire cites Thomas Aquinas, *Summa Theologica*, 1–2, q.40, a.6.
19. Maguire, *The Moral Core of Judaism and Christianity*, 203.
20. Ibid. Maguire cites Thomas Aquinas, *Summa Theologica*, 2–2, q.17, a.1.
21. Maguire, *The Moral Core of Judaism and Christianity*, 204.
22. Ibid.
23. Daniel C. Maguire, *The Moral Choice* (San Francisco: Winston/Harper & Row, 1979), 430–2.

24. Maguire, *The Moral Core of Judaism and Christianity*, 205.
25. Ibid., 207.
26. S. M. H. Shirvani, "'Raising Hope' in Quran and Psychology," *HTS Teologiese Studies/Theological Studies* 74/1 (2018): 2, https://doi.org/10.4102/hts.v74i1.4828. Citations of passages from the *Holy Qur'an* appear in parentheses. *The Qur'an*, trans., M. A. S. Abdel Haleem, *Oxford World's Classics* (Oxford: Oxford University Press, 2005).
27. Shirvani, "'Raising Hope' in Quran and Psychology"; ibid.
28. Ibid.
29. Ibid.
30. Ibid., 3.
31. Fatemeh Bahmani, Mitra Amini, Seyed Ziaeddin Tabei, Mohamad Bagher Abbasi, "The Concepts of Hope and Fear in the Islamic Thought: Implications for Spiritual Health," *Religion and Health* 57 (2018): 57–71, DOI: 10.1007/s10943-016-0336-2, at 57.
32. Ibid.
33. Ibid., 59.
34. Ibid.
35. Ibid., 60.
36. Ibid.
37. Ibid. The authors cite M. Khorchide and U. Topkara, "A Contribution to Comparative Theology: Probing the Depth of Islamic Thought," *Religions* 4/1 (2013): 67–76.
38. Bahmani et al., "The Concepts of Hope and Fear in the Islamic Thought," 61.
39. Ibid., 61, cite V. Al-kulaynī, *al-Usul min al-Kafi* (Tehran, Iran: Dar al-Kutub al-Islamiyyah, 1968).
40. Bahmani et al., "The Concepts of Hope and Fear in the Islamic Thought," 61.
41. Ibid.
42. Ibid., 62 cites, A. H. al-Ghazālī, In trans Al-Haj Maulana Fazlul, Ihya Ulum-id-din Karim (ed.), Vol. 4, 113–45 (New Delhi, India: Islamic Book Service, 1991).
43. Franklin Foer, "Greta Thunberg Is Right to Panic," *The Atlantic*, September 20, 2019, https://www.theatlantic.com/ideas/archive/2019/09/greta-thunbergs-despair-is-entirely-warranted/598492/.
44. Katie O'Reilly, "To Have or Not to Have Children in the Age of Climate Change: Dispatches from One Millennial's Uterus," November 1, 2019, *Sierra*, https://www.sierraclub.org/sierra/2019-6-november-december/feature/have-or-not-have-children-age-climate-change. "Climate 'Apocalypse' Fears Stopping People Having Children—Study," https://www.theguardian.com/environment/2020/nov/27/climate-apocalypse-fears-stopping-people-having-children-study.

45. Thomas Homer-Dixon, *Commanding Hope: The Power We Have to Renew a World in Peril,* ISBN: 9780307363169, Knopf Canada, 2020, 464 pages, hardcover, ebook, and audiobook.
46. Arno Kopecky, "There May Yet Be Hope: Our Future Is Not Set in Stone," *Literary Review Canada—A Journal of Ideas,* Climate Crisis, November 2020, https://reviewcanada.ca/magazine/2020/11/there-may-yet-be-hope/.
47. Homer-Dixon, *Commanding Hope,* 6.
48. Ibid., 8.
49. Ibid., 56.
50. Ibid.
51. Ibid., 61, 81–3.
52. Ibid., 66.
53. Ibid., 83.
54. Ibid., 84.
55. Ibid., 85–6.
56. Ibid., 86.
57. Ibid., 86–7.
58. Ibid., 88.
59. Ibid., 89.
60. Ibid.
61. Ibid., 93. Homer-Dixon illustrates: "The present & known—His young son's horror at the random slaughter of sharks when they are unintentionally caught by commercial fishermen. The future—Sharks should not be killed, and perpetrators penalized. The reality inside: sympathy for the sharks; outside: slaughter. Challenge of the impossible and the inevitable: create a device to cut the lines of the shark killers."
62. Homer-Dixon, *Commanding Hope,* 94.
63. Ibid., 96.
64. David Tracy, *The Analogical Imagination: Christian Theology and the Culture of Pluralism* (New York: Crossroad Publishing, 1998). David Tracy, *Blessed Rage for Order: New Pluralism in Theology* (Chicago: University of Chicago Press, 1995).
65. Homer-Dixon, *Commanding Hope,* 99–100.
66. Ibid., 102.
67. Ibid.
68. Ibid., 103.
69. Ibid., 38–9, at 38: "In simplest terms, a worldview is a densely connected network of concepts, beliefs and values in a person's mind. Each of us has one that's in some ways unique since it's largely a product of our own first hand experiences."

70. Homer-Dixon, *Commanding Hope*, 39–40.
71. Ibid., 40.
72. Ibid.
73. Ibid., 41.
74. Ibid., 99–100.

1

Hopeful Hebrew Testament Stories of Original Creation and Covenants

Introduction: St. Francis, St. Clare, and Biblical Stories of Creation and Redemption

St. Francis of Assisi had such great reverence for the Sacred Scriptures that he would pick up from the ground pieces of paper that contained any lettering on them. He reasoned that the letters on such scraps could, literally, be put together to form the texts of the Word of God.[1] A similar reverence for the Bible is seen in St. Clare's *Second Letter to Blessed Agnes of Prague*. Praying with the Scriptures and meditating on their message was central to the prayer of the Poor Ladies of San Damiano (Poor Clares). Sacred Scripture was their guide for following the example of Jesus or, as Clare put it, "[holding] fast to the footprints (1 Pt. 2:21) of Him to Whom you have merited to be joined in Marriage."[2]

The Scriptures were central in the life of St. Francis and St. Clare.[3] The sacred texts revealed Jesus Christ, the Incarnate Word in whose footprints all must follow.[4] To follow in the footprints of Jesus meant to conform one's ways of being, thinking, and acting to the life, teachings, and example of Jesus. And so, like St. Francis and St. Clare of Assisi, we reverently begin our study of Franciscan sources for ecological understandings with the Hebrew Testament and Christian Scriptures. We ask how these texts inform Christian theology, ethics, and spirituality when addressing today's "Climate Emergency."

St. Francis' deep regard for the Scriptures is visible in his *Testament*, the document he gave to the first friars, explaining his most important teachings.[5] Further, St. Francis regarded the Gospel itself as the very heart of the *Rule* for the Friars and the Poor Ladies.[6] Clare and the Poor Ladies of Assisi joined Francis in taking up a life in pursuit of Gospel perfection.[7] The daily practice of the Poor Ladies included several times when they all meditated on the Scriptures together, and only then did they engage in the ordinary tasks of communal living and assisting the poor—actively integrating the insights from the Word that had grasped their heart during their contemplation.[8]

Finally, it is rare to find something written by St. Francis or St. Clare that does not include at least a paraphrase of some portion of a biblical text. In thirteenth-century Assisi, lacking today's exegetical tools for interpreting biblical texts, Francis and Clare understood the biblical texts as a narrative or story of faith, in a literal[9] or analogical[10] sense, and as a means of providing authority to what they claimed concerning the topic at hand.[11] Significantly, Francis and Clare were "at home" with Scripture as one is comfortable with a good friend. Unfortunately, we have less of St. Clare's writings than those of St. Francis. Thus, most of what we say here will be from his perspective.[12] Yet there is ample evidence that Clare had considerable influence on Francis' thought.[13]

The various works of Francis and Clare—the rules for the First, Second, and Third Franciscan orders, prayers, letters, poems, etc.—reveal extensive use of Scripture texts, showing God as the Creator of the universe, who is revealed through the natural world.[14] Such knowledge was readily absorbed into the lifeblood of the saints, when growing up in the lush landscape of Umbria, Italy. Intuitively, Francis wove those revelations from Scripture and nature together with his personal knowledge of Jesus the Christ Incarnate, the One who became part of the material world and through whom the world was brought into existence.

Francis knew the natural beauty of Umbria; he had memorized many biblical passages and had an intimate relationship with Jesus. Thus, God's relationship to the world was a living reality for him. That relationship began from the first moment of creation, continued through the many moments when people rejected God, but then returned to God with renewed promises and covenants. That story climaxed with the birth, life, death, and resurrection of Jesus. Today, theologians talk about this reality as the relationship between the Christian doctrines of creation and redemption. Unfortunately, what was so obvious for St. Francis was not always so clear for theologians and the Church, and it was nearly lost.

Biblical Texts and Science: Interpretation and Use

Early Christians, Francis and Clare, and medieval theologians including St. Augustine, St. Bonaventure of Bagnoregio, St. Thomas Aquinas, and Bl. John Duns Scotus saw the created world as a "second book of revelation" about the God who created and saved us. But creations' message was explained and clarified by Sacred Scriptures. Sadly, later theologians and biblical scholars grossly neglected the numerous biblical texts about the natural world. Thus, a strong disproportionate emphasis on the "saving of human souls" became common, and the role of the natural world beyond a human-focused story of salvation was rendered insignificant.

Only when it seemed that scientific theories conflicted with a literal reading of the Bible did the Church and Christian theologians deal with the natural world and scientific matters. It was left to science to address the natural world.[15] Some Catholic Scripture scholars developed a theory of "special revelation" and joined debates of the nineteenth and twentieth centuries and attempted to defend the literal reading of the Bible against biological evolution.[16] They claimed that God acted directly to create every new species. Another debate focused on the meaning of Genesis 1:28 concerning humans having "dominion over all living creatures."[17]

Three important developments took place that allowed Catholic Scripture scholars to return to a more authentic way of understanding the Bible in relation to the environment, ecology, and the whole creation. Firstly, in his encyclical, *Divino Afflante Spiritu* (1943), Pope Pius XII directed biblical scholars to use studies of the ancient languages of the original ancient biblical manuscripts (e.g., Hebrew, Greek, Aramaic) and other modes of modern biblical criticism to interpret the Scriptures.[18] Secondly, *Dei Verbum*, "The Dogmatic Constitution on Divine Revelation" of the Second Vatican Council (1965) reiterated that Sacred Scripture, taken together with the Church's tradition, is the supreme rule of Catholic faith.[19] Subsequently, those advances opened opportunities for a third development, namely conversations between science and religion.

The science–religion dialogue established that, while scientific methods stress explaining the workings of the universe, and religion and biblical studies focus on uncovering the meaning of the universe, the two methods mutually inform and enrich one another.[20] Indeed, substantial numbers of scientists acknowledge that there is meaning concerning all creatures to be found in God or an ultimate Other (beyond science).[21] There is no *necessary* conflict between religion and science.[22] Today, centuries beyond the lifetime of St. Francis and St. Clare, as Pope Francis teaches, we can confidently follow their example of seeking biblical wisdom to address the global climate emergency using current biblical exegetical methods that also engage with science.[23]

The Unity of the Stories of Creation and Redemption

When Christians think about the Bible, environment, ecology, or the natural world, they usually think only of "Genesis" and tend to understand creation in anthropocentric terms.[24] Sadly, biblical creation accounts such as those in Job, Sirach, Proverbs, and Wisdom are neglected. Thus, the larger Christian story of redemption, the major focus of the Bible, becomes disconnected from the story of creation. However, taken together, these stories give us a rich and deep vision of the thorough-going interrelationship of God: humans: living beings: nonliving beings throughout the entire universe.

It is important to recall that biblical evidence shows that the God who created is the same God who redeems. "And this God creates not only Israel, but all other peoples and the whole world in which human history is enacted."[25] If we are to understand what the Bible has to say about environmental and ecological issues, we need to see how the biblical texts deal with the interactions between God, humans, living, and nonliving beings.

Clearly, for the Hebrew Testament writers, the only divine being was the God of Israel (Exod. 20:2-17; Deut. 5:6-21). And significantly, everything God created was "good and beautiful" (Gen. 1, Hebrew = *tob*), capable of revealing something about God. God's creation was to be shared among the creatures and respected because it was "of God." Second, there was no absolute separation between the spiritual and the material because "[t]he earth is the Lord's and all that is in it, the world, and those who live in it" (Ps. 24:1). Humans and all creation are to serve God and follow the divine commandments. Human service to God is not enslavement but a loving exchange in a covenanted relationship for the flourishing of the entire creation. Various expressions of the covenant are woven through the entire

Bible, but especially in the Hebrew Testament. There, God is the origin of goodness and life, while evil and sin originate in human history when people have responded negatively to God.[26]

Creation—Redemption in Genesis 1-11

The Hebrew Testament book of Genesis opens with two creation stories. The older narrative is found in Gen. 2:4b–2:25. Scripture scholars refer to this version as the "Yahwist source," written about 1010–930 BCE.[27] God is the main character in this story. A human being is formed by God out of the mud of the Earth, and God breathes the very breath of life (Hebrew = *rûah*) into its nostrils, making it a living person (v. 7).[28] This creature was needy, so God placed it in the Garden of Eden, a lush place of plenty, and directed the person to cultivate and care for it (v. 15).[29] God also created the animals, and notably animals and the humans share in the status of being "living souls" or "living creatures" (Hebrew = *nefesh chayah*).[30] Further, the human is asked to give the animals names and find a companion among them (v. 19). This act of naming was considered an act of intimacy (Buber's *I-Thou*), of creating an orderly bond and caring relationship between the human and the other creatures.

Scripture scholars date the Genesis 1 "Days of Creation" account at about the sixth-century BCE and as authored by the Priestly writer. It is an example of what Franciscan theologian Zachary Hayes called "a physical cosmology which manifests clear parallels with the accounts of origins in other religions of the ancient world, though these elements have been shaped and reformed by the confrontation with Israel's own religious experience."[31] Notably, because the sun was not created until the fourth day (1:16), Rabbi Sholom Berezovsky taught the "light" (1:3) was a spiritual light and "that 'without this holy light there is no merit in sustaining creation.'"[32] The original creation was a holy place for healthy creatures.

Genesis 1 contains God's directives to humans, to "subdue" the Earth and to have "dominion over" it. But proper biblical interpretation requires us to understand this frequently abused text in its original context before applying it today.[33] The Priestly writers stressed Israel's belief that God created order out of chaos and authorized a day of rest for praising the Creator. This emphasis on order and the co-creative role of humans with God and other creatures is significant, especially when we recall that this text was written during Israel's captivity in Babylon.[34]

The Genesis 1 story is like the Babylonian creation myth, *The Enuma Elish*,[35] but the differences are striking.[36] In the myth, the vengeful god Marduk brutally murders the goddess Tiamat and then creates the world using her carcass. By contrast, Israel's God creates order out of chaos by simply speaking a word while the Spirit of God (*rûah*) moves over the waters giving the life energy to all of creation (v. 2). "On days three, five, and six, God invites creatures to be involved in further creative acts."[37] In Genesis, the heavenly bodies and the fertility of the natural world are simply creatures of God, not sacred (Babylonian deities). In the *Enuma Elish*, an evil god was killed by other gods. Then, humans were created from the victim's blood and enslaved by the murders. But in Genesis 1:26-27, on the sixth day God created humans and animals and called them "very good, beautiful" (Hebrew = *tob*). Humans need to remember their common creaturely status *with* the animals, as St. Francis did and respect them accordingly. How creation lives and develops is mutually dependent on us *with* God and other creatures.

The Hebrew Testament tells us that humans were created in God's "image and likeness" (Gen. 1:26-27). This depiction reflects language used about ancient Egyptian and Mesopotamian kings, who were considered representatives of their gods or as trustees of the gods' possessions.[38] This understanding reminded exiled Israelite people of their dignity, of being entrusted with the privilege of representing God, and delegated to care for creation as God cares for Israel.[39] Indeed the human's dignity is comprised of their spiritual capacity to relate to God in a distinct way, while remaining creatures among others of God's creation.[40]

After declaring humans to be made in the image of God, the text states: "God blessed them, and God said to them, 'Be fruitful and multiply, and fill the Earth and subdue it; and have dominion over the fish of the sea and over the birds of the air and over every living thing that moves upon the Earth'" (Gen. 1:28). These words have spiritual and moral implications for humans so blessed.

In Genesis, humans are created for the service (Hebrew = *abad*) of other living creatures with whom humans share an earthly kinship (2:15).[41] To keep the meaning of "subdue" and "dominion" in perspective, it is helpful to recall that these stories were written during the Neolithic age, when likely little was known about egalitarian relationships. So humans (Hebrew = *adam*) are to rule over the biota (Gen. 2:19), the Leviathan over the sea (Job 40:25-32; 41:1-22), and the Behemoth over the land (Job 40:15-24). But those "ruling" humans are ultimately accountable to God, who is their Creator, and the loving God of the covenant.[42]

Scripture scholars have shown how all the creatures are involved with different kinds of relationships with each other.[43] The human role of "dominion" is held in perspective by the "mocking of the human inability to understand nature beyond that which has been domesticated."[44] Humans need to be humble before creation.[45] The plants and animals empathize with human joys and sorrows.[46] Isaiah 34–35 illustrates how nature chastises humans, sympathizes with them, and rejoices in their redemption.

> And the streams of Edom shall be turned into pitch,
> and her soil into sulfur;
> her land shall become burning pitch. (34:9)
> … the hawk and the hedgehog shall possess it;
> the owl and the raven shall live in it. … (34:11)
> And the thorns shall come up in their places,
> Thorns shall grow over its strongholds, nettles and thistles in its fortresses … (34:13)
> Wildcats shall meet with hyenas,
> goat-demons shall call to each other … (34:14)
> … there too the buzzards shall gather, each one with its mate. (34:15)

During Israel's future salvation, however, "[t]he wilderness and the dry land shall be glad, the desert shall rejoice and blossom; like the crocus it shall blossom abundantly and rejoice with joy and singing" (35:1-2). The environment deteriorates when people sin; nature is often God's tool of reward and punishment. Nature's beneficence depends on human morality. Humans' dominion over nature, then, is strictly conditioned on their moral fitness. Humans who sin bestialize the divine image and diminish their authority over nature (Gen. 9:7). The full meaning of "dominion" emerges later in Genesis in the story of the Great Flood.

In Genesis 6, God grieves over the immense wickedness of humans, initiating the onslaught of an ecological disaster of worldwide proportions. Only Noah and his family were faithful and thus exempted from the great flood that destroyed all other humans, "together with animals and creeping things and birds of the air" (v. 7). Noah followed God's instruction to build an ark and bring "two of every kind … to keep them alive" (v. 20). This action exemplified the true meaning of "having dominion"—to affirm morality and to care and save the other living creatures.[47]

With the flood ended, God indicated that from that time forward, a reckoning will be required from humans and from every beast alike

(Gen. 9:1-4). Then God established a covenant with Noah's family, their descendants, and all living creatures (vv. 9-11) that is symbolized by God's "bow in the clouds" (v. 13).[48] The story of Noah and the flood illustrates that human offenses potentially threaten the rest of creation. "Dominion," enacted by a representative of God in Noachic covenant partnership, clearly ruled out anthropocentrism or the exploitation of nonhuman nature. Today, with every "bow in the clouds," we too are invited to recall this Noachic covenant that God made with the earth and all its inhabitants.

Genesis 1:28 also includes God's command that humans "fill the Earth and subdue it." The Hebrew term for "subdue" (*kābās*) means "to bring into bondage." However, according to biblical scholar James Barr, and considering the use of the term throughout the Bible, "subdue" simply means to inhabit the land that God has given as a gift, transforming it into a home where God can be worshiped.[49] Subduing the Earth cannot be equated with a license for humans to exploit God's creation. In fact, the premeditated decimation of nature is uniquely God's prerogative, not that of humans (Ps. 29:5-6, 9; Zech. 11:1-3; and Hab. 3:5-8). Human arrogance against nature is considered blasphemous against God (2 Kgs 19:23-24; Isa. 9:9-11; 10:13-19; 14:24; Hab. 2:17; Judg. 6:3-6; Ezek. 29:3-59). Humans indirectly bring about environmental destruction as an outcome of sin; thus, to do so directly is foolish arrogance.

In the Hebrew Testament crimes against God are also crimes against the natural landscape in which they were committed (Gen. 4:10; Lev. 18:25; Ezek. 12:19; Hos. 1:1-3). Reciprocal justice governs human–nature relationships. All moral and immoral deeds have a positive or a negative impact on the land in which they are perpetrated, and the land responds accordingly. Humans do not commit evil in isolation or without effects on the entire community. The masses suffer for the crimes of a few. This reality places a heavy weight on individuals to act responsibly and morally. "The entire Torah could be considered as a guidebook for environmental maintenance. The belief that all human offenses potentially imperil nature is the Bible's strongest statement about human domination over the environment."[50]

In summary, Genesis 1 declares a belief in a God who creates, bringing order out of chaos in a nonviolent manner. In this context, the commission given by God to humankind, made in God's image, is to protect the balance of life that God's ordering word has built into the universe and to promote the continuation of all species having a place in that delicate earthly balance.

Creation—Redemption beyond Genesis

Second Isaiah

The place that most clearly connects the themes of Creation/Redemption is the second part of the book of Isaiah, known as "Second Isaiah" (Chapters 40–50). This text was composed at about the same time as Genesis 1, about 538 BCE.[51] The context of its writing is that the author is directed by God to "speak tenderly to Jerusalem [because] her service [as an exile in Babylon] is at an end" (Isa. 40:1). Here we have some reflections on the theological significance of the end of Israel's exile and the new exodus to the Promised Land. The prophet links God's redemption of Israel and God's re-creation of the earth. An important Hebrew word that shows this connection is *bara*. This word is used frequently in the creation stories of Genesis and in Second Isaiah. It means "making full" or literally "fattening" in a way that only God can perform. "The same word is used for the original creation as for God establishing his loving kindness toward Israel."[52] Both actions are very personal and responsive acts of God.

God leads the Israelites through the wilderness to a new occupation of the Promised Land, a kind of redemption that is God's gift. During this new exodus, valleys are filled in and mountains leveled so that the glory of God can be revealed anew (40:4-5). The new creation is also God's gift. Echoing Genesis 1, Second Isaiah encourages a depressed and impoverished Israel to trust in God: "For thus says the Lord, who created the heavens (he is God!), who formed the earth and made it (he established it; he did not create it a chaos, he formed it to be inhabited!): I am the Lord, and there is no other" (45:18). The word "chaos" (Hebrew = *tohu*) is a clear reference to the origins of creation, when the Earth was "a formless void" and without God's ordering (Gen. 1:2). For Second Isaiah, God continues to call order out of chaos through his caring involvement with all creatures, sustaining them and their survival. God invites: "Turn to me and be saved, all the ends of the Earth! For I am God, and there is no other" (v. 22). Clearly, in Second Isaiah *creation and redemption* are *complementary* in the deepest sense of the word.

The Prophets: Hosea and Jeremiah

The connection between creation and redemption is sometimes made in a negative way in the Hebrew Testament. Two examples of this are found in the pre-exilic writings of Hosea and Jeremiah. The first instance in Hosea recalls the Noahic covenant: "On that day I will answer, says the Lord, I will answer the heavens and they shall answer the earth; and the earth shall answer the grain, the wine, and the oil, and they shall answer" (2:21-22). Here even the animals were given commandments by God (Hebrew = *mitzvot*) in Gen. 1:22 and 8:17. But later, Hosea points out, because the people sinned, violating the covenant, God has a legal suite against Israel: "Therefore the land mourns, and all who live in it languish; together with the wild animals and the birds of the air, even the fish of the sea are perishing" (4:3).

A century later Jeremiah proclaims the extension of the covenant to the earth: "Give them this charge for their masters: Thus says the Lord of hosts, the God of Israel: This is what you shall say to your masters: It is I who by my great power and my outstretched arm have made the earth, with the people and animals that are on the earth, and I give it to whomever I please" (27:4-5). The people suffer because they have failed to honor the sacred Noahic covenant relationship and thus the land also suffers. Jeremiah calls for a "mournful dirge" on behalf of the despoiled land and all that dwell on it:

> Shall I not punish them for these things? says the Lord; and shall I not bring retribution on a nation such as this? Take up weeping and wailing for the mountains, and a lamentation for the pastures of the wilderness, because they are laid waste so that no one passes through, and the lowing of cattle is not heard; both the birds of the air and the animals have fled and are gone
> (Jer. 9:9-10)

Jeremiah (8:4-10:25) maintains the people have brought this ecological crisis upon themselves by their own life choices, and thus a lament is required.[53]

Israel's infidelity and failure resulted in defeat by Nebuchadnezzar, king of Babylon (Jer. 27:5-6). Yet hope remained. What God created and what has been reduced to chaos by sin, Jeremiah suggests, can be re-created. He announced a time of a new creation is coming, when Nebuchadnezzar's kingdom will collapse (27:7), ending Israel's long period of exile (25:11-12; 29:10; 28:1).

The Psalms

God the Creator and the natural world as the occasion of praise of God are common themes in the Psalms. Psalm 104, commonly known as the "Franciscan Psalm," because it closely resembles St. Francis' "Canticle of the Creatures," recalls the creation stories of Genesis 1 and 2, honoring God the Creator. The psalmist responds with wonder and awe to the beauty of creation (24-34), in some detail: God's splendor in the heavens (1-4), how the chaotic waters were tamed to fertilize and feed the world (5-18), and how primordial night was transformed into a gentle time of refreshment (19-23). Then the *rûah*, the Spirit of God, again appears: "When you hide your face, they are dismayed; when you take away their breath, they die and return to their dust. When you send forth your spirit, they are created; and you renew the face of the ground" (vv. 29-30). Psalm 104 ends with hope: "Let sinners be consumed from the earth, and let the wicked be no more. Bless the Lord, O my soul. Praise the Lord!" (v. 35).

Psalm 146 speaks most clearly of the one and the same God who is the Creator and the Redeemer of all. There is no other source of salvation (v. 3) than God the Creator, the Maker of heaven and earth, the sea, and all that is in them (v. 6). It is this same God who "executes justice for the oppressed; who gives food to the hungry. The Lord sets the prisoners free; the Lord opens the eyes of the blind. The Lord lifts up those who are bowed down; the Lord loves the righteous."

"The Lord watches over the strangers; he upholds the orphan and the widow, but the way of the wicked he brings to ruin" (vv. 7-9). In each activity, God responds to the creatures most in need, offering them the freedom of a redeemed life.

The Wisdom Literature

Another important set of texts about the environment and creation is the Wisdom literature.[54] Wisdom literature includes the biblical books of Job, Sirach, Proverbs, and the Book of Wisdom. In the wisdom literature, we find the themes of creation and redemption united in wisdom (*Hôkmah* = Hebrew and *Sophia* = Greek, both feminine nouns). Today Scripture scholars understand that "wisdom theology is creation theology." Wisdom represents the human effort to relate to creation as God has intended. The theme of redemption is closely intertwined with creation because people always struggle with the forces of chaos in their lives.

Today we usually think of "wisdom" as an accumulation of insights people create or gather through experiences over a lifetime. But the Israelites thought of wisdom as a separate creation of God, and something that guided the cosmos as well as humans. The way people gained access to wisdom was through "fear of the Lord"—extending deep reverence and respect to God. Wisdom is the key to understanding the universe, but also the way of proper action and the moral living before God. According to Scripture scholar Gerhardt von Rad, a characteristic of the wisdom literature is "the determined effort to relate the phenomenon of the world, of 'nature' with its secrets of creation, to the saving revelation addressed to man."⁵⁵ Throughout the book of Proverbs, for example, the teacher consistently links the themes of creation and redemption in profound and penetrating ways. In Proverbs 3, the teacher asserts: "The Lord by wisdom founded the earth" (v. 19).

Wisdom (*Hôkmah/Sophia*) is personified as a woman in the first nine chapters of Proverbs with strong suggestions of divinity.⁵⁶ Sophia is she who is the giver of life (Prov. 4:23). In Proverbs 8, Sophia describes her character and works: "Ages ago I was set up, at the first, before the beginning of the earth" (v. 23). Sophia presents herself as existing before the rest of creation, and as the very first of God's creative works, and not of the ordinary created order (vv. 22-26). She explains:

> The Lord created me at the beginning of his work, the first of his acts of long ago. Ages ago I was set up, at the first, before the beginning of the earth. When there were no depths I was brought forth, when there were no springs abounding with water. Before the mountains had been shaped, before the hills, I was brought forth—when he had not yet made earth and fields, or the world's first bits of soil (vv. 27-30).

Sophia is a creature of God and a co-creator with God. She is involved in the activity of creation as a designer and master craftswoman: "when he assigned to the sea its limit, so that the waters might not transgress his command, when he marked out the foundations of the earth, then I was beside him, like a master worker; and I was daily his delight, rejoicing before him always" (vv. 29-30). Sophia is the model or exemplar of God's works. She is also the one who executes the creative activity of God—through her creation happens, and she takes delight in creation. Sophia sustains the order of creation by opposing evil for the sake of justice (v. 13). Lady Wisdom, Sophia invites her followers to listen to her and obey her directives. Those who follow them find life, but those who neglect her ways die (vv. 35-36).

Gleanings from Hebrew Testament Texts

The prevailing viewpoint of the Hebrew Testament is that of choosing life over death.⁵⁷ As we have indicated, to "choose life" meant to keep God's commands (Hebrew = *mitzvot*). If one fulfilled the commandments, then one would have: the means to produce or find enough food to eat; protection for the extremes of weather; freedom from life-threatening dangers; sufficient capacity for human, animal, and plant reproduction; and sufficient shelter.

All this security would be accounted for as the work of God the Creator and the spiritual force (*rûah*) within all living beings. Choosing life would be continued through the capacity to have a sufficient livelihood to pass on to future generations. Today we might well call this a life based on sustainability.

Humans share the *nefesh chayah* and the *rûah* with all animate life. Jeanne Kay explains the implications of this:

> Judaism's belief in nature dependent on a single Creator God is therefore a belief in the fundamental unity of nature, rather than in its fragmentation under different powers as depicted in some forms of pantheism [worship of the objects of nature—plants, animals, rocks, rivers, etc.]. There is no textual or archaeological evidence that ancient Jews believed that God commanded humanity to deplete the environment to such an extent that its life-supporting capabilities deteriorate. In contrast, a life-sustaining environment, with sufficient rainfall and fertile soil is considered among the most desirable of God's gifts. It is a principal reward for the demands of a Jewish life (Deut. 11:14-17).[58]

The Hebrew Testament, including the creation stories of Genesis 1 and 2 and related texts, clearly shows that creation and redemption are intimately related and that there is a genuine kinship between humans and all other creatures of God. Throughout salvation history, the God whose creative love overflows in the universe also redeems, continuing to bring order out of the chaos caused by sin—all the work of a loving God.

Long before Ernest Haeckel first defined the science of ecology in 1866, the Bible presented humans and earth's other life forms as interconnected and interdependent on religious grounds. Humans are distinct among creatures, but they are *also* profoundly *related* to all creatures. This is what St. Francis and St. Clare knew so well, exemplified with their lives, and passed on to us. Saint Francis called each entity of creation "brother" or "sister" and his story reveals how even the wild animals came running to him as their friend and companion. Similarly, Saint Clare taught that we must respect all the creatures—"whether a person, a tree, or a paper wasp"—because they all are made and loved by God.[59]

In the next chapter, we will examine the Christian Scriptures—the New Testament, focusing on the theme of creation and the "new creation." We will see how the promises God made to the people of Israel are fulfilled in Jesus, the "Wisdom of God." Jesus' life and ministry involved rich relationships with creation. We will examine how the Wisdom Woman of the Hebrew Testament and the parables, proverbs, and prayers of Jesus all play a part in the Christian understanding of the environment and ecological ethics.

From the Writings of St. Francis
Francis of Assisi, *The Admonitions VII*
Let Good Action Follow Knowledge[60]
The apostle says, *the letter kills, but the spirit gives life.*

Those people are put to death by the letter who only wish to know the words alone—that they might be esteemed the wiser than others and be able to acquire great riches to give to their relatives and friends.

And those religious are put to death by the letter who are not willing to follow the spirit of the divine letter but, instead, wish only to know the words and to interpret them for others.

And those people who are brought to life by the spirit of the divine letter who do not attribute every letter they know, or wish to know, to the body, but by word and example return them to the most high Lord God to Whom every good belongs.

Reflection and Application

The "Admonitions" of St. Francis are a collection of his teachings intended to guide Christians trying to live according to the Good News of Jesus. "Admonition VII" emphasizes the best approach to a Christian's study of Sacred Scriptures, and it points to the life-giving responses such study elicits.

Citing St. Paul, the apostle (I Cor. 3:6) St. Francis insisted that Christians not be concerned with only "the letter" of the Sacred Scriptures, i.e., learning facts and information *about* the biblical texts or priding themselves in memorizing numerous passages, with the intent of outsmarting opponents in, e.g., argumentative climate policy debates. Such use of Sacred Scripture (proof-texting) is an abuse that empties biblical texts of their "spirit." Self-centered boosting, drawing attention to ourselves, makes it impossible for us or anyone else to hear God's voice in the texts. Thus, "the letter kills."

Instead, St. Francis cautions, it is necessary to live out in one's daily life what one learns from contemplating the Scriptures. As we saw, the Scriptures show us a loving and generous God who created a good and beautiful universe for us and our sisters and brothers of all kinds. A reflective attitude characterizes the most fruitful approach to Bible. One must be open and attentive to what in the sacred text touches our heart as we read. Then, with the help of God's grace, one will be able to make the changes necessary to conform one's life to "following in the footprints of Jesus." We must love and care for creation as God the Creator loves and cares for us. This includes engaging in respectful dialogue with others.

In his landmark encyclical, *Laudato Si'—On Care for Our Common Home*, Ch. 2, "The Gospel of Creation," §s 62-100, Pope Francis models the proper use of Sacred Scripture as a theological, spiritual, and moral source of wisdom and motivation for addressing issues of the "Climate Emergency."[61] He cites numerous texts (including those examined above) especially Gen. 1:28. Genesis reveals that "human life is grounded in three fundamental and closely intertwined relationships: with God, with our neighbour and with the earth itself" (66). These relationships are ruptured by sin, namely "by our presuming to take the place of God and refusing to acknowledge our creaturely limitations" (66). Noting Exodus 23:12, Pope Francis states: "Clearly, the Bible has no place for a tyrannical anthropocentrism unconcerned for other creatures" (68). Creation is an intentional act of a loving God (Wis. 11:24), yet God created "a world in need of development" and "counts on our cooperation" (80). Each person and creature is unique in ways not fully explained by evolution and praises God in its unique irreplicable manner (87).

"Concern for the environment thus needs to be joined to a sincere love for our fellow human beings and an unwavering commitment to resolving the problems of society" (91). Pope Francis stresses: "Everything is related, and we human beings are united as brothers and sisters on a wonderful pilgrimage, woven together by the love God has for each of his creatures and which also unites us in fond affection with brother sun, sister moon, brother river and mother earth" (92). This requires a revolution in our perspective on the fundamental rights of the poor and the underprivileged. It requires that private property be subordinate to "the universal destination of goods, and thus the right of everyone to their use" (93). Pope Francis recalls, "The Christian tradition has never recognized the right to private property as absolute or inviolable, and has stressed the social purpose of all forms of private property" (93). He concludes that "[t]he natural environment is a collective good, the patrimony of all humanity and the responsibility of everyone. If we make something our own, it is only to administer it for the good of all. If we do not, we burden our consciences with the weight of having denied the existence of others" (95).

Hope is readily ours to have, even amid the "Climate Emergency." Indeed, Christianity's treasure trove of teachings, texts, and exemplars bears the light of hope, and Christians can freely offer those in dialogue with other believers and people of good will for the common goal of healing the Earth and returning to sustainable living (62-63). Noah's story illustrates how it takes only one good person to bring hope to the planet and its people. Israel's renewed faith in God and new life emerging from their wretched captivity in Babylon bring hope beyond adverse circumstances (74). Thus, Pope Francis proclaims: "God has written a precious book, whose letters are the multitude of created things present in the universe." "From panoramic vistas to the tiniest living form, nature is a constant source of wonder and awe. It is also a continuing revelation of the divine" (85).[62] Therein lies Christian hope!

Questions for Reflection and Discussion

1. When thinking about the "Climate Emergency," in what way do you value or regard the Bible compared to other books, as a source for wisdom relevant for resolving it? Compare your experience with that of St. Francis' attitude toward Sacred Scripture and creation.
2. Have you ever heard a Christian homily on the doctrine of creation? Do you recall how (if at all) the preacher related the doctrine of creation and the doctrine of redemption?
3. Compare the ways science describes the kinds of positive relationships between humans, animals, plants, and other natural elements such as rivers, lakes, rocks, hills, or plains with the way the Hebrew Testament describes those within God's creation. Notice the ways there is commonality, uniqueness, or complementarity in the descriptions.
4. What influence might the Hebrew Testament creation texts have on how you think about "natural resources"? What you buy? How you invest your money?
5. If the ultimate purpose of other creatures is not to be found in us, how do humans and other creatures fit into God's plan (*Laudato Si'* §83)?

Suggestions for Action

1. Read Psalm 104. Then sit quietly for a while and bask in God's generosity. In gratitude praise God for the gift of your life within such a marvelous creation.

2 Go outside and observe your favorite plant, animal, daytime or nighttime sky, or earth element. Then express your "psalm" telling its "creation story," giving praise and thanks to God.
3 Check out the Franciscan Action Network website and see how you can participate in caring for the Earth: http://www.franciscanaction.org/.
4 Use reusable or biodegradable items—save trees and reduce plastic waste that endangers animals who become entangled in it or mistake its fine degraded particles for food.
5 Select a plant or animal and research how it relates to other creatures within the ecosystem where you live, bringing life to all other elements of creation in your locale.

Sources for Further Study

Bergant, Dianne. *Genesis: In the Beginning.* Collegeville: Liturgical Press, 2013.

Edwards, Denis. *Partaking of God: Trinity, Evolution, and Ecology.* Collegeville: Liturgical Press, 2014.

Habel, Norman C. *Finding Wisdom in Nature: An Eco-Wisdom Reading of the Book of Job.* Sheffield: Sheffield Phoenix Press, 2014.

Hayes, Zachary. *Window to the Divine: A Study of Christian Creation Theology.* Quincy, IL: The Franciscan Press, 1997.

Nothwehr, Dawn M., ed. *Franciscan Theology of the Environment: An Introductory Reader.* Quincy, IL: The Franciscan Press, 2002.

Notes

1. Thomas of Celano, "The Life of Saint Francis" (1228–1229), Chapter XXIX:82, in FA: ED, Volume I—*The Saint*, 251-2.
2. Clare of Assisi, "Second Letter to Blessed Agnes of Prague," in *TL:CA:ED*, 47.
3. Works by St. Francis FA:ED, Volume I—*The Saint*, 40-167. Works by St. Clare in in *TL:CA:ED*.
4. Francis of Assisi, "A Letter to Brother Leo (1224–1226)," in FA:ED Volume I—*The Saint*, 122-3.
5. "The Testament (1226)," in FA: ED, Volume I—*The Saint*, 124-6.
6. Francis of Assisi, "The Undated Writings—Admonitions," VII, in FA:ED Volume I—*The Saint*, 132. Also Francis of Assisi, "The Testament (1226),"

14–15, in FA: ED Volume I—*The Saint,* 124–7. Regis J. Armstrong and Ignatius C. Brady, trans. and eds, *Francis and Clare: The Complete Works* (New York: Paulist Press, 1982), 4, 12, 17–18, 108 n.2.
7. Armstrong & Brady, *Francis and Clare,* 170, 172, 178.
8. Ingrid J. Peterson, *Clare of Assisi: A Bibliographical Study* (Quincy, IL: Franciscan Press, 1993), 279, 283–4.
9. The *literal sense* of Scripture refers to a way of interpreting the biblical texts stressing the obvious common meaning of each word in light of the kind of work (poem, song, historical record, etc.) it is. *Litera* is the Latin word for "letter."
10. The *analogical sense* of Scripture is a way of interpreting the biblical texts by finding a symbolic meaning for the words concerning human destiny or purpose (beyond the literal meaning). *Anagein* is the Greek word for "to refer."
11. Thomas of Celano, "The Major Legend of St. Francis of Assisi" (1260–1263), Chapter XI:2, in FA:ED Volume II—*The Founder.*
12. Margaret Carney, "Franciscan Women and the Theological Enterprise," in *The History of Franciscan Theology*, ed. Kenan B. Osborne, 331–45, especially at 333 (St. Bonaventure, NY: The Franciscan Institute, 1994).
13. Peterson, *Clare of Assisi.*
14. Examples: Francis of Assisi, "The Later Admonition and Exhortation to the Brothers and Sisters of Penance," 61; Francis of Assisi, "Exhortation to the Praise of God," 138; Francis of Assisi, "The Praises to Be Said at All the Hours," 161; and Thomas of Celano, "The Life of Saint Francis" (1228–1229), Chapter XXIX:80–1, in FA:ED Volume I—*The Saint*, 49, 138, 161–2, 250–1. Also Thomas of Celano, "The Major Legend of St. Francis (1260–1263)" Chapter VIII, in FA: ED Volume II—*The Founder,* 586–95.
15. Elizabeth A. Johnson, *Creation and the Cross: The Mercy of God for a Planet in Peril* (Maryknoll: Orbis Books, 2018).
16. Don O'Leary, *Roman Catholicism and Modern Science: A History* (New York: The Continuum Publishing Group, Inc., 2006).
17. Anthropocentric theology still prevails. Dawn M. Nothwehr, "For the Salvation of the Cosmos: The Church's Mission of Ecojustice," *International Bulletin of Mission Research* 43/1 (2019): 68–81.
18. An encyclical is a pastoral teaching document circulated to the whole Church by the Pope. Pope Pius XII, *Divino Afflante Spiritu,* http://www.vatican.va/content/pius-xii/en/encyclicals/documents/hf_p-xii_enc_30091943_divino-afflante-spiritu.html.
19. Vatican Council II, *Dei Verbum,* https://www.vatican.va/archive/hist_councils/ ii_vatican_council/ documents/vat-ii_const_19651118_dei-verbum_en.html. *Dei Verbum* presents three broad principles for interpreting biblical texts: 1) The primary message of any biblical text is the

meaning intended by its author(s) … the language, history and culture of the Bible must be studied. (No. 12). 2) … [I]t is important to examine … themes in light of how the Bible as a whole treats them. 3) Taking into account the entire tradition of the Church … the interpreter should study how a particular passage was used and understood in the earlier life of the Church (No.12).

These three principles of biblical interpretation affirm of Roman Catholicism as an ever-evolving tradition concerned with illuminating and responding to the changing signs of the times.

20. John F. Haught, *Science and Faith: A New Introduction* (Mahwah, NJ: Paulist Press, 2012). Also, Francis Schüssler Fiorenza, "Systematic Theology: Task and Method," in *Systematic Theology: Roman Catholic Perspectives*, ed. Francis Schüssler Fiorenza and John P. Galvin (Minneapolis: Fortress Press, 2011), 1–78.
21. Dawn M. Nothwehr, "The Quest for Interconnectedness: Cosmic Mutuality," in *Plural Spiritualities—North American Experiences*, ed. Robert J. Schreiter, Christian Philosophical Studies, XIV (Washington, DC: The Council for Research in Values and Philosophy, 2015), 11–33.
22. John Paul II reaffirmed this relationship in *Letter of His Holiness John Paul II to Reverend George V. Coyne, S.J. Director of the Vatican Observatory*, http://www.vatican.va/ content/john-paul-ii/en/letters/1988/documents/ hf_jp-ii_let_19880601 _padre-coyne.html. F. LeRon Shults, "Religion and Science in Christian Theology," *Routledge Companion to Religion and Science* (New York: Routledge, 2012), 3–11.
23. Pope Francis, LS, §s 62, 102, 110, 114, 131, 199, 200. *Laudato Si'* is a papal encyclical, a religious and ethical teaching document. In the Roman Catholic tradition, a papal encyclical originates with the Bishop of Rome, the Supreme Pontiff, the Church's universal teacher of faith and morals. It thus bears the highest authority and it obliges Catholics to follow its teaching—at the level of conscience. The content of *Laudato Si'* is a formal part of official Catholic social teaching. As such, this document is a work in moral theology, social ethics, and environmental ethics. The word "encyclical" comes from Late Latin *encyclicus* (from Latin *encyclius*, a Latinization of Greek *enkyklios* meaning "circular," "in a circle," or "all-round"). Hereafter, numbers in parentheses indicate the paragraph of the encyclical.
24. Bryan L. Moore, *Ecological Literature and the Critique of Anthropocentrism* (Cham: Palgrave Macmillan, 2017), 7–12.
25. Zachary Hayes, *A Window to the Divine: A Study of Christian Creation Theology* (Quincy, IL: Franciscan Press, 1997), 18.
26. Ibid., 19.

27. Peter Enns, "When Was Genesis Written and Why Does It Matter? The BioLogos Foundation," https://wp.biologos.org/wp-content/uploads/2019/02/enns_scholarly_essay3.pdf.
28. Also Ps. 104:30; Eccles. 3:19, 21; and Gen. 1:24-26.
29. Rabbi Lord Jonathan Sacks, "The Stewardship Paradigm," in *Eco Bible,* Vol. 1. An Ecological Commentary on Genesis and Exodus, ed. Rabbi Yonatan Neril and Rabbi Leo Dee (Jerusalem: Interfaith Center for Sustainable Development, 2020), 11. Sacks explains that the first human is set in the Garden of Eden "to work it and take care of it." Two significant Hebrew verbs are *le'ovdah* = "to serve it"; the human is both master and servant; an *le'shomrah* = "to guard it"—same language is used in legislation for guarding property belonging to someone else; requires vigilance, and protection; and is personally liable for losses that occur through negligence.
30. Jeanne Kay, "Concepts of Nature in the Hebrew Bible," in *Franciscan Theology of the Environment: An Introductory Reader*, ed. Dawn M. Nothwehr (Quincy, IL: Franciscan Press, 2002), 27. Sachs, "Learning from Animals," *Eco Bible,* 13–14.
31. Hayes, *A Window to the Divine*, 20–1.
32. "Sustainability and Spiritual Awareness," *Eco Bible,* 4.
33. LS, §67.
34. Anne Katrine Gudme and Ingrid Hjelm, eds, *Myths of Exile: History and Metaphor in the Hebrew Bible* (London: Routledge, 2015).
35. Bernard W. Anderson, *Creation Verses Chaos: The Reinterpretation of Mystical Symbolism in the Bible* (New York: Association Press, 1967). Also Alexander Heidel, *The Babylonian Genesis* (Chicago: University of Chicago Press, 1951).
36. Bratton, "Christian Ecotheology and the Hebrew Scriptures," in *Franciscan Theology of the Environment: An Introductory Reader*, ed. Dawn M. Nothwehr (Quincy, IL: Franciscan Press, 2002), 51–2.
37. Terrence E. Fretheim, "Issues of Interdependence in Matters of Creation: An Old Testament Perspective," in *Eco-Reformation: Grace and Hope for a Planet in Peril*, ed. Lisa E. Dahill and James B. Martin-Schramm (Eugene, Or: Wipf & Stock Publishers, 2016), at 127: "Gen. 1:11-13—'let the earth bring forth' … Gen 1: 20, 24—'Let the earth bring forth … Let the waters bring forth' …; Gen 1:26—'… Let us create humankind …' only in Gen 1:28 are humans specifically invited into the process."
38. Claus Westermann, *Genesis 1-11: A Commentary*, trans. John J. Scullion (Minneapolis: Augsburg Publishing House, 1974), 153.
39. Rabbi Isaac Karo explains: The language of 1:26, for "ruling" fish, birds, and animals, does not mean killing them for human food (Gen. 1:29).

Rabbi Gil Marks shows that over most of history meat was a flavoring agent; instead, people used sheep's milk and wool for clothing; cattle for plowing and turning mechanical wheels for drawing water; pulling plows; trodding grain. *Eco Bible*, 6 and 187–8, notes 54 and 55.
40. Bratton, "Christian Ecotheology," 56.
41. Norman Habel, *An Inconvenient Text: Is a Green Reading of the Bible Possible?* (Adelaide: AFT Press, 2009), 68–77. Habel insists the better translation (Gen. 2:15) is "to serve," not "to till and keep." Also note 29 above.
42. In v. 26, *ve-yir-du* = "They shall rule." But in v. 28 = *u-re-du* the command form. "Thus, Rabbi Chanina interpreted the Midrash to say: 'If humankind is worthy, God says *u-re-du*' [you rule!]; while if humankind in not worthy, God says, '*yé-ra-du*'—he will be taken down (or let others [the animal] rule over him." Humans will be ruled by animals if we are not worthy; i.e., we do not cultivate God-like qualities. *Eco Bible*, 7 and 188, notes 57–61.
43. Clarence J. Glacken, *Traces on the Rhodian Shore: Nature and Culture in Western Thought from Ancient Times to the End of the Eighteenth Century* (Berkeley: University of California, 1967). Gen. 1:30; Ps. 104:14-20; Ps. 145:16; Ps. 147:8-9; Job 38:39-41; Job 39:1-8,28.
44. Kay, "Concepts of Nature," 29. Job 38: 25-27; 39:9-12; and Eccl. 11:5.
45. Denis Edwards, *Partaking of God: Trinity, Evolution, and Ecology* (Collegeville: Liturgical Press, 2014), 167–9. Beldon C. Lane, "Biodiversity and the Holy Trinity," *America* 185/20 (2000): 8.
46. Joel 1:12; Amos 1:2; Jon. 3:7-7; and Isa. 14:7-8.
47. The Ark in Gen. 6:16, the Ark was a "green building" with three decks. One deck was for humans, another for animals, and a third for manure needed for post flood recovery to fertilizer farmlands that the flood waters drained of nutrients. Gen. 6:19, Midrash tells that Noah planted the trees for the Ark 120 years before the Flood. Gen. 6:21, concerning care for the creatures, Rabbi Meir Leibush explains that God forewarned Noah of the need to provide for animals because their capacity to care for themselves would be disrupted by the flood. *Eco Bible*, 19–23 and 190–1, notes 112, 117–20.
48. Several rabbinic interpretations of the bow: The inverted warrior's bow was a sign of surrender in battle. Thus, the bow was a reminder of peace. The bow is a kind of half circle that God provides, and humans are free to complete the circle—or not. God cannot guarantee that humanity will not destroy itself. *Eco Bible*, 24–5 and 191, notes 129–32.
49. James Barr, "Man and Nature: The Ecological Controversy and the Old Testament," in *Ecology and Religion in History*, ed. David and Ellen Spring (New York: Harper and Row, 1974), 63–4.
50. Kay, "Concepts of Nature," 36.

51. Joseph Blenkinsopp, *Isaiah 40-55*, The Anchor Yale Bible Commentaries, Volume 19A (New Haven: Yale University Press, 2002), 54.
52. Bratton, "Christian Ecotheology," 53.
53. Terrance E. Fretheim, "Divine Dependence upon the Human: An Old Testament Perspective," in *What Kind of God? Collected Essays of Terrance E. Fretheim*, ed. Michael J. Chan and Brent A. Strawn, 25-39. Siphrit: Literature and Theology of the Hebrew Scriptures (Winona Lake, IN: Eisenbrauns, 2015), 33-4.
54. John H. Hayes, *Introduction to the Bible*, chapter 14 (Philadelphia: Westminster Press, 1971).
55. Gerhardt von Rad, *Old Testament Theology*, Vol. 1 (New York: Harper and Row, 1962), 449.
56. Roger N. Whybray, *Wisdom in Proverbs: The Concept of Wisdom in Proverbs 1-9* (London: SCM Press, Ltd., 1965). Also Roland E. Murphy, *The Tree of Life* (New York: Doubleday; The Anchor Bible Reference Library, 1990).
57. Kay, "Concepts of Nature," 39. Also Deut. 30:15-20.
58. Kay, "Concepts of Nature," 41.
59. Elizabeth A. Dreyer, "'[God] Whose Beauty the Sun and the Moon Admire:' Clare And Ecology," in *Franciscan Theology of the Environment*, ed. Nothwehr, 133.
60. Francis of Assisi, "The Undated Writings—Admonitions," VII, in FA: ED Volume I—*The Saint*, 132.
61. *LS*, see note 23, above.
62. Pope Francis cites: John Paul II, *Catechesis* (January 30, 2002), 6; *Insegnamenti* 25/1 (2002): 140. Canadian Conference of Catholic Bishops, Social Affairs Commission, Pastoral Letter *"You Love All that Exists ... All Things are Yours, God, Lover of Life"* (October 4, 2003), 1.

2

Hopeful Christian Testament Stories of a New Creation and Covenant

Introduction: Hope from a Rich Heritage

Most people have never heard of British composer Sir John Stainer (1840–1901) or his oratorio *The Crucifixion* (1887). A professor of music at Oxford, he was never considered a "first rank" composer of his time. Nonetheless, today his "God So Loved the World," a movement from his oratorio, is a standard classic in the repertoire of most church choirs.[1] Its velvet-soft, reverent, yet supple vocal harmony conspires to penetrate any listener's heart, offering a visceral experience of the profound message: "God so loved the world, that he gave his only begotten Son, that Whosoever believeth in Him, should not perish, but have everlasting Life. For God sent not his Son into the world to condemn the world; But that the world through Him might be saved" (Jn 3: 16-17). Today many argue those words only expound a romantic myth of days gone by. This message seems but nonsense as we experience today's "Climate Emergency." If a loving God has "saved world" why are we experiencing its utter destruction—reaching and exceeding known ecological tipping points? Can we uncover any new insights as we reflect on these words in light of evolution, quantum physics, or ecology? What do all of these have to do with St. Francis and finding sustainable ways of living today?

Rich Heritage: The God Who Creates

God Created and Continues to Sustain the World

In the Hebrew Testament, the belief that God created the world and continues sustaining it holds center stage. Turning to the Christian Scriptures, Jesus Christ, whom Christians confess to be the Son of God and Savior of the world, is predominant. Significantly, early Christians experienced the Creator God of Genesis and understood the original goodness of creation through Jesus, his teaching, and his actions.[2] Thus, the New Testament presents the themes of creation and redemption as two related aspects of God's one engagement with the world in the Incarnation. Simply put, through Jesus' life, death, and resurrection, God's creative activity continues in our lives as a work of redemption (healing, renewal, recreation). The theme of creation is constantly in the background of all that Jesus said and did and it undergirds how the early Christians viewed Jesus as the bringer of the New Creation. According to Scripture scholar Barbara Bowe, "notions of the New Creation (*kainē ktisis*) and ultimate destruction of the world undergird the whole apocalyptic schema in Hellenistic Jewish and early Christian thought."[3]

Notions concerning the original creation are found in the New Testament Pauline and post-Pauline traditions and the Johannine writings.[4] Bowe illustrated this utilizing study of the Greek *ktizō* word group and the *kosmos* word group. *Ktizō* means "to intentionally establish" or "to found."[5] God, like a Roman Emperor who founded a city, intentionally brought order out of chaos. The use of this term *ktizō* is significant because in non-Christian sources, that founding action is indicated using the term *dēmiourgeō*, meaning "to engage in the construction of something."[6] Comparatively, the two terms bear an important qualitative difference in meaning. God's act of creation (*ktizō*) is not simply pragmatic or utilitarian but rather it is personal, loving, and intentional.

Generally, *kosmos* indicates the "arrangement" or the "order" of our world or universe.[7] That term originated in Hellenistic Judaism to tell of God's creating the world "out of formless matter." *Kosmos* thus indicates the "Earth" that humankind inhabits, but also "humankind itself" (Wis. 6:24; 4 Macc. 17:14). In the Gospel of John, and in First Corinthians, "this world" refers to creation as a temporary place of sin that is marked by the absence of salvation and the knowledge of God. Other uses of the term *kosmos* indicate creation as the place where God's activity takes place through Jesus; in John, the One Sent and, as Paul claims, through the Spirit.

The meaning of *kosmos* is further specified by Scripture scholar, Sandra Schneiders.[8] First, "world" refers to this earth as God spoke all things into being (Gen. 1:1–2:4a); the very place of God's revelation (Wis. 6:24; 4 Macc. 17:14). This universe emerged at God's expression through the Word, and it is a world God called "very good." Second, the "world" refers to "the theater of human history," this place of material existence where we humans live among other creatures. Into this history the "Word made flesh" was born (Jn 1:14). Third, and particularly significant for Christians, the world is the place where the Reign of God unfolds and where disciples of Jesus over the ages are sent (Jn 17:15). And fourth, the "world" refers to "a synonym for evil" or the one Jesus calls Satan, and who is the one with whom Jesus and his disciples struggle in the pursuit of God. God's creative love bursts into this malevolent world, first as the emergence of creation and then it continues in the redemptive action of the New Creation. Taken together, the world, "the *kosmos*," is the place where God is revealed through what God created, and it is the object of God's abundant love, a love that dynamically continues to grow and deepen in each particular moment, bringing forth ever new and renewed life.

Linking Original Creation and New Creation

Jesus' "Inaugural Address"

Beyond the Genesis creation stories, the Christian Scriptures abound in texts that address creation. The Synoptic Gospels (Matthew, Mark, and Luke) are brimming with various kinds of creation references. For example, in Luke 4:16-21, at the beginning of his ministry in what is sometimes referred to as his "Inaugural Address," Jesus announced his mission and its purpose.

He read from Isaiah 61, which ends with a proclamation of a Sabbath Year (every seventh year), "the year of the Lord's favor." In the Sabbath Year, slaves were freed, and debts canceled, but planting, pruning, and harvesting crops for storage were forbidden. The earth itself was given Sabbath rest in honor of the Creator (Lev. 25:2-7 and Deut. 15:7-11). Throughout the Jubilee Year (every fiftieth year) mandates, especially considering Leviticus

25:23, we see that ecological well-being of the land is intimately tied to the spiritual and material well-being of the people of Israel.[9] God, who owns the land, is attentive to the needs of the poor and of the land, for rest. When the Levitical laws of holiness are heeded, all of creation, including humans, abound in wholeness.

The original creation and the New Creation are thus linked in the Christian Scriptures. When Jesus read Isaiah 61:1-2 in the temple (Lk. 4:18-19), he also identified himself with an additional text, Isaiah 58:6, which is referenced therein. Both Isaiah texts point to the Jubilee Year. Thus, Jesus claimed all of what it outlined, as his own prophetic mission. Subsequently, Jesus' teaching and ministry empowered his followers for liberating, enlightening, and saving actions, bringing about the Kingdom of God. All such activities are life-giving. Such language harkens back to the great prophetic promises and talk of the New Covenant (Jer. 31:31-34), the Resurrection (Ezek. 37:1-4), and the New Creation (Isa. 65:17-25). All of these point to the fulfillment of the Reign of God—the New Creation.

Similarly, even a cursory reading of the Gospels shows they are filled with sacred memories of Jesus carrying out actions that Psalm 146 attributed to the Creator. As Jesus announced it, his mission was to do what "the Lord their God, the maker of heaven and earth" had done (Ps. 146:6). The widow and the orphan of Psalm 146 are among the poor to whom Jesus brought glad tidings, the prisoners for whom he proclaimed liberty, the blind to whom he gave sight, and the oppressed for whom he secured justice (Lk. 4:18).

From the Synoptic Gospels

If we read the accounts in the Synoptic Gospels of the life, teachings, and ministry of Jesus with an eye toward ecological sensitivity, we readily see how "earth friendly" Jesus was.[10] Clearly, we cannot impose or insert today's specific issues upon the biblical texts. However, we can assert that Jesus was highly attentive to the natural world; indeed, matter mattered to him! Elizabeth A. Johnson observed: "The point is that his life and ministry were filled with orientations that open to the physical, earthy dimensions without strain, once the question is raised."[11]

Jesus was an excellent teacher who explained who God is for us, by using examples from the material world God created. Just as we can know something about an artist, by examining her/his work—paintings, sculpture, drawings, poems, or choreography—so too something of who God is can be discovered through every creature in creation (panentheism). Indeed, the natural world is a dwelling place of God. The examples of Jesus' engagement with physical healing of the sick, lame, or mentally ill as well as his teachings using natural "visual aids" fill the pages of the gospels. His parables, sayings, and sermons are intentionally familiar—wildflowers, trees, grain, miniscule seeds, birds, fish, children, women, enemies, sheep, foxes, ants, wind, rain, sunrises, and more.

Acknowledging a world overflowing with God's grandeur, Jesus and his disciples frequented natural out-of-doors settings, especially for prayer and reflection. They had life-changing encounters with God (*Abba*) in deserts, hilltops, beaches, or gardens. (See Lk. 6:12; Mk 1:15-35.)

Jesus consistently shows us a radically relational God (*Abba*) who loves all of creation unconditionally, with grace, compassion, and tender mercy. Indeed, all creation is loved by God and revelatory of God. Jesus admonished that we need not only love our neighbor *as ourselves*, but that we *love as God loves*. And *that* includes our "ecological neighbors"—those who live downwind and downstream from us![12]

Beyond the Synoptics: Lady Wisdom and Jesus, the Wisdom of God

The New Testament writers built on the Jewish prophetic tradition but also on the Wisdom tradition.[13] Recall that Lady Wisdom was present at the foundation of the world. Early Christians recognized Jesus as a Wisdom teacher and soon attributed to him the role of *Hôkmah/Sophia* (Sir. 24:23; Prov. 8). Among numerous Christian writers, St. Paul is most explicit when he speaks of Christ as the best revelation of God's wisdom (I Cor.1: 24, 30). Similarly, Matthew sees Jesus as Wisdom because of his healing and all-encompassing presence (Mt. 11:20, 28). But the role of Jesus as Wisdom is particularly poignant in the Gospel of John, "the Franciscan Gospel."[14]

Jesus the Wisdom of God in the Gospel of John

In order to understand the Gospel of John, particularly the Prologue (Jn 1:1-14) some background information from the Hebrew Testament is necessary. The Hebrew Testament speaks about God as the "wise" creator

(Ps. 104:24; Prov. 3:19; Job 38:4-11). God is a divine artisan or skilled craftsperson who fashioned a good and beautiful universe (Sir. 39:16; Gen. 1:4, 10, 12, 18, 21, 25, 31).[15] The fact that God created "with wisdom" became personified over several centuries, as "Wisdom Woman" who originated with God and who had a mission directed to humans on earth (Prov. 8:22; Sir. 24:3, 9). She clearly says she is not God (Sir. 24:3-6). Among Wisdom Woman's activities are that she beckons us, drawing us in and through the world (Prov. 1, 8, 9), and promises life and blessing for those who embrace her (Prov. 1:32; 3:13-18). Through her, God is present in the world.

When discussing of the ways of Wisdom in Job 28, the author clearly states that "God knows the way to it and he knows its place" (Job 28:23). Then in Prov. 1-9, Wisdom Woman makes her appearance as "one more precious than jewels"; "beyond compare"; and a "tree of life"—for "the Lord by Wisdom founded the earth" (Prov. 3:15-19). Further, in Proverbs 8 Wisdom Woman speaks of being God's first creature; of her presence in and through all divine creative actions; and that she delights and rejoices in her presence in the created world, including the human race (Prov. 8:22-31).

Beyond all of this, the book of Sirach offers a further development. In Sirach 24, Wisdom Woman now seeks a "resting place" (v. 7), and God chose a spot for her tent "in Jacob" (v. 8). More specifically, though Wisdom continues to be present throughout creation, she rests in the "book of the covenant" the Torah, the Law of Moses (vv. 22-23). So now we also see that the Torah also preexisted creation (cf. Job 28:12, 20). Subsequently, we read in John 1, "In the beginning the Word (*logos*) was with God" (Jn 1:1a)—but not created, because "the Word was God" (Jn 1:1b). As Christians believe, Jesus is the fullness of the law; he is the "Word made flesh"; God incarnate (Jn 1:14).

As Michael D. Guinan points out, what God created was the entire universe (Prov. 3:19-20), and Wisdom provided the supporting pillars (Prov. 14:31). She actually rejoices and delights in the human race (Prov. 8:31) and invites all creation to feast with her (Prov. 9:2-6). Wisdom opens for us a joyful way of living—to follow in her way, the way of Wisdom, is to follow the One who John's Gospel identifies as Jesus Christ, the Wisdom of God.

Scripture scholar Barbara Bowe utilized the work of Josephine Massynbaerde Ford to break open additional insights, linking the original Creation and the New Creation (creation, incarnation, and redemption) themes in the Gospel of John.[16] Bowe began with the "Prologue" of the Gospel (Jn 1:1-14).

The opening words sound familiar—"In the beginning ..." (Gen. 1:1) but the ending of the phrase is different "... was the Word" (Jn 1:1). Here Jesus' story is presented as a new story of creation.[17] The structure of the Prologue is patterned as "celestial-divine/terrestrial-human, alternating between realms."[18] In v. 14, Jesus the (*logos*) Word of God is identified as the one (like Wisdom) who "pitched a tent with us" joining the divine and human realms for eternity. It is through the Word (*logos*) that "all things came into being" ... [and emphatically] "without him not one thing came into being" (v. 3). Jesus is the creative agent whose divinity is the light infused in the world (1:5), making way for the rebirth of the Spirit (3:6), the bringer of regenerating energy to the world.[19]

Bowe continued, showing how John 1 and 2 expand on the creation motif (1:29, 35, 43, and 2:1), intimating that Jesus' story begins a new week of creation (cf Gen. 1-2:4). Jesus' act of revealing God's glory begins "on the third day" at Cana (Jn 2:1) evoking the memory of God coming to the people of Israel at Saini "on the third day" (Exod. 19:9). The fact that the occasion of Jesus' action is the wedding banquet at Cana suggests further, the messianic banquet that crowns creation (2 Bar. 29:5-8). That recollection, moreover, points to the "Bread of Life" discourse of John 6, especially vv. 51 and 58, where the "Word made flesh" gives himself "for the life of the world" so that the person "who eats will live for ever."[20] In all of these instances, renewal, regeneration, and recreation of life are brought about.

Bowe then returned to Ford's interpretation of John 19—the death of Jesus on the cross. Ford offers the provocative insight from the Syriac tradition concerning the significance of the flow of blood and water from Jesus pierced side. She connects the piercing of Jesus' side with the opening of Adam's side (Gen. 2:21-23) as a kind of act of giving birth to new life. In Ford's words: "I suggest that Jesus goes to his passion and death ... as a woman to give birth to her child by blood and water."[21] Ford suggests a similar strain of rebirthing can be seen in the giving of the Spirit (Jn 19:30; 20:22). Jesus "breathes upon the disciples to bring them new life and the Paraclete ... It may also be possible that the insufflation reflects the action of the midwife helping the newborn child to breathe."[22]

Bowe pointed out that at the conclusion of John's Gospel (Jn 20:11-18), Mary Magdalene met Jesus in a garden (*kēpos*—Jn 19:41; compare with *paradeisos* Gen. 2-3). Bowe suggests that Magdalene's encounter with Jesus brings the theme of "new birth" proclaimed in the Prologue (1:12) full circle. "Mary, the *apostola apstolorum* (female apostle to the other apostles) becomes the herald, the midwife of the new creation in the family of God."[23] Indeed, the Gospel of John shows us how God's love poured out in the original creation is expressed in the incarnation and is the link that brings forth life-giving redemption into the world.

Creation and New Creation: Insights from an Evolutionary Worldview

Over the past centuries, most Christian teaching about creation and redemption utilized Aristotelian and neo-Pationic models of metaphysics, the theological framework of Thomas Aquinas or Bonaventure of Bagnoregio, and later, scientific models of Isaac Newton. These patterns helped us understand much about God and the known world. In recent decades, evolution, quantum physics, and ecology opened new vistas that have enriched, renewed, and revised our understanding of God, creation, and redemption, providing insights for Christian life and our participation in the Reign of God—amid our "Ecological Emergency."

Preeminent Bonaventure scholar Zachary Hayes set out four characteristics that opened the way to such renewed theological reflection on creation.[24] First, he noted that Creation is *immense* in size and duration—well beyond human capacities to fathom. Current science indicates the age of the universe is 13.7 billion years old, and of such proportions that staggers the limits of human imagination—we know of billions of galaxies and billions of stars in each of them![25]

Secondly, Hayes noted this immense universe is yet *unfinished*; in fact, it is actually expanding. Amazingly, the Big Bang Theory asserts the amazing possibility that all of creation burst forth from a concentration of energy the size of a pin head. Through a process of emergence of subatomic particles, protons, neutrons, and electrons, which then cooled, the cosmos as we know it today came forth.[26]

Thirdly, current physics attests that creation is *interrelated* at every point.[27] From the smallest fractal to the expanses of the universe, everything is related to everything else, and "what we think of as matter, is actually the manifestation of energy, what physicists call *quanta* or little packets or lumps of energy manifesting themselves out of an infinite field."[28] Similarly, biologists see the world as "living systems as interrelated wholes ... a 'part' becomes identified as a pattern in an inseparable web of relationships."[29] Where Newton understood the world as the result of forces and trajectories, today we must think in terms of change, growth, and development, or considerations of complexity.

Fourthly, in its production of the vast diversity of life, ranging from the simple to the complex, *planet Earth is unique*. Remarkably, the whole evolutionary process became fine-tuned to support carbon-based life as we know it. Even more amazing is the assertion that humans are this universe come to consciousness![30] Scientists call this reality evidence of the "strong anthropic principle."[31] Had the process developed "a trillionth of a thrillionth of a trillionth of one percent faster, the cosmic material would have been flung too far apart for anything significant to happen."[32]

Considerations of evolution and ecology place humanity in a new light as well. Early humans appeared about 150,000 years ago.[33] This view does not negate the biblical story of human origins but rather gives us "an understanding of how the mechanics within nature promote species diversity and development and on a cosmic level, how the universe progresses from the Big Bang to human life."[34] Basically, current evolutionary theory holds that life can be explained by a combination of law, chance, and deep time. In the case of humans, this process took billions of prior forms, cataclysmic events, and extinctions before "humans" evolved. Beyond their evolution into *Homo sapiens*, humans are also products of emergence. "Philip Clayton defines emergence as 'genuinely new properties which are not reducible to what came before, although they are continuous with it.'"[35] Humans developed in complexity in a world of grace to become self-conscious beings, aware of their divine origins.

Reign of God—New Creation—Emergence

The "New Creation" or the "Reign of God" is at the heart of the Christian Scriptures and the activity of Jesus. As Leonardo Boff and Mark Hathaway explain, the actual Aramaic term Jesus used to name the Reign of God or the Kingdom of Heaven is *malkuta*. The term is related to *malkatuh*, a Middle Eastern name for Mother Earth.[36] The ancients perceived a divine quality about the Earth, which they found dynamic and empowering. Thus, the *malkuta* is that which provides an empowering vision rooted in the divine presence in the cosmos. Today we can understand this empowerment in terms of "liberation, as a process leading the cosmos toward ever greater communion, differentiation, and interiority."[37] As Dougas-Klotz puts it, the image evoked is "of a fruitful arm poised to create, or a coiled spring that is ready to unwind with all the verdant potential of the Earth."[38] Jesus reminds us, the Reign of God is here, but not yet; within us, yet beyond us and around us (Lk. 17:21). The moral implications for caring for the Earth especially amid a "Climate Emergency" are vast.

Throughout Christian history, believers have compared God and God's love to common experiences and knowledge, including models from contemporary science or philosophy. Today, we can understand God as the Creator in light of "emergence theory."

Danish theologian Niels Henrik Gregersen suggested that we can see a simpler version of emergence theory in Aristotle's principle of *entelechy* or Plotinus' doctrine of *emanation*. Plotinus' neo-platonic notion of creation as all things flowing from the One greatly influenced Christian thought.[39] The occurrence of new things took place as *devolution* or a kind of dissipation of the power of the being, that is, in the divine principle before creation takes place. In Plotinus' thought "emanation from the One is a sharing of being from Being and hence, participates in Being without becoming something new."[40]

Currently, as Delio explains, "emergenists subscribe to a robust scientific naturalism, according to which mental processes supervene on biological processes, and biological processes on physical processes. Emergence is irreducible novelty of increasing complexity, a combination of holism with novelty in a way that contrasts with both physical reductionism and dualism."[41]

In light of this, we can no longer speak of God primarily as the Neoplatonic *cause* of creation (as does much of Church teaching on creation). Rather, we need to think about God as the *goal* toward which all things are moving. Harkening back to the Big Bang, and the (approximate) 13.7 billion-year history of the universe, God's creative activity can be understood as enabling things to evolve into something ever new.[42] The notion of emergence revises our understanding of what creation really is and also suggests a far more dynamic image of God (than recognized in the past). Our current knowledge about the physical creation gives us renewed insights about God, the Creator of an emerging Creation. We have a fresh understanding of God's dynamic, overflowing, generous, reconciling, and healing love in all of creation. We can build on ideas that are nascent in 2 Cor. 5:17 and in Rev. 21:1-8. These passages speak of God who "makes all things new" and the reality that we have "new life" in Jesus Christ. Observing the ongoing emergence of the creation is a way we, like Sts. Francis, Clare, and Bonaventure, can "follow in the footprints of Jesus" today.

God's dynamic love affirms an open process of (sometimes uncertain and painful) evolution. Literally everything in the universe participates in the process of creation. In *Laudato Si'*, Pope Francis affirmed what St. Francis knew so well through faith and intuition, and St. Bonaventure explained in neo-platonic terms that everything in creation is related and moves to ever greater perfection (read—emergence, evolution, movement toward complexity) drawn forth by God's love.[43] Delio suggests that in light of the theory of emergence and evolution, we could rephrase St. Bonaventure's notion of *circumincessio* as "the movement from within to be for another so as to become more than the other."[44] She continues: "The emergent Trinity may be described as love yielding to love, an eternal movement toward personal, complexified union in love. Thus, every divine person is nested in every other person so that every divine person recapitulates God who is eternally coming to be. Thus, we can say, God is that which no greater is coming to be for it is in the coming to be that God is."[45]

We know from our own experience of genuine human love that love of persons "in love" grows, deepens, and changes in its expression in different situations and on different occasions across time. So it is with the Triune God; change is integral to God because God is love. Since God actively loves what God creates, we can know God in relationship to evolutionary creation as novelty and future. This dynamic activity of the Triune God is the way the Creator constantly pours out life to the world. As Delio concludes: "Creation is always more than the present moment can hold. Creation therefore thrives on the threshold of the future endowed with freedom, promise, and openness to new emergent life. … [C]reation moves forward, driven by the power of love into an ever-new horizon of God, a future of newness in love, and our hope that love alone will endure."[46]

Indeed, God so loved the world that from the moment of creation divine dynamism was infused into everything to "become" until it reached its fullest potential. God, with atoms, through variations of their valences, set life into motion to become and emerge, and the Divine continues to draw the beloved creation forward to perfection. God invites people to cooperate in change in positive ways that respect their own integrity and that of fellow creatures. But this "becoming" of humans in the world involves the constant mutual exchange with the Divine, a free reciprocal offer of love by humans in relationship with God and God's creation. Deplorably because humans knowingly harm created things, St. Francis' lament is fitting for our moment is history. There is voluminous evidence that "[t]hese creatures minister to our needs every day; without them we could not live; and *through them the human race greatly offends the Creator*."[47]

From the Writings of St. Francis

Thomas of Celano, "The Life of St. Francis," XXIX, 81 [48]

How great do you think was the delight the beauty of flowers brought to his soul whenever he saw their lovely form and noticed their sweet fragrance? He would immediately turn his gaze to the beauty of that flower, brilliant in springtime, sprouting *from the root of* Jesse (Isa. 11:1). By its *fragrance* (I Cor. 2:14) it raised up countless thousands of dead. Whenever he found an abundance of flowers, he used to preach to them and invite them to praise the Lord, just as if they were endowed with reason.

Reflection and Application

In our ecologically threatened age, repentance, conversion, reconciliation, and renewal need to take pride of place. The August 9, 2021, *IPCC Working Group I report, Climate Change 2021: The Physical Science Basis Scientists* vividly asserted that "scientists are observing changes in the Earth's climate in every region and across the whole climate system that are unprecedented in thousands, if not hundreds of thousands of years, and some of the changes already set in motion—such as continued sea level rise—are irreversible over hundreds to thousands of years."[49] Even a cursive examination of the IPCC document makes clear that these changes are human caused and destructive of any semblance of loving relationships of people and God's planet!

This reality is tremendously frightening, unfamiliar, discomforting, even repulsive for many of us. Nonetheless, it is a truth that we no longer have luxury to avoid. Serious, immediate, and large-scale reversal (conversion) of our neglectful ways is ours to embrace! While increasingly urgent warnings have been sounded from innumerable sources, we have been satiated by the material comforts (that arguably have gotten us in to this mess in the first place)! There is ample room for both personal and communal changes: repentance, conversion, and *metanoia* by humans at all levels of planetary existence. The IPCC has sounded a "Code Red" for humanity; there is some reasonable chance to limit our harm—*but will we act this time*?[50]

St. Francis of Assisi—Mentor and Model

The desire for continual *personal* conversion was constantly at the forefront of St. Francis' prayer and action.[51] Yet it is highly significant that when explaining his motivation for writing his classic *Canticle of the Creatures*, his moral imagination and concern expanded to *also* address offences expressly by *humankind* against God's creatures. He stated:

> God has given me such a grace and blessing that he has condescended in his mercy to assure me, his poor and unworthy servant, still living on this earth, *that I would share his kingdom.* Therefore, for his glory, for my consolation, and the edification of my neighbor, I wish to compose a new "Praises of the Lord," *for his creatures.* These creatures minister to our needs every day; without them we could not live; and *through them the human race greatly offends the Creator. Every day we fail to appreciate so great a blessing, by not praising, as we should, the Creator and dispenser of all these gifts.*[52]

Notably St. Francis' moral insight concerning the communal offences of humankind against God's creatures developed *after*, and is *directly linked with*, Divine assurance that eternal life would be his.[53] His spiritual realization held tremendous moral relevance that moved him to action!

It is remarkable how Francis' moral sensitivity grew out of the profound visceral revulsion he experienced when seeing the harms people inflicted on those companion creatures he knew so well as his fellow beings amid God's creation. On the one hand—Francis was so awestruck at the beauty, mystery, and profound dignity of those creatures which he affectionately and reverently acknowledged in his *Canticle* as expressions of the Divine. Yet on the other hand, he was deeply disturbed by the egregious debasement of their nobility and goodness when humans idolized them, granting them godlike powers—beyond their creaturely status—effectively committing idolatry.

Recognition of human harm to fellow creatures as offenses against the Divine occurred *after* St. Francis *first acknowledged* that each creature is the artwork of the Divine. Today amid our current "Climate Emergency," as we increasingly experience the global obliteration of our common home and our dwellings—as well as the habitats of our fellow creatures and their surroundings—like St. Francis, we need to shift our gaze to *really see* and *experience* the wondrous beauty and mystery of God's creation *beyond ourselves*. Only then will we be able to widen our vision and deepen our moral imagination to comprehend how our passive and active degradation of fellow creatures is an egregious offence against God. What we do not know we cannot love, and what we do not love we will not care for and defend!

The Church's numerous calls for ecological care and environmental justice have too often fallen on deaf ears. In the twentieth century every pope forewarned us of our threats to the planet and our unjust treatment of God's creation.[54] Over more than six decades, individual bishops and bishop's conferences issued ever more focused warnings of our planetary-sized sinfulness, but sufficient catechesis was often absent.[55]

On March 10, 2008, the Apostolic Penitentiary listed "ecological" offences among the "New Forms of Social Sin."[56] However, while claiming that wonton destruction of God creation is never a moral good, the Catholic Church has never definitively defined ecological sin. One significant move toward correcting this lack occurred on May 14, 2014, when Pope Francis and the Ecumenical Patriarch Bartholomew signed a landmark declaration that stated the mistreatment of the planet is "tantamount to sin."[57]

Then in *Laudato Si'* §s 7 and 8, Pope Francis provided Catholics with a more explicit explanation of the "sinful nature" of our planetary destruction by affirming the Ecumenical Patriarch's call for repentance for crimes against the planet destroying biodiversity, damaging earth's climate, stripping earth of its natural forests, and destroying its wetlands. Indeed, "to commit a crime against the natural world is a sin against ourselves and a sin against God."[58] Pope Francis quoted the Patriarch: "As Christians we are called to 'accept the world as a sacrament of communion, as a way of sharing with God and our neighbors on a global scale. It is our humble conviction that the divine and the human meet in the slightest detail in the seamless garment of God's creation, in the last speck of dust of our planet.'"[59]

On November 15, 2020, at a meeting of the International Association of Penal Law in Rome, and following the Synod of Bishops for the Amazon, Pope Francis indicated that a definition of "ecological sins"—"sin against ecology, ecological sin against the common home" —would be included in the *Catechism of the Catholic Church*.[60]

Pope Francis and *Querida Amazonia*

To date, the best description of "Ecological Sin" is found in *The Final Document of the Amazonian Synod* §82:[61]

> 82. We propose to define ecological sin as an action or omission against God, against one's neighbour, the community, and the environment. It is

sin against future generations, and it is committed in acts and habits of pollution and destruction of the harmony of the environment. These are transgressions against the principles of interdependence, and they destroy networks of solidarity among creatures (cf. *Catechism of the Catholic Church*, 340–4) and violate the virtue of justice. We also propose to create special ministries for the care of our common home and the promotion of integral ecology at the parish level and in each Church jurisdiction. Their functions include, among others, the care of the territory and of the waters, as well as the promotion of the encyclical *Laudato Si'*, taking up the pastoral, educational and advocacy program in its Chapters V and VI at all levels and structures of the Church.

This definition is supported in the *Final Document* by a detailed discussion of egregious failures and involvements of social, political, economic, and ecclesial entities that not only disempowered humans but wreaked irreparable destruction to entire Amazonian ecosystems.[62] Pope Francis also provided a clear-eyed admission of the Catholic Church's complicity in such egregious violations; the Church "did not always take the side of the oppressed" in the Amazon (§19). Deplorably, some Catholics continue to be "part of networks of corruption" by silence bought through financial donations. Thus, the Pope, citing Jn 3:5, devoted Chapter Two of the document to outlining a wide array of "Paths of Pastoral Conversion."[63]

Thus, beyond any previous Church social teaching documents, the Amazon documents express what St. Francis lived and taught, namely that ecological harm is perpetrated by humans, including willful disregard and violation of the God-given dignity of each entity of Creation. Such harmful activity is a sin—a foundational fracturing of our relationship with the Divine! Ecological destruction is now understood to include far more than undignified maltreatment of animals![64]

Ecocide—A Crime against Humanity?

The movement to define "ecocide" as the Fifth "Crime against Humanity" is an unprecedented, alarming signal of the dire state of the global "ecological emergency." Pope Francis endorsed the global international law initiative to add "ecocide" as the Fifth "crime against humanity" (four crimes are named in the 1998 Rome Statute, to be prosecuted and condemned by the ICC: war crimes, crimes against humanity, genocides, and aggression).[65] The pope explained ecocide as "the massive contamination of air, land and water resources, the large-scale destruction of flora and fauna, and any action capable of producing an ecological disaster or destroying an ecosystem."

The Stop Ecocide Foundation published a legal definition of ecocide for the first time: "Ecocide means unlawful or wanton acts committed with knowledge that there is a substantial likelihood of severe and either widespread or long-term damage to the environment being caused by those acts."[66] That carefully crafted definition aligns well with four crimes of the Rome Statute. This wide and formal recognition of human criminality affirms, from a Catholic ethics "natural law" perspective, what St. Francis saw as our need to admit our sinfulness and engage personal and communal conversion.[67] God's gift of creation can be the "word" that draws us to change our ways—as was the case with St. Francis. Such change and conversion begin with choosing to open ourselves to the love of God as St. Francis did.

St. Francis of Assisi was not always a model for creation care. Only *after* his conversion did St. Francis truly delight in creation.[68] Falling in love with Christ drastically shifted Francis' capacity to see and to know. Through prayer and *experiencing* the wonders of *God's love through creation*, Francis made the connection between God as the Creator and Jesus, the "Word made flesh," as the Gospel of John so beautifully tells us.

Jesus Christ is the Word through whom the world was created, but he was human like us. He also lived on this Earth as part of the material universe. (Indeed, as current science tell us, we are made of stardust!) St. Francis made a deep spiritual connection between Incarnation (Jesus, the "Word made flesh"), Creation, (the entire universe), and Redemption (God's offer of the gift of conversion and eternal life). Only then did he realize that humans are also part of the natural world and that to love God is also to love God's creation.[69] And only then did Francis see the footprints of Jesus everywhere!

With St. Francis, we are called to protect and preserve the Earth and all creatures, which, in their beauty and complexity, draw us in, give us joy, inspire us to praise, and lead us to the heart of God. St. Francis' vision of kinship of creation expands the meaning Jesus' command to love both God and neighbor (Mt. 22:37-39). Our neighbor is everyone, including every creature, plant, and cosmic element. Today, our lifestyle and daily choices reveal our values and affect the health of the planet. The "New Creation" is not yet here, but it is present within us and among us. In this "Code Red" moment it is our work to open ourselves to God's love and to create the conditions for the "New Creation" to emerge!

Questions for Reflection and Discussion

1. Describe your best experience of loving or of being loved. How does love remain the same over time? In what ways does love change? How is the love you experience like/unlike God's love expressed in creation?
2. Does thinking about creation as a process of emergence give life any less dignity than it has in your previous understanding of the origins of life? In what ways do your actions of loving or being loved assist or detract from the emergence of God's New Creation?
3. Growing up, what were you taught about "sin"? What have you learned about different "kinds of sin"? What have you learned about "forgiveness" and "reconciliation"?
4. How well do you know the place where you live? What is its evolutionary and ecological history? How has it emerged over the years? How has human intervention shaped it—for good or for ill?
5. How does the Word of God take on the flesh of the piece of God's creation where you live?

Suggestions for Action

1. Visit a science or natural history museum or search online for websites to learn about the geological and ecological evolution of your local area.
2. Read the Gospel of John and consider the ways in which the natural world reveals "the Word made flesh."
3. What animals and plants in your areas of the planet are endangered by human intervention in their habitats? Join or organize a group to advocate on their behalf.
4. Where do the "poor people" live in your community? What access do they have to beauty, clean air, water, or land that is free from pollution? Consult with the people who live in environmentally unsafe areas concerning how you might become allies in fighting for justice.
5. When you prepare to receive the Sacrament of Reconciliation, reflect on the ways you have participated in "Ecological Offenses" against God's creation. Pray for ecological conversion and a more sensitive heart.

Sources for Further Study

Coloe, Mary L. PBVM. "John 1-10." Vol. 44a, *Wisdom Commentary*, Mary Ann Beavis, Volume Editor. Barbara E. Reid, OP, General Editor. A Michael Glazier Book. Collegeville: The Liturgical Press, 2021.

Guinan, Michael D. *The Franciscan Vision and the Gospel of John*. The Franciscan Heritage Series, Vol. 4. St. Bonaventure, NY: The Franciscan Institute, 2006.

Johnson, Elizabeth A. *Creation and the Cross: The Mercy of God for a Planet in Peril*. Maryknoll: Orbis Books, 2018.

Nothwehr, Dawn M. "Called to Ecological Conversion." *New Theology Review* 22, no. 1 (February 2009): 84–7.

Sorrell, Roger D. *St. Francis of Assisi and Nature: Tradition and Innovation in Western Christian Attitudes toward the Environment*. New York: Oxford University Press, 1988.

Notes

1. "God So Loved the World," performed February 9, 2009, by St. Paul's Cathedral Choir, London, http://www.youtube.com/watch?v=X5Akz6J8Rw0.
2. Michael D. Guinan, *The Franciscan Vision and the Gospel of John: The San Damiano Cross | Francis and John | Creation and John*, The Franciscan Heritage Series, Vol. 4 (St. Bonaventure, NY: The Franciscan Institute, 2006) 32.
3. Barbara Bowe, "Soundings in the New Testament Understandings of Creation," in *Earth, Wind & Fire: Biblical and Theological Perspectives on Creation*, ed. Carol J. Dempsey and Mary Margaret Pazdan (Collegeville: The Liturgical Press, 2004), 59.
4. Ibid., 59–60.
5. Ibid., 59.
6. Ibid., 60.
7. Ibid. *Kosmos* appears 186 times in the New Testament, thirty-seven times in the Pauline writings, and seventy-eight times in the Johannine corpus.
8. Sandra Schneiders, "God So Loved the World … Ministerial Religious Life in 2009," talk on vowed religious life given to the IHM Congregation, June 14, 2009, 22–4, https://scholarcommons.scu.edu/cgi/viewcontent.cgi?article=1153&context=jst.
9. Moshe Greenberg, Shmuel Safrai, and Aaron Rothkoff, "Sabbatical Year and Jubilee," in David L. Lieber, *Encyclopedia Judaica*, ed. Michael Berenbaum and Fred Skolnik, Vol. 17, 2nd ed. (Detroit: Macmillan

Reference USA, 2007), 623–30, at 623: "Sabbatical Year and Jubilee (Heb. שְׁמִטָּה, shemittah; יוֹבֵל, yovel). According to the Bible, during the seventh year, all land had to be fallow and debts were to be remitted (Exod. 23:10–11; Lev. 25:1–7, 18–22; Deut. 15:1–11). The close of seven sabbatical cycles instituted the Jubilee (Lev. 27:16–25; Num. 36:4)."

10. Dianne Bergant, *A New Heaven a New Earth: The Bible and Catholicity*, Catholicity in an Evolving Universe Series (Maryknoll: Orbis Books, 2016), esp. 117–36.
11. Elizabeth A. Johnson, "An Earthy Christology: 'For God so Loved the Cosmos,'" *America* 200/12, Whole No. 4852 (April 13, 2009): 28.
12. Jeanne Kay Guelke, "Looking for Jesus in Christian Environmental Ethics," *Environmental Ethics* 26/2 (2004): 123.
13. Bergant, *A New Heaven a New Earth*, 89–116, esp. 102–6.
14. According to Kajetan Esser, the Gospel of John is the most influential source for St. Francis' vision of his way of life. See *Opuscula Sancti Patris Francisci Assisiensis*, ed. K. Esser, OFM (Rome: Grottaferrata, 1978). Optatus van Asseldonk, OFM Cap. "Favored Biblical Teachings in the Writings of St. Francis," *Greyfriars Review* 3 (1989): 287–314, especially 295–305. Thaddée Matura, OFM, "How Francis Reads and Interprets Scripture," in *The Gospel Life of St. Francis of Assisi Today* (Chicago: Franciscan Herald Press, 1980), 31–44. James P. Scullion, OFM, "The Writings of St. Francis and the Gospel of John," in *Franciscans and the Scriptures: Living in the Word of God*, Washington Theological Union Symposium Papers, 2005, ed. Elise Saggau, OSF (St. Bonaventure, NY: Franciscan Institute Publications, 2006).
15. Michael D. Guinan, "Images of God in the Wisdom Literature," *Bible Today* 38 (2000): 223–7.
16. Bowe, "Soundings in the New Testament Understandings of Creation," 61. She cited Josephine Massynbaerde Ford, *Redeemer, Friend, and Mother: Salvation in Antiquity and in the Gospel of John* (Minneapolis: Fortress, 1997).
17. Bowe, "Soundings in the New Testament Understandings of Creation," 61.
18. Ibid.
19. Ibid.
20. Ibid., 62. Bergant, *A New Heaven a New Earth*, 136–40.
21. Josephine Massynbaerde Ford, *Redeemer, Friend, and Mother*, 198.
22. Ibid., 200. Insufflation means the action of breathing or blowing into or on.
23. Bowe, "Soundings in the New Testament Understandings of Creation," 63.
24. Zachary Hayes, "New Cosmology for a New Millennium," *New Theology Review* 12/3 (1999): 29–39.
25. In 1999 the age of the planet was thought to be between 15 and 20 billion years old.

26. Ilia Delio, *The Emergent Christ: Exploring the Meaning of Catholic in an Evolutionary Universe* (Maryknoll: Orbis Books, 2011), 13–17.
27. This concept is like the notion of integral ecology as in *Laudato Si'*, §s 10, 11, 62, 124, 137 159, 225, and 230.
28. Delio, *The Emergent Christ*, 24.
29. Ibid., 25.
30. Ibid., 17.
31. Ibid.
32. Judy Cannato, *Radical Amazement: Contemplative Lessons from Black Holes, Supernovas, and Other Wonders of the Universe* (Notre Dame: Sorin Books, 2006), 42 cited by Delio, *Emergent Christ*, 17.
33. Smithsonian National Museum of Natural History, "Homo Sapiens," https://human origins.si.edu/ evidence/human-fossils/species/homo-sapiens.
34. Delio, *Emergent Christ*, 21. Also see her discussion about the compatibility of evolution with Catholic Church teaching at 21–4. There is no inherent conflict between evolution and Christian doctrine.
35. Delio, *Emergent Christ*, 20.
36. Leonardo Boff and Mark Hathaway, *The Tao of Liberation: Exploring the Ecology of Transformation* (Maryknoll: Orbis Books, 2009), 331. Boff and Hathaway cite Neil Douglas-Klotz, *Prayers of the Cosmos: Meditations on the Aramaic Words of Jesus* (San Francisco: HarperSanFrancisco, 1990), 20.
37. Boff and Hathaway, *The Tao of Liberation,* 131.
38. Ibid.
39. Ilia Delio, "Godhead or God Ahead? Rethinking the Trinity in Light of Emergence," in *God, Grace, & Creation*, ed. Philip J. Rossi, College Theology Society Annual Volume 55 (2009), note 91, at page 20: "Entelechy refers to the internal principle of growth and perfection that directs the organism to actualize the qualities that it contains in a merely potential state."
40. Ibid., 7.
41. Ibid., 7–8.
42. Chelsea Gohd, "Astronomers Reevaluate the Age of the Universe," January 8, 2021, https://www.space.com/universe-age-14-billion-years-old: "The current 2021 measure of the age of the universe is 13.77 billion years."
43. See "integral ecology," in *LS* §s 10, 11, 62, 137, 159, 225, 230. More on Bonaventure is in Chapter 5.
44. Delio, "Godhead or God Ahead?," 14. *Circumincession* describes the relationship between each person of the triune God. Denis Edwards indicates, Bonaventure used this term in its Latin translation as *circumincessio* (*circum-incedere*), which points to the three divine persons' dynamic movement around one another in their mutual intimacy. Denis

Edwards, *Jesus the Wisdom of God: An Ecological Theology*, ed. Australian (Homebush, NSW: St. Pauls, 1995), 104; Bonaventure, 1 Sent., d.19, p.1, a.u., q.4, conc. (I, 349). See also Part III, Chapter 5 below.

45. Delio, "Godhead or God Ahead?," 14.
46. Ibid., 19.
47. "The Assisi Compilation (1244–1260)," 83, FA:ED Volume II—*The Founder*, 186. Emphasis added.
48. Thomas of Celano, "The Life of St. Francis," XXIX, 81 in FA:ED Volume 1—*The Saint*, 251.
49. "Climate Change Widespread, Rapid, and Intensifying—IPCC," Press Release, https://www.ipcc.ch/2021/08/09/ar6-wg1-20210809-pr/.
50. Kelly Levin, David Waskow, and Rhys Gerholdt, "5 Big Findings from the IPCC's 2021 Climate Report," August 9, 2021, World Resources Institute, https://www.wri.org/insights/ipcc-climate-report.
51. Thomas of Celano, "The Life of Saint Francis" (1228–1229), Book I, Chapter 1, in FA: ED, Volume I—*The Saint*, 184. Julian of Speyer, "Life of St. Francis (1232–1235)," Chapter 2, in FA: ED, Volume I—*The Saint*, 377–8. "The Sacred Exchange between St. Francis and Lady Poverty (1237–1239)," Prologue, in FA:ED, Volume I—*The Saint*, 530. Bonaventure of Bagnoregio, "The Minor Legend of St. Francis (1260–1263)," Chapter 2, "His Conversion," in FA:ED, Volume II—*The Founder*, 684–8. Bernard of Besse, "A Book of Praises of St. Francis, (1277–1283)," Chapter 4, "Poverty," in FA:ED, Volume III—*The Prophet*, 45.
52. "The Assisi Compilation (1244–1260)," 83, in FA:ED Volume II—*The Founder*, 186. Emphasis added.
53. Sin is defined in the *Catechism of the Catholic Church* in Part Three: Life in Christ, Section One—Man's Vocation Life in the spirit, Chapter One: The Dignity of the Human Person, Article 8, Sin, https://www.vatican.va/archive/ ENG0015/_INDEX.HTM.
54. Numerous citations at Catholic Charities of St. Paul Minneapolis—Environment https://www.cctwincities.org/education-advocacy/catholic-social-teaching/notable-quotations/environment/.
55. Early statements: US Appalachian Bishops (1975), the US Heartland Bishops (1980), the Bishops of the Dominican Republic (1987), The Philippines and Lombardy, Italy (1988).
56. Philip Pullella, "Vatican Lists 'New Sins,' Including Pollution," *Reuters*, March 10, 2008, https://www.reuters.com/article/us-pope-sins/vatican-lists-new-sins-including-pollution-idUSL1096023 20080310.
57. *Common Declaration of Pope Francis and the Ecumenical Patriarch Bartholomew I*, https://www.vatican.va/content/francesco/en/speeches/2014/may/documents/papa-francesco_20140525_terra-santa-dichiarazione-congiunta.html, "6. It is our profound conviction that the

future of the human family depends also on how we safeguard—both prudently and compassionately, with justice and fairness—the gift of creation that our Creator has entrusted to us. Therefore, we acknowledge in repentance the wrongful mistreatment of our planet, which is tantamount to sin before the eyes of God."

58. *LS* §8.
59. Francis cites the Patriarch's "Global Sustainability and Ecological Responsibility," Closing Remarks, Halki Summit I, Istanbul, June 20, 2012.
60. Junno Arocho Esteves, "Catechism will be updated to include ecological sins, pope says," *Catholic News Service*, November 15, 2019, https://www.ncronline.org/news/earthbeat/ catechism-will-be-updated-include-ecological-sins-pope-says. To date, no revision has occurred.
61. Synod of Bishops Special Assembly for the Pan-Amazonian Region, *The Amazon: New Paths for the Church and for an Integral Ecology—Final Document*, Vatican, October 26, 2019, https://www.vatican.va/roman_curia/synod/documents/rc_synod_doc_20191026_sinodo-amazzonia_en.html.
62. Ibid., §9.
63. Ibid., §s 20–40.
64. *Catechism of the Catholic Church*, #s 2415–18, https://www.vatican.va/archive /ENG0015/__P8B.HTM.
65. Address of his Holiness Pope Francis to Participants of the World Congress of the International Association of Penal Law November 15, 2019, in Rome, https://www.vatican.va/content/francesco/en/speeches/2019/november/documents/papa-francesco_20191115_diritto-penale.html.
66. Julie Gaubert, "Top International Lawyers to Make 'Ecocide' a Crime against Nature," June 22, 2021, euronews.green, https://www.euronews.com/green/2021/06/22/top-international-lawyers-to-make-ecocide-a-crime-against-nature. Ecocide is defined here: Legal Definition of Ecocide Completed, https://www.stopecocide.earth/legal-definition. There are numerous resources available related to this movement—see for example, Stop Ecocide, https://www.stopecocide.earth/who-we-are-.
67. Ford, *St. Mary's Glossary*, s.v. "natural law." The term refers to that part of the moral law that can be known through human reason and so is said to be inscribed on the human heart.
68. Roger D. Sorrell, *St. Francis of Assisi and Nature: Tradition and Innovation in Western Christian Attitudes toward the Environment* (New York: Oxford University Press, 1988), especially 57 and 67–8.
69. As St. Bonaventure tells us in "The Major Legend of St. Francis (1260–1263)," in FA:ED Volume II—*The Founder*, 596–7: "In beautiful things [Francis] contuited Beauty itself … [and he] savored in each and every creature that fontal goodness."

Part II

St. Francis and St. Clare: Models of Faith and Sustainable Living

3

St. Francis of Assisi—From Birdbath to Patron Saint to Papal Encyclical

Introduction: More than Your Garden Variety

On November 29, 1979, Pope John Paul II proclaimed St. Francis of Assisi the Patron Saint of Ecologists.[1] The 266th pope of the Roman Catholic Church, elected on March 13, 2013, Jorge Mario Bergoglio took the name Francis (Francis of Assisi). On May 24, 2015, Pope Francis promulgated his encyclical, *Laudato Si'—On the Care of Our Common Home*. Therein, he roundly condemned the over 150-year human injection of greenhouse gases into the atmosphere that has resulted in horrendous environmental devastation and especially the failure of the Church (and ordinary believers) to provide sustained, substantive, religious critique of that impunity.[2] Indeed something new was afoot here!

Five years later, this leader of the world's 1.3 billion Catholics addressed executives of the world's biggest multinational oil companies, challenging them to curtail fossil-fuel production and develop sustainable energy—to "avoid a climate emergency." Failure to act urgently to reduce greenhouse gases would be "a brutal act of injustice toward the poor and future generations."[3] Yet subsequent challenges to date have had various and mixed results.

Laudato Si' is popularly known for its environmental critique. But its most central and profound challenge is its call to spiritual conversion. At its heart *LS* calls all people of good will to rediscover the God of All Creation who inspired and animated St. Francis' spiritual depth and mutual care of the for all creatures and "Our Sister, Mother Earth." Indeed, living from the values and vision of St. Francis is our singular pathway to overcoming the "Climate Emergency" of the twenty-first century.[4]

St. Francis of Assisi is best characterized as an ontological poet and a nature mystic who discovered the transformation of the universe and the interrelatedness of all beings through a spiritual journey of conversion, penance, and praise. The journey to his conversion was arduous and the subject of his entire life. Yet, in our "Climate Emergency," we need to attend to St. Francis' internal spiritual encounter and the ecological ethical effect of his spiritual journey. That journey points the way to our own conversion toward becoming sisters and brothers in the cosmos. Thus, later in this chapter, we explore Brazilian theologian Leonardo Boff's three main explanations for how Francis "arrived at sympathy and synergy with all things."[5]

William Short, OFM, helpfully explains, there are several important themes that run through St. Francis' life and work.[6] The first is the reality of the Incarnation. At the heart of Franciscan theology stands Jesus, the Incarnate Word of God. God's goodness moves the Creator to create the entire world. The crowning glory of creation is Jesus, the Word, and the whole created world is modeled after him. Each being—living and nonliving—in some way resembles the model, Jesus Christ, but humans bear the Divine image (*imago Dei*). St. Paul tells us the Incarnate Word, Jesus of Nazareth, is the pattern or "image of the invisible God" (Col. 1:15) through whom the entire universe was created. These amazing realities led Franciscan scholars and mystics to develop theological reflections on Christ's centrality for everything that lives. Indeed, Christ became the answer to the philosophical question, "Why is there something and not nothing?"[7] According to Short the early Franciscan theologians provided additional insights into just how the Christocentric theology and spirituality are rooted in the New Testament and are relevant to Christian life. Our challenge today is to make St. Francis' Christocentric teaching meaningful in our daily life and stop confining him to birdbaths and garden statues! Like St. Francis, our Christian life needs to focus on the goodness of God, Christ the Image of God, the Christocentric universe, the Imitation of Christ, and love.

The radical desire to live the *"full Gospel"* marks the distinctive Franciscan way (charism) of living the Christian life. Living that way stresses the challenge to balance the active and the contemplative aspects of life. Such a balance enables us to respect, reverence, and care for creation and to seek the optimal conditions of justice and mutual relationship among all creatures in the world. As Pope Francis shows in *LS*, II, *The Globalization of the Technocratic Paradigm* [106–14], this attitude is all but absent from the dominant cultures in today's technologically dependent world. The pope speaks of a "technological paradigm" which creates the absence of an *attitude of reverence* for creation in relationship with the human. This absence is at the heart of the current "Ecological Emergency."[8]

As for St. Francis, it is in prayer that we meet the Poor Christ who deified (made whole and holy) us and the material world by becoming part of it, and it is in the activity of daily living that we meet Christ in our neighbors. It is Christ, not humans desiring power or wealth, who stands at the center of the universe. Both contemplative action and the active contemplation that is engaged with the realities of the world are necessary for just and mutual relationships among the human family and for their relationships with all of creation.

St. Francis readily acknowledged that it was through God's work of conversion in him that he was able to move beyond the false promises of wealth and power that was within his grasp as the son of an upwardly mobile cloth merchant of the early twelfth century.[9]

We are left to wonder what it was exactly that allowed St. Francis to be open to such a conversion. According to theologian Thomas Murtagh, St. Francis' capacity for fostering nature developed as a part of his growth in the love of the Lord Jesus.[10] St. Francis' biographer, Thomas of Celano, explained, Francis embraced a life of penance as a pathway to coming to know the love of God.[11]

Francis was quite a literalist in that he readily personalized and gave religious definition to objects from the natural world around him, associating them with Scripture texts that spoke of those things or with liturgical and sacramental meanings associated with various objects or articles.[12] For example, water reminded Francis of the sacrament of baptism and, in turn, also of Christ. Many also observed a mutual bond of trust and affection between animals and Francis. Proof positive that St. Francis was not a simple romantic or pietist is easily found in the early Franciscan sources. We can see evidence that Francis struggled with his human limitations in dealing with the natural world.[13] Francis, at times, was annoyed by mice and flies, and he was *not* a vegetarian! Thus, though Francis sought God in all things, there is evidence that he too had his limits. And as for humans, Francis noted that though all creatures praise God, humans are particularly annoying in their refusal to praise God in a fitting way.[14]

Poetry, Prayer, and Poverty

Brazilian theologian Leonardo Boff suggests three main explanations for what made Francis so open to sympathy and synergy with all of creation.[15]

Poetic Sensitivity

First, Francis grew in his self-understanding as a poet who was able to grasp the essence and sacredness in all of creation. As "the Troubadour of the Great King," he did not shy away from the erotic enchantment, wonder, and desire for and with all things in the universe.[16] Francis was awestruck by the love of God seen in the Incarnation and demonstrated by Christ's death on the Cross. God's profound and faithful love, shown from the stable to the cross, drew Francis to first "follow in the footprints of Jesus" and ultimately into union with the Crucified One.[17] That union with the Crucified Jesus was most fully realized when Francis received the stigmata at Mount LaVerna.[18]

Standing before the crucified Christ, Francis was keenly aware of his creaturely status with all of its imperfections. Nonetheless, in the *Fifth Admonition* Francis exhorts: "Consider … how excellent the Lord made you, for he created and formed you to the image of his beloved Son according to the body and to his own likeness according to the spirit."[19] The depth of such passionate love disposed Francis to be free of possessiveness and to extend himself in relation to all of creation because he saw Christ's presence in everything and everyone, especially the poor and the lepers. As Pope Francis stressed, it is human failure to stand in wonder within creation, seeking oneness with God and all creatures, that has brought us to the brink of the collapse of Earth's ecosystems—now a "Climate Emergency."[20]

Even a cursory reading of the early Franciscan sources reveals St. Francis' unique love affair with all of creation.[21] These passages, especially the Franciscan classic, the *Canticle of the Creatures*, must always be read considering Francis' profound personal insight into the significance of the Incarnation.[22] Indeed, the events immediately prior to the composition of the *Canticle*, recounted in the *Assisi Compilation*, are important for our understanding.[23] Suffering from an eye disease that had left him blind and in excruciating pain, Francis lay in a mouse-infested cell. There he had a vision in which he was offered a golden globe of the earth in exchange for his infirmities, and he was assured of eternal life. The alchemical symbolism of the earth changing to gold stood for Francis' conversion. That conversion was brought about by two critical experiences.[24]

The First Event

First was Francis' renunciation of his father, Pietro Bernadone before the Bishop of Assisi. There Francis cast himself in all his nakedness, totally into the care of his Heavenly Father saying: "Until now I have called you father here on earth, but now I can say without reserve, 'Our Father who art in heaven,' since I have placed all my treasure and all my hope in him."[25] Having embraced radical poverty, a rejection of the possession of anything in any form, Francis was now able to embrace the common Source of all creation and thus know as well the radical relatedness of the entire cosmos. As St. Bonaventure writes of Francis: "From a reflection on the primary source of all things, filled with even more abundant piety, he would call creatures, no matter how small, by the name of 'brother' or 'sister,' because he knew they shared with him the same beginning."[26] Francis realized that humans stand among the other creatures.

In the *Salutation of the Virtues*, Francis shows that the fitting relationship among all creatures is one of obedience; that is, carefully attending to the other: "[The person who possesses holy Obedience] is subject and submissive to everyone in the world, not only to people but to every beast and wild animal as well that they may do whatever they want with it so far as it *has been given* to them *from above* by the Lord."[27]

The Second Event

His encounter with the Crucified One at San Damiano was the second event toward Francis' conversion. There he discovered that not only is God the glorious Creator, but God loves to the extent that "the Word of God became flesh" (Jn 1:14, Gk. *sarx*) part of the material universe. This realization served to deepen Francis' sense of the sacredness of creation, and he wrote: "Oh, how holy and how loving, gratifying, humbling, peace-giving, sweet, worthy of love and above all things, desirable: to have such a Brother and such a Son: our Lord Jesus Christ, Who laid down His life for His sheep" (cf. Jn 10:15).[28] Francis realized that not only was he a brother to other people, he and they are sisters and brothers of Jesus. And beyond that Jesus is related to the rocks and the worms. Thus, humans are sisters and brothers to rocks and worms as well!

Thomas of Celano, St. Francis' biographer, wrote: "He used to call all creatures by the name 'brother' and 'sister' and in a wonderful way, unknown to others he could discern the *secrets of the heart* of creatures like someone who has already passed *into the freedom of the glory of the Children of God*."[29]

Francis' union with nature is distinct from the parabolic *associations* of God with nature in the New Testament, pantheistic *identification* of God and Nature of the Renaissance, or the ecstatic joy *over* Nature of the Greeks.[30] Francis' union was *with* God manifest *within* nature.

Prayer Experience of the Common Origin of Things

While at prayer, Francis had a religious experience that allowed him to understand the *common origin* of all things. This second aspect of Francis' self-understanding gave him a deeper insight into his kinship with all of creation. That everything in the world comes from the same Creator was not a dry dogmatic tenet for St. Francis. Rather, it was more like a love song that drew all beings to "the heart of the Father, through the Son in the enthusiasm of the Holy Spirit."[31] In light of this understanding, Leonardo Boff claims that it is more in the spirit of St. Francis to translate his famous *"Deus meus et omnia,"* not as it is usually translated—"My God and my all"—but as "My God and all things."[32] Indeed, as Bonaventure recounts, Francis was most delighted to sing *with* the creatures: "Our sisters the birds are praising their Creator; So we should go among them and chant the Lord's praises and the canonical hours."[33]

Radical Poverty

Francis' radical poverty is the third and final characteristic of his life that enabled him to be kin to all of creation. Not selfishly holding on to anything, but rather meeting life with open hands and heart, Francis was able to set aside usual human tendencies toward subordination or domination and meet everything and everyone as one utterly available and completely focused on the need of the other. As Bonaventure claims, Francis was able to return to the state of "primeval innocence," a place of full mutuality in relationship with God and all creatures.[34] Indeed, Francis saw himself as a son of the Loving and Generous Creator and Great King, a brother to Jesus, and the entire family of God's creatures.

Francis came to *know* God and *know about* God through an integrated life of contemplation and action, choosing to live the Gospel, "following in the footprints of Jesus." Thus, he gave us both a *method* for theological reflection (seeking to understand our faith) and a *content* (topics or subject matter) of theology that is very "earth friendly." Now, we will first examine St. Francis' theological reflection process (method) and then highlight the content of a Franciscan ecotheology.

A Franciscan Theological Reflection Method

Just how did St. Francis approach learning to know God and the things God desires us to care about in creation? Regis J. Armstrong selected three starting points or ways which, when taken together, reveal how St. Francis sought to know God and God's will, namely penance, poverty, and prayer.[35]

Penance

In his *Testament* Francis bears witness to his call from God to do penance.[36] To do penance Francis embraced a life of loving relationship with God, viewed the world as an expression of the Creator's goodness, and lived in hope of the fulfillment of the Reign of God. Francis showed us how a life of penance is a journey of faith which climaxes in conversion, a new way of knowing, and a greater sensitivity to the voice of God within ourselves and all of creation. Most importantly, this conversion leads to action.

In his *Testament* (1 and 2), Francis described his experience of embracing a leper, a moment of true conversion in his life. In that moment, he became conscious of God's unconditional largess, and he responded by embracing the leper "with a heart sensitive to misery."[37] St. Bonaventure's account of that embrace of the leper also includes Francis' encounter with a beggar and a poor knight, and he calls Francis' responses acts of *pietas*—"an act of devotion to God and of compassion."[38] Penance is a process of engaging in a spirit-filled life which draws one, in the fullest sense, into the very heart of God—the goal of all theology. Living the lifestyle of a penitent readily leads one to an attitude of poverty—Armstrong's second prism of a Franciscan theological method.

Poverty

When one has glimpsed the infinitely loving and gracious God, by contrast, one is confronted with one's human limitations of sin, arrogant self-centeredness, or an unhealthy lack of self-confidence, and the deceptions of our restrictive biases and prejudices. In this moment of recognizing that we humans are all weak and imperfect, it is possible to comprehend the necessity of choosing to face the world with open head, heart, and hands, not clinging to anything as exclusively one's own. *Our* power to control others and the natural world is often shortsighted and selfishly motivated. In his *Second Admonition,* Francis pointed out that the Fall of humanity into sin had *everything* to do with human desires to grasp things and use them in an arrogant and selfish manner.[39] This grab for power and security is the injustice of appropriating for ourselves what is rightfully the Creator's.

Another aspect of poverty is material poverty. There is a sense in which material poverty is sacramental for Francis: "it is an outward sign of an inner reality, spiritual poverty, and, more importantly, an outward sign that leads to a deeper reality."[40] As we embrace material poverty more seriously, we are prompted to identify more honestly our other appropriations until when we are bereft of everything, God alone becomes our treasure which we can both cherish and give away. Typically, Francis insisted that the brothers attend to the prompting of the Spirit in all things. This kind of dependence comes through a consciousness of one's own poverty—sinfulness and limitations—and utter reliance on God's ever abiding love and goodness.

Prayer

Prayer, Armstrong's third prism of the Franciscan theological reflection method, can be described as the process of attending to one's relationship with God. Francis reminds us that we are empowered to see, know, and believe by the same Holy Spirit which animates the very life of the triune God. Indeed, it is the Holy Spirit who enables Christians to recognize the human Jesus as the Christ, and the bread and wine of the Eucharist as the Body and Blood of Our Lord Jesus Christ. Beyond the Eucharist, the Spirit enables one to perceive *ordinary earthly things* as reflections of God, not as objects of one's egotistical self-aggrandizing grasp for power.[41]

When describing Francis' capacity to grasp and know things beyond what he could see, Bonaventure used an interesting and unusual Latin verb, *contuere.* When one knows something through the Holy Spirit, one "co-intuits" (*conituita*) both the contingent particulars, for example, the size, shape, color, smell of a rose, but also the eternal reasons in those particulars—the love of God the Creator imaged in the beauty of the rose. So Bonaventure explained Francis' perception of the world:

> In beautiful things he [St. Francis] contuited Beauty itself and through the footprints impressed in things he followed his Beloved everywhere, out of them all making himself *a ladder* through which he could climb up to lay a hold of him *who is utterly desirable*. With an intensity of unheard devotion

he savored in each and every creature—as in so many rivulets—that fontal Goodness, and discerned an almost celestial choir in the chords of power and activity given to them by God, and like the prophet David, he sweetly encouraged them to praise the Lord.[42]

The more deeply Francis lived in the Spirit, the more he grew in his capacity as a "contuitive," delighting in the world as a revelation of the divine. Indeed, "Prayer, then, a principal activity of the Spirit, must be the starting point of our theologizing, but it must also be its culmination. For the contuitive person, one who gazes upon the world with the eyes of the Spirit, every moment becomes, to borrow Thomas Merton's words, 'a seed of contemplation.'"[43]

Three Elements of Content for a Franciscan Ecotheology

To complement Armstrong's three prisms for a Franciscan theological method—penance, poverty, and prayer—we now explore the content, topics, or subject matter of Franciscan theology and see what we can glean from this for a Franciscan ecotheology.

The World Is Good

First, we find St. Francis' strong intuition that the world is good, and it will provide for every authentic human need. The vast variety and abundance in creation is, for Francis, ample evidence of the nature of God. Francis constantly speaks of God in superlative terms. His God is both powerful and profoundly intimate, loving, and generous. Chapter twenty-three of *The Earlier Rule* illustrates this typical way of naming God:

> Therefore, let us desire nothing else, let us want nothing else, let nothing else please us and cause us delight except our Creator, Redeemer and Savior, the only true God, Who is the fullness of Good, all good, every good, the true and supreme good, *Who alone is good*, merciful, gentle, delightful and sweet, Who alone is holy, just, true, holy, and upright, Who alone is kind, innocent, clean, from Whom, *through Whom* and in Whom is all pardon, all grace, all glory of all penitents and just ones, of all the blessed rejoicing together in heaven.[44]

And Francis goes on and on naming God in superlative terms.

The Incarnation Deifies Creation

The meaning of the human Christ is a second insight forming the content of a Franciscan ecotheology. This insight both flows from and suggests a positive worldview. Francis' understanding of creation was that creation manifests Christ.[45] Everything—flowers, lambs, worms, lepers, poor women—recognized in the incarnate Christ, the human "babe from Bethlehem," portrayed at Greccio.[46] Because Christ chose human form and the limits of time and space of *this* world, the goodness of this world is affirmed. Indeed, as humans and as followers of this Christ, our place, too, is in *this* world. We don't have to escape this world to be in the presence of Christ.

Authentic Humanness Requires Relationship with Christ

The third intuition that reveals Francis of Assisi's theology is found in Celano's account of Francis receiving the *stigmata*.[47] When in prayer, the Crucified One gave Francis "a kind and gracious look," and he was frightened at seeing Christ's pain and suffering. From this experience Francis drew insight into the meaning of the human person. People are fragile, limited, and vulnerable. Yet it is this very condition of fragility, limitedness, and vulnerability that reveals human creatureliness and the wondrous love of God. *Authentic humanness is revealed in relationship with Christ.*

Thus, we see Francis' insights, about how we *know* God and what we *know about* God in creation, form a pattern of conversion, action, and contemplation. Through that threefold pattern, we can be transformed and converted and then repeatedly recycled through the process, moving ever more deeply into the heart of God. This is the pattern and content of Francis' ecotheology—living the Gospel and following "in the footprints of Jesus."

Thomas of Celano and the first Franciscan theologians understood St. Francis and St. Clare to be the embodiment of this theology in which God is a compassionate Lover made manifest in the Incarnation and revealed in all of creation. Though marred by sin and finitude, the world is a good place. As God in Christ looks lovingly upon vulnerable humanity, so too must humans reach out to those viewed as the lepers of our day—the poor, the oppressed and forgotten, the polluted environment, and threatened species. We must value the entire cosmos and cherish its every member, in its particularity, and for its own sake, insofar as each reveals something of God who is Good, the Highest Good.

Thus far, we have seen that Francis was open to sympathy and synergy with all things because he had a poetic heart, he experienced God as the common origin of all creation, and he embraced radical poverty. Francis discovered his *relationship with* and *knowledge of* God, by actively practicing the virtues of *penance* and *poverty* and engaging in a vibrantly active life of *prayer*. Through all of this activity, Francis gained three important insights, namely God is Good, the Highest Good; because of the Incarnation, all of Creation is deified, made holy and sacramental; and a relationship with Christ is necessary for the most authentic human living. With this background in mind, we now turn to an examination of St. Francis of Assisi's *Canticle of the Creatures*.

From the Writings of St. Francis
The Canticle of the Creatures (1225)[48]

Reflection and Application

The Canticle of the Creatures (1225) by St. Francis of Assisi is a literary and religious classic.[49] This well-known composition of St. Francis is no mere fanciful, lyrical poem tritely romanticized in birdbaths and garden statues. Scholarly study reveals it is a profound call for spiritual conversion and behavioral change.

In his book, *The Analogical Imagination*, theologian David Tracy claims that there are many works—art, music, literature, dance—recognized in every culture as timeless that capture meaning, that express the *very soul* of a people.[50] These expressions are identified as "classics" by five fundamental characteristics. They are excellent, universalizable, shocking, hope inspiring, and fecund.

Classics are most excellent, more than period pieces or fads. They express far more meaning than what is momentary or provincial, and they are in no way merely glitzy or tawdry. Because classics hold such deep truths and density of content, it takes time and effort to appreciate their wealth. A classic cannot be reduced simplistically; to do so is to do it violence by making it something it is not. We must first know a classic's particularity before we can comprehend its universality.

Secondly, a classic helps us to look deeply at life and its meaning. The Bible and the Scriptures of the world's religions, similarly, exemplify this characteristic. These world-renowned texts teach life's meaning, give moral guidance, treat major themes that touch the very core of human existence such as human rights, power, the shape of a just society, compassion, tragedy, hope, human solidarity, or the reverence due creation, and much more.

Throughout life, people interpret what they experience; indeed, knowing is an active enterprise. Culture, myths, metaphors, associations, symbols, memory, cognitive moods—all become lenses which influence, constrict, or dominate human imagination, or knowing. Classics shock us into a deeper reality, cutting through our narrowness, pettiness, and jostle our cognitive smugness and stretch us to the highest potential of our human capacities.

Classics are ultimately hope-inspiring. They pull us above the fray toward our very best selves and away from indifference—the greatest form of violence humans can exert. As the philosopher Albert Camus put it, "All literature is hopeful; silence is the produce of despair."[51]

Finally, Classics have a kind of fecundity. They have a way of moving us into both internal and external action. They draw us into the heart of the intensity of the game of life. As Tracy puts it, "In reacting to a classic, we must abandon our own self-conscious intellectual control, so that the energy of the game can take over. In every game, I enter the world where I play so fully, that finally, the game plays me."[52] We can begin to understand what Tracy means; if we recall that often, one of the first things that happens when a totalitarian regime takes over is that they ban the classics in their state. Classics hold the deepest memory of a people, and in that sense, they are subversive to any other way of being. Classics are antidotal to any form of slavery of the mind, imagination, or the will.

Thus, to claim that *The Canticle of the Creatures* is a religious classic is to say it retains meaning that Francis intended in the twelfth century, but there is also wisdom for us in our present context. Because this is so, we will briefly review the circumstances surrounding Francis' composition of the *Canticle*, seeking to glean further insights from this classic.

Curiously distinct from the wide repertoire identified in Francis' other works, the *Canticle* names only a few creatures. Significantly, the *Canticle* is built primarily around the four classical elements: earth, air, water, and fire. The circumstances of three different occasions for which Francis wrote the various parts of the *Canticle* are also important for understanding its full impact.

Francis wrote verses 1–9 of the *Canticle*, shortly after he had received the *stigmata*, a sign of his profound intimacy and identification with Jesus. Having recently relinquished his role as founding Minister General of the

Order of the Friars Minor, Francis realized that it was not he but God who would determine its future. Verses 10 and 11 were written as part of a peacemaking strategy which required the friars to sing before the quarreling civil and religious authorities of Assisi. Verses 12 and 13 were composed, when Francis was weak and suffering from a painful eye disease that left him sensitive to light, almost blind, and near death. Verse 14 is thought to be the refrain to be sung after each verse.

Clearly, Francis' relationship with God was the governing factor for understanding his bond with all creatures. Francis had no unusual scientific understanding of the natural world. Yet his insight into relations—humans and God, God and creatures, humans and creatures—was unique. That universal kinship of all creation with God and one another makes humans and all creatures sisters and brothers—and that makes all the difference!

The dynamics of Francis' spiritual conversion is more than hinted at in the *Canticle*.[53] Franciscan theologian Eric Doyle called the *Canticle* the work of St. Francis, the poet-mystic. Poets use words in ways that point beyond the usual meanings assigned to them. The *Canticle* expresses beautiful poetic praise of the God, the Creator, and "the authentic Christian attitude toward creation which is to accept and love the creatures as they are."[54] The creatures are not mere objects of human power or control. Rather, like us, they are the expression of God's goodness and love. In our creaturehood, humans are equal with all other creatures. Recall that, in the Noahic Covenant, God purposefully established a relationship with humans *and every living creature* (Gen. 9:12-13). Each creature uniquely reflects God and God's goodness. As God loves each creature uniquely, so too must we. Francis learned this way of the Divine first by entering into a contemplative union with God, and coming to recognize evidence of God, in and through all other beings and elements of creation. In union with God and all the creatures, Francis found his own uniqueness as one ever more original.

The realization of his singularity among the creatures, yet his likeness to them as a recipient of the love of God was, in turn, a source of Francis' great love of God's creation. To reflect on this immersion in love is to encounter Mystery, "the 'never-the-last-wordness' of our existence."[55] We are always seeking and searching for something more, yet every human attempt to satisfy the "more" ends in more seeking. Francis' "heart sight" told him he had found the "more" in God, and God was ever present in the here and now and all around him.

The words of the *Canticle* express the depth of Francis' spiritual integration and the inner reaches of his soul. As Doyle holds, "All beautiful words and music come from the mystery of personhood, welling up from the inner depths. It is not so remarkable that Francis, though blind, was able to write a song about the beauty and unity of creation. He was already one with himself and with the world, and the world was one in him."[56] This integration provided Francis with an inner confidence and a cure for alienation from all "others" that could threaten him. The path to such integration for Francis was prayer, the first step of self-surrender.

Francis struggled to embrace poverty as a way to freely open himself to God and all of creation. Through meeting God in prayer, he learned to love *as* and *what* God loves. To love authentically is to love and accept other humans and all creatures on their own terms. Particularly noteworthy for our "Climate Emergency" is that Francis was able to find himself, and true peace and harmony, not in warfare or wealth but through spiritual means. Today, when we are experiencing a spiritual malaise, prayer and spiritual practices are necessary to assist us in reversing the devastation of the planet.[57] This is *not* a call to escapism! It is to move to the depths of our being—to confront the foundational human truth, namely that we are creatures who stand in relationship with both God and our fellow earth creatures. To realize we are surrounded with wondrous manifestations of God's love and care, personal integration can take place, alienation vanishes, and we can be motivated to act.

To understand one's relationship to all of creation through prayer and contemplation is also a political act.[58] What we do not know, we cannot love. What we do not love, we will not defend. To be in a love relationship with all of creation is to risk being motivated to act in defense and protection of those we love. If we claim to love God, we cannot tolerate injustice or abuse of the environment because everything in creation is our "sister" or our "brother" in God, the Creator. When one is motivated to defend another, one's focus shifts from self to the other. It is often risky to be so motivated; it is a move toward poverty, indeed perhaps the ultimate poverty of losing one's own life for the sake of another.

Significantly, Francis even called death, "Sister," because he understood death as integral to life. Indeed, death is the ultimate journey into poverty, a letting go of all possessions including life itself. Having given his life completely to Christ, Francis had nothing to fear from death. Death was, for Francis, a passage into the fullness of life with Christ. In our day when fears of the "small deaths" of life such as personal limitations or the inability to achieve wealth or position are frequently the cause of discord, abuse, or other kinds of violence, we can learn much from Francis' embrace of "Sister Death" as a friend who opens the way to new life beyond imagination.

Cosmic Elements and the Human Person

Franciscan ethicist, Thomas A. Nairn, sees St. Francis of Assisi's *Canticle of the Creatures* as an exercise of the moral imagination and a call to moral conversion.[59] He noted that expositor of medieval popular culture, Aron Gurevich, claimed the *Canticle*'s four cosmic elements—earth, air, water, and fire—had great importance in St. Francis' day. Human beings were considered a "microcosm," reflecting the larger "macrocosm" of the world and revealed a parallelism between the person and the world. People of the Middle Ages understood the heavenly objects "sun, moon, stars" as powers which affected human destiny. Indeed, people believed that the four elements affected a person's very identity. The goal of both medicine and natural philosophy was to restore the disease or temperamental problems caused by an imbalance among the four elements—earth, air, water, fire. With this in mind, Nairn engages us in an exercise of moral imagination.

Moral Imagination for the Future

Nairn noted how the verses naming the four elements differ from the rest of the *Canticle*. In each strophe the earth elements relate to God but also serve humanity. Most likely Francis wished to show contemporaries that when confronted with the powerful cosmic elements, they must remember the elements are *merely* creatures of God. Further, Nairn suggests, the terms "brother" and "sister" show the relationship of the elements to God and humans, but those terms serve "a relativizing function, as well."[60] In the medieval context then, Francis' use of the four elements "[brought] the cosmic elements, understood as elements which influence humanity, down to a human level."[61]

Nature was valuable because it contributed to humanity knowledge of God and drew humans to God. Nature was evil if it hindered humanity's quest for God. If the elements do not move humans to praise God, they are misused. "If the proper role of the elements points humanity to God, then God and not the elements is the true influencer of humanity … But as humanity accepts its place in the microcosm of this universe it must also appreciate its own vocation in serving God. It is in serving God that humanity finds true freedom."[62]

Amid our "Climate Emergency" the *Canticle* loudly summons us to especially take up our ecological vocation to care for God's creation. Our moral imagination must be converted to the very mind of God. We must treat the planet as does God, living in proper relationship to all of God's creatures. The *Canticle*'s "relativizing function" declares we are God's unique servants caring for sister and brothers!

As Pope Francis points out in *LS*, especially Chapters One and Three, human abuse of the natural environment has pushed vast bioregions of the world to their breaking point and increasingly past any reasonable measure of their carrying capacities. This is clearly confirmed in the 2021 *Sixth Assessment Report of the U.N. Intergovernmental Panel on Climate Change*.[63] Some scholars contend that the carrying capacity of the Earth was already breached in 1986.[64] We continue to reap the results.

Implications for Praxis

Our habitat Earth, this *oikos,* our home, is protected by a high concentration of stratospheric ozone (O_3), which absorbs much of the harmful incoming solar radiation called UVB, linked to skin cancers, cataracts, and harm to crops and marine life.[65] Forces beyond human control unite all earthly life in one household (Greek—*oikos*). All Earth creatures and elements constitute one family who must find the economy of laws or rules (Greek—*nomos*) that will allow the survival and thriving of the entire family, *if indeed* any *one* being would fulfill its potential. This is what Pope Francis indicated by "integral ecology," a twenty-first-century name for Francis of Assisi's notion of the kinship of creation.[66]

In 2021, the International Union for Conservation of Nature (IUCN) reported that of 134,425 species that were assessed, 35,000 are "Red Listed"— at immediate threat of extinction.[67] This included 25 percent of all mammals; 13 percent of all birds; 41 percent of all amphibians; 33 percent of warm water reef-building corals; 63 percent of cycads, and 34 percent conifers.

The UN Convention on Biological Diversity's August 8, 2020, *Global Biodiversity Outlook 5* report indicated that the world is failing to address a catastrophic biodiversity collapse that not only threatens to wipe out beloved species and invaluable genetic diversity but endangers humanity's food supply, health, and security.[68] At the global level, only six of the biodiversity convention's twenty targets were partially achieved and none were fully achieved. Of 196 countries, 167 submitted national reports on their efforts. The United States did not report because it was not a party to the treaty.[69] Sadly, this news is not that new![70] We have been living in a false reality!

The long pattern of neglecting limits and disrespecting the cyclical patterns through which the natural world renews itself is at its breaking point. We are now in an "Ecological Emergency." We have violated the goodness of God and the integrity of creation which requires we recognize each member as having intrinsic value and thus moral status. We now are reaping the results.[71]

Clearly the human species is not excluded from this disturbing picture. At the start of this millennium, the United Nations Development Program reported that if the world population was divided into quintiles according to income, the *richest fifth* of the population received *82 percent* of total global income, while the *poorest fifth* received *1.4 percent* of the income.[72] In 2021 an estimated 698 million people, or 9 percent of the global population, were living in extreme poverty—that is, living on less than $1.90 a day. Over two-fifths (3,293 million people) lived below $5.50 a day. By 2020, the number of people living in extreme poverty increased by an estimated 50 million due to the Covid-19 pandemic and resulting global economic downturn.[73]

To be human—created in the Divine Image and Likeness, loved, and redeemed by the Lord Jesus—and to be poor is an oxymoron. But today, as in recent centuries, especially for people of color and indigenous peoples, to be poor is/was to be powerless in the face of government and corporate collusion to exploit the only home they knew—food, clothing, shelter, land, the entire way of life taken by a bulldozer, a drill, or the pollution of industry and technology.

Theologian Leonardo Boff experienced this kind of poverty among the indigenous peoples of the Brazilian Amazon region. His insights can help us understand the relationship between issues of economic poverty and ecological issues. Following his Franciscan roots, he argued that liberation theology and ecology must become partners in light of the current state of affairs of the poor.

After Ernest Haeckel first formulated the notion of ecology in 1866, ecology was soon understood as the unity of three ecologies: *Environmental ecology, social ecology*, and *mental ecology*.[74] *Environmental ecology* is concerned with the relations that various societies and individual human beings have with the environment. *Social ecology* explores the reality that humans are both earth creatures and social beings. Depending on how humans organize themselves, there will be exploitation, collaboration, or respect and reverence for the natural world. *Mental ecology* starts from the recognition that nature is *within* human beings—in their minds, in the form of psychic energy, symbols, archetypes, and behavior patterns that embody attitudes of aggression or of respect and acceptance of nature.

As classical liberation theologies claim, people stand in need of a threefold liberation: First, as an integral human person; second, as a social being who participates in political, economic, and social relations; and third, as a spiritual person in need of redemption from sin. Notice how the three levels of liberation align well with the three ecologies. They also find a correlative in the threefold Franciscan method of doing theological reflection by engaging in penance, poverty, and prayer. Human persons thrive when they are at home, in a place where they are at peace, in right relationship with God and neighbor, and respectful of the integrity of creation. Boff rightly contends that when any of these relationships are broken, we *also* see the emergence of dehumanizing poverty, oppression, and injustice of all sorts.

What holds all these relationships together is a sense of the sacredness of creation like that held by St. Francis. If humanity, indeed the planet, is to live through the Third Millennium, we must face the reality that *science* taken to its depths brings us to *mystery*, and *mystery* brought to intelligibility moves to *concreteness*. Indeed, our Sister Mother Earth nourishes and sustains everything. So too, in our contemporary world of work, which has removed itself from the Earth into concrete jungles and cyberspace, we must find ways to touch the Earth from which we came—attuning body, mind, and spirit to the rhythms of this Earth which reveals God the Generous Creator so that we also will come home to the heart of God.

Today we stand at a crossroads. We must make a radical turn to the Earth, do penance as Francis did, and be converted to live *with* nature, not *from* nature.[75] Like St. Francis, we must take seriously the foundational moral experience—reverence for persons and their environment. In *LS* §139, Pope Francis invites us to do just that:

> When we speak of the "environment," what we really mean is a relationship existing between nature and the society which lives in it. Nature cannot be regarded as something separate from ourselves or as a mere setting in which we live. We are part of nature, included in it and thus in constant interaction with it. …
>
> We are faced not with two separate crises, one environmental and the other social, but rather with one complex crisis which is both social and environmental. Strategies for a solution demand an integrated approach to combating poverty, restoring dignity to the excluded, and at the same time protecting nature.[76]

Questions for Reflection and Discussion

1. In what way does St. Francis' *Canticle of the Creatures* inform Pope Francis' notion of integral ecology?
2. St. Francis was moved and motivated by the fact of the Incarnation, and nature became holy to him. What difference does the fact of the Incarnation make in how you deal with environmental issues?
3. Compare St. Francis' understanding of "poverty" with your own perception of poverty. In what way does St. Francis' understanding impact how we treat God's people and our common home?
4. In what way is Franciscan theologian William Short's definition of "sin" as "the will to possess" helpful in thinking about the environmental crisis?
5. How do you see Haeckel's three dimensions of ecology operative in your own daily life?

Suggestions for Action

1. Daily recall that we *Homo sapiens* are daughters and sons of the Earth; the Earth itself becomes self-aware, animated by the very breath of the Spirit of God, in communion and solidarity with other species in the community of living beings.
2. Reflect on the 13.7 billion years of the evolution of the universe and the sacred, astonishing wonder that we exist at all! We are latecomers to the Earth; it existed before us, and it likely can exist without us!!!
3. Take 8 minutes to experience the Sun. It takes each ray of sunlight, traveling at 186,000 miles per second, eight minutes to reach you! Such are the dimensions of the universe!
4. On a clear night, lie on the ground and look *down and out* into space. Become conscious of gravity—like the arms of our Sister, Mother Earth gently holding you to herself, preventing you from falling off into space.
5. Find a spot in creation that you can visit once a week. At each visit, spend 15 minutes in quiet contemplation of creation. Like St. Francis, be amazed at what you learn!

Sources for Further Study

Secondary Sources

Bodo, Murray. *Francis, The Journey and the Dream*. 40th Anniversary ed. Cincinnati, OH: St. Anthony Press, 2011.

Boff, Leonardo. *Cry of the Earth, Cry of the Poor*. Ecology and Justice Series. Maryknoll: Orbis Books, 1997.

Cocksedge, Simon, Samuel Double, and Nicholas Alan Worssam. *Seeing Differently: Franciscans in Creation*. London: Canterbury Press, 2021.

Dalarun, Jacques. *The Canticle of Brother Sun: Francis of Assisi Reconciled*. Trans. Philippe Yates. Paris: Alma Editeur, 2014.

Doyle, Eric. *St. Francis and the Song of Brotherhood and Sisterhood*. [Reprint of St. Francis and the Song of Brotherhood, New York: Seabury Press, 1981.] St. Bonaventure, NY: The Franciscan Institute, 1997.

Notes

1. https://www.vatican.va/content/john-paul-ii/la/apost_letters/1979/documents/hf_jp-ii_apl_19791129_inter-sanctos.html.
2. *LS*, https://www.vatican.va/content/francesco/en/encyclicals/documents/papa-francesco_20150524_enciclica-laudato-si.html. *LS* is a 200-page encyclical.
3. "Pope Francis Declares 'Climate Emergency' and Urges Action," June 14, 2019, https://www.theguardian.com/environment/2019/jun/14/pope-francis-declares-climate-emergency-and-urges-action.
4. Brian Roewe, "Why Is Francis of Assisi the Patron Saint of Ecology?," October 2, 2020, https://www.ncronline.org/news/earthbeat/why-francis-assisi-patron-saint-ecology.
5. Leonardo Boff, *Cry of the Earth, Cry of the Poor*, trans. Phillip Berryman (Maryknoll: Orbis Books, 1997), 213–16.
6. William Short, "The Franciscan Spirit," in *Franciscan Theology of the Environment*, ed. Nothwehr, 111–27.
7. Ibid., 118.
8. Boff, *Cry of the Earth, Cry of the Poor*, 1–34. *LS* §s 101,109, 111, 112, 122.
9. "The Testament (1226)," 1–3, in FA:ED, Volume I—*The Saint*, 124.
10. Thomas Murtagh, "St. Francis and Ecology," in *Franciscan Theology of the Environment*, ed. Nothwehr, 143–54.

11. "The Remembrance of the Desire of a Soul by Thomas of Celano (1245–47),"
    IX: 14, in FA:ED, Volume II—*The Founder*, 253.
12. "Mirror of Perfection," 118 in *St. Francis of Assisi: Writings and Early Biographies, English Omnibus of Sources for the Life of St. Francis*, ed. Marion A. Habig (Chicago: Franciscan Herald Press, 1983), 1256–7. "The Beginning of the Mirror of Perfection of the Status of a Lesser Brother (Sabatier Edition)," 118, in FA:ED, Volume III—*The Prophet*, 366.
13. *The Legend of Perugia*, 43 and *2 Cel* 75. Cf. "The Assisi Compilation (1244–1260)," 83, in FA:ED, Volume III—*The Founder*, 184–7. Thomas of Celano, "The Remembrance of the Desire of a Soul (1245–1247)," 45:75, in FA:ED, Volume III—*The Founder*, 297.
14. Francis of Assisi, "The Undated Writings—The Admonitions," V, in FA:ED, Volume I—*The Saint*, 131.
15. Boff, *Cry of the Earth, Cry of the Poor*, 213–16.
16. Boff cites the *Legend of Perugia*, 64. See "The Assisi Compilation (1244–1260)," 99 in FA:ED, Volume II—*The Founder*, 202–3. See also "A Mirror of Perfection of the *Status* of a Lesser Brother (Sabatier Edition, 1928)," 121, in FA:ED, Volume III—*The Prophet*, 369–79.
17. Francis of Assisi, "The Earlier Rule" (Without the Papal Seal 1209/10-1221) 1:1, in FA:ED, Volume I—*The Saint*, 63–4.
18. The Legend of the Three Companions (1241–7), Chapter XVII, 69–70, in FA:ED, Volume II—*The Founder*, 108.
19. Francis of Assisi, "The Undated Writings—The Admonitions," 5, in FA:ED, Volume I—*The Saint*, 131.
20. LS § 11.
21. "The Life of St. Francis by Thomas of Celano (1228–1229)," Book I, 21:58–61, in FA:ED, Volume I—*The Saint*, 234–6. "The Remembrance of the Desire of a Soul (1245–1247)," Book II, 124: 165–6; 168–71 in FA:ED, Volume II—*The Founder*, 353–7. "The Assisi Compilation (1244–1269)," 88 and 110 in FA:ED, Volume II—*The Founder*, 192 and 217. "The Remembrance of the Desire of a Soul (1245–1247)," Book II, 124: 165–6; 168–71 in FA:ED, Volume III—*The Founder*, 192; 217–8.
22. Francis of Assisi, "The Canticle of the Creatures (1225)," in FA:ED, Volume I—*The Saint*, 113–14. The canticle is more popularly known as *Canticle of Brother Sun*. See *St. Francis of Assisi: Writings and Early Biographies, English Omnibus of Sources*, ed. Habig, at 128–9.
23. "The Assisi Compilation (1244–1269)," 83, in FA:ED, Volume II—*The Founder*, 184–7. This document was formerly known as the *Legenda Perugina*, 43. See Ewert Cousins, *Christ of the 21st Century* (Rockport, MA: Element, Inc., 1992), 143–4.
24. Zachary Hayes, "St. Francis of Assisi and Nature: A Model for a 21st Century Spirituality," unpublished manuscript, 8–16.

25. Bonaventure of Bagnoregio, "The Major Legend of St. Francis (1260–63)," Chapter 2: 4 in FA:ED, Volume II—*The Founder*, 538. Alessandro Vettori, *Poets of Divine Love: The Rhetoric of Franciscan Spiritual Poetry* (New York: Fordham University Press, 2004).
26. Ibid., Chapter 8:6, in FA:ED, Volume II—*The Founder*, 590.
27. Francis of Assisi, "The Undated Writings—A Salutation of the Virtues," 14 in FA:ED, Volume I—*The Saint*, 165.
28. Francis of Assisi, "The Earlier Exhortation to the Brothers and Sisters of Penance [The First Version of the Letter to the Faithful] (1209–1215)," 1:13, in FA:ED, Volume I—*The Saint*, 42.
29. "The Life of St. Francis by Thomas of Celano (1228–1229)," 28:81 in FA:ED, Volume I—*The Saint*, 251.
30. Max Scheler, *The Nature of Sympathy*, trans. Peter Heath (Hamden, CT: The Shoestring Press, Inc., 1970), 90.
31. Ibid.
32. Boff, *Cry of the Earth, Cry of the Poor*, 66.
33. Bonaventure, "Major Legend of St. Francis (1260–1263)," VIII, 9, in FA:ED, Volume II—*The Founder*, 592–3.
34. Ibid., VIII, 1, 586–7.
35. Regis J. Armstrong, "Francis of Assisi and the Prisms of Theologizing," *Greyfriars Review* 10/2 (1996): 179–206. See also Giovanni Iammerrone, "Franciscan Theology Today: Its Possibility, Necessity, and Values," *Greyfriars Review* 8/1 (1994): 103–26.
36. St. Francis, "The Testament," 1–3, FA:ED, Volume I—*The Saint*, 124. For Clare's *Testament* see "The Testament (1247–1253)," TL:CA:ED, 59–65. See Margaret Carney, "Franciscan Women and the Theological Enterprise," in *The History of Franciscan Theology*, ed. Kenan B. Osborne (St. Bonaventure, NY: The Franciscan Institute, 1994), 331–45.
37. Armstrong, "Francis of Assisi and the Prisms of Theologizing," 185.
38. Bonaventure, "The Major Legend of Saint Francis (1260–1263)," 1: 5–6, in FA:ED, Volume II—*The Founder*, 533–5.
39. Francis of Assisi, "The Undated Writings—The Admonitions," 2:1–2, in FA:ED, Volume I—*The Saint*, 129.
40. Armstrong, "Francis of Assisi and the Prisms of Theologizing," 189.
41. Francis of Assisi, "The Undated Writings—the Admonitions," 6, in FA:ED, Volume I—*The Saint*, 131.
42. Bonaventure, "The Major Legend of Saint Francis (1260–1263)," 9:1, in FA:ED, Volume II—*The Founder*, 596–7.
43. Armstrong, "Francis of Assisi and the Prisms of Theologizing," 199.
44. Francis of Assisi, "The Earlier Rule (1209/10–1221)," Chapter XXIII, in FA:ED, Volume I—*The Saint*, 81–6. Quote is at 85.

45. "The Life of Saint Francis by Thomas of Celano (1228–1229)," Book I, 28:77, in FA:ED, Volume I—*The Saint*, 248.
46. "The Life of Saint Francis by Thomas of Celano (1228–1229)," Book I, 30:84, in ibid., 254–7.
47. "The Life of Saint Francis by Thomas of Celano (1228–1229)," Book II, 3:94, in FA:ED, Volume I—*The Saint*, 263–64. *Stigmata* comes from the Greek *stigma*, meaning "mark" or "brand" and is used to describe the physical marks the resemble the wounds of the crucified Christ.
48. See text "The Canticle of the Creatures (1225)," FA:ED, Volume I—*The Saint*, 113–14, https://www.franciscantradition.org/francis-of-assisi-early-documents/writings-of-francis/the-canticle-of-the-creatures/129-fa-ed-1-page-113.
49. "The Canticle of the Creatures (1225)," in FA:ED, Volume I—*The Saint*, 113.
50. David Tracy, *The Analogical Imagination* (New York: Crossroad, 1981), 108–65.
51. Camus cited by Daniel C. Maguire, *The Moral Core of Judaism and Christianity: Reclaiming the Revolution* (Minneapolis: Augsburg Fortress Press, 1993), 65.
52. Tracy, *The Analogical Imagination*, 114.
53. Eric Doyle, *St. Francis and the Song of Brotherhood and Sisterhood*, [reprint of *The Song of Brotherhood* (New York: Seabury Press, 1981)] (St. Bonaventure, NY: The Franciscan Institute, 1997).
54. Eric Doyle, "'The Canticle of Brother Sun' and the Value of Creation," in *Franciscan Theology of the Environment*, ed. Nothwehr, 158.
55. Doyle, St. *Francis and the Song of Brotherhood and Sisterhood*, 47.
56. Ibid., 49.
57. Boff, *Cry of the Earth, Cry of the Poor*, 187–202.
58. Politics deals with how we all live together and how we organize our actions for the common good of all creation. Kenneth R. Himes, *Christianity and the Political Order: Conflict, Cooptation, Cooperation*, Theology in Global Perspective Series, Gen, ed. Peter C. Phan (Maryknoll: Orbis Books, 2013), 2–5.
59. Thomas A. Nairn, "St. Francis of Assisi's *Canticle of the Creatures* as an Exercise of the Moral Imagination," in *Franciscan Theology of the Environment*, ed. Nothwehr, 175–87.
60. Ibid., 183.
61. Ibid.
62. Ibid.
63. *AR6 Climate Change 2021: The Physical Science Basis*, https://www.ipcc.ch/report/ar6/wg1/.

64. Tim Flannery, *The Weather Makers: How We Are Changing the Climate*, 246, cited in Sallie McFague, *A New Climate for Theology: God, the World, and Global Warming* (Minneapolis: Fortress Press, 2008), 20.
65. National Aeronautics and Space Administration, Goddard Space Flight Center, https://ozonewatch.gsfc.nasa. gov/facts/SH.html.
66. LS §s 10, 11, 62, 124, 137, 159, 225, 230.
67. https://www.iucn.org/resources/conservation-tools/iucn-red-list-threatened-species#RL_index.
68. https://www.cbd.int/gbo5
69. Catrin Einhorn, "A 'Crossroads' for Humanity: Earth's Biodiversity Is Still Collapsing," *New York Times*, September 15, 2020, https://www.nytimes.com/2020/09/15/climate/biodiversity-united-nations-report.html?smid=em-share.
70. Guy Beney, in *Global Ecology*, ed. Wolfgang Sachs (London: Zed Books, 1993), 181–2, cited in Larry Rasmussen, *Earth Community, Earth Ethics* (Maryknoll: Orbis Books, 1996), 91–2.
71. Brad Plumer, "Humans Are Speeding Extinction and Altering the Natural World at an 'Unprecedented' Pace," *New York Times*, May 6, 2019, https://www.nytimes.com/2019/05/06/climate/humans-are-speeding-extinction-and-altering-the-natural-world-at-an-unprecedented-pace.html.
72. The United Nations Development Project cited in Daniel C. Maguire, *Sacred Energies* (Minneapolis: Augsburg Fortress, 2000), 27.
73. Elena Suckling, Zach Christensen, and Dan Walton, *Poverty Trends: Global, Regional and National*, https://devinit.org/resources/poverty-trends-global-regional-and-national/.
74. F. Guattari, *As Três Ecologias* (Campinas: Papirus, 1988).
75. Ibid., 128.
76. LS § 139.

4

Wisdom from St. Clare of Assisi for a "Climate Emergency"

Introduction: Why Consider St. Clare?

The life and writings of Lady Chiara di Favarone di Offreducio, St. Clare of Assisi (July 16, 1194–August 11, 1253), open a pathway to spiritual empowerment and wholesome sustainable living through engaging in prayer and contemplation. Clare's lifestyle is ecologically healthy, moral, and Christ-centered.[1] She models a way of being and living that is counterintuitive to the near frenetic activity we associate with alleviating an "emergency." Her spiritual wisdom provides a process toward the personal transformation and communal changes imperative for correcting our current ecocidal course.[2] We focus on Clare's life at San Damiano. Then we examine her contemplative prayer that holds great promise for building our moral capacity for mitigating our "Climate Emergency."

St. Francis of Assisi received Lady Chiara into religious life as a penitent.[3] Later, Clare, her mother Lady Ortulana, blood sisters Beatrice and Catherine (religious name Agnes), and several other women moved to San Damiano, a cloister that St. Francis prepared for them, just outside of Assisi.[4] There, the "Poor Ladies" became known for their radically austere lifestyle.[5] In a world increasingly bent on materiality, power, and wealth, Clare's ideal was to emulate "the Poor Christ, who had nowhere to lay his head."[6] She believed that in contrast to God, who is the eternal, and ultimate source of our security, the created world is fleeting and filled with spiritual temptation.[7] Yet Clare's belief in Christ Incarnate enabled her to exemplify ways of being and acting that are vital for true ecological living.

Clare's Community-Minded Living

In Clare's day, the Umbrian economy was shifting to the mercantile system. Around 1197, citizens of Assisi established a *commune* and elected city Councils.[8] As a child, Clare experienced war for political control and new economic access to wealth that pitted the *Majores* against the *Minores*. That warfare required the Offreducio household (*Majores*) to flee to Perugia until the Peace of Assisi was signed (1210). The trauma of that violence, her religious training, and at-home meetings with pious women, steeped Clare in Gospel values. She established a life with her sisters at San Damiano characterized by mutual regard, respectful admiration, humility, and delight.[9]

Reverence and Respect

As the founding Abbess, Clare modeled the pace and tone for the life of the Poor Ladies. A young woman of nobility, she was likely literate and a gifted writer of Letters, a Rule, and Testament.[10] Clare's self-deprecating manner and courtesy, particularly evident in her letters to Agnes of Prague, was widely acknowledged by all who knew her.[11] Clare's letters reflected the deepest affection and respect, communicated a sense of profound love, urged self-esteem, invited courage, and like-minded treatment of others.[12] Such words bring to life the Christian belief that humans are created in the *imago Dei* and thus bear an inviolable dignity.

Clare's Example of Humility

Clare's salutations reflect genuine humility to the extent that they can even seem unhealthy to our ears.[13] Clare's humility was deeply grounded in her experience of God's unfathomable and steadfast love demonstrated in the Incarnation. She accepted her creatureliness, as one made in the *imago Dei*, and that she was loved by others as well. Clare was thus free to set aside her noble socioeconomic status and respectfully affirm all others.

The virtues of poverty, charity, and humility reoccur consistently in Clare's *Form of Life* (1253), *The Testament* (1247–53), and *Letters to Agnes of Prague*. But Clare was known primarily for her humility.[14] As the Abbess, at San Damiano, Clare lived as a humble servant to others.[15] Clare washed the mattresses of her sick sisters, cared for them, and even washed their feet.[16]

Engaging the Heart

Clare's most intimately revealing works are her letters to Agnes of Prague. Therein, Clare expressed her profound appreciation for Agnes' qualities and virtues. Both daughters of nobility, the two women shared much in common on their spiritual journeys. Clare was thrilled that Agnes had become a faithful lover of God, and she desired that Agnes would know the fullness of God's friendship. In her fourth and final letter to Agnes, Clare expressed her delight in their spiritual friendship.[17] These respectful and complementary words from Clare, the Abbess, to Agnes her subject reveal Clare's characteristic desire that Agnes—and all others—receive her words with deep and unrestricted regard, fondness, and reverence. Clare does not hesitate to establish genuine bonds of adult friendship.

What does all of this have to do with a "Climate Emergency"? Clare's primary focus was on God. But significantly, in Clare's day the dominant Christian spirituality and worldview were dualistic, setting "spiritual things" over against "material things." Yet Clare described Christ using images of heavenly luminaries (material things) positively: "Him Who gave Himself totally for your love, At Whose beauty the sun and the moon marvel, Whose rewards and their preciousness are without end."[18] For Clare, worship of God definitely included reverencing God's creation in all its splendor. Sister Angeluccia testified that Clare instructed the Poor Ladies to "praise God when they saw beautiful trees, flowers and bushes; and likewise, always to praise Him for, and in all things when they saw all peoples and creatures."[19]

Similarly, when Clare blessed her sisters with water she would say, "My sisters and daughters, you must always remember and recall this blessed water that came from the right side of our Lord Jesus Christ as He hung upon the cross."[20] Through the eyes of faith, like St. Francis, Clare understood the sacredness of creation, as reflecting her incarnate Redeemer as Creator.

Perhaps most significant for our current "Climate Emergency," in her *Testament*, Clare entrusted to the Poor Ladies the values she hoped they would maintain after her death. She wrote directing how the sisters were to care for each other: "And loving one another with the love of Christ, may you demonstrate without in the love you have within so that, compelled by such an example, the sisters may always grow in love of God, and in mutual charity."[21]

A Community of Footwashers

Influenced by Lady Ortulana's gathering of strong women for prayer and doing pious deeds, St. Francis, and the Lesser Brothers, Clare was innovative when she structured life in the San Damiano community.[22] Clare's *Form of Life* (1253) outlined her "way" as a horizontal set of relationships.[23] She promoted gentle, mutual care; power-sharing; compassion for sinners; and special treatment for the ill among the Poor Ladies.[24] Clare's *Form of Life* provided for all of the sisters being involved in decision-making, and when that was not possible, Clare turned to a special group of consulters.[25] All of the Poor Ladies, including the Abbess, openly confessed their faults and sought forgiveness from one another.[26] Most telling was that, while under political pressure, Clare reluctantly accepted the title "Abbess," but she never used it.[27] Rather, *The Legend of Saint Clare* (1254–55) provides details of Clare's hands-on care for the Poor Ladies.[28] All of Clare's reverential love and respect for her sisters was inspired by her profound comprehension of human dignity, Christ Incarnate, and her own sense of being held in the heart of God, her loving Creator.

Lady Clare's Lessons for Intervention in a "Climate Emergency"

Today we are painfully aware of the alarming, irreversible destruction and loss of potable water, clean air, and arable soils; poisoning of rivers, streams, and oceans; vast extinctions destroying the earth's biodiversity, threatening, and fragmenting all life—including human life.[29] Yet there is much to learn from Clare's simple, courteous, and contemplative ways of relating to God and all of God's creation.

Courtesy and Civility

St. Clare grew up amid the institution of knighthood—its rituals of warfare, religion, and society. In Clare's family, seven knights embraced the premiere virtue of courtesy.[30] The central knightly virtues were strength, fidelity, and courage.[31] Courtesy embraced solidarity in war, fidelity to one's word in peacetime, and openness to communication with enemies for sustaining the possibility of peaceful settlements of disagreements. Knights presumed truth telling by another until it was proven otherwise. Courage required knights to be generous and liberal, exerting their considerable power on behalf of vulnerable persons. The primary virtues of noble women were beauty, courtesy, and wisdom. *The Acts of the Process of Canonization* (1254) prove Clare was exemplary in these virtues.[32]

In her *The Testament* (1247–53) Clare mentions the courtly gesture of bowing. There speaking of the *Privilege of Poverty* for which she fought all her life, and which was granted by Pope Innocent at the time of her death, Clare stated: "For this reason, *on bended knees and bowing low with both [body and soul]*, I commend all my sisters, both those present and those to come, to holy Mother the Roman Church to the supreme Pontiff, and especially, to the Lord Cardinal who has been appointed for the religion of the Lesser Brothers and for us."[33] Clare's stance is one of gratitude—expressed in the most respectful courtly gesture of the day. She gave herself away to raise up another's dignity and worth in the name of holy poverty.

In our pandemic-stricken, ecologically threatened world, daily we experience divisive and vitriolic language in political debate, and life-threatening lack of compliance with basic health and safety measures. We fail to extend a courtly bow to one another and Sister, Mother Earth; to deal with others kindly; to be prudent about how we treat the air, water, and soil; and to extend courtesy to protect and restore Earth's beauty. Basic courtesy can be a first step toward healing and upholding the intrinsic value of God's creation.

Clare may have had similar thoughts today. She certainly would agree with St. Francis. In his *The Undated Writings—A Salutations of the Virtues* he proposed that a fitting relationship among humans and between humans and animals was that of obedience: "[The person who possesses holy Obedience] is subject and submissive to all persons in the world and not to man only but even to all beasts and wild animals so that they may do whatever they want with him inasmuch as it *has been given* to them *from above* by the Lord."[34] Francis refers to "mutual deference." Like medieval knights, who exercised "a mutual regard and deference between brothers serving God together," so too Francis' view of the relationship among humans and animals was familial, "sisters" and "brothers" serving the Creator.[35]

Humans: Beloved Ones among Many

As previously noted, within the graced story of the universe we humans are the fruits of billions of years of intense activity on the part of the matter that preceded us. Humans are unique, yet we remain interdependent with everything else in the universe. Without clear air, potable water, and arable soil and intact global systems that keep the earth's bioregions in ecological balance, no human could survive to live and love. Indeed, God is the common ground behind the creation story of evolution (*how* creation emerged) and the Genesis creation accounts (*why* creation emerged). In the Covenants with humans and all of creation God models for us the way toward global environmental well-being and sustainability. The Scriptures present a holistic, interdependent relationship between God and all creation and among all the elements of creation.

Heart Sight

St. Clare's contemplative prayer and lifestyle show us personal and communal pathways to spiritual and moral formation necessary for dealing with our "Climate Emergency." Her ethics of power, modeled in the structures of mutuality contained in her *Rule*, can guide us in living in a respectful sustainable manner.

Clare was simply in love with God. And, like all people who are in love, she saw the world differently. The source and motive for Clare's optimism were her participation in the very life of God—open to all of creation. What made Clare's perception different was that she had, what Franciscan theologian Eric Doyle called, "heart sight."[36] But what does it mean to see things that way?

As already noted, in Clare's day Christian theology and spirituality were understood through the lens of Neoplatonic philosophy.[37] That perspective drove religious monastics into isolated and insulated ways of life and unhealthy escapism. But St. Clare did not renounce the world, only her social and economic status in the world. She and the Poor Ladies encountered this world in an even more radical way through focusing on the Incarnation of Jesus Christ, the One through whom the world was created (Jn 1:1-18). It is Jesus' example of the poverty of God that opened for Clare the way to graced sustainable living.

Even today, at San Damiano in Assisi, one can see the San Damiano cross.[38] It is this iconic image of the love of God, made known through the Incarnation, that was St. Clare's focus in contemplative prayer. In contemplating Christ's image, Clare saw the totality of the love of God-become-human, God incarnate, through whom the world was created, a generous pouring forth of love, creativity, and beauty. Clare came to see that the world is fully embraced by God; we need not escape this world to find God!

Clare recalled Matthew 5:3, which shows us God's offer of the Reign of God to the truly poor. Here we see the crux of Christian spirituality, namely that by a kind of self-emptying (poverty) we make room within ourselves for God, our true source of wealth and empowerment. When we do that, we also make room for other persons and fellow creatures.

Today, poverty is understood primarily as deprivation or lack of the necessities of a life of dignity and good health. But Clare's notion of poverty was deeper. For her, poverty was a good. Clare understood what current studies of economic wealth have shown, namely that there is a threshold for genuine happiness achieved through economic wealth alone.[39] Buttressing the self with external wealth alone leaves people empty of spirit, often spiraling into destructive self-medication of various sorts or even suicide.

Clare's poverty was rooted in wisdom found in the universal paradoxes of the mysteries of human life: death/life, time/eternity, goods of the earth/things of heaven. Clare's focus was learning through contemplation from the One who lived these mysteries fully, Jesus Christ. For Clare, the poverty of God is known through experiencing the fountain fullness of God's love—all relationships established by God's self-gift. Similar kinds of relationship are known with humans' self-gift in situations of natural disasters where neighbors and strangers give what they can to help—even at some considerable cost to themselves. Here we see the poverty of God, enacted as the immensity of human love.

Clare used the image of a mirror to explain the Christian life. We are to become mirrors, reflecting Jesus Christ. Humans are created in the Divine image (Gen. 1:27). To become an ever more complete image of God is to become personal as God is—loving, compassionate, and relational. In Christ, the Word of God (Jn 1:1) who is the Image of God (Col. 1: 15-23) we see how we can become whole and holy people. A mirror shows the external image of a person.

But by reflecting on the image of Jesus on the cross, we can learn the depths of his mind, soul, and heart. It is to Christ's inward image and shape that we are called to conform. Clare wrote to Agnes of Prague concerning this.[40] By gazing at the cross, we begin to see and understand what internally motivated Christ and what must motivate us—the all-embracing living glory and brilliance of God's eternal love.

To gaze is to take more than a glancing look. It is to intentionally focus and be drawn into the object or person that we see and visually make an embrace. What constitutes such an embrace is to open oneself to create a space inside oneself; to understand the other on their own terms; to allow the identity of the other to affect us, change us; or to remain a mystery to us. To gaze is to become poor, open-minded, and openhearted, ready to receive God's grace. This kind of enacting is challenging in today's materialistic technocratic world.[41]

In today's "Climate Emergency" God's suffering earth is the place of God's deep incarnation.[42] It is an entry point for the Holy Spirit's appeal to our ecological vocation.[43] Each of us is compelled to go out of ourselves to see and embrace the suffering of other people and creatures of all kinds. And then, like Clare, through the process of letting go of status and power, we can recognize our *inter*dependence. With the God-like generosity of Clare, we need to *choose* to use our personal, economic, and political power to truly love and nurture humans and otherkind.

Clare understood creation to be permeated with the presence of God. Why else would she have asked the "extern sisters" to notice the beauty and wonder of creation when doing their work outside the enclosure of San Damiano? To ignore, or even abuse such evidence of God, would be the equivalent of negating God's revelatory self-expression—and thus sinful.

To Have a Voice

In Clare's community, each sister had a voice determining the life of the sisters—including the youngest sister.[44] According to Clare's *Rule*, 4:15, the Abbess met with the sisters "at least once a week." And, throughout her *Form* of *Life* (1253), Clare used the possessive form—"*our* profession," "*our* poverty," "*our* life."[45] In these ways "Clare insured a sense of mutuality" within the community.[46]

Considering the virtue of mutuality, today we must ask—who hears the voices of the glaciers, the rainforests, or the polluted air, streams, or soils? Indeed, "the Earth is the Lord's" (Ps. 24). We humans are to be the guardians giving voice to the needs of creation. According to the Noachic Covenant,[47] all plants and animals have value and moral standing before God. With Pope Francis and the Ecumenical Patriarch Bartholomew, we assert that human destruction of Creation is not only foolish, but also blasphemous against God and therefore sinful.[48] We are not destined to be masters and mistresses of the universe to rule over creation in utilitarian ways. Today environmental impact studies, scientific models, and our own observations of the natural world allow us to "hear" the voices of the created world.[49]

Ignoring Clare's kind of reverence for God and all others is a violent stance infecting our very character and identity, distorting, and warping it.[50]

Our attitude toward the nonhuman world directly shapes our development and excellence as persons.[51] We, like Clare, can genuinely care for creation, experience empathy with it, rather than attempt to control it. Inspired by a vision of cosmic harmony, we can put ourselves at the service of the cosmos in a spirit of sacrificial love. "To live in hope as we face possible ecological disaster is a difficult and revolutionary activity. But the mandate of the gospel demands that we use the graces of the tradition—St. Clare of Assisi is one example—and the graces of our own commitment and creative imagination in the service of the universe."[52]

From the Writings of St. Clare
The Acts of the Process of Canonization[53]

THE FOURTEENTH WITNESS

9. [37]She also said when the most holy mother used to send the serving sisters outside the monastery, she reminded them to praise God when they saw beautiful trees, flowers, and bushes; [38]and, likewise, always to praise Him for and in all things when they saw all peoples and creatures.

Reflection and Application

For centuries, the industrialized Western nations have exercised power over the "resources" of the earth with virtually no regard for limits. David Toolan defined the "imperial ecology" of Bacon and Descartes; the shift to economic materialism; and belief in the clockmaker god of Deism as models of the exercise of "power-over."[54] Underpinning "power-over" was the assertion of human superiority in all areas of life. In *Laudato Si'*, Chapter 3, Pope Francis provides a similar critique using the prophetically insightful work of Romano Guardini, *The End of the Modern World*.[55]

Imperial Ecology

Francis Bacon (1561–1626) and Rene Descartes (1596–1650) initiated what environmental historian David Worster called "Imperial Ecology."[56] In Bacon's view, humans are lords and masters over nature. The agricultural revolution instituted thoroughgoing exploitation of the earth, with the various earth elements constituting parts of a machine that could be remade, according to the reason and the imagination of "Man the Maker" (*homo faber*). Science, he claimed, could restore the world to the biblical "New Jerusalem."[57] Technology was the means to that end. Bacon claimed the new science would produce a "blessed race of heroes and supermen."[58]

René Descartes held that nature is a machine, comprehensible by analyzing its various parts.[59] He sought to understand nature by formulating its relationships into mathematical equations. His aim was to formulate laws to serve human interests.[60]

Isaac Newton (1642–1727) was Francis Bacon's dream of the "superman" come true! Newton was a genius at taking what had previously only been known as facts and novelties and formulating them into general laws and principles that could be broadly applied. "If Descartes embodied the new detached ego of the modern West, Newton gave us its objective correlate: an objective world of deterministic law."[61]

Eventually, Newton's student Pierre Simon LePlace (1749–1827) argued that the universe is completely determined—"so we no longer require the hypothesis of God."[62] Today we are reaping the results of the arrogance and idolatry of scientific materialism. The current water, energy, food, and "Climate Emergency" evidences the scale and size of the abuse human "power-over" has wrought, forcing Earth's ecosystems to their breaking point.

Power and Kinds of Power

So how do we move from abusive power to mutuality, as Clare understood it? Put simply, we need to shift our self-understanding and the focus of our choices from our presumed superiority to what we hold in common with others in God's creation.[63]

Respectful of the particularity of each creature, we must honor the reality that in the moral sense, each element of creation has God-given worth and power. Humans have power to manipulate the natural order on a scale distinct from other creatures. Humans can choose how we use that power—for good or for ill.

Beverly Wildung Harrison stated concerning power: "it is the goal of a genuinely transformative social ethic, to identify social policies that will enhance shared, reciprocal, accountable social power, so as to press beyond zero-sum power toward more inclusive shared power and participation."[64] She defined power as "the ability to act on and effectively shape the world around us, particularly through collective and institutional policy. To have power means to have access to physical resources and wealth, to knowledge, and to loci of social decision-making and to be able to impact institutional and social policy."[65]

Our "Climate Emergency" requires the use of "power-with," exemplified by St. Clare. That is, one's "ability to move, effect, make a difference" as "shared, reciprocal and constrained by, the limits that respectful interrelationship imposes."[66] Power engaging all parties in a relationship—plants, animal, air, water, soil, as well as people—is to be prized and pursued in contrast to "Power-over," that is, the possession of control, authority, or influence over others from a hierarchical stance.[67]

But why is the use of power important? The key to genuine love is not discounting and objectifying someone or something as merely worthless toward whom indifference can justifiably be directed. Rather, following St. Clare, when making daily decisions affecting God's creation, we must engage that "other" as a partner—whether human or otherkind. Such engagement must take place on the level of the personal and the concrete. Christians need to consider all the virtues, especially norms of love, justice, and mutuality—the dynamics of power operative in all relationships.

Clare's virtue and norm of mutuality is the moral standard that can help us make better moral decisions, regarding all relations. Considerations of mutuality seek out the threads of common human needs and desires, placing everything and everyone, in the context of a history, a developmental continuum, with a beginning, middle, and end. When utilizing the norm, mutuality, one constantly involves the potential "Other"—whether through a personal conversation or an environmental impact study—leaning toward forming a consensus that maximizes the flourishing of everyone and everything involved in the situation.[68] Christian feminist ethicists have carefully defined "mutuality" as a formal norm for Christian social and environmental ethics and uncovered its probative value.[69] "Mutuality" as a standard of measure helps us to examine the dynamics of power in all kinds of relationships: gender, generative, social, and cosmic. Here we focus on "cosmic mutuality."

Mutuality Defined

All relationships are known to have boundaries, the set of limits and capacities that define the being or system we are engaging, as well as the patterns or dynamics of the exchange of power. For example, Clare knew and respected the needs of the individual sisters, and she cared for them accordingly. In the case of mutuality, boundaries are distinct, but the critical difference is that their definition and engagement are determined *with* the other(s), and thus they are often more flexible and fluid. Clare's *Form of Life* required the participation of all the sisters in making decisions about all dimensions of life in the monastery. The means and the end of exchange must be geared to the common flourishing of all parties involved. How we cross boundaries in our relationships, and what we *do* once we have breached a boundary, is certainly significant. In Clare's case, she treated all her sisters courteously, and open confession and reconciliation were frequently practiced in the life of the Poor Ladies.

Mutuality is a concept found in classical Christian theology, and it defines the maximum flourishing of humanity in relation to four areas—the cosmos, gender relationships, divine-human co-generativity, and human sociality. The basic definition of mutuality is "the sharing of 'power-with' by and among all parties in a relationship in a way that recognizes the wholeness and particular experience of each participant toward the end of optimum flourishing of all."[70]

The form of mutuality that is most relevant to our discussion of environmental issues is "cosmic mutuality." As we saw in Clare's *Form of Life* (1253), the relationships she spoke about in her *Testament*, and the *Letters to Agnes of Prague*, all model the social dimension of mutuality. We also can find glimpses of the other forms of mutuality in Clare's work as well (though admittedly she never used the term).[71]

Cosmic Mutuality

Evidence for cosmic mutuality is advanced in astrophysics, ecology, and quantum physics and demonstrates a foundational kinship of everything in the entire cosmos. When mutuality is violated, strong ecological evidence shows that the natural environment asserts itself as living systems that "answer back" to the human defilement.[72] Humans violate the ecosystem to their own detriment. The most effective social analysis considers how any form of power impacts the most disadvantaged, while looking toward the well-being of all. Beyond that, as noted in previous chapters, theologians have recovered a renewed understanding of the deep relationship between creation and God—"integral ecology."[73]

The phrase "God in the world and the world in God" expresses the ancient Christian belief that the entire creation is revelatory of God.[74] The reality, which Christians proclaim in their creeds—that God is Creator, Vivifier,

Redeemer, and more—is possible only in relation to creation and shows, in a certain analogous sense, God's need for relationship with the cosmos.[75] The kinship of all creation shapes the command "love thy neighbor" to include all created elements in a manner that reverences the God-given capacities of each.[76] Given all of this data, a form of mutuality can be defined as "Cosmic Mutuality—the sharing of 'power-with' by and among the Creator, human beings, all earth elements, and the entire cosmos in a way that recognizes their interdependence and reverences all."[77]

St. Clare of Assisi and Cosmic Mutuality

Clare of Assisi never studied theology or ethics, and she lived within the dualistic neo-platonic worldview of the twelfth to thirteenth centuries, but she keenly understood the meaning of the Incarnation. Through her profound knowledge of the Poor Christ, who humbled himself to become part of this material world, Clare understood the deepest meaning of what we know as mutuality. A humble servant of God, she connected the praise of God, the beauty of creation, and reverence for the human person as related to the same source of power.

We have forgotten that this is God's planet and that we are the humble guardians charged with its care. We have arrogantly appropriated "power-over" one another, our fellow creatures, or the planet itself, and thus we find ourselves in a "Climate Emergency." So let us heed the example of the Poor Lady, St. Clare of Assisi and take her words to heart when she exhorts: "praise God when you see beautiful trees, flowers and bushes; and likewise, always praise Him for and in all things when you see people and creatures."[78] Then, with St. Clare, we can follow in the footprints of Jesus, taking new steps to alleviate our "Climate Emergency."

Questions for Reflection and Discussion

1. What are your experiences of being held in esteem?
2. What does it feel like to be on the receiving end of someone's courteous regard and care?
3. Who do you know as someone especially careful and respectful of the Earth's creatures—beyond humankind?

4 When are you most reverent toward others—plants, animals, soil, water, air?
5 In what ways do your "needs" lead to pollution, abuse, or destruction of air, water, soil, or even human life?

Suggestions for Action

1 Take a walk around your immediate neighborhood. Listen to the voices of your fellow Earth creatures. Then respond to their cries and groaning with a courteous, loving, healing action.
2 Explore the internet or libraries for sources that explain how ocean and air currents across the globe create weather patterns or the geological history of the place where you live. Pay attention to how all the various parts are interdependent and interrelated.
3 Clare was known as a healer. Search the internet for a pediatrician's view on the effects of pollution and climate change on human health—especially pregnant women and unborn children.
4 Clare was known for her humility—doing the "dirty jobs" necessary to care for her sick sisters. The word "humility" is derived from the Latin word for "earth" = *humus*. Humans are "earth creatures"; we have our origins in dirt (Gen. 2:7). Those who do the "dirty jobs" in our society are often looked down upon. Treat your trash collector, food processing and service workers, grocery cashier, or custodian with personal courtesy and advocate for just working conditions for them, so they can have a life of dignity.
5 Go to the website of the Catholic Climate Covenant at https://catholicclimatecovenant.org/ and find ways you can take action to alleviate our "Climate Emergency."

Sources for Further Study

Secondary Sources

Carney, Margaret. *The First Franciscan Woman: Clare of Assisi & Her Form of Life*. Quincy, IL: Franciscan Press, 1993.

Dreyer, Elizabeth A. "[God] 'Whose Beauty the Sun and the Moon Admire:' Clare and Ecology." In *Franciscan Theology of the Environment: An*

Introductory Reader, edited by Dawn M. Nothwehr, 129–41. Quincy, IL: Franciscan Press, 2002.

Meany, Mary Walsh and Felicity Dorsett, eds. "Her Bright Merits." In *Spirit and Life, Essays on Contemporary Franciscanism*, Essays Honoring Ingrid Peterson, OSF, Vol. 17. St. Bonaventure, NY: Franciscan Institute Publications, 2012.

Mooney, Catherine M. *Clare of Assisi and the Thirteenth-Century Church: Religious Women, Rules, and Resistance*. Philadelphia: University of Pennsylvania Press, 2016.

Peterson, Ingrid J. *Clare of Assisi: A Biographical Study*. Quincy, IL: Franciscan Press, 1993.

Primary Source in English Translation

Armstrong, Regis J., ed. and trans. *The Lady—Clare of Assisi: Early Documents*. Revised ed. New York: New City Press, 2006.

Abbreviations of Clarian Texts

Abbreviation	Source
1LAg	The First Letter to Blessed Agnes of Prague (1234)
2LAg	The Second Letter to Blessed Agnes of Prague (1235)
3LAg	The Third Letter to Blessed Agnes of Prague (1238)
4LAg	The Fourth Letter to Blessed Agnes of Prague 1253)
FLCl	The Form of Life of Clare of Assisi (1253)
TestCl	The Testament (1247–1253)
BlCl	The Blessing (1253)
PC	The Acts of the Process of Canonization (1253)
LCl	The Legend of St. Clare (1255)

Notes

1. Regis J. Armstrong, ed. and trans., "Introduction," in *The Lady—Clare of Assisi: Early Documents*, revised ed. (New York: New City Press, 2006), 13–28. Catherine M. Mooney, *Clare of Assisi and the Thirteenth-Century Church: Religious Women, Rules, and Resistance* (Philadelphia: University of Pennsylvania Press, 2016), 16–19.

2. Cambridge Dictionary, https://dictionary.cambridge.org/dictionary/english/ecocide: "Ecocide Is Destruction of the Natural Environment of an Area, or Very Great Damage to It." "Stop Ecocide International—Legal Definitions" at https://www.stopecocide.earth/videos-definition.
3. Ingrid J. Peterson, *Clare of Assisi: A Biographical Study* (Quincy, IL: Franciscan Press, 1993), 109. See LCl, III and IV in *TL:CA: ED*, 283–8. Also PC, "The Twelfth Witness," 2 in *TL:CA: ED*, 183–5.
4. LCl, V in *TL:CA: ED*, 287–8.
5. Peterson, *Clare of Assisi*, 168.
6. 1LAg, 17–18 in *TL:CA: ED*, 45. 4LAg, 15–23 in *TL:CA: ED*, 55–6. FLCl, VI-VII, 5–15, in *TL:CA: ED*, 117–2. Also see Matthew 8:20.
7. 1LAg, 22–3, in *TL:CA: ED*, 45–6. 2LAg, 15–23 in *TL:CA: ED*, 48–9. 4LAg, 7 in *TL:CA: ED*, 54.
8. Peterson, *Clare of Assisi*, 55–65.
9. Peterson, *Clare of Assisi*, 17–106. See Jn 13:4-5 and Jn 15:15.
10. Mooney, *Clare of Assisi*, 89–94. Leslie Knox, "Clare of Assisi and Learning," *The Cord* 46/4 (1996): 171–9.
11. Timothy Johnson, "'To Her Who Is Half of Her Soul': Clare of Assisi and the Medieval Epistolary Tradition," *Magistra; Atichison* 2/1 (Summer 1996): 24, https://go.openathens.net/redirector/bc.edu?url=https://www.proquest.com/scholarly-journals/her-who-is-half-soul-clare-assisi-medieval/docview/216909091/se-2?accountid=9673.
12. 1LAg, 1 in *TL:CA: ED*, 43. 3LAg, 1 in *TL:CA: ED*, 50. Examples: "To the esteemed and most holy virgin, Lady Agnes …" or "To the Lady most respected in Christ, and the sister to be loved before all mortals, Agnes …."
13. 3LAg, 2 in *TL:CA: ED*, 50. Also, 4LAg, 2 in *TL:CA: ED*, 54.
14. PC, Prologue, in *TL:CA: ED*, 141–4; The First Witness, 144–9; The Fourth Witness, 162–6; The Fifth Witness, 166–7; The Sixth Witness, 167–71; The Seventh Witness, 171–3; The Eighth Witness, 173–4; and The Tenth Witness, 177–80. Also, LCl, VII, 5 in *TL:CA: ED*, 290; LCl, VIII, 291–2; and LCl, XI 295–6.
15. Peterson, *Clare of Assisi*, 144. See LCl, VIII, 12, in *TL:CA: ED*, 291–2.
16. PC, The First Witness, 12 in *TL:CA: ED*, 144–9; The Second Witness, 3, 150; The Third Witness, 9, 157; The Seventh Witness, 5, 172; The Tenth Witness, 6, 178. Also see Peterson, *Clare of Assisi*, 144.
17. 4LAg, 33, in *TL:CA: ED*, 57.
18. 3LAg, 16, in *TL:CA: ED*, 16.
19. PC, The Fourteenth Witness, 9, in *TL:CA: ED*, 189.
20. PC, The Fourteenth Witness, 8, in *TL:CA: ED*, 188.
21. TestCL, 56–60; quote at 59–60, in *TL:CA: ED*, 64.
22. LCl, I:1, in *TL:CA: ED*, 280. Also Armstrong, ed. and trans., "Introduction," in *TL:CA:ED*, 14–16. See also Peterson, *Clare of Assisi*,

29–38; 67–78. Mooney, *Clare of Assisi*, 196. Margaret Carney, *The First Franciscan Woman: Clare of Assisi & Her Form of Life* (Quincy, IL: Franciscan Press, 1993), 150–9.
23. FLCl, IV, 9–12 in *TL:CA: ED*, 114–5. Also, TestCl, 61–73, in *TL:CA: ED*, 4–65. Carney, *The First Franciscan Woman*, 146–9. Mooney, *Clare of Assisi*, 173–4.
24. FLCl, X, 4–5, in *TL:CA: ED*, 123. Also LCl, VIII, 6–11, in *TL:CA: ED*, 292. Peterson, *Clare of Assisi*, 144.
25. Carney, *The First Franciscan Woman*, 171. FLCl, IV, 15–17, in *TL:CA: ED*, 115.
26. FLCl, IX, 6–10, in *TL:CA: ED*, 121–2. FLCl, IV, 16, in *TL:CA: ED*, 115.
27. PC, The First Witness, in *TL:CA: ED*, 144–9; The Sixth Witness, 167–71; The Tenth Witness, 14, 177–80. Also LCl, VIII, 4–5 in *TL:CA: ED*, 291–2. See Carney, *The First Franciscan Woman*, 67–68. Peterson, *Clare of Assisi*, 146–7.
28. LCl, XXV, 1–4, in *TL:CA: ED*, 312.
29. LS § 19.
30. *Gale Virtual Reference Library Dictionary*, s. v. "courteous": **1**. marked by polished manners, gallantry, or ceremonial usage of a court **2**: marked by respect for and consideration of others; consideration, cooperation, and generosity in providing something (as a gift or privilege).
31. Marco Bartoli, *Saint Clare: Beyond the Legend*, trans. Frances Teresa Downing (Cincinnati, OH: St. Anthony Messenger Press, 2010), 29–43.
32. PC, VIII, 4: the witness spoke of Clare's integrity and mature judgment; PC, II, 2 and XVI, 2 the witness spoke of Clare's gentleness, kindness, and courtesy that revealed the nobility of her soul; and PC VIII, 2. It was publicly known that she refused the proposal of marriage by men who admired her great beauty. Also 1LAg, 9.
33. TestCl, 44, in *TL:CA: ED*, 62–3. Emphasis added.
34. Francis of Assisi, "The Undated Writings—A Salutation of the Virtues," 14 in in FA:ED, Volume I—*The Saint*, 165.
35. Roger D. Sorrell, *St. Francis of Assisi and Nature* (New York: Oxford University Press, 1989), 74.
36. Eric Doyle, "'The Canticle of Brother Sun' and the Value of Creation," in *Franciscan Theology of the Environment: An Introductory Reader*, ed. Dawn M. Nothwehr (Quincy, IL: Franciscan Press, 2002), 163.
37. The National Gallery, London, s.v. Neo-Platonism, "Neo-Platonism was a philosophical movement inaugurated by Plotinus (AD 204/5–270), which reinterpreted the ideas of the ancient Greek philosopher Plato. It argued that the world which we experience is only a copy of an ideal reality which lies beyond the material world. This ideal reality is comprised of three levels; the final level cannot be grasped by philosophy, and can only be reached through mystical experience."

38. Anne's Italy: The original San Damiano cross is in the Basilica di Santa Chiara. The replica is at San Damiano, https://www.annesitaly.com/blog/san-damiano-in-assisi/.
39. Steve Branton, "The Well-Being Theory: How Much Happiness Can Money Truly Buy?" March 11, 2021, https://privateocean.com/the-well-being-theory-how-much-happiness-can-money-truly-buy/.
40. *The Third Letter to Agnes of Prague*, 12–15, CA:ED, 51, https://www.Franciscantradition.org/clare-of-assisi-early-documents/the-third-letter-to-agnes-of-prague/227-ca-ed-1-page-51. Regis J. Armstrong, "Clare of Assisi: Mirror Mystic," *The Cord* (1985): 195–202.
41. LS §106–14.
42. Duncan Reid, "Enfleshing the Human: An Earth-Revealing, Earth-Healing Christology," in *Earth Revealing Earth Healing: Ecology and Christian Theology*, ed. Denis Edwards (Collegeville: Liturgical Press, 2001), 69–83. Niels Heinrich Gregersen, "The Cross of Christ in an Evolutionary World," *Dialog: A Journal of Theology* 40 (2001): 192–207.
43. Elizabeth A. Johnson, *Ask of the Beasts: Darwin and the God of Love* (London: Bloomsbury, 2014), 281–4.
44. FLCl, 4:15-24 in *TL:CA: ED*, 115–16.
45. Carney, *The First Franciscan Woman*, 168. Emphasis is mine. Mooney, *Clare of Assisi*, Chapter 8, "The 1253 Forma Vitae, ca. 1250–1253," 190–3.
46. Carney, *The First Franciscan Woman*, 168.
47. Everlasting covenant = (Hebrew) *b'rith 'olam*.
48. LS §s 2, 8, 66, 239.
49. See Romans 8:18-27.
50. In this understanding of Christian virtue ethics, people become good (virtuous) by doing what is good or evil (vicious) by doing what is not good or evil. Richard M. Gula, "The Shifting Landscape of Moral Theology," *Church* 25/1 (Spring 2009): 44–53.
51. Elisabeth A. Dreyer, "'[God] Whose Beauty the Sun and Moon Admire': Clare and Ecology," in *Franciscan Theology of the Environment*, ed. Nothwehr 139.
52. Ibid.
53. *Clare of Assisi: Early Documents (1216–1254)*, The Acts of the Process of Canonization (1253), The Fourteenth Witness, https://franciscantradition.org/clare-of-assisi-early-documents/the-acts-of-the-process-of-canonization/366-ca-ed-1-page-189.
54. David Toolan, *At Home in the Cosmos* (Maryknoll: Orbis Books, 2001), especially 41–74.
55. Ramono Guardini, *The End of the Modern World* (Wilmington: Intercollegiate Studies Institute, 1998).
56. Toolan, *At Home in the Cosmos*, 48.

57. Ibid., 49.
58. Ibid.
59. Ibid., 49–50.
60. Ibid., 50.
61. Ibid., 52.
62. Ibid., 53.
63. *LS* § 83, 89–93.
64. Beverly Wildung Harrison, "The Politics of Energy Policy," in *Making the Connections: Essays in Feminist Social Ethics*, ed. Carol S. Robb (Boston: Beacon Press, 1985), 174. Dawn M. Nothwehr, *Mutuality a Formal Norm for Christian Social Ethics* [(San Francisco: Catholic Scholars Press, 1998) Reprinted Eugene, OR: Wipf & Stock Publishers, 2005], 7.
65. Beverly Wildung Harrison, "Keeping the Faith in a Sexist Church," in *Making the Connections: Essays in Feminist Social Ethics*, ed. Carol S. Robb (Boston: Beacon Press, 1985), 290. Nothwehr, *Mutuality a Formal Norm*, n. 177 at 67.
66. Harrison, "The Politics of Energy Policy," 175.
67. Carter Heyward, *Touching Our Strength: The Erotic and the Love of God* (San Francisco: Harper & Row, 1989), 191.
68. Martin Buber, *Between Man and Man*, trans. Ronal Gregor Smith (London: Kegan Paul, 1947), 41–2.
69. For an extensive treatment of mutuality in all its forms, see Nothwehr, *Mutuality: A Formal Norm*.
70. Nothwehr, *Mutuality: A Formal Norm*, 233.
71. PC, The Fourteenth Witness, in *TL:CA:ED*, 9.
72. Rosemary Radford Ruether, *Gaia and God: An Ecofeminist Theology of Earth and Healing* (San Francisco: Harper, 1992), 2–3.
73. *LS* §s 10, 11, 62, 124, 137, 159, 225, 230.
74. Bonaventure of Bagnoregio, *Hexaemeron*, XII, 14 in José de Vinck, trans. and ed. *The Works of Bonaventure: Cardinal Seraphic Doctor and Saint*, Vol. V, Collations on the Six Days/*Collationes in Hexaemeron*, 178. Thomas Aquinas, *Summa Theologiae*, Part One, Question 47, Saint Thomas Aquinas, *Summa Theologiae*, trans. Fathers of the English Dominican Province, https://www.logoslibrary.org/aquinas/summa/1047.html.
75. Elizabeth A. Johnson, *She Who Is: The Mystery of God in Feminist Discourse* (New York: Crossroad, 1992), 232.
76. Elizabeth A. Johnson, *Woman, Earth, Creator Spirit*, 1993 Madelava Lecture (New York: Paulist Press, 1993), 59–60, 66–7.
77. Nothwehr, *Mutuality: A Formal Norm*, 233.
78. PC, The Fourteenth Witness, in *TL:CA:ED*, 9.

Part III

From Vernacular Theology to Scholastic Theology

5

St. Bonaventure of Bagnoregio—Creator, Christ, Creatures, Cosmos

Introduction: The Seraphic Doctor

Born in 1217 in Bagnoregio, in the Papal States, St. Bonaventure was baptized Giovanni di Fidanza. As a youth, between ages seven and fourteen, his mother, Maria di Retellio, dedicated him to St. Francis.[1] Giovani attended classes at the Faculty of Arts at the University of Paris in 1236–42. In 1243, as a Franciscan novice, Bonaventure began theological studies in Paris.[2] In 1248 he professed Perpetual Vows and began studies under Franciscan scholar, Alexander of Hales, his "father and master."[3] As a doctor of theology, in 1254–57 he was officially recognized by the university as Regent Master of the Franciscan School.[4]

While acting as Regent Master, Bonaventure's academic career was truncated when on February 2, 1257, he was elected Minister General of the Franciscan Order. As Minister General, he integrated Franciscan spirituality with speculative theology, creating a unique synthesis.[5] Today Bonaventure's integrated theology and powerful spirituality gives his work great promise for our time.[6]

Grounding his highly relational worldview in the teachings of St. Francis, Bonaventure developed a Trinitarian creation theology. He understood St. Francis' teaching concerning the life-sustaining virtue of mutual obedience among all the creatures: "[the obedient one] is subject and submissive to everyone in the world, and not only to people, but to every beast and wild animal as well so that they may do whatever they want with [that person], insofar as it *has* been given to them *from above* by the Lord."[7] Further, Francis denounced abusive relationships that humans create with other creatures.[8] Humans abuse other creatures when meeting daily survival needs, remaining ungrateful to these "sisters and brothers" and failing to recognize the Creator of such gifts and blessings.

Bonaventure's philosophical and theological synthesis and teachings enhanced and systematized the mystical experience and spiritual reflection of the Poverello. St. Francis' influence is visible primarily in Bonaventure's Christ-centered theology, which illuminates the Poverello's profound reverence for Christ. Bonaventure interpreted St. Francis' religious experience and adopted his custom of naming God "Supreme Good."[9] But Bonaventure also drew upon the theologian Pseudo-Dionysius who asserted that "goodness is self-diffusive."[10] Thus, Bonaventure called God "*fontalis plenitude*" (Font of All Goodness). Bonaventure developed these linkages between Christ, creation, creatures, and humans solidifying an inseparable connection between the Franciscan theology, spirituality, and ethics.[11]

The poetic and aesthetic nature mystic, Francis is far from absent from Bonaventure's work. But Bonaventure gave St. Francis' spirituality a philosophical and theological framework. Bonaventure's thirteenth-century insights serve to deepen our understanding of the relationship of God, the cosmos, and human identity. In this chapter, we will explore how Bonaventure's understanding of Christ in relation to the Trinity finds a place in his Franciscan creation theology and how that informs our experience of our "Climate Emergency." In Bonaventure's work we find grounds, not only for the sacredness of creation in general, but particularly for the value of each cosmic element.

In our complex, conflicted world, it is especially important to note Bonaventure's work, "*Reduction of the Arts to Theology*." There he shows how all forms of true knowledge have their source in God, the Creator, and he promoted interdisciplinary engaged learning for attaining truth.[12] Today we must follow his example. Today the story of creation is best told in an interdisciplinary way, yielding a fuller truth.

Something about St. Bonaventure's Thought

To understand Bonaventure, one must be aware of the many dimensions of his thought and the way he employed the languages of the imagination and of metaphysics.[13] Bonaventure saw the imagination and metaphysics as interconnected, and he understood that they impact one another. The preeminent Bonaventure scholar of the English-speaking world, Zachary Hayes showed that the Doctrine of the Trinity forms the core of Bonaventure's theology.[14] Using the philosophy of Neo-Platonism, Bonaventure understood the Trinity as divine *exemplarity*. The immense fecundity of the Goodness of God is expressed in the outward movement (*emanation*) of the Three Persons, flowing into the created cosmos.

At the level of the imagination, the world outside ourselves impacts our consciousness through our five senses and we make judgments about what we experience. Bonaventure held that because God created all things, we can know something about God by experiencing the created world.[15] However, our intellect is also involved in knowing. As we reflect on the information given us by our senses, we raise the *metaphysical* questions about interpretation and meaning. We move to the *ontological* level of exploring the nature of the One (God) reflected in the encounters brought by the senses.[16] Here we see Bonaventure's use of Plato's philosophy to show that the nature of the Creator influences the nature of the created order, and thus, all created reality is grounded (originates) in God.

Bonaventure explains the existence of the created world as the result of the tremendous creative productivity of God's goodness. He addresses divine exemplarity by building on Pseudo-Dionysius' neo-Platonic principle that goodness is necessarily self-diffusive and Richard of St. Victor's understanding of ecstatic love.[17] The Triune God expresses a dynamic creative love within the Godhead that is the *emanation* (giving out) of the Three Persons. The divine life of the Godhead flows outward and is reflected in the created cosmos. The created world is, therefore, *theophanic*—it images and reveals God in varying degrees. As we will see, the theophanic nature of creation is at the heart of a Franciscan ecotheology.

All created things resemble God in some way.[18] Franciscan philosopher Phil Hoebing explained: "All living things are *vestiges* (footprints) of God whereas man who represents God closely and distinctly is an image of God. The man conformed to God by grace is a similitude [necessary likeness] because such a person represents God most closely."[19] Divine exemplarity is most perfectly found in the figure of Christ, who is also the Incarnation of the Divine Word—the Art of the Father.[20]

> So, when the divine exemplarity is focused so sharply in the self-expressive Word; when that Word enters into the most profound relationship to creation in the humanity of Jesus, this conjunction of the divine archetype and what Bonaventure calls the macrocosm (because something of all creation is in

human nature) when that comes together, this is the synthesis of all that makes up the created cosmos. It is at that conjunction when the divine aim for all creation is brought to fruition.[21]

This is the reason *why* God created—so that through love, the creation can be brought into a kind of transforming fullness in union with the divine.[22] Put simply, God desired to express divine love. And that happens first, and to the fullest extent, in Jesus. Given this vision, we could say that the world of creation has its own truth and beauty.[23] However, there is much more to this story. "Beyond this, each creature and the whole of creation is in its truest reality, an expressive sign of the glory, truth, and beauty of God. Only when it is seen in these terms is it seen in its most profound significance."[24] Here is the basis upon which we can hold that each element of creation has intrinsic value, in itself.

Bonaventure's metaphysics grounds a whole series of metaphors about how the cosmos reveals things about God and which express his understanding of creation. The Seraphic Doctor employed metaphorical language to show the relationship between God and the cosmos. Zachary Hayes selected seven of Bonaventure's many metaphors "circle, water, song, book, window, micro/macrocosm, and the cross" to further illustrate the Seraphic Doctor's vision of the created world and how it reveals God.[25] God is like an intelligible circle, whose center is everywhere and whose circumference is nowhere.[26] God, as Trinity, is like a gushing fountain, that is the source from which the river of all reality flows and to which it ultimately returns. Again, God is like the water of an overflowing fountain, generously showering all of creation with love. Or, like the expansive deep oceans that are like the vast depth of God's faithful love.[27] Like a song—where all the notes, in a carefully crafted order, must be heard for the song to be known—so too, in its wide diversity, the various dynamic cosmic elements make up the interrelated cosmos.[28] God's self-revelation is like a book—first "written" within in the consciousness of God in the form of the Divine Word (cf. Plato's divine ideas)—which becomes the book "written without" as the whole creation; all created things are the expression of the Divine Artist.[29] Or the Book of Creation is God's primeval revelation to which people became blinded through the Fall; the Scriptures are given to sinful humanity to guide and enlighten them and entice them away from sin, and the Book of Life is the revelation of the fullness of God in Christ.[30]

Then there is Bonaventure's window metaphor. Each element of creation reveals something of the Creator like the array of colored glass in a stained-glass pane, which flashes with dynamic hues as sunlight passes through them, setting up an orgy of color.[31] Finally, there is the metaphor of the macro/microcosm. The medievals believed that the macrocosm was made up of the four elements: earth, air, water, fire, and beyond that—the spiritual order. Each human is a microcosm made up of the four elements, and each has a spiritual dimension as well. Bonaventure believed that through the resurrection of the Incarnate Christ, the transfiguration of the entire cosmos began.[32]

Bonaventure's vision of the world of creation given at the level of metaphor and symbol is summarized by Hayes in this way:

> [F]or Bonaventure, the relationship between creation and God can be expressed in two words: manifestation and participation. All things in the cosmos exist so as to manifest something of the mystery of God. And all things exist by virtue of some degree of participation in the mystery of being that flows from the absolute mystery of the creative love of God. An appropriate reading of the book of the cosmos, therefore, gives us some sense of the divine goodness and fecundity; of the divine wisdom and beauty; of the divine intelligence and freedom; and of the relational character of the divine mystery of the Trinity in which all of creation is grounded. It gives us some sense of the pain and tragedy of existence in a fallen condition.[33]

But the good news for us is that Bonaventure's integrated understanding of God's creation also holds important clues toward our ecological conversion and sustainable living in our "Climate Emergency." We turn now to Bonaventure's Christ-centered theology to find those clues.

Christ at the Center—"The Firstborn of All Creation"

Situating Bonaventure's Christology in the Franciscan Theological Tradition

Franciscan theology is characterized by a particular set of core values and beliefs, namely conversion, peacemaking, the emphasis on divine love and freedom, the primacy of Christ, the centrality of the Incarnation, Christ crucified, the sacramentality of creation, the goodness of the world, the human person as the image of God, emphasis on poverty and humility, and the development of *affectus* (goodwill, emotion, disposition of mind).[34] The "common thread" sustaining the Franciscan theological tradition across time is the person and witness of Francis of Assisi, "the Patron of Ecology."[35] St. Francis' theological authority originated in the gift of his graced experience of God and so he became known as a "vernacular theologian."[36] Three major themes in Francis' vernacular theology irrevocably link Franciscan spirituality and Franciscan theology: the humanity of Christ, the mystery of God as generous love, and the sense of creation as family.[37] Bonaventure develops these linkages between Christ, creation, creatures, and humans solidifying an inseparable connection between the Franciscan theology, spirituality, and ethics.[38]

St. Bonaventure's Christology and Creation

Some Major Sources

Bonaventure of Bagnoregio stands as the founder of the formal Franciscan theological tradition, and the most clear interpretive Christological voice of St. Francis of Assisi.[39] Along with the aforementioned sources, Pseudo-Dionysius and Richard of St. Victor, St. Augustine is included.[40] These ground and support an evangelical theological synthesis, faithful to the intuitions of Francis, and a rigorous intellectual structure and method.[41] The integration of a rigorous systematic theology and a powerful spirituality gives Bonaventure's work great promise for our time.[42] The three themes of St. Francis' Christocentric spiritual vision run deep in the speculative theology of Bonaventure.[43]

Bonaventure's Christology: Creation and the Incarnation

While clearly we cannot simply dust off Bonaventure's theology and then impose it on ethical challenges of today's "Climate Emergency," Bonaventure's Christology opens a horizon to a renewed image of God intimately concerned with creation, an understanding of the human person, and "earth friendly" moral living. Bonaventure's theological insights provide the basis for formal ecological ethical norms (values, standards, or principles) of mutual relations that compel us to take seriously God's mandate to care for creation and to live sustainably.[44]

Bonaventure began his Christological discussion with the faith claim that "the Word became flesh" (Jn 1:14), and he asked "why?" He then proceeded to probe this question from God's perspective and from the human perspective.[45] Bonaventure found the answer rooted in the ways God reveals the divine self. The Incarnation (union of human and divine natures) is grounded in the possibility of God as the Creator. God created out of self-diffusive and self-communicative love. God's self-revelation is given in its broadest sense in all of creation. The Divine is revealed more specifically in human nature (*imago Dei*). But, beyond that, the most complete revelation of God is in the human-and-divine, Jesus Christ.[46]

In Bonaventure's Logos-centered (Word-centered; Christ-centered) theology, the Word, God's revelation, is given in the entirety of the universe. Also, within creation, God's revelation is found in humans as the *imago Dei*. Notably, in Bonaventure's Trinitarian theology, the Son is also known as the Image. "Thus, in the mystery of the incarnation, the created image is filled with the eternal exemplary Image. In this way humanity reaches its fullest participation in the divine archetype and thus, the deepest fulfillment of its potential."[47] Humans are unique among the creatures (as is each creature) in that by virtue of their spiritual dimension, they have an inner ordering to immediacy with God. When this capacity is brought into act by divine initiative, "the created order finds its highest form of fulfillment."[48]

Zachary Hayes recapped all of this (above) showing the relationship of the incarnation and creation:

> In this sense, when God comes into the world, God comes into his own (Jn 1:11). This coming is not a change of physical place. It is, rather, a matter of spiritual presence to that which, by virtue of the act of creation, was formed as a potential recipient of the divine. In such a world, an incarnation is not an unwelcome intrusion of a foreign God. It is, in fact, but the fullest realization of the most noble potential in the created order.[49]

Here we see in Bonaventure a kind of evolutionary worldview that later theologians would name "Christogenesis."[50]

Bonaventure's Christology: Cosmic Dimensions

Following the long tradition of the Franciscan school, Bonaventure did not limit his discussion of the meaning of Christ to the reality to the cross. Rather, he "perceive[d] the possible relations between the story of Jesus and the larger picture of the world."[51] The Incarnation must be thought of as God's intent from the very moment of creation; it was not an afterthought, subject to human sin.[52] Rather, the meaning of the cross is situated within the context of the broader cosmic vision.

Bonaventure's Franciscan cosmic Christology provides a framework for a hope-filled rediscovery of the fact that, in Jesus, we find the divine clue to the structure and meaning not only of humanity but of the entire universe. Central to Bonaventure's understanding of Jesus is its intimate and necessary integration with an incarnational spirituality. Through the divine-human person, Jesus, our relationship with God, one another, and all of creation forms an interconnected whole. This understanding of Jesus Christ is helpful as we face the moral and spiritual malaise that undergirds the human-caused ecological problems of our day.[53]

Bonaventure came to understand the Incarnation of Jesus Christ as not an isolated event but as integral to creation itself. Christ is not an accident or an intrusion in creation. As Franciscan theologians put it, "a world without Christ is an incomplete world, that is, the whole world is structured Christologically."[54] Three New Testament texts gave Bonaventure insights for understanding of Jesus Christ, the relationship of creation and incarnation. Understanding this can assist us in our moral choices about our "Climate Emergency" and sustainable living.

Wisdom Sophia—Colossians 1:15-20

We consider first the early Christological creation hymn in Colossians 1:15-20. Here, Christ is God's preeminent and supreme agent in creation. Feminist Scripture scholars, Cynthia Briggs Kittredge and Claire Miller Colombo, see this hymn as reflecting the Jewish prototype of Lady Wisdom, and they envision both women and men praising Christ as the cosmic mediator.[55] The cosmic Christ promotes harmony between humans and all earth elements and creatures. Christ creates the conditions for harmonious community and is its redeemer and rescuer.[56] Christ also holds the fabric of the universe together, and thus, human acts constantly affect and are affected by it.[57]

This hymn has its roots in Genesis 1 and Proverbs 8. Franciscan Scripture scholar, Robert J. Karris, reflects: "Yes, Colossians 1:15-20 invites us, challenges us to take flight in our religious imagination back to the beginning, nay, before the beginning and to see Christ thoroughly enjoying creating and longing to become human to express tangibly God's unconditional love for all human and nonhuman creation."[58]

Jesus is also the mediator of redemption: "to reconcile all things for him, making peace by the blood of his cross" (Col. 1:20). The whole cosmos—all things on earth and in heaven—finds reconciliation and peace in

Jesus Christ. The saving activity of God in Jesus is the unfolding of God's purpose in creation and the beginning of its transformation in, as the passage continues, "his fleshly body" (v. 22). As Australian theologian Denis Edwards explained:

> Here the cosmic Christ is celebrated as both the *source* of creation and its *goal:* all things have been *created* in Christ and all things are *reconciled* in him. The words "all things" are repeated like a refrain. All things are created in Christ, who is the image (*icon*) of the invisible God. As in the wisdom literature *Sophia* is with God in creation and continually sustains all things, so in Colossians, the risen Christ is the one in whom all things are created and in whom all things hold together. The Colossians hymn continues, asserting that in Christ and Christ's cross, God has reconciled all things to God's self. Everything in creation, is created in Christ, sustained in him, and reconciled in him.[59]

Throughout Colossians 1:15-20, the truly universal role of Christ is repeatedly made clear. As Karris points out, in the ancient context, the "principalities and powers" are initially good but have fallen and now require reconciliation.[60] But even the cosmic powers—"whether thrones or dominions or rulers or powers" are subject to Christ's rule (Col. 1:17-18). This was likely reassuring to the Pauline community who lived in an "age of anxiety" in which angelic beings were thought of as controlling earth, air, water, and fire, as well as the movements of the sun, the moon, and the stars.[61] But "in Him" all cosmic forces are taken up and transformed in the power of the cross and resurrection. The entire universe is to be transfigured in Christ, "Who is the image of the invisible God" (Col. 1:15). In Colossians, Christ's death and resurrection are understood as the beginning of the transformation of the whole of creation. This is possible because of "the primacy of Christ"—the belief that God's will and grace are primary over the role of human sin (secondary). God's will predominates in six different ways, according to Scripture scholar Jean-Noël Aletti:[62]

- ✓ Eminence—1:5a "image;" 1:15b "firstborn"; 1:18 "preeminent"
- ✓ Universality—in 1:15-20 "all things" is mentioned eight times
- ✓ Uniqueness—that it is solely and uniquely Jesus Christ who does what the hymn says
- ✓ Totality—on all levels of creation, in every level of being, all is reconciled for Christ and through Christ
- ✓ Priority—1:15 "firstborn"; "before all things"; 1:18b "the beginning"; "Firstborn from the dead"

✓ Definitive accomplishment—The hymn celebrates what Christ has already accomplished.

This leaves us with great hope!

Deep Incarnation—John 1:1-14

Already as a student Bonaventure had an affinity for the Gospel of John. The Prologue of John (1:1-18) presents us with the amazing reality of the Incarnation. For Bonaventure, the Incarnation was a central Christian belief, uniting the doctrines of creation and redemption. Indeed, the great theologians of the first centuries of Christianity such as Irenaeus and Athanasius taught that, in the "Word made flesh," God became human so that the whole of humanity might be healed, taken up into God and deified—that is, made whole and holy—in God. The meaning of the Incarnation, of Christ becoming flesh, includes the whole interconnected material world in some way.

Scripture scholar, Mary L., Coloe, PBVM notes that in the opening verses of John, Jesus is identified with Wisdom/Sophia as portrayed in Proverbs, Sirach, and Wisdom.[63] She shows three "stories" are told in the Prologue: cosmological—creation; historical—Johannine community; and eschatological—future consummation of the world.[64] The Word (Jesus), one birthed from a woman, permeates the entire cosmos, the lives of believers, and anticipates the future consummation of the world. All flesh owes its existence through Christ, is empowered by Wisdom, and is given new life through Him.

Further, Australian theologian Duncan Reid suggested that God's embrace of humanity in the incarnation must be understood in context of the wider claim in John's Gospel that the Word has become flesh.[65] The Greek term "*sarx*" often translated as "flesh" also points beyond the humanity of Jesus and us, to the world of biological life, and it calls forth the entire interwoven web of life that God sustains and embraces in divine love.

New Zealand theologian Neil Darragh builds on Reid's thought: "To say that God became flesh is not only to say that God became human, but to say also that God became an Earth creature, that God became a sentient being, that God became a living being (in common with all other living beings), that God became a complex Earth unit of minerals in the carbon and nitrogen cycles."[66] Edwards elaborates, "In Jesus of Nazareth, God becomes a vital part of an ecosystem and a part of the interconnected systems that support life on

Earth. Danish theologian Niels Henrik Gregersen, calls this the idea of *deep incarnation.*[67] Gregersen explains further that "in Christ, God enters into biological life, in a new way, and is now with evolving creation, in a radically new way."[68] Christ's suffering on the cross is not only a redemptive act for humans. It is also God's act of suffering with the limitations of all life forms in creation—God's identification with all of creation in all its complexity, struggle, and pain.

Gregersen writes:

> In this context, the incarnation of God in Christ can be understood as a radical or "deep" incarnation, that is, an incarnation into the very tissue of biological existence, and system of nature. Understood this way, the death of Christ becomes an icon of God's redemptive co-suffering with all sentient life as well as with the victims of social competition. God bears the cost of evolution, the price involved in the hardship of natural selection.[69]

Faithful to the Christian tradition, these insights of Coloe, Reid, Darrah, Edwards, and Gregersen provide a timely understanding of what St. Paul claims in Rom. 8:19-23 that the whole creation waits with "eager longing" for its liberation from "bondage to decay" and for "the freedom associated with the glory of the children of God."

All Creation Groaning—Romans 8:18-27

As Anne M. Clifford illustrated, in Romans 5:12-21, Paul recalls Genesis 2-3 and discusses the justification of human beings in Christ, whom he calls the "New Adam."[70] In Romans 8, Paul presents a vision of the future of the earth as intimately bound to the future of humanity. Paul reflects on a theme of Genesis 6–9, Hosea, and Jeremiah, and describing that "[f]or the creation waits with eager longing for the revealing of the children of God; for the creation was subjected to futility, not of its own will but by the will of the one who subjected it, in hope" (8:19-20). Because of human sin, the created world became subject to a kind of fruitlessness that results in decay (v. 21). St. Paul states: "We know that the whole creation has been groaning in labor pains until now; and not only the creation, but we ourselves, who have the first fruits of the Spirit, groan inwardly while we wait for adoption, the redemption of our bodies" (8:22-3). But Paul provides a glimpse of God's generous, creative, compassion when he writes that it is not only creation that groans but "[l]ikewise the Spirit helps us in our weakness; for we do not know how to pray as we ought, but that very Spirit intercedes with sighs too deep for words" (8:26). Not only do humans groan inwardly in longing for redemption, but creation in its entirety does as well. There is great hope amid the groaning of creation; the Spirit that gives life in an outpouring of compassion groans with all of creation.

Bonaventure clearly understood that the entire world was transformed from the moment of the Incarnation—when the Divine became part of the material world. Just how widely and deeply are the various elements of creation related to one another? Bonaventure replied:

> All things are said to be transformed in the transfiguration of Christ. For as a human being, Christ has something in common with all creatures. With the stone he shares existence; with plants he shares life; with animals he shares sensation; and with the angels he shares intelligence. Therefore, all things are said to be transformed in Christ since—in his human nature—he embraces something of every creature.[71]

From the Writings of St. Bonaventure

The Journey of the Soul into God, 1.15 [5:299][72]

Open your eyes, alert your spiritual ears, unseal your lips, and apply your heart so that in all creatures you may see, hear, praise, love, serve, glorify and honor God, lest the whole world rise up against you. For the "universe shall wage war against the foolish." On the contrary, it will be a matter of glory for the wise who can say with the prophet: "For you have given me O Lord, a delight in your deeds, and I will rejoice in the work of your hands. How great are your works, O Lord! You have made all things in wisdom. The earth is filled with your creatures."

Reflection and Application

Although, after the Fall (Gen. 3), the human view of God's self-revelation in creation was obscured, it was not lost. Biblical and historical revelation supplements and clarifies what we see in nature and enables us to read the cosmic revelation with greater accuracy. The story of the love of God expressed in creation is elaborated in the Scriptures and modeled most perfectly in the person, life, ministry, death, and resurrection of Jesus. In the end, there is little excuse for those who do not heed the call to return to the Fountain Source of all Goodness.

The Dialogue between Science and Theology

Now it is one thing to speak about creation this way in a medieval setting where Christian theology and belief formed and contextualized the daily life for the vast majority. How does this fit with the contentions of some who claim that religion and theology have nothing to say to each other? Already in the 1990s, Zachary Hayes challenged Timothy Ferris' claim that cosmology could tell us nothing about God.[73] Hayes carefully argued that the real focus of concern is what questions we can expect religion and science to answer. Science and religion each rightfully address questions utilizing specific methods. The danger comes when either science or religion makes exclusive claims of having the entire truth and that one or the other discipline can interpret all levels of meaning. As noted, Bonaventure utilized and conversed with the scientific knowledge of his day. So, too, we need to be conversant with the information made accessible to us through methodologies such as quantum physics, astrophysics, or ecology, and use that data as the subject of our theological reflection.

From Dialogue to Contemplation and Right Action

Franciscan philosopher Phil Hoebing pointed to the early work of scientist J. Baird Callicott, who recognized the real and necessary contribution of theological ethics in defining the intrinsic value of the natural world/creation, not only its instrumental value.[74] Certainly Bonaventure's vision, of the Creator and God's creation, offers reason for Christians of today to assign intrinsic value to all in the created world. Hoebing showed how this assessment can be made by grounding one's reasoning in Bonaventure's philosophy and theology. Bonaventure so eloquently stated,

> [T]he entire world is a shadow, a road, a vestige, and it is also a book written without. (Ex 2:8; Ap 5:1) For in every creature there is a shining forth of the divine exemplar but mixed with the darkness. Hence, creatures are a kind of darkness mixed with light. Also, they are a road leading to the exemplar. Just as you see a ray of light entering through a window is colored in different ways according to the colors of the various parts, so the divine ray shines forth in each and every creature in different ways and in different properties; it is

said in Wisdom: *In her ways she shows herself* (Wis 6:17). Also, creatures are a vestige of the wisdom of God. Hence creatures are a kind of representation and statue of the wisdom of God. And in view of all of this, they are a kind of book written without.[75]

Bonaventure teaches us that "contemplation deepens the more we feel the workings of God's grace within our hearts, and the better we learn to encounter God in creatures outside ourselves."[76] In *Laudato Si'* § 239, Pope Francis, citing Bonaventure's *Quaest. Disp. de Myst. Trinitatis*, 1, 2 concl., reminds us:

> 239. For Christians, believing in one God who is trinitarian communion suggests that the Trinity has left its mark on all creation. Saint Bonaventure went so far as to say that human beings, before sin, were able to see how each creature "testifies that God is three". The reflection of the Trinity was there to be recognized in nature "when that book was open to man and our eyes had not yet become darkened." The Franciscan saint teaches us that *each creature bears in itself a specifically Trinitarian structure*, so real that it could be readily contemplated if only the human gaze were not so partial, dark, and fragile. In this way, he points out to us the challenge of trying to read reality in a Trinitarian key.[77]

In our "Climate Emergency," may we be wise enough to engage Bonaventure's vision of creation, and the accompanying ethics of cosmic mutuality, to guide us in our role as caretakers of creation. In the next chapter, we will take up those two considerations by examining the work of John Duns Scotus.

Questions for Reflection and Discussion

1. How do you understand the Incarnation? What is the relationship between the Incarnation and creation?
2. Considering Bonaventure's understanding of the "theophanic nature" of creation, what does creation tell you about God?
3. Bonaventure calls Christ the "Art of the Father." Explain what you understand about this and how thinking about Christ in this way can influence how you value the created world.

4 Read Colossians 1:15-20. How do you see Christ's work of redemption helpful in your efforts to live sustainably?
5 In what ways do you consider science a source for theological reflection or prayerful contemplation?

Suggestions for Action

1 Visit a science museum. When you return home, reflect on what you learned. What new insights about Christ come to mind? View short films produced for the American Association for the Advancement of Science, Dialogue on Science, Ethics and Religion at https://sciencereligiondialogue.org/resources/sciencethewideangle/.
2 Bonaventure held that because Christ became incarnate, the entire material world was deified. Walk through your neighborhood. How does what you see, hear, smell, touch, or taste reflect the value people place on creation? List ways you can act to improve your care for creation.
3 Do an internet search on sustainable living. Pick one way to change your lifestyle to express your care for the earth.
4 Buy "Fair Trade" beverages, food, and household items that are produced using sustainable methods.
5 Expand your "earth literacy quotation." Study composting, pollution of various kinds, the life cycle of butterflies or the hydrocycle in your region. Act on what you learn.

Sources for Further Study

Delio, Ilia. *Simply Bonaventure: An Introduction to His Life, Thought, and Writings*. New York: New City Press, 2001.

Zachary, Hayes. *The Hidden Center: Spirituality and Speculative Christology in St. Bonaventure*. St. Bonaventure, New York: The Franciscan Institute, 1992.

Zachary, Hayes. *What Manner of Man? Sermons on Christ by Bonaventure*. Chicago: Franciscan Herald Press, 1974.

Monti, Dominic V. and Katherine Wrisley Shelby, eds. *Bonaventure Revisited: Companion to the Breviloquium*. St. Bonaventure, NY: Franciscan Institute Publications, 2017.

Nothwehr, Dawn M. "The 'Brown Thread' in *Laudato Si'*: Grounding Ecological Conversion and Theological Ethics Praxis." In *Integral Ecology for a More Sustainable World: Dialogues with Laudato Si'*, edited by Dennis O'Hara, Matthew Eaton, and Michael T. Ross, 111–26. Langham, MD; Lexington Press, 2020.

Notes

1. I follow John F. Quinn, "Chronology of St. Bonaventure (1217–1274)," *Franciscan Studies* 32 (1972): 173. J. Guy Bourgerol, *Introduction to the Works of Bonaventure* (Patterson, NJ: St. Anthony Guild Press, 1964), 3. Ewert Cousins, *Bonaventure, The Classics of Western Spirituality*, ed. Richard J. Payne (New York: Paulist Press, 1978), 4.
2. Bourgerol, *Introduction*, 5–10. John F. Quinn, "Chronology of Bonaventure's Sermons," *Archivum Franciscanium Historicum* 67 (1974): 151–2.
3. Bourgerol, *Introduction*, 4.
4. Quinn, "Chronology of Bonaventure's Sermons," 151–2.
5. Zachary Hayes, "The Life and the Christological Thought of St. Bonaventure," in *Franciscan Christology: Selected Texts, Translations and Introductory Essays*, ed. Damian McElrath, Franciscan Sources No.1 (St. Bonaventure, NY: The Franciscan Institute, 1980), 62–3.
6. *Aeterni Patris,* Encyclical of Pope Leo XIII on the Restoration of Christian Philosophy (1879) §14, https://www.vatican.va/content/leo-xiii/en/encyclicals/documents/hf_l-xiii_enc_04081879_aeterni-patris.html. Pope Leo XIII named Bonaventure a preeminent theologian of the Church but promoted Thomism, nearly destroying Franciscan and other orthodox theologies. Gerald A. McCool, *From Unity to Pluralism: The Internal Evolution of Thomism* (New York: Fordham University Press, 1989), 163, 171–2, 190, 196–7.
7. Francis of Assisi, "A Salutation of the Virtues," 14–18, in *Francis of Assisi: Early Documents*, Volume I—The Saint, trans. and ed. Regis J. Armstrong, J. A. Wayne Hellmann, and Wm. J. Short (New York: New City Press, 1999), 165.
8. "A Mirror of Perfection of the *Status* of a Lesser Brother [The Sabatier Edition, 1928]," in *Francis of Assisi: Early Documents*, Volume III—*The Prophet*, trans. and ed. Regis J. Armstrong, J. A. Wayne Hellmann, and Wm. J. Short (New York: New City Press, 2001), 278–86.

9. Zachary Hayes, "Bonaventure: Mystery of the Triune God," in *The History of Franciscan Theology*, ed. Kenan B. Osborne (St. Bonaventure, NY: Franciscan Institute, 1994), 45. Regis J. Armstrong, "Francis of Assisi and the Prisms of Theologizing," *Greyfriars Review* 10/2 (1996): 196–8.
10. Bernard McGinn, *The Foundations of Mysticism*, Vol. 1, *The Presence of God: A History of Western Christian Mysticism* (New York: Crossroad, 1991), 157–82. *Stanford Encyclopedia of Philosophy*, s. v. "Pseudo-Dionysius the Areopagite," https://plato.stanford.edu/entries/pseudo-dionysius-areopagite/. The basic idea is that goodness tends to inspire more goodness. If something good happens to a person, it is rare that she or he would tell no one else about it; in fact, they may tell everyone who will listen!
11. Zachary Hayes, "Christ, Word of God and Exemplar of Humanity," *Cord* 46 (1996): 6.
12. Zachary Hayes, "The Cosmos: A Symbol of the Divine," in *Franciscan Theology of the Environment: An Introductory Reader*, ed. Dawn M. Nothwehr (Quincy, IL: Franciscan Press, 2002), 255–6, 266 notes 9–12 where Hayes cites Bonaventure's *Collations in Haexemeron*, 2, 20 (V, 339–40); and 12, 15–16 (V, 386). Bonaventure, *On the Reduction of the Arts to Theology*, Translation with Introduction and Commentary, Zachary Hayes (St. Bonaventure: Franciscan Institute, 1996). Dawn M. Nothwehr, "The 'Brown Thread' in *Laudato Si'*—Grounding Ecological Conversion in Theological Ethics Praxis," in *Integral Ecology for a More Sustainable World—Dialogue with Laudato Si'*, ed. Dennis O'Hara, Matthew Eaton, and Michael T. Ross (Lantham, MD: Lexington Books, 2020), 111–26. John Haught, *Science and Faith: A New Introduction* (Mahwah, NJ: Paulist Press, 2012), 9–20.
13. Hayes, "The Cosmos," 250–2. *St. Mary's Press Glossary of Theological Terms*, ed. John T. Ford, Essentials of Catholic Theology Series, Winona, MN: St. Mary's Press, 2006, at 120, s.v. "metaphysics." "This word (from the Greek *metaphysika*, which literally means 'after physics') was originally used by editors to describe the section of the works of Aristotle that came after the section on physics. Because this section addresses the *nature of being*, 'metaphysics' has come to mean the philosophical study of being in terms of its most foundational aspects such as *matter* and *form*."
14. Hayes, "Bonaventure: Mystery of the Triune God," 53–60.
15. In Chapter 2 of *The Journey of the Soul into God*, Bonaventure shows how the senses bring us in contact with God.
16. *St. Mary's Press Glossary* s.v. "ontology" at 133: "This word (from the Greek *onta* meaning 'things that exist,' and *logos* meaning 'word') refers to the branch of philosophy that considers *being* and *existence*."

17. *Internet Encyclopedia of Philosophy*, s.v. "Neoplatonism," https://iep.utm.edu/neoplato/. *New Catholic Encyclopedia*. Vol. 12. 2nd ed. (Detroit: Gale, 2003), s.v. "Richard of St. Victor," 234-5. Hayes, "Bonaventure: Mystery of the Triune God," 56.
18. Bonaventure, *Breviloquium* 2.12 [5:230], cited in Zachary Hayes, *Bonaventure: Mystical Writings*, Spiritual Legacy Series (New York: Crossroad Publishing Company, 1999), 90. All citations Hayes gives in this work are his translations from *Doctoris Seriphici S. Bonaventurae opera omnia*, 10 vols, Quaracchari: Collegium S. Bonaventurae, 1882-1902. The first two numerals indicate the section of the text; the bracketed numerals indicate the volume and the page in that volume.
19. Phil Hoebing, "St. Bonaventure and Ecology," in *Franciscan Theology of the Environment*, ed. Nothwehr, at 276.
20. Bonaventure, *Collations on the Six Days of Creation*, 1.13 [5:332], cited in Hayes, "Bonaventure: Mystery," 74.
21. Zachary Hayes, a lecture "Of God's FULLNESS We Have All Received: The Teaching of St. Bonaventure on Creation," June 12, 1997, at the National Franciscan Forum—*Franciscans Doing Theology*, Franciscan Center, Colorado Springs, CO. The videocassette of the lecture is included in Mary C. Gurley, "An Independent Study Program to Accompany *The History of Franciscan* Theology," Kenan Osborne, ed. (St. Bonaventure, NY: The Franciscan Institute, 1999).
22. Hayes, "Bonaventure: Mystery of the Triune God," 63-4.
23. Bonaventure, *The Collations on the Six Days of Creation* 3.8 [5:344], cited in Hayes, *Bonaventure: Mystical*, 73.
24. Hayes, "The Cosmos," 252-3.
25. Ibid., 253-8.
26. Ibid., 253.
27. Ibid., 253-4.
28. Ibid., 254.
29. Ibid., 254-5.
30. Ibid., 255.
31. Ibid., 256.
32. Ibid., 257.
33. Ibid., 258. Hayes, "Bonaventure: Mystery of the Triune God," 65.
34. Ilia Delio, "The Franciscan Intellectual Tradition: Contemporary Concerns," in *The Franciscan Intellectual Tradition*, ed. Elise Saggau, CFIT/ESC-OFM Series No. 1, Washington Theological Union Symposium Papers, 2001 (St. Bonaventure, NY: The Franciscan Institute, 2002), 1-19.
35. November 29, 1979, John Paul II proclaimed Francis of Assisi the Patron saint of ecology. Ioannes Paulus Pp. II, Litterae Apostolicae, *Inter Sanctoss, Franciscus Assisiensis Caelestis Patronus Oecologiae Cultorum Eligitur,*

https://www.vatican.va/content/john-paul-ii/la/apost_letters/1979/
documents/hf_jp-ii_apl_19791129_inter-sanctos.html.
36. Congregation for the Doctrine of the Faith, "Instruction on the Ecclesial Vocation of the Theologian," *Origins* 20/8 (July 5, 1990): 119. United States Conference of Catholic Bishops, "Doctrinal Responsibilities: Approaches to Promoting Cooperation and Resolving Misunderstandings between Bishops and Theologians," *Origins* 19/7 (June 29, 1989): 101. Bernard McGinn, *Meister Eckhart and the Beguine Mystics* (New York: Continuum, 1983), 6–7 and his *The Flowering of Mysticism: Men and Women in the New Mysticism—1200-1350* (New York: Crossroad, 1998), 21.
37. John 14:6-9 and St. Francis, *Admonition* I:1-4 in Regis Armstrong and Ignatius Brady, *Francis and Clare* (Mahwah, NJ: Paulist Press, 1982), 25–6.
38. Zachary Hayes, "Christ, Word of God and Exemplar of Humanity," 6.
39. Kenan B. Osborne, ed., *The History of Franciscan Theology* (St. Bonaventure, NY: The Franciscan Institute, 1994), vii–ix. Hayes, "The Life and the Christological Thought of St. Bonaventure," 62–4. Timothy Johnson, "Lost in Sacred Space: Textual Hermeneutics, Liturgical Worship, and Celano's *Legenda ad usum chori*," 12. E. R. Daniel, *The Franciscan Concept of Mission in the High Middle Ages* (New York: The Franciscan Institute, 1975), 48.
40. J. Guy Bougerol, *Introduction to the Works of Bonaventure*, Vol. 1, trans. José de Vinck (Patterson, NJ: St. Anthony Guild Press, 1964), especially 23–49.
41. Delio, "The Franciscan Intellectual Tradition," 8. Ilia Delio, *Crucified Love: Bonaventure's Mysticism of the Crucified Christ* (Quincy, IL: Franciscan Press, 1998).
42. The encyclical, *Aeterni Patris.* McCool, *From Unity to Pluralism,* 163, 17.1–2, 190, 196–7. It is noteworthy that the foundational theology grounding *Laudato Si'* is Franciscan.
43. Ilia Delio, *Simply Bonaventure* for Bonaventure's method and metaphysics; Trinitarian theology; and doctrine of creation.
44. Dawn M. Nothwehr, *Mutuality: A Formal Norm for Christian Social Ethics* [(San Francisco: Catholic Scholars Press, 1998). Reprinted Eugene, OR: Whipf & Stock Publishers, 2005].
45. Zachary Hayes, "Bonaventure: The Mystery of the Triune God," 87.
46. Ibid., 83.
47. Ibid., 86.
48. Hayes, "Bonaventure—The Mystery of the Triune God," 87. *St. Mary's Press Glossary of Theological Terms,* s.v. "hypostatic union," at 94: "This term (from the Greek *hypostasis*, meaning 'what lies beneath,' and the Latin *unio*, meaning 'oneness,' or 'unity,') refers to the union of the divine and the human natures in the one divine person of Jesus Christ the Son of God (See *CCC,* 494–69)."

49. Ibid., 88.
50. Leonardo Boff, Cry of the Earth, Cry of the Poor, Ecology and Justice Series (Maryknoll: Orbis Books, 1997), 174–86, especially at 185. For Teilhard de Chardin, Christogenesis is the notion that Christ would be the start and the end of evolution, its Alpha and Omega. All the energies of the universe would be continuously rising to some superior level that would be a movement toward Christ.
51. Hayes, "Christ Word of God and Exemplar of Humanity," 6.
52. More will be said concerning this as developed by John Duns Scotus.
53. Hayes, "Christ, Word of God and Exemplar of Humanity," 16–17. Ilia Delio, Christ in Evolution (Maryknoll: Orbis Books, 2008), especially Chapters 3 and 7.
54. Hayes, "Christ, Word of God and Exemplar of Humanity," 6.
55. Cynthia Briggs Kittredge and Claire Miller Colombo, "*Colossians*," in *Philippians, Colossians, Philemon, Wisdom Commentary*, ed. Elsa Tamez et al., Vol. 51 (Collegeville, MM: Liturgical Press, 2017), 151.
56. Ibid., 154.
57. Ibid., 155.
58. Robert J. Karris, "Colossians 1:15-20—Jesus Christ as Cosmic Lord and Peacemaker," in *Franciscan Theology of the Environment*, ed. Nothwehr, 86.
59. Denis Edwards, *Ecology at the Heart of Faith* (Maryknoll: Orbis Books, 2006), 56.
60. Karris, "Colossians 1:15-20," 90.
61. Ibid., 75.
62. Karris, "Colossians 1:15-20," 81–3.
63. Mary L. Coloe, PBVM, *John 1-10*, Wisdom Commentary, Volume 44A (Collegeville, MM: Liturgical Press, 2021), 1–9.
64. Coloe, PBVM, *John 1-10*, at 9 cites, Adele Reinhartz, *The Word in the World: The Cosmological Tale in the Fourth Gospel*, SBLMS 45 (Atlanta: Scholars Press, 1992), 4.
65. Duncan Reid, "Enfleshing the Human," in *Earth Revealing-Earth Healing: Ecology and Christian Theology*, ed. Denis Edwards (Collegeville, MN: Liturgical Press, 2000), 69–83.
66. Neil Darragh, *At Home in the Earth* (Auckland: Accent Publications, 2000), 124. See discussion of "deep incarnation" in Denis Edwards, *Ecology at the Heart of Faith* (Maryknoll: Orbis Books, 2006), 58–60.
67. Edwards, *Ecology at the Heart of Faith*, 59. See Neils Henrick Gregersen, "The Cross of Christ in an Evolutionary World," *Dialog: A Journal of Theology* 40 (2001): 205.
68. Edwards, *Ecology at the Heart of Faith*, 59.
69. Ibid.

70. "Foundations for a Catholic Ecotheology of God," in *"And God Saw It Was Good:" Catholic Theology and the Environment*, ed. Drew Christiansen and Walter Grazer (Washington, DC: United States Conference of Catholic Bishops, Inc., 1996), 36.
71. Bonaventure, *Sermo I, Dom II*, in Quad. IX, 215–19, quoted in Hayes, "Christ, Word of God and Exemplar of Humanity," 13.
72. Bonaventure, *The Journey of the Soul into God*, 1.15 [5:299], in Hayes, *Bonaventure: Mystical*, 77.
73. Hayes, "The Cosmos," 258–65.
74. Hoebing, "Bonaventure and Ecology," 270. See the American Association for the Advancement of Science, Dialogue on Science, Ethics, Religion (DoSER) program: https://www.aaas.org/programs/dialogue-science-ethics-and-religion/about.
75. Bonaventure, *Hexaemeron*. XII, 14, quoted in Ewert Cousins, *Christ of the 21st Century* (Rockport, MA: Element, Inc., 1992), 152.
76. Bonaventure, II *Sent*, 23, 2, 3 cited in *LS* § 233, note 160.
77. LS § 239, https://www.vatican.va/content/dam/francesco/pdf/encyclicals/documents/ papa-francesco_20150524_enciclica-laudato-si_en.pdf.

6

Bl. John Duns Scotus—Sacred Subtle Thoughts Concerning Creation

Introduction: The Subtle Doctor[1]

Born in 1265 at Duns, Berkwickshire, Scotland, and raised in a devout Christian family, John Duns Scotus was named after St. John the Evangelist. In 1280 he completed the novitiate of the Franciscan Friars Minor at Dumfries, Scotland. Following priestly ordination in 1291, he studied philosophy at Cambridge and Oxford. He lectured on Peter Lombard's *Sentences* at Oxford until 1302 and then did further study at Paris. From June 1303 to April 1304, he was at Oxford. He returned to Paris and served as Regent Master in Theology from 1305 to 1307. In 1307 took charge of the Franciscan House of Studies at Cologne, until his death, November 8, 1308.

Something about Bl. John Duns Scotus' Thought

Scotus: The Metaphysical Wing of St. Francis

Precise and subtle philosophical distinctions define Scotus' work, earning him the designation the "Subtle Doctor." His thought frequently combined philosophical ideas and theological notions, integrating them to form new understandings. Yet he was a true son of St. Francis and St. Clare: John Duns Scotus might be called "the metaphysical wing of St. Francis."[2] Any careful reading of John's work readily reveals that Love dominates his thought. His conclusions are colored with Franciscan spirituality, expressed in metaphysical terms. Scotus is a person who is in love with Love, and the ultimate purpose in his thinking and writing is union with God. Scotus is one utterly amazed at the intensity of God's love revealed in creation, the Scriptures, theology—and ultimately in Christ. He had a beautiful mind, able to express truths about God, creatures, creation, and the cosmos in the language of metaphysics with the same passion and brilliance found in the mystical language of St. Francis or St. Bonaventure.

Scotus: Metaphysician

Metaphysics is a specialized area of the study of philosophy.[3] The term "philosophy" literally means "love of knowledge" or "love of wisdom" (Grk. *philosophia*). Philosophers use logical reasoning rather than empirical investigation. Metaphysics deals with *the study of being* in its most foundational aspects of *matter* and *form*. Metaphysicians understand *matter* to be the potential or underlying reality, while *form* is what individualizes or actualizes matter.

In this chapter Franciscan metaphysician John Duns Scotus offers important ideas relevant for ecotheology for today. With St. Francis and St. Bonaventure, Scotus recognized God as the creator of all and thus viewed creation as a source of God's self-revelation. Scotus' reflections provide distinct insights that can assist us as we wrestle with our current "Climate Emergency."

Scotus: The Realist
God as First Principle
To appreciate how John Duns Scotus understood the created world we need first to comprehend his view of God's relationship to creation, the value placed on the created world in general, and the dignity of creation overall. Scotus was a Christian realist who understood that everything in the created world somehow had its source in God.[4] Scotus began his reflections

with empirical (experiential) observation of the created world in its totality, attempting to discover what he could identify through observation and experience. He first accepted that reality includes the natural environment—its physical nature, its vegetative and animal life—as well as good and evil, virtue and sin, the angelic and the demonic. He then asked, what kind of a credible God would allow this wildly diverse reality to exist? What does all of this tell us about God? As a Christian, Scotus realized that *nothing* created lasts forever and that *everything* was ultimately dependent on God for its life and existence. He expressed this insight using the metaphysical concept of *contingency*, that is, the reality that things or situations in life (a) don't have to exist *at all* nor (b) do they need to exist *as* they exist. They *are all utterly dependent on something else or someone* else to bring them to life or to make them happen. For example, a rose could be red, yellow, or pink. If the gardener does not water the rosebush, it will die; or the gardener may care for the plant so well that its blossoms win a prize at a garden show. On the other hand, there is only so much the gardener can do to make the rosebush grow in a particular way; all else depends on its God-given capacity to live and grow. Scotus reasoned that *if* something *exists* (e.g., a stone), that means that it is somehow *possible* for it *to* exist if the conditions are right (e.g., lava from a volcano cools and becomes obsidian). He traced backward through a series of causes that could make something exist or happen until he reached the ultimate point of origin where a Being existed, but it had no cause, yet it had the potential to cause other things, and he ended up with *only* God. For Scotus, the only being that is *not contingent*, i.e., uncaused and *necessary*, is God.

God is *necessary* simply because there is *nothing* that could bring about God or "make God happen." The Divine exists because God *chooses* to exist and the creation exists because God artistically, freely, and lovingly calls it into being in the act of creation. That God is *love* was most important for Scotus and for us.[5] Because God is absolutely free, God is absolutely loving, and this love is absolutely immanent (present, here with us). If anything exists, God is present to sustain it.

God is not known only through empirical observation (human experience) but also through divine revelation (e.g., sacred Scriptures). The vast diversity of creation led Scotus to a wonderful conclusion, namely that the God revealed in such a creation is the First Principle, *absolutely necessary*, yet utterly free, and that the created world is equally *utterly contingent*. Such a totally free God did not *have* to do anything! Just think of it—everything we have ever known and loved did not have to be created—you and I included! In fact, the entire created world is pure grace and gift! This knowledge stands in contrast with the Enlightenment philosophers or Deists of the past.

Loving Creator, God

Further, Scotus held that God has primacy in three ways: of efficiency, finality, and eminence.[6] God is *necessary* simply because there is *nothing* that could bring about God or "make God happen." However, what was most important for Scotus (and for us) is that God is more than the "uncaused cause" of created things—God is *love*.[7] Because God is completely free, God loves absolutely, and this love is utterly immanent. This insight speaks loudly to the kind of attitude we need to have in relation to the created world. If the entire creation is God's free gift of love, how dare we abuse it? If in absolute divine freedom God generously provides such vast diversity and abundance in creation, how dare we withhold what is needed for the flourishing of our human sisters and brothers *and* entire ecosystems? Deplorably, at present, nearly all the world's economic systems operate on the presupposition of scarcity with an eye only toward satisfying the opulent excesses of a few human elites who profit from the unsustainable harvesting of vital elements of the earth's wealth.[8]

Why and How Did God Create?

Scotus explained the kind of power that God has and how that power was used to bring about the creation. God's power is manifested in two ways: first, *potentia absoluta* that allows God to act with indifference toward creation. Such power, viewed in fallible human terms, could seem threatening. However, because God *is always* loving and rational, the exercise of divine power *is always* rational and loving and never arbitrary. *Potentia ordinata* refers to what God has chosen to do or has in fact done, and so it requires conformity to rules predetermined by divine wisdom or motivated by the divine will.[9] To be sure, things work the way God created them to work, and God respects the requirements of this world because they express the divine creative intent. This consistency in God and in God's actions serves as an affirmation of humanity in that it inspires trust, fidelity, and orderliness, making possible a loving human—divine relationship. Divine revelation and personal accounts of salvation history witness to the fact that God *is loving and faithful* through all times and circumstances. God chose to create to make divine glory known (Eph. 1:3-10). God did not *have* to do anything. The entire created world is pure grace and gift.

Haecceitas

There is one very important aspect of creation that is the focus of Scotus' attention and that reveals the great dignity of God's creation. The Subtle Doctor claims that for one subject (person, thing, or idea) to be related to another, it must *first* be known and understood for what it is *in itself*. Scotus' principle of *haecceitas* (individuation or "thisness") provides the philosophical foundation for everything in created reality to be specified (identified as specific entities).[10] Osborne explains, "Scotus makes the claim that individuation must be based in the very substance of a thing or a person, not in some accidental aspect of a thing or person."[11] *Haecceitas* makes a singular thing what it is and differentiates it from all other things (of common nature) to which it may be compared (because of its commonality).[12]

For example, the principle of *haecceitas* holds that if I have a bouquet of twenty-two flowers (items of a common nature) made up of roses and daisies, I not only have a bouquet (things of a common nature) of roses (that can be compared because of their commonality), and daisies (that can be compared because of their commonality), but I have *twelve distinct individual flowers* (that we judge to be enough alike as to call them roses) and *ten distinct individual flowers* (that we judge to be enough alike as to call them daisies). In Scotus' thought a rose is a rose and not a daisy, and each rose or each daisy is distinct from every other rose and every other daisy. So too it is with all of creation, humans included. Each person (or thing or idea) is unique in all time and eternity—there never has been nor will there ever be another human being identical to you or me; no, not even a clone! A human person's identity cannot be reduced to her or his physical makeup or their current embodied existence. Mary Beth Ingham explains:

> *Haecceitas* points to the ineffable within each being. The sacredness of each person, indeed of each being is philosophically expressed in this Latin term. According to Scotus, the created order is not best understood as a transparent medium through which divine light shines (as Aquinas taught) but is itself endowed with an inner light that shines forth from within. The difference between these two great scholars can be compared to the difference between a window (Aquinas) and a lamp (Scotus). Both give light, but the source of light for Scotus has already been given to the being by the creator. Each being

within the created order already possesses an immanent dignity; it is already gifted by the loving Creator with sanctity beyond our ability to understand.[13]

Not only does the *entire* creation have dignity because of its vastness and diversity, it is profoundly valued for its particularity—*each* being, *itself*. Thus, from observing creation and from divine revelation Scotus uncovers a Creator, who is powerful, artistically free, loving, and who sustains that creation in general and in an ordered perfectly loving way. Significant for us is that *haecceitas* makes it possible for each person, plant, animal, earth, or cosmic element (or idea) to be distinct, one from the other. Without individuation, in which there are at least two distinct entities, no authentic relationships—interpersonal or otherwise—are possible.

The implications that *haecceitas* holds for ecology and environmental ethics are vast, especially for biodiversity.[14] *Haecceitas* potentially affects human relating in general because it affects how we understand contingent reality as thoroughly laced with God's utterly free and loving intent. Humans are created by God with freedom to choose good/evil, right/wrong, yet are unconditionally loved by God. Humans are not loved by God simply as a species, but each is loved in her/his person—their individual essence. Just as human value is enhanced by such intimate regard, so too the value of all elements of the cosmos is revered. Not only is each element of the cosmos different in its *accidental* characteristics, but each is distinct in its very *essence*. If this is the case, then for Christians, issues of biodiversity must be considered in this light. Not only are entire species of great worth, but each *particular being* also is *valued uniquely* for its own sake.

Intended before All Time: The Incarnation as God's Masterpiece

But Scotus' insights draw us into an understanding of God that is deeper still. The reality of the humanity of Jesus as exposed in Scripture is also included in the reality with which Scotus dealt. Without a doubt, the most profound and perfect self-revelation of God took place in the Incarnation. God, the Divine Artist, conceived of the best way in which the fullness of divine glory could be shared. Before the beginning of time, and like a diligent artist who envisions a gorgeous landscape, and who then begins to execute the design by creating the background that will support the whole of the work, so too, before the beginning of time, Scotus contends, God freely planned the

Incarnation.[15] This teaching is known as the Primacy and Predestination of Christ (Eph. 1:3-10; Col. 1:15-18). In a sense we can say that Jesus Christ is "the *haecceitas* of God"—God's Masterpiece!

Simply stated, according to Scotus, the reason for the Incarnation, in the first place, was God's free and eternal decision to have (outside himself) someone who could love him perfectly. Through the humanity of Jesus, God expressed the absolutely free divine desire to communicate divine love in a contingent and finite world.

And so it was that the world was created through the Word (Jn 1:1-18). Humans were created as those having the capacity to respond freely to God's invitation and who could enter a personal relationship with God and one another. As Scotus sees it, humans were not only created in the image and likeness of God (*imago Dei*), but they were also created in the image of the incarnate Son (*imago Christi*). Scotus sees Christ as the pattern after which all creation is fashioned. Likewise, the Subtle Doctor holds that progress in the spiritual life is a process of *christification* as well as *deification*; the more Christ-like one becomes, the more God-like one is. Indeed, human union with God is mediated through the Incarnation.

The Subtle Doctor joins a long line of Franciscan scholars in maintaining that the Word would have become incarnate even if *Adam* had not sinned.[16] *Adam*'s sin was not the *sine qua non* for the Incarnation. In Scotus' view, the Incarnation was not necessitated by human choice to sin, for that would effectively subject God (who is absolutely free) to the permission of sin.[17] Also, if the Incarnation had been the result of sin, contrary to charity, humans would have reason to rejoice at the sinfulness of others.[18]

Rather, the Incarnation represents the manifestation of God's eternal glory and God's intent to raise human nature to the highest point of glory by uniting it with divine nature (Prov. 8:30). Understood in this way, the Incarnation is a paradigm for divine-human mutuality. As Ingham stresses: "Mutuality between God and humanity was foreseen from eternity, begun in the Incarnation and is to be fully realized in the future when Christ will be 'all in all.' The summit of creation is the communion of all persons with one another and with God. ... Christ is the very person in whom the human and divine achieve mutuality."[19] Christ embodies the divine message that human actions are pleasing to God, human persons are pleasing to God, and humans are loved by God. The fact that, according to Scotus, God's freedom and liberality inspired the Incarnation provides a positive enhancement of human nature that is not possible in a sin-centric understanding of the doctrine. God, in Scotus' view, is a creative artist who selected the human nature as the "material" most fitting to receive the highest glory of subsisting in the person of the Word.[20] Because Jesus Christ became human, part of this material created universe, the entire created cosmos is divinely affirmed. Understood in this way, the Incarnation is a paradigm for human beings and all created reality as partners with God in the ongoing co-creation and co-redemption of the world.

One strong implication for ecology suggested by this understanding of the Incarnation is that humans have a particularly Christ-like role to play in the cosmos. That role is to love God and everything in the entire cosmos, which is God's self-expression. Because the entire cosmos in some way resembles Christ, the "first born of all creation" (Col. 1: 15-20), we must cherish creation with reverent care, just as we reverence Christ.

From the Writings of John Duns Scotus
De Primo Principio[21] *[A Treatise on God as First Principle]*
Chapter One

1.1 May the First Principle of things grant me to believe, to understand and to reveal what may please his majesty and may raise our minds to contemplate him.
1.2 O Lord our God, true teacher that you are, when Moses your servant asked you for your name that he might proclaim it to the children of Israel, you, knowing what the mind of mortals could grasp of you replied: "I am who am," thus disclosing your blessed name. You are truly what it means to be, you are the whole of what it means to exist. This, if it be possible for me, I should like to know by way of demonstration. Help me then, O Lord, as I investigate how much our natural reason can learn about that true being which you have predicated of yourself.

Reflection and Application

A Spirituality of *Haecceitas*

Séamus Mulholland claims that foremost among Scotus' teachings are his unique doctrine of *haecceitas* and the Primacy and Predestination of Christ, and these bear unique implications for Christian spirituality. At the heart of each of these notions is Love, which is God. Mulholland states: "They [the teachings] are the conclusions of a man of prayer and deep spiritual serenity, for in Scotus, the ultimate aim of all theology is union with God, and this is also the ultimate aim of spirituality."[22]

In absolute freedom,

> God's will is that he be loved outside himself by someone who can love perfectly. He foresees the intensity of the union between Christ and himself who loves him *as* he loves himself. Christ, therefore, one concludes from this, is the center of all creation, all of which has its beginning, source, and end in the love God has for himself in Christ most perfectly.[23]

Creation, Christ, and the human family are formed in love and drawn toward the end of ultimate union with God.

But it is to a very specific and individual intimacy that we are drawn. Scotus' *haecceitas* "concerns itself ... with the absolute unique individual distinction of originality that is the result of God's free loving creative activity and effects every animate and inanimate thing."[24] It is in this utter uniqueness that God loves each and every thing for its own sake in and of itself. There is no insignificant being! A spirituality based on "thisness" calls forth a profound regard for life, hope, and respect for the uniqueness of God's creation and the ever-present love of God.

It is this spiritual celebration of *God's freely expressed love in creation* and the Primacy of Christ that Franciscan theologian William Short finds in the poetry of Gerard Manley Hopkins: "The world is charged with the grandeur of God."[25] As the first born of all creation, Christ is the model after which all the created world is fashioned. The materiality of Jesus, and the materiality of all of creation alike, is the result of the absolutely free, loving expression of God. As Short points out, as each distinct created thing or person lives, each enacts themselves. In the process of each being enacting itself into existence, each thing or person is simultaneously enacting or manifesting something of Christ (in his human materiality).[26]

Scotus' understanding of nature stands in contrast to other scholastics such as Thomas Aquinas, whose "theory of the analogy of being ... held that true being exists only in God and all other being is derivative, pointing toward true being, but only weakly and indirectly."[27] Scotus' *theory of the univocity of being* holds that each created being in its own singular manner expresses the total image of the Creator.[28] So when we observe the natural world or other persons, we see "things are/do themselves. That doing/being themselves is their doing/being Christ."[29]

In contrast to Thomas Aquinas' view that things have two components, matter and form, Scotus claims everything has a third component: "This" (*haec*).[30] "Here is the corollary of the incarnation—God became *this* Jewish carpenter: this unique, unrepeatable, specific creature is the incarnate Creator. From this belief one can conclude that things are God-like in their specificity. Things deserve the respect of our attention, for whatever *is* is because of Christ."[31]

Essential Order: Human and Divine Relationship Made Possible

As Scotus sees it, both in creation and through salvation history, God sets out a design for human life to be lived in relationship with the Divine and with others. In fact, Scotus' principle of *essential order* explains this design, using the language of metaphysics. Another way to talk about this relational design is to use the language of *natural law*. Reasoning human beings can observe a kind of order in the created world without any kind of special divine revelation. People can see cycles in nature, or they might observe that treating human beings in a disrespectful manner lowers their self-esteem, perhaps even leading them to a psychotic break.

However, Scotus explains that the Scriptures (revelation) fine-tune what we can know about relationships with God and other creatures from the natural law and place it in the context of God's love for humanity. Thus, there is a qualitative difference in how we live. Knowing God's love for us, we need to take into consideration not only whether an action is reasonable (rational judgment) but also whether the act is motivated by love (affective motivation). For example, at Christmas time, Person "A" may donate to the Boys and Girls Club because she genuinely cares about the quality of life children have. This is a reasonably good thing to do. In another instance, Person "B," who is a caring person, wants to make life better for poor children. However, she knows some of the children because she meets them on her way to work every day. She has grown attached to them and though she can't afford to give each child what she or he might need, she knows they all participate in the Boys and Girls Club. Thus, she can help all of them by giving to the club. In either scenario, a good deed was done. However, the deed in the second scenario is qualitatively (subjectively) distinct from the first because "B" has a relationship with the children.

When Scotus discusses the summary of God's covenant with the people of Israel, given in the Ten Commandments, he explains that the first table (Commandments 1-3) deals with our relationship with God, while the second table (Commandments 4-10) deals with relationships between neighbors. The Franciscan claims that the meaning of the first three commandments is obvious to anyone who recognizes that God is the highest most perfect being, namely that God is to be loved, unconditionally (*Deus diligendus est*).[32] Significantly, the commandments of the second table could be known through the natural law. Yet, if they are understood considering the first table, one can see that the reason we are to act lovingly toward our neighbors (including our other-than-human neighbors) is not because we are models of generosity or great humanitarians, but rather because God deeply loves us and desires that we love one another. In this light, the Ten Commandments are no longer chapters of a legal code but themes of a love song about our relationship to God, neighbors, and all creatures.

Scotistic Ethics and Our "Climate Emergency"

Human Free Will and Affections

A central notion of John Duns Scotus' ethical thought is that human persons are created by God, and each has a free will. According to Scotus, our human will has two affections or orientations. The first, the affection for possession or happiness (*affectio commodi*), is directed inward at a healthy kind of self-preservation or happiness. This is not "selfishness," but rather it is a healthy kind of self-interest.[33] It is a mature self-esteem that enables and requires a person to grow in personal integrity and to place themselves in perspective with others, while not permitting disrespect or abuse.[34] The second, affection for justice (*affectio iustitiae*), is directed outward toward others and seeks what is just and to love each individual according to his or her worth (what is rightly due them).[35] Right living requires that we balance these two affections when making choices about things that we do or things that will shape our character. If we do follow our affection for justice, Ingham states, "The result is a dynamic of mutual love and expanding inclusivity."[36] Such a stance would also enable us to live into the right relationships characteristic of the Reign of God. This, according to Ingham, would require each of us to develop *a self-reflexive stance* toward our own lives, *a critical awareness of injustice* around us, and the *courage to act as quickly as possible* on behalf of justice.[37] This moral capacity is critical for developing sustainable habits of living and being as we encounter our "Climate Emergency."

Human Will and Freedom of Choice

In Scotus' ethical thought, the focus is on the human person. The objective of ethics is the perfection of the moral person.[38] For Scotus, the *will* is the sole rational faculty capable of self-determination and self-movement. The "will" is a term for the human person's capacity for desires, loves, and choices.[39] It can will, nil, or refrain from (affirm, renounce, or not make a choice) passing judgment on any object.[40] The "intellect" is the term for the human cognitive capacity to know and to understand. While these faculties (powers) are formally distinct, they work together in the human process of choosing. Like a host who introduces a speaker to an audience, the *intellect* presents an idea or an object to the *will*. The *will* then considers the possibilities and makes a choice. The significant point here is that *the will also* has access to the *intellect* in the process of choice making. Thus, we can place any one particular choice in perspective with other factors and choose intelligently and wisely. Scotus was clear that nothing outside of the *will* determines its choice. This means that even though humans can be forced to act against their *will*, each person is responsible for the choices they make. Human freedom then is set in the context of moral rationality in the form of self-control and self-determination according to the light of reflection.[41]

The morally good act and its circumstances are determined by the virtues of right reason or prudence and must be suitable to the agent, have a suitable object, and be performed under suitable circumstances (end, manner, time, and place).[42] Love for God is, for Scotus, the self-evident first principle of praxis (acting). He demonstrates in *De Primo Principio* that God is infinite being and therefore also infinite goodness.[43] Then he restates the Aristotelian/Stoic maxim, "Good is to be pursued, evil avoided," as the theological principle, *Deus diligendus est*. That God is to be loved is necessarily true because God is infinite goodness and as such is worthy of all love.

The Triune God: A Basis for All Reality and Relationships

For Scotus all of reality is better understood if we think about it considering the Christian doctrine of the Trinity. He gives particular attention to the likenesses and differences between the activity of the Trinity *ad intra* and *ad extra*. The life of the Trinity *ad intra* is the internal aspect of Trinitarian life (the necessary relationship between the Father, Son, and Holy Spirit with and among each other). The life of the Trinity *ad extra* is that aspect whereby the Trinity expresses its divine will, freely choosing to enact the creation, Incarnation, and *acceptatio*.[44] Scotus asserts that the essence of God involves both aspects of Trinitarian life, however.[45]

In Scotus' view, the basis for the relationship among the three persons reveals an important aspect of God's essence. Not only are there three distinct persons in the God-head but the very interaction of those persons form and shape one another and actively give each other life.[46] Scotus held that each of the persons and the relationship or communion of the three persons are essential to the divine life.[47] There can be no relationship without at least two terms joined in interaction.[48] In his discussion of the topic in the fourth of the *Quodlibetal Questions*, Scotus is most clear about how God's essence is also communion.[49]

Scotus' discussion of the Trinity is significant for understanding godly *mutuality* as fundamental to human relationship for several reasons: First, the Trinity can be understood as a model for human relations—all members of the Godhead are distinct and of equal value, but they share a mutually life-giving life with one another. Second, the individuality Scotus claims for each person of the Trinity provides the metaphysical basis for mutuality; the persons of the Trinity are constituted *as persons* through the relationship (*ad intra*) of mutuality. Insofar as the Trinity is a communion of persons that models the goal for human community, the Trinity exemplifies the relationship of mutuality as the ideal and goal of all human activity.[50]

Scotistic Wisdom for Sustainable Economic Life

Trinitarian life is the basis for Scotus' understanding of the love of neighbor. While each person of the Trinity is distinct, each is constituted in relation to one another. This interrelatedness also applies to relationships among human, as well as among all planetary beings. We become the persons we are because of the influences that shape us in relationship with one another, God, and the entire creation.

At the heart of human relationships with God and one another is a dynamic, reciprocal love that empowers and enhances life. This love is expressive and inclusive.[51] Since the nature of God's love requires the lover to seek only what enhances the well-being of the beloved, we find that Scotus' understanding of love is that it consists in a radical, generous, overflowing identification with the needs of the other (including any beings or things considered of a lesser status) by the lover.

Scotus wrote no systematic treatise on society, politics, or economics. However, we find an interesting discussion in his treatise on the sacrament of penance. There he responds to the question of whether restitution is necessary prior to receiving the sacrament. Within this discussion, we also find his treatment of the origins of civil authority and the use and ownership of property.[52] Scotus insists that the best form of government is a form in which the people who are the subjects of governance participate in determining its structure and give it authority over them.[53]

In the realm of economic life, Scotus' assumptions are that "the earth is the Lord's and all that is in it" (Ps. 24:1) and it is only human law that allows the existence of the concept of "mine" in the human vocabulary.[54] True to Francis of Assisi, who admonished that we live in the world as strangers and guests (Lev. 25:23), Scotus did not identify "use" with "ownership," even in the case of fungibles.[55] According to Scotus, money is to be viewed as a fungible because by its nature it is essentially a medium of exchange, which is "consumed" in the process of exchange for other goods.

While Scotus' approach to economics is simple, and seemingly even naïve for such a great thinker, in practice, if his very basic principles were followed, they could radically and positively impact the quality of political, economic, and ecological status of human and planetary life. The participation of the governed in a context where there is no absolute ownership, and where material wealth and goods are considered the generous bequest of God, the Gracious Host, suggests a radical contrast to our present-day political, economic, and ecological reality. In Scotus we find acknowledgment of the contingent nature of wealth and a radical recognition of the sole purpose of material goods, namely the divinely ordained well-being of the entire cosmos. Both political and economic decisions must be made through participation of the community with the common good of the whole as the first and foremost criterion.

At the heart of Scotus' economic and political philosophy is the common good and special consideration of the poor that acknowledges the interrelationship between ecology and economics. Because all humans are but caretakers and borrowers of a common creation—a generous gift from God—to use material goods unjustly is to effectively steal, especially from the poor. As current economic data bears out, the poor suffer the repercussions of injustice and "Climate Emergency" disproportionately. Thus, it is the poor who require repayment when circumstances prevent the person who has been wronged from being repaid directly.[56]

Scotus' Fundamental Considerations Today

The basic aspects of Scotus' fundamental considerations are still true today. On October 24, 2011, the Pontifical Council for Justice and Peace issued: "Towards Reforming the International Finance and Monetary Systems in the Context of Global and Public Authority."[57] Just economic relations require an ethic of solidarity:

> This implies abandoning all forms of petty selfishness and embracing the logic of the global common good which transcends merely contingent, particular interests. In a word, they ought to have a keen sense of belonging to the human family which means sharing the common dignity of all human beings: "Even prior to the logic of a fair exchange of goods and the forms of justice appropriate to it, there exists something which is due to man because he is man, by reason of his lofty dignity."[58]

This ethic, together with the principle of subsidiarity, which requires involvement of people at the local level, enables adapting policies to care for the earth while providing sufficient goods for the health and well-being of all.

In *Laudato Si'* Pope Francis shows many past and current violations of Scotus' economic principles still prolong the "Climate Emergency." Industrial activity and transportation are major sources of greenhouse gases, causing global warming which leads to destruction of habitats and loss of potable water sources (*LS* § 23-26). Contrary to Scotus' understanding of mutual relatedness, today, leadership, political will, a sense of care for people who are poor, and concern for vital planetary systems are lacking (*LS* § 48, 53). Private property is a good only when it is held lightly, and in perspective with the notion of the "common destination of goods," especially the reality that the natural environment is the patrimony of all humanity, as Catholic social teaching stresses (*LS* § 93, 95). Technology and the market have been a blessing to humankind but also sources of a threat to planetary life when for some entrepreneurs, their behavior shows that for them maximizing profits is enough (*LS* § 109).

A vibrant politics that follows the principles of subsidiarity and solidarity is necessary to check the power of some economic sectors that hold more power than some nation-states. "What is needed is a politics which is farsighted and capable of a new, integral and interdisciplinary approach to handling the different aspects of the crisis" (*LS* § 196-197).

Importance of Scotistic Theology and Philosophy for Ecotheology

As we have suggested, Scotus is relevant for our day on several counts. His moral vision is rooted in an optimistic view of the human capacity to act morally in the world. Our will for self-preservation and our affection for justice can work together to respond rationally to the command to love God, neighbor, and self. Scotus is also optimistic about creation. The created world has God's all-powerful, free, generous love as its source. Thus, all reality is good and beautiful. The moral life involves everything in our environment and our efforts to strengthen and enhance our mutual relations with it. Scotus' view is both organic and dynamic. All reality progresses through the present toward a future that potentially includes greater integration and awareness. Ingham concludes: "If relationship and mutuality are appropriate human goods, then they are moral goals. Accordingly, all persons have a right to share equally in the resources of the earth."[59]

We can sum up the significance of John Duns Scotus' philosophy and theology for ecotheology and ethics as follows: God created the world in absolute freedom. But, more, God is Love. Out of a desire to be loved perfectly God chose the human form as the material in which to express the Masterpiece of Creation, Jesus Christ. Each unique being in creation is an expression of God in its own right. The created world and all that is in it is good, and thus, there is great hope for humans and the entire cosmos.

In our global "Climate Emergency," humans need to follow their affection for justice and inclination to live in mutual relation with all of creation. These two ways of being provide a necessary kind of asceticism for us today. Our actions need to be within the life-giving limits of the Franciscan "*usus pauper*" (poor use) or self-restrained use of the earth's goods that frame the natural birthright of each person.[60]

The orientation of the Franciscan tradition is positive, but it is not naive. When acknowledging the utter urgency of global warming, and the accompanying human, plant, and animal suffering and threats of extinction, Franciscan theology requires praxis. The primary theological question is: "In the face of this moment, this suffering, what am I called to do as a follower of Jesus, right here and now?"[61] If we act positively, we, like St. Francis, will be following in the footprints of Jesus as we find them in our world today.

Questions for Reflection and Discussion

1. Words describing the properties of God mean the same thing as when they apply to people or things (the univocity of being). How does this change your understanding of creation?
2. Scotus held that God is both "absolutely necessary" and "absolutely free." Discuss the implications of this belief for how we understand the created world.
3. How would Scotus answer: Why did God create? Why does his answer matter?
4. Recall Scotus' notion of *haeccietas* ("thisness"). Discuss your understanding of this principle and its relation to present-day issues of biodiversity.
5. What difference does Scotus' understanding of economics make in your approach to environmental issues?

Suggestions for Action

1. Explore the internet for the most recent data on biodiversity and the extinction of species.
2. Explore the meaning of "common good" in Catholic Social Teaching. See the website, Catholic in Alliance for the Common Good, https://socialjusticeresourcecenter.org/?s=common+good.
3. How might God be calling you to conversion of heart? Through self-preserving actions or actions that serve others?
4. List several plants, animals, or earth elements. Recall Scotus' point—each originates in God.
5. Consider the political and economic power relationships that govern environmental policies in your local. How can you participate to achieve environmental justice?

Sources for Further Study

Bonansea, Bernardino M. and John K. Ryan. *John Duns Scotus 1265–1965*. Paperback ed. Washington, DC: Catholic University of America Press, 2018.

Horan, Daniel P. *Postmodernity and Univocity a Critical Account of Radical Orthodoxy and John Duns Scotus*. Baltimore, MD: Project Muse, 2014.

Ingham, Mary Beth. *Scotus for Dunces: An Introduction to the Subtle Doctor*. St. Bonaventure, NY: Franciscan Institute Publications, 2003.

Ingham, Mary Beth. *Understanding John Duns Scotus: of Realty the Rarest-Veined Unraveller*. St. Bonaventure, NY: Franciscan Institute Publications, 2017.

Shannon, Thomas A. *The Ethical Theory of John Duns Scotus: A Dialogue with Medieval and Modern Thought*. Quincy, IL: Franciscan Press, 1995.

Notes

1. See my *The Franciscan View of the Human Person: Some Central Elements*, The Franciscan Heritage Series, Volume Three, CFIT/ESC-OFM (St. Bonaventure, NY: The Franciscan Institute, 2005), 45–62.
2. Séamus Mulholland, "Christ: The *Haecceitas* of God: The Spirituality of John Duns Scotus' Doctrine of *Haecceitas* and the Primacy of Christ," in *Franciscan Theology of the Environment: An Introductory Reader*, ed. Dawn M. Nothwehr (Quincy, IL: Franciscan Press, 2002), 307.
3. John T. Ford, ed., *St. Mary's Press Glossary of Theological Terms*, Essentials of Catholic Theology Series (Winona, MN: St. Mary's Press, 2006), 118, 120, 144.
4. Kenan B. Osborne, "Incarnation, Individuality, and Diversity," in *Franciscan Theology of the Environment: An Introductory Reader*, ed. Dawn M. Nothwehr (Quincy, IL: Franciscan Press, 2002), 296–7.
5. Ibid., 299.
6. Osborne, "Incarnation, Individuality, and Diversity," 298.
7. Ibid., 299.
8. L. Chancel, T. Piketty, E. Saez, G. Zucman et al., *World Inequality Report 2022* (World Inequality Lab, 2021). Creative Commons Licence 4.0., https://wir2022.wid.world/www-site/uploads/2021/12/WorldInequalityReport2022_Full_Report.pdf.
9. John Duns Scotus, *Ordinatio III*.37, trans. Allan B. Wolter, *Duns Scotus on the Will and Morality* (Washington, DC: Catholic University of America Press, 1986), 269. John Dun Scotus, *Tractatus de primo principio*, 4:15 trans. Allan B. Wolter, *A Treatise on God as First Principle* (Chicago: Franciscan Herald Press, 1981), 82. John Duns Scotus, *Ordinatio* I.44, trans. Wolter, *Will and Morality*, 255.
10. *John Duns Scotus: God and Creatures, The Quodlibital Questions*, Paperback ed., trans. Felix Alluntis and Allan B. Wolter (Washington, DC: Catholic University of America Press, 1981), "Glossary," 511.

11. Osborne, "Incarnation, Individuality, and Diversity," 301.
12. Eric Doyle, "Duns Scotus and Ecumenism," in De *Doctrina I. Duns Scoti*, Vol. III, *Acta Congressus Scotistici Internationalis Oxonii et Edimburgi*, September 11–17, 1966, *celebrati*, ed. Camille Bérubé (Roma: Cura Commissionis Scotisticae, 1968), 460.
13. Mary Beth Ingham, *Scotus for Dunces: An Introduction to the Subtle Doctor* (St. Bonaventure, NY: The Franciscan Institute, 2003), 55.
14. Kevin J. O'Brien, *An Ethics of Biodiversity: Christianity, Ecology, and the Variety of Life* (Washington, DC: Georgetown University Press, 2010).
15. Scotus' position on the Incarnation is articulated in his *Reportatio* and *Ordinatio* III.7.3. Allan B. Wolter, "John Duns Scotus on the Primacy and Personality of Christ," in *Franciscan Christology: Selected Texts, Translations and Essays*, Franciscan Sources No. 1, ed. Damian McElrath (St. Bonaventure, NY: Franciscan Institute Publications, 1980), 147–55. Antonio Aranda, "La Cuestión Teológica de la Encarnatión del Verbo: Relectura de Tres Posiciones Características," *Scripta Theologica* 25 (1993): 49–94.
16. "The Scotist Cosmic Christ," in *De Doctrina Ioannis Duns Scoti*, Vol. III, 194–8.
17. *Reportatio* I, d. 41, n.72 in John Duns Scotus, *The Examined Report of the Paris Lecture: Reportatio* I-A, ed. A. B. Wolter and O. Bychkov (St. Bonaventure, NY: Franciscan Institute, 2008) 2, 506, cited in Mary Elizabeth Ingham, "The Testimony of Two Witnesses: A Response to Ask of the Beasts," *Theological Studies* 77/2 Jun 2016: 472.
18. John Duns Scotus, *Ordinatio* III, d. 7, in *Four Questions on Mary*, 25 cited in Ingham, *Scotus for Dunces*, 77. Ingham, "The Testimony of Two Witnesses," cites Francis of Assisi, "Admonition XI," in *Francis of Assisi: Early Documents*, Volume I—The Saint, trans. and ed. Regis J. Armstrong, J. A. Wayne Hellman, and William J. Short (New York: New City Press, 1999), 133.
19. Mary Elizabeth Ingham, "Integrated Vision," in *The History of Franciscan Theology*, ed. Kenan B. Osborne (St. Bonaventure, NY: The Franciscan Institute, 1994), 222.
20. John Duns Scotus, *Ordinatio* III.7.q.3, trans. Wolter "On the Primacy," 151.
21. John Duns Scotus, *John Duns Scotus—A Treatise on God as First Principle*, Second ed., trans. Allan B. Wolter (Chicago: Franciscan Herald Press, 1966), 3.
22. Séamus Mulholland, "Christ the *Haecceitas* of God: The Spirituality of John Duns Scotus' Doctrine of *Haecceitas* and the Primacy of Christ," in *Franciscan Theology of the Environment*, 307.
23. Ibid., 309. John Duns Scotus, *Opera Omnia, Editio nova*, 26 vols., Parisiis: L. Vivès, 1895—(Farnborough, England: Gregg International Publishers, 1969). See *Ordinatio* III, d.7 (Vivès edition, XIV, 348–9, 354–5) and *Reportatio Parisiensis*, III, d. 7, q.4 (Vivès edition, XXIII, 301–4).

24. *Reportatio Parisiensis*, III, d. 7, q.4 (Vivès edition, XXIII, 310-1.
25. William Short, "Pied Beauty: Gerard Manley Hopkins and the Scotistic View of Nature," in *Franciscan Theology of the Environment,* 316. See "God's Grandeur, #8," in *Poems and Prose of Gerard Manley Hopkins*, ed. W. H. Gardner (New York: Penguin Books, 1985).
26. Short, "Pied Beauty," 317.
27. Ibid.
28. Ingham, *Scotus for Dunces,* 320-1.
29. Ibid., 319.
30. Ibid., 320.
31. Ibid.
32. *Ordinatio*, IV, d.46, q.1, n.10.
33. Ingham, *Scotus for Dunces*, at 226.
34. John Duns Scotus, *Ordinatio* II.d.6.q.2.n.8. (Vivès 12:353), trans. Wolter, *Will and Morality*, 463.
35. Ingham, *Scotus for Dunces*, 225-6.
36. Mary Elizabeth Ingham, "A Certain Affection for Justice," *The Cord* 45/3 (1995): 15.
37. Ibid. Mary Beth Ingham, "Presence, Poise, and Praxis: The Three-Fold Challenge for Reconcilers Today," *The Cord* 53/6 (2003): 303–14.
38. *Ordinatio* prol.5. q.1-2.n.262 (Vatican I 177.11-12).
39. Ingham, *Scotus for Dunces*, 94. Ingham defines will and intellect in the context of faculty psychology.
40. John Duns Scotus, *Quaestiones Metaphysicam IX,* q.15, trans. Wolter, *Will and Morality*, 145–7. See also *Ordinatio* IV.49.1.10.n.10. (Vivès 21:333b). Wolter views this position considering self-determination or rational self-direction, which ideates the will from potency to act. See Wolter, "Native Freedom of the Will Key to the Ethics of Scotus," in *The Philosophical Theology of John Duns Scotus*, ed. Marilyn McCord Adams (Ithaca: Cornell University Press, 1990), 152.
41. Ingham, *Scotus for Dunces*, 96.
42. John Duns Scotus, *Quodlibet* 18.1.n.3.18.8, trans. Alluntis/Wolter, 400.
43. John Duns Scotus, *Tractatus de primo principio*, 4:87-4:94, trans. Wolter, *First Principle*, 146–51. Also *Ordinatio* III.suppl.d.27, trans. Wolter, *Will and Morality*, 425.
44. *Acceptatio* is the acceptance of a human act by God as a meritorious act.
45. Of the two dimensions, the incommunicable (internal) dimension is seen as the logical *suppositum* which is necessary for the *ad extra* relationship. For a definition of the term, *suppositum*, see Ingham, *Scotus for Dunces*, at 230: "A general name for a *per se* being which has its ultimate actuality. In the case of a rational or intellectual nature, such a being is called a person.

This term is a translation of hypostasis, the Greek term used to refer to the persons of the Trinity." See also her example at 110.

46. In the *Lectura* discussion of *Ordinatio* I, 26 on the constitution of the divine persons, Scotus argues for some kind of constitutive cause for each person of the Trinity. By insisting on the integrity of each person of the Trinity in the absolute sense, he designates the basis upon which he can later assert that God's essence is also communion.
47. Mary Elizabeth Ingham, "John Duns Scotus: An Integrated Vision," 213. Ingham cites *Lectura* n.54.
48. Ingham, "Integrated Vision," 214. Ingham cites *Quodlibet 1*.n.3. (Alluntis 1:5-6) trans. Alluntis/Wolter, 6–7.
49. Ingham, "Integrated Vision," 217. Ingham cites *Quodlibet* 4.n.28 (Alluntis 4:61) trans. Alluntis/Wolter, 103–4.
50. Ingham, "Integrated Vision," 218.
51. *Oridinatio* III.suppl.d.37.10, trans. Wolter, *Will and Morality*, 283: "Hence it follows that if God is to be loved perfectly and orderly, then the one loving God must will that his neighbor love God; but in so willing, he is loving his neighbor."
52. *Oridinatio* IV, in *Duns Scotus' Political and Economic Philosophy: Latin Text and English Translation* with Introduction and Notes by Allan B. Wolter (St. Bonaventure, NY: The Franciscan Institute, 2001).
53. *Oridinatio* IV.1, trans. Wolter, *Duns Scotus' Political and Economic Philosophy*, 39.
54. *Oridinatio* I, trans. Wolter, *Duns Scotus' Political and Economic Philosophy*, 35.
55. *Oridinatio* IV.1, trans. Wolter, Duns Scotus' Political and Economic Philosophy, 51. See ibid., 105, ns 5 and 6. St. Francis of Assisi, *Regula Bulata* (1223), Chapters 5–6, trans. Regis J. Armstrong and Ignatius C. Brady, in *Francis and Clare: Complete Works*, The Classics in Western Spirituality (New York: Paulist Press, 1982), 140–1. Also see *Wikipedia*, s.v. "fungibility," http://en.wikipedia.org/wiki/Fungibility.
56. *Oridinatio* IV.4, trans. Wolter, *Duns Scotus' Political and Economic Philosophy*, 79–87.
57. The Pontifical Council for Justice and Peace, "Towards Reforming the International Finance and Monetary Systems in the Context of Global and Public Authority," https://www.vatican.va/roman_curia/pontifical_councils/justpeace/documents/rc_pc_justpeace_doc_20111024_nota_en.html.
58. Ibid., § 2.4.
59. Ingham, "A Certain Affection for Justice," 18.
60. Ingham, The Testimony of Two Witnesses, 473.
61. Ibid., 474.

Part IV

Ecological Vocation: What Is Ours to Do?

7

Anthropogenic Climate Change: A Leper Awaiting Our Embrace

Introduction: Embracing a Leper

In St. Francis' day, leprosy presented a public health crisis. Because leprosy was not properly understood, lepers were socially stigmatized as immoral, sanctioned, and met with hostility by anxiety-ridden citizens. Such vicious treatment denied lepers their God-given dignity (*imago Dei*). Within this environment St. Francis encountered the leper. From a deeply spiritual place, and empowered by the Spirit of God, St. Francis overcame his fears and he embraced and kissed the man.[1] Francis' gesture presented a groundbreaking spiritual and social challenge to injury against lepers. It reawakened his society to its shared humanity with Christ Incarnate and thus also a common God-given creaturehood and dignity of each member of God's creation.

Today we are called to encounter a different public health crisis, a "Climate Emergency," and to make a similar embrace. Just as lepers were denied their proper human dignity, we have objectified and brutalized people and our other-than-human fellow planetary creatures, denying their proper dignity. Just as St. Francis' divinely empowered embrace of the leper brought renewal of social regard for the dignity of lepers, we must now renew our embrace of the common nobility of all of God's creation. We must take up our unique ecological vocation to stop the ecocide, heal, and care for Earth, our common home.[2]

Christian faith compels us (all believers) to respond to today's "Climate Emergency."[3] Our conversion must be internal and spiritual shifting our dispositions and attitudes, as well as external and moral, changing our daily behaviors and practices. The case is closed—99.9 percent of the world's scientists agree the "Climate Emergency" is caused by humans.[4] We already *know* what needs to change. The question is, when will we make significant lifestyle changes for sustainable living and healing our planet? To not act is to insult God and blaspheme God's gift of creation. Denial and delay are not realistic options.

The Sixth IPCC Assessment Report

The world's climate has warmed by about one-degree Celsius since the Industrial Revolution. Fossil-fuel use is incontrovertibly changing the global climate.[5] A one-degree Celsius increase in temperature is significant. As the *Sixth Assessment Report* indicates, the changes of global warming are "unprecedented." Earth's sensitive ecosystem has already suffered devastating consequences.[6] UN Secretary-General António Guterres properly characterized the *Sixth Assessment Report* as "a code red for humanity. The alarm bells are deafening, and the evidence is irrefutable … the internationally-agreed threshold of 1.5 degrees above pre-industrial levels of global heating is 'perilously close.'"[7] Multiple century-old indicators justify this alarm.

Many hoped that the November 2021 Glasgow COP26 would respond adequately to this "Code Red."[8] However, indications signaled a less than adequate response.[9] Obstruction of the necessary thoroughgoing action was enacted by the oil and fossil-fuel lobby and is highly influential in US politics.[10] Yet positive indicators include a growing body of Catholics, spiritual persons, religious groups, and youth who are increasingly active and influential.[11] A Vatican statement noted several positive COP26 commitments but stressed that much more action is vital.[12] A substantive and growing body of influential faith-based organizations remains committed to saving God's creation.[13] At the COP26, over 100 countries signed the "Global Methane Pledge," initiated by the United States and EU to reduce global methane emissions by at least 30 percent by 2030. That bolsters the European Green Deal strategy on methane reduction.[14]

Why Christians Care, and What Must We Do?

Simply put, Christians must act out of love for the poor and for the preservation of God's planet. The COP26 presentation by Minister for Justice, Communication & Foreign Affairs, Simon Kofe of Tuvalu standing knee-deep in water inundating that country due to climate-induced sea rise, starkly illustrates realities of climate change impact on the poorest and most vulnerable of the world.[15]

People in industrialized regions have had the luxury of indifference because until now, they could "adapt" with life relatively unchanged! But now the *real impact* of *our own current* pollution is compounding *previous generation's input*. Indeed, the United States now tastes the effects of unchecked emissions. Between 1980 and 2021, 20 wildfires, 29 droughts, 152 severe storms, 57 tropical cyclones, 36 floods, 20 winter storms, and 9 billion-dollar freeze disaster events affected the United States.[16] There is likely much more to come!

Abuse of God's creation raises the specter of complex issues of morality, justice, and human rights. People forced to become refugees due to a storm, drought, flood, fire, or famine must assert "assistance to survive" as a human right. Yet, to date, the UN High Commission on Refugees does not recognize a category of "Climate Refugee." Thus, the struggle for survival can turn violent.[17] For Christians, such moral and spiritual matters are interrelated and affect our journey toward salvation (Mt. 25:3-46). But how do we bring all these issues to practical action? Let me begin with a story.

A Story

Gerry walked with a Native American friend during the buzzing lunch hour in Washington, DC. The traffic noise and the bustling crowds made it difficult to hear anything else. Amid that ruckus, Gerry's friend stopped and said, "Hey, a cricket!" "What?" said Gerry. "Yeah, a cricket," said his friend. "Here, look," and he pulled aside some nearby bushes abutting the government building. There in the shade was a cricket chirping away! "Wow," said Gerry, "How did you hear that with all this noise and traffic?" "Oh," said the Native man. "It was the way I was raised ... what I was taught to listen for. Here, I'll show you something." The Native man reached into his pocket and pulled out a handful of coins and dropped them on the sidewalk. Everyone who was rushing by stopped ... to "listen."[18]

Our listening to the drone of the dominant, economistic, Western culture has deafened us to cricket chirps—drowning out the cries of the poor and the Earth! Continuing to attend to the same old things, in the same old ways, we will never overcome our "Climate Emergency!" We must learn to value and attend to life differently.[19]

Ecological Conversion: From Impunity to Justice

In 1971, Pope Paul VI defined destroying the Earth's natural environment and ecosystems as "immoral."[20] In his 1972 address in Stockholm, he asserted, "[M]an and his environment are more inseparable than ever." He condemned "the disorderly exploitation of the physical reserves of the planet" and called for "clear-sightedness and courage" when tackling environmental problems that have intergenerational impact.[21] Thereafter, ecology, environmental degradation, and climate change increasingly populated the Church's Social Teachings.[22]

The US Bishops' *Global Climate Change* (2001) insisted on immediate and *significant* life changes toward halting global warming![23] March 10, 2008, Archbishop Girotti of the Vatican Office of the Apostolic Penitentiary listed "ecological" offences, among the "New Forms of Social Sin."[24] In 2009 St. John Paul II called for "ecological conversion," Christian simplicity—a relational vision and way of living.[25] Today, the Vatican is exemplary as the only nearly "carbon neutral" state on the planet![26]

Laudato Si'—On Care for Our Common Home (2015)

Pope Francis' landmark encyclical, *Laudato Si'* Chapter One, assessed climate change and global warming and its numerous effects. Citing Ecumenical Patriarch Bartholomew, Francis asserts that "to commit a crime against the natural world is a sin against ourselves and a sin against God."[27] The climate is a common good that belongs to all and is meant for all, and thus the effects of climate change will harm every creature.[28] The poor and those directly dependent on the natural world for a living, unable to access mitigation of climate change, are most profoundly harmed.[29] Deplorably, "those who possess more resources and economic or political power seem mostly to be concerned with masking the problems or concealing their symptoms, simply making efforts to reduce some of the negative impacts of climate change."[30] Citing the Catholic Bishops of the United States and Bolivia, the pope asserted the "differentiated responsibilities" of more powerful, wealthy, and technologically developed nations to share the wealth and knowledge to empower and provide for the needs of lesser endowed peoples.[31] The heaviest moral responsibility for resolving climate change lies on the shoulders of those more powerful countries who have polluted and benefitted most from technologies, social, economic, and political practices.[32]

Pope Francis is not naive about the heavy demands and huge technological, social, political, economic, and spiritual changes that saving the planet will entail, but the costs of this will be low, compared to the devastation of climate change. "In any event, these are primarily ethical decisions, rooted in solidarity between all peoples."[33] Halting climate change and reversing its harms is a multigenerational task that requires sustained personal action and public pressure on civic institutions, political authorities, governments, and more.[34] Beyond changing knowledge and beliefs, it is yet another thing to alter our lifestyle and act morally.

In Chapter Six of *Laudato Si'* Pope Francis offers key ideas for education and spiritual development for our ecological vocation. We must first understand the psychosocial aspects driving our responses concerning climate change and ecocide. Our moral disposition, attitude, and concrete daily activities *do matter*! First, we must admit our limitations and that—wittingly or not—we are complicit in ecological destruction, and resolve to change. To this we now turn.

Why Do We Resist Dealing with Global Warning and Climate Change?

Human-Induced Global Warming: From Denial to Ethical Engagement

Climate change denial takes various forms when people perceive it as a serious threat to the status quo and their way of life.[35] In April of 2009, G-20 leaders did not shift to a sustainable economic system. They simply reconfigured the same old ecologically destructive global economic methods![36] This typical *illusionary frame of mind* fails to confront the size, scale, and complexity of global warming. Framing global warming in singularly scientific terms, requiring only technological fixes, failed because deeper human psychosocial, spiritual, and ethical issues were not addressed.[37]

Personal Psychosocial Dynamics of Denial

Humans have the capacity for objective (unbiased) reasoning, but subjective reasoning arises from stronger emotions and instincts. The prioritization and decision-making concerning weighty matters outlining our "Climate Emergency" require a level of self-discipline and all-encompassing lifestyle changes. Those entail hard work toward the hereto for unpresented ends. Every known dimension of planetary life is now threatened. These conditions are a classical setup for *motivated reasoning* and *denial*.

In *motivated reasoning*, people direct their thinking to accommodate their comfort level, regardless of objective reality. Having evolved in small groups requiring cooperation and persuasion for survival, people still respond automatically and defensively to ideas that threaten their communal ideological worldview. They exercise *confirmation bias*—they rationalize and select evidence—crediting experts they agree with and eliminating outright those they disagree with.[38] They think in ways that suit their group and comfort level, but which may not accurately fit objective reality.

When people *deny* anything, they attempt to protect themselves from something. *Denial* is a coping mechanism that allows a person time to adjust to destressing situations. But concerning global warming, any delay in deciding and acting is counterproductive. Delays make mitigation more difficult and complex. Factors that determine one's denial capacity are primarily religious, political, ethnic identity, and beliefs. Sustaining one's decisions based *only* on those factors, not seriously considering objective factors, one is engaging in *motivated reasoning*.[39]

Sadness and helplessness often accompany *Denial*. Objectively, what is to be feared is *inaction* concerning elimination of GHG emissions. Positive actions, currently well underway toward a just, inclusive, climate-sustainable economy, offer millions of safe well-paying sustainable jobs.[40]

Psychological and Cognitive Limits

Human sensate capacities are not designed to perceive long-term temperature rise that occurs in small increments, only quantifiable in tenths of degrees per decade, but highly significant. Thus, anyone who accepts that empirically observed scientific evidence of Earth's incremental temperature changes is primarily predisposed to overall trust of empirical science. With little climate and/or weather literacy concerning their region, people often misunderstand extreme short-term changes as "proof" for or against anthropogenic global warming. Many struggle to grasp that the Earth's atmosphere is not simply empty space into which any toxic emissions can randomly be pumped. It is a thin, fragile, multilayered system that changes in composition and dynamics over planetary history. There is only one atmosphere for the entire planet! Whatever is forced into *the atmosphere* by humans affects *everything on* Earth. Unequivocally, our *denial and resistance* to human-caused global warming *itself* bring about a self-fulfilling prophecy. Some imagine that the necessary scale of change is regression to "the lifestyle of the caveman." Such dread results in inaction, while GHGs emissions grow and heating increases. This lack of personal accountability has resulted in a "tragedy of the commons" scenario.[41]

Denial Writ Large and Inaction by Nation-States

Particularly egregious is denial of global warming by the more industrialized nations (e.g., the United States) and/or the politicized refusal to take responsibility for the multiple, ecocidal activities since the 1850s, that produced ever-increasing destruction of people and ecosystems in lesser industrialized nations (global south).[42] A clear appalling record exposes ecological devastation that disproportionately still ravages the poorest, women, and people of color.[43]

Many still engage in serious "double-think syndrome." They partake in activities that devour fossil fuels—the most egregious sources of CO_2 emissions.[44] "Double-thinkers" support candidates who publicly proclaim their approval of stringent CO_2 emissions reduction targets but enact no means to enforce them! When "reduction efforts" fail, they revert to the political adage "Nobody ever rioted for the cause of austerity!"[45] Others succor their conscience by buying carbon off-sets before flying, purchasing green products, or supporting carbon trading. But, as Jess Worth put it, "It's like finding out that you've got cancer, but then delaying going to the doctor for treatment for a few months because you want to paint your house!"[46]

Sociopolitical and Economic Dynamics of Denial

Focusing on applied scientific and technological GHG reduction, urgency requires us to wrestle simultaneously with *ethical and spiritual issues* of climate injustice and ecocide. We must go beyond surface behaviors to *moral transformation.* It demands facing the terrific and all-encompassing nature of the problem and drawing deeply from our richest religious and spiritual treasures, seeking fortitude to change.

The Status Quo: Human Limitations and Education for Problem Solving

For decades many presumed the cure for anthropogenic climate change was merely "education." But environmentally literate people do not necessarily follow the science or change behaviors sufficiently. This approach defined the problem too simplistically.[47]

Authentic "environmental literacy [is] the acquisition of information about the environment [that] rests on a political substrate, as well as critical social practices, linked to the concept of citizenship."[48] Thus, the content of environmental education needs to include mentoring in spiritual practices that equip people to restore their relationships with the web of life and revolutionizing social, political, and economic structures that have ignored the totality of human ecological interdependence. Engaging ethics, spiritual, and religious content is necessary to support people in facing the new and challenging phenomena in a world of erratic, unfamiliar—but very real—change.[49]

The Role of Media

Early media messages offered in only sound bites could not adequately explain climate change complexities. Even today, despite warnings by Pope Francis or the UN Secretary General of a "Climate Emergency," most climate facts are left untold by politicians seeking approval or by commercialized news outlets dependent upon corporate revenue.

Recently, people in industrialized nations began to personally experience more numerous vicious, costly, unprecedented weather events attributed to the warming climate. Then media outlets were motivated to provide more adequate and forthright reporting about causes of climate extremes. The climate *is indeed* changing and often earlier than scientific models predicted! Thus, in February 2022 the Associated Press organized a sweeping climate initiative, employing a global network of twenty for climate coverage in areas such as food, agriculture, migration, housing and urban planning, disaster response, the economy, and culture.[50] Even on Earth Day, April 22, 2022, Twitter© announced it would ban advertisements that deny climate crisis data.

Individualism, Consumerism, and the "Technocratic Paradigm"

Certainly, each person has a role to play and small changes in daily living can contribute, though minimally, to the bigger project of halting the uptick in global warming. Recycling, buying electric cars, or halogens, light-emitting diodes (LEDs), or compact fluorescent lamps (CFLs) do help. But unless the dangerous "consumer mentality" is changed, the *minimal level of impact* is lost. People easily "backslide" into old ways. The *net cost* to Earth's climate *increases*!

Pope Francis warns, we must set aside "consumerism and the technocratic paradigm" that got us into the "Climate Emergency" in the first place![51] A consumer mentality presumes we can buy enough technological fixes to save the planet. But the dominant economic model of development is *still*, ultimately sustained by *fossil-fuel consumption*. Thus, consumptive lifestyles continue to unjustly suck life and sustenance from our neighbors across the globe. The ecological reality is that carbon emissions from coal-burning power plants in Chicago contribute to droughts and food insecurity in sub-Saharan Africa.

Difficulties Climate Complexity Poses

Most challenging for ordinary people to comprehend is the reality that human-caused global warming takes place as the result of an *aggregate effect*. It is difficult to predict the effect of any *one* human action *by itself*, beyond the immediate moment. For many this is discouraging and confusing. However, there is a vast scientific certainty that the cumulative effect of emissions of GHGs from billions of people across the globe and over the centuries have altered (and are still substantially altering) Earth's climate system.

Further, climate change is *differentiated in time and space*. If we consider the natural evolution of climate, compared to the human-induced changes in the atmosphere, then over the last decades, changes have been extremely rapid—post 1880's Industrial Revolution and post-Second World War industrial expansion and globalization. Yet, if we look *only* at the human scale, from the 1850s to the present, the change was rather slow. This is because there is a *lag time* between when GHG emissions occur and their *differentiated or cumulative effect* of changing the surface air temperature and causing global warming.[52] Thus, it is hard for people to imagine that the emissions from "Coal-Fired Power Plant A" are responsible for a rise in the surface air temperature on the other side of the globe or that even if "Plant A" were shut down today, its past emissions would continue to contribute to global warming for years.

Also, global warming effects of GHG emissions do not take place in linear time. Rather, crucial changes take place as "*threshold effects.*" This means that the effects of day-to-day progressive additions of GHGs into the atmosphere are often barely perceivable. Yet any one addition of more GHG may suddenly cause a sharp shift in the established equilibrium of the atmosphere, causing air surface temperature warming across the globe. These patterns do not grab headlines, yet they are vitally important. The consequences of not paying attention are deadly. Like a frog, basking in a pot of water that sits on a fire, that fails to detect the gradual increases in temperature until the water boils, we humans ignore these important realities to our peril!

Pope Francis insists: "Everything is connected!"[53] People fail to grasp that interrelatedness of global air, water, and soil systems or the basic chemistry of GHGs. Through obliviousness or in denial, they fail to act to reduce GHS emissions, thus narrowing the possibility of overcoming the devastation of the biophysical environment and human communities. Further, what science documents as overall trends in the totality of climatic systems does not always manifest that way in the *local scene*. For example, global warming has caused climate changes that effectively reduced the total potable water available on the planet—especially in sub-Saharan Africa. However, people who experience flooding in Chicago will find that reality is difficult to believe!

Early use of the technical scientific term "uncertainty" confused unschooled persons and remains so today. That term was used in scientific reports that were based primarily on models and projections. Scientists use "uncertainty" as a technical term that is distinct from the word "risk." While "risk" involves *what is **known**, or a reliably estimable probability;* "uncertainty" arises *when such probabilities are not available, **unknown**.* Thus, to say that there was scientific "uncertainty" surrounding global warming was to simply claim that we did not know and could not reliably estimate the probability that climate change would occur, nor its extent, if it did occur. But times have changed, and so has scientific certainty! It is highly significant that, already in their 2001 *Scientific Assessment*, the data scientists offered the world was given in terms, "very likely," that meant a *probability of 90–99 percent!*[54] With greater accuracy in their 2022 *AR Six Report*, the Intergovernmental Panel on Climate Change (IPCC) *did assign probabilities* to its main climate predictions, making the situation one of *risk*, rather than *uncertainty*.[55] Those probabilities are of considerable magnitude. Current data is from actual empirical measurements from the field, gathered from thousands of sites across the globe![56] We fly planes, drive cars, or gamble with less "certainty"!

Moral Issues—Navigating the Terrain

Pope Francis noted there are "differentiated responsibilities" for achieving climate justice.[57] The same high GHG-emitting nations consumed the highest levels of fossil fuel. Historically, the emissions produced by lesser industrialized nations were largely for industrial processes benefiting the "first world." Today, lesser industrialized nations are trying to "catch up" to current technological standards. For the sake of *all* of us, they must choose sustainable technologies. The World Economic Forum and the World Bank are assisting this effort to enable transition to sustainable sources.[58] But far more is needed.

Many smaller national economies remain dependent upon the extraction and export of natural resources; most of these strategies severely affect ecological balance, e.g., forestry, mining, or mono-crop agriculture. In their poverty, these nations remain ill equipped to mitigate negative climate impacts on general safety, water supplies, new diseases, economic breakdown, or food security.

"Out of Sight and Out of Mind"

Most people do not know the energy sources powering their daily lives. They rarely care that the coal firing the local power plant comes from blown-up mountaintops of Appalachia, or that constructing an oil pipeline requires ripping through thousands of acres of carbon-absorbing ancient boreal forest in Canada or polluting and violating treaty rights to indigenous tribal homelands.[59] Energy prices never reflect the real extraction costs and use in terms of environmental or societal damage to local or regional ecosystems. Few US residents know that federal subsidies are paid to the petroleum industry.[60] What a difference it could make if ordinary people were enabled to connect the real environmental costs that accrue from their personal way of life! We ignore these practical considerations to our peril.[61]

Today world leaders *know* that any emission of GHGs from even one source brings global warming to all. Drastic reduction of GHGs requires some sacrifices from all nations (though justice demands differentiated responsibilities). Considering global warming in light of psychologist Abraham Maslow's hierarchy of needs, that issue is foundational to meeting our most important survival needs.[62] If we allow unchecked emitting GHGs, we will not have access essentials for human life at the base of Maslow's hierarchy. The slow progress of COP26 indicates this is a moral challenge of the highest order that remains for the foreseeable future.

Embracing True Sustainability

From Intoxication to Sustainability

In 1987 the UN Brundtland Commission published *Our Common Future*.[63] Brundtland defined sustainable as "development that meets the needs of the present without compromising the ability of future generations to meet their needs."[64] They presumed that "sustainable development" meant raising productivity, accumulation of goods, and technological innovations.[65] But such thinking overlooked key sources of poverty—exploitation of workers and pillaging of nature. Brundtland's notion of "sustainable development" was economic growth for its own sake, and the primary goal was profit-making. Today we reap the exploitative results.

By contrast, biology and ecology define "sustainability" as "the trend of ecosystems toward equilibrium, sustained in the web of interdependencies and complementarities flourishing in ecosystems."[66] Genuine "sustainability" requires social and economic structures that support "*social justice*—the right relationship between persons, roles, and institutions"—and "*ecological justice*, the right relationship with nature, sufficient access to resources, and the assurance of quality of life."[67] St. Francis promoted this kind of sustainability. Reawakening his society's embrace of the inviolable dignity of lepers and all creation through their relationship in the incarnate Christ, he showed us how dignified relationships of care and concern create true wealth.

A renewed vision of community is essential for interdependent sustainability.[68] In *Laudato Si'*, Chapter Two, "The Gospel of Creation," Pope Francis elaborates such a vision. He cites the Bible, Early Christian writers, the *Catholic Catechism*, Catholic Social Teaching, and the witness of St. Francis and St. Bonaventure.[69] The rich meaning of the Greek root *oikos* links notions of economy, ecology, and ecumenicity to shape the habitability of the Earth which is a central reality, deep in Christian theology. Economy is the ordering of the household for the sustenance of its members. The contrast between this Christian understanding of sustainability and that of the Brundtland Commission is remarkable.

Brundtland exemplifies how deeply a consumer mentality had permeated the highly industrialized world. Sue McGregor explained this reality well: "People behave as they do in a consumer society because they are so indoctrinated into the logic of the market that they cannot 'see' anything wrong with what they are doing … they actually contribute to their own oppression. … Consumerism is a way to self-development, self-realization, and self-fulfillment. In a consumer society, identity is tied to what she or he consumes."[70] Pope Francis warns: "The environment is one of those goods that cannot be adequately safeguarded or promoted by market forces."[71]

Quantum physicist David Bohm compared uncritical adherence to growth and treating everything other than human as mere "natural resources" or "natural capital" to a man who lost the key to his house: "He was found to be looking under the light. He looked and looked, and he couldn't find it. Finally, someone asked where he had lost the key. Pointing to another area of his yard, he said, 'Over there.' Asked why he had not looked 'over there,' the man responded, 'Well, it's dark over there, but there's light here for me to look.'"[72]

Quantum theologian Diarmuid O'Murchu speaks of "cultural intoxication," the Western world's addiction to material acquisition that drowns out an alienation from the life and death realities of the world, thus maintaining the illusion of power and control.[73] But the raw truth is that this addiction simply signals a desperation and deep denial of its opposite.

The Way Out Is the Way Through

Joanna Macy asserts that many in the industrialized West live in a state of "apathy."[74] Westerners facing global warming data become paralyzed, move to denial, and inaction.[75] Macy explains, the West has lost many of the values, attitudes, and skills required to resolve global warming. People repress the overwhelming pain of ecocide because culturally expressing pain is thought dysfunctional! They ignore the complexities. On the one hand, Westerners fear human intellectual inadequacy for developing solutions to the problem. On the other, they are overcome with guilt, knowing that they live in opulence, disproportionately consuming the world's goods—so they "leave it to the experts!"

The resolution of this paralysis is to realize that the guilt and pain are not only real but also healthy! Awareness of our "Climate Emergency" allows space for hope engendering action against the pain. People can choose to live within limits, break their isolation, and begin the healing, restoration, and renewal for themselves and the Earth. This awakening provides opportunities for virtuous living—humility, poverty, obedience, and love—a life of Christian simplicity.

Toward Christian Simplicity: *Laudato Si'* and Social Sciences

In Chapter Six, of *Laudato Si'*, Pope Francis called forth our ecological vocation, beginning with an "ecological conversion" a realignment of our lifestyles, attitudes, convictions, and actions.[76] Failure to change our individual and communal attitudes and lifestyles will render solutions to our global ecological crisis impossible.

Pope Francis called Catholics, Christians, and believers in God to rid themselves of "a whirlwind of needless buying and spending."[77] He challenged everyone to a lifestyle of greater sobriety, less obsessiveness, more moderation and inner peace, and ultimately greater fulfillment.[78] Pope Francis suggests "less is more" is a biblical mantra.[79]

The overall health and well-being of the planet's natural and human-built environments require fulfilling our pleasures by ecofriendly means. Every economic choice is a moral choice affecting creation and the dignity of workers and local cultures.[80] Those awarenesses and the small, daily gestures that flow from them create the desirable transformative "culture of care."[81]

For Catholics, active daily practices of faith open a Christian ecologically conscious spirituality. The Eucharist, other Sacraments, and Sabbath observance shape our awareness of God visible through the created world. These provide times of rest, celebration, and renewal of relationships with our neighbor, Creation, and God. Creation and the Scriptures reveal God to us and unite us in love. Jesus, the Incarnate One through whom creation came to be (Jn 1:1-18), will provide the strength and light needed to find our way and "impel us to find new ways forward."[82]

Environmental Education

Seasoned environmental educator David Selby modeled "education for contraction," a systematic and organic way of transforming human living to less exploitative earth-sustaining ways.[83] Ecological awareness, frugal consumption, and personal spiritual growth are essential to sustaining life. Duane Elgin stressed that life needs to focus on achieving a balance of the material with the spiritual.[84] This requires conservation, need-limiting frugality, and living life in cooperation with others. Personal identity must flow from our various relationships, including earth elements. Though unique, ultimately each person is inseparable from the whole of humanity and the cosmos. The cosmos must be seen as a precious living organism with its own integrity. Personal behaviors need to include only sufficient self-sustaining activity to remain healthy, while thriving in connected communities.

This confirms what St Francis knew well, namely, we live in an interdependent, connected world and that people need to care for it in ways respectful of interrelationships between and among all things. St. Francis, the Patron of Ecologists, stands as the supreme example of Christian simplicity.

From the Writings of St. Francis

The Testament (1226), 1–3[85]

The Lord gave me, Brother Francis, thus to begin doing penance in this way: for when I was in sin, it seemed too bitter for me to see lepers. And the Lord Himself led me among them and I showed mercy to them. And when I left them, what had seemed bitter to me was turned to sweetness of soul and body.

Reflection and Application

Embracing the Leper was life-changing for St. Francis and ultimately for his society. In a vitally healthy way, that Spirit-led encounter deepened his awareness of the true source of human dignity and wealth, namely the mercy of God and the healing such love of God and neighbors—human and otherkind—can bring into the world. St. Francis cared deeply for creation because he saw in each creature the one common Source of Life.

We are called to a similar kind of conversion. We must admit that our drive to material wealth continues to inflict disproportionate suffering on people and the planet. The "American Dream" often becomes the "Global Nightmare" as we consume fossil fuels in our cars, homes, industries, and rape ecosystems destroying their capacity to function properly. Our GHGs cause destruction and death far from our shores. Denying our complicity can drive us into even deeper delusional negation of our responsibility. *Now is the time* to let go of our false securities and allow God's mercy to heal us! Quantum theologian O'Murchu says it well: "We are compelled to assert what seems initially to be an outrageous claim: a radically new future demands the destruction and death of the old reality. It is from dying seeds that new life sprouts forth. Destruction becomes a precondition for resurrection: denigration undergirds regeneration."[86]

Confronting Spiritual Malaise

For decades, scientists and theologians have identified unfettered materialism and consumerism as rooted in deep spiritual malaise.[87] Conveniences, unspeakable variety, and abundance overshadow, blind, satiate, and pacify people against the deeper longings of the human spirit. In our self-inflicted ignorance, we nonsensically recycle ourselves through denial and consumption, aggravating and threatening everything—especially the poor. We need a new moral and spiritual formation on limits, accepting death as part of life and of the common good.

Moral Formation and Death Acceptance: Francis of Assisi as Model

As Pope Francis asserted, St. Francis of Assisi, the Patron Saint of Ecology, is a model of conversion worthy of our attention.[88] St. Francis, like us, often wrestled with his inner "angels and demons." He had moments of doubt, being overwhelmed and discouraged *(Pathos)*. Yet Francis modeled the true dynamic of life—"desire" or *Eros*. *Eros* is the dynamic force of life within us that calls out to life and invites us to live forever. This is the drive to totality. Brazilian theologian Leonardo Boff tells us: "By their very nature, *Eros* and *Pathos*—because they constitute the basic energy of human life—expand in all directions. Because of this, we must always recognize that, as a force, they lend themselves as much to constructive, as well as to destructive purposes."[89] We can see this operative in our "Climate Emergency."

Fortunately, the human capacity for reasoning and meaning-making *(Logos)* allows us to direct our God-given energies toward the good. For St. Francis, we see this *(Logos)* in action in his gentleness, compassion, and care for all of creation that characterized his holiness. Francis embraced his demons, and thus, with God's grace, the negativity in his life was also his source of great joy. As Boff puts it, "accepted negativity loses its virulence and behaves like a house pet."[90]

Deep Joy and the Mercy of God

Today Western industrialized culture has lost a genuine quality of joy. In our misguided spiritual striving, we try to "create" our security, happiness, and pleasure consuming ever more "stuff," which drives more pollution. Yet just as reading the black text on a white page would be impossible without the black/white contrast, so too genuine joy is often most clearly understood after knowing its opposite—sadness, grief, sorrow, and gloom. St. Francis allowed himself to know and experience such things. He chose to confront, embrace, and integrate negative experiences as part of life. Like Jesus, Francis took his hard, overwhelming, or painful experiences to God in prayer and to his brothers in community. He spent time reflecting on what he might learn from the limits he faced. Indeed, the key to St. Francis' joy was his profound experience of the mercy of God.[91] And in his suffering and death, when his ultimate limits were reached, St. Francis surrounded himself with the love and compassionate care of his brothers and sisters.[92]

If we are to reach human maturity, each of us needs to accept the reality of certain limits beyond our control in our human existence: suffering, misunderstanding, and absurdity that is inherent in human life. There are definite limits to our drive to totality (*Eros*). Daily we are confronted with "small deaths"—frustrated desire, the need to deny ourselves something; the obligation to accept something else; or we face a situation we must overcome. Yet such limits allow us opportunities to grow by experiencing the joy of generosity and sharing for the sake of others and the common good.

"A sign of human and religious maturity is, to integrate the trauma of death in the context of life. Death is dethroned from its status as lord of life and ultimate reality. *Eros* triumphs over *Thanatos*, and desire wins the game. But there is a price to pay for this immortality: the acceptance of death, the frustrating of empirical and superficial desire that demands eternal life, is the condition by which, desire achieves its truth of living forever, in absolute triumph."[93] We find this process of acceptance of death in a marvelous manner in the life of St. Francis. Two dimensions illuminate St. Francis' reconciliation with death: (1) acceptance of death as part of life and (2) his identification with the Source of Life.

True Freedom—Acceptance of Death as Part of Life

When we observe creation from an evolutionary perspective, we see that the structure of God's creation thrives amid cycles of life, death, and rebirth.[94] Though we rarely allow ourselves to think this thought, from the moment we are born, we begin to die! Contrary to popular understanding, mortality did not arise with sin as punishment.[95] As Boff rightly notes, from a Christian viewpoint, within the mortality of life, humans walk toward eternal life. What sin introduced to humankind was "the closing off of understanding, shuttering off a vision of mortal life, making life and death enemies."[96] Thus, death became the negation of life. Humanity clung to "life," so it could escape death. Frequently, fear of death blossoms and desperation rises at the first hint of death's proximity. Key to dealing with death acceptance is how we deal with its signs—e.g., limitations, illness, ignorance, corporal or spiritual weakness, or loss of power, prestige, and status.

Identification with the Source of Life

St. Francis' genuine joy developed over the course of his lifetime. His joy had a deep source. His link with life, nature, and all people was so radical that it reached the Source of what gives life to all, God who is loving, just, and merciful. Gabriel Marcel characterized such a relationship thus: "If you love me, I know it, I will never die."[97] Can Christians come to such a place on our spiritual journey that we can genuinely entrust our lives to our loving, merciful God in this way? Did Christ not promise us the constant sustaining presence of the life-giving and Communion-building Holy Spirit? How simple life could be if our focus moved from our own self-preservation to care for the planet and the common good of *all* our sisters and brothers? Those who come to integrate death with life in this way certainly achieve fulfillment in the Reign of God. Nothing can threaten them anymore because they have no enemies. Our true joy is in sustaining loving relationships with ourselves, God, all neighbors, and the cosmos.

In his *Canticle of the Creatures*, Francis names Death, "Sister"—a fellow creature, of the life-giving female gender. She is the necessary *transitus* toward a new and definitive birth. A shift to this stance of accepting death as part of life was a profound conversion for Francis, and can be ours, as well. We are called to a similar conversion. Such change can be painful—as is all birth—but it makes possible a new advent with life—now with God in a different way.

Called to Be and to Do New Things

The primary causes of anthropogenic climate change are the predatory technocratic paradigm and consumerism. The 2015 promulgation of *Laudato Si'—On Care for Our Common Home* revived work to care for the Earth at all levels of Catholic Church life. Two outstanding efforts are *Journeying towards Care for Our Common Home—Five Years after Laudato Si'*, and work of the Economy of Francesco, begun in 2020.[98]

Journeying towards Care for Our Common Home (*JCTOCH*), by the Interdicasterial Working Group of the Holy See on Integral Ecology, is intended to promote dissemination, detailed study, and the implementation of *Laudato Si'*. The 227-page volume presents reflections on some operational proposals of the encyclical through an action-oriented text addressed to the local Churches, their communities, political leaders, and all people of good will. Its primary focus is described in *LS* §16.[99] *JCTOCH* has two chapters addressed to the world and global Church: *Chapter I, Education and Ecological Conversion* and *Chapter II, Integral Ecology and Integral Human Development*.

A social encyclical, *LS* requires action, based on conscientious reflection on its content, along with "divine revelation, natural law, and Christian theological anthropology, grounded in the dignity of the person as an intelligent being endowed with free will, and as the subject of rights and obligations, called to self-mastery and the responsible exercise of our primacy over other creatures."[100] *JCTOCH* supports both dimensions.

"The Economy of Francesco" was a global virtual gathering of over 2,000 young entrepreneurs (under 35) and laureate-level economists, environmental activists, international development experts, liberation theologians, and Vatican officials. Salesian Sr. Alessandra Smerilli, an economist on the Pontifical Faculty of Educational Sciences, and expert in behavioral economics, who served in several advisory roles for the pope, led the event.

Invited by Pope Francis, in May 2019, the event's ultimate end was to formulate a new economic vision, rooted in integral ecology, that deemphasizes growth and profit and prioritizes justice, equality, and caring for the poor and the earth. The task is to continue to explore the practical implementation of the heterogeneous notion of "ecological economics" described in *Laudato Si'*, especially in §s 140–1, 143, 147, and 156.[101]

November 19–21, 2020, virtual sessions were hosted from the Basilica of St. Francis in Assisi, Italy. St. Francis rejected a life of wealth to become "*il poverello*" and the fifteenth-century Franciscan Friars' *montes pietatis* established small lending institutions like modern micro credit banks, offering low-interest loans to the poorest when usury was rife.

Prior to November, participants met in thirty preparatory conferences in twelve thematic villages, each focused on specific aspects, e.g., work and care; finance and humanity; agriculture and justice; energy and poverty; policies and happiness; and women for economy. The November event brought participants from 120 nations together in 4-hour sessions each day for presentations and mentoring by a "Who's Who" roster of experts.

Upon the event's conclusion participants issued a "prophetic" statement that outlined twelve points of action to guide a reanimation of the global economy.[102] The twelve points mirror the twelve thematic village hubs that identified key topics. The work has been sustained, and the movement continues to develop, including with annual global conferences in 2021 and 2022.[103]

Now, dear reader, what is yours to do?

Questions for Reflection and Discussion

1 Calculate your carbon footprint at the US Environmental Protection Agency website: https://www3.epa.gov/carbon-footprint-calculator/.
2 How does your carbon footprint fit with the "footprints of Jesus" and his care for the poor and the marginalized?
3 What other religious social teaching documents concerning the current "Climate Emergency" do you know of?
4 What does it mean to be prudent? How can you become more prudent in consuming less?[104]
5 What biblical texts, stories of saints, or heroes/heroines of faith can help you confront the "small deaths" that can free you to accept God's mercy and a life of Christian simplicity?

Suggestions for Action

1. Review the "6 Interactive Tools to Better Understand the Climate Crisis," https://www.climaterealityproject.org/blog/6-interactive-tools-better-understand-climate-crisis.
2. Insulate your home and be thrifty with heating and cooling.
3. Learn about the disruption of Earth's climatic systems and how that affects your region of the world. See US Environmental Protection Agency: https://www.epa.gov/climate-change.
4. Lean how to communicate about climate: https://catholicclimatecovenant.org/resource/communicating-climate-change-people-faith.
5. Join the Catholic Climate Covenant at http://catholicclimatecovenant.org.

Sources for Further Study

Delio, Ilia, Keith Douglas Warner, and Pamela Wood. *Care for Creation: A Franciscan Spirituality of the Earth*. Cincinnati, OH: St. Anthony Messenger Press, 2008.

Miller, Vincent J., ed. *The Theological and Ecological Vision of Laudato Si'—Everything Is Connected*. New York: Bloomsbury T&T Clark, 2017.

O'Hara, Dennis, Matthew Eaton, and Michael T. Ross, eds. *Integral Ecology for a More Sustainable World: Dialogues with Laudato Si'*. Lanham: Lexington Books, 2020.

Schaefer, Jame, ed. *Confronting the Climate Crisis: Catholic Theological Perspectives*. Milwaukee, WI: Marquette University Press, 2011.

Schreiter, Robert J., ed. *Plural Spiritualities—North American Experiences*. Cultural Heritage and Contemporary Change Series VIII. Christian Philosophical Studies, Vol. 14. Washington, DC: The Council for Research in Values and Philosophy, 2015.

Notes

1. "The Remembrance of the Desire of the Soul," chapter V, FA:ED, Volume II—*The Founder*, 248–9.
2. *Laudato Si'—On Care for Our Common Home, Chapters 1 and 2,* https://www.vatican.va/content/francesco/en/encyclicals/documents/papa-francesco_20150524_enciclica-laudato-si.html. NASA, Global Climate

Change: Vital Signs of the Planet, "What Is the Greenhouse Effect?" https://climate.nasa.gov/faq/19/what-is-the-greenhouse-effect/.
3. UNEP and Parliament of the World's Religions, *Faith for Earth: A Call for Action* (Nairobi: United Nations Environment Programme, 2020). *LS*, Chapters 1 and 2.
4. US EPA, Climate Change Science, "Basics of Climate Change," https://www.epa.gov/climatechange-science/basics-climate-change. "NASA—What's the Difference between Weather and Climate?" February 1, 2005, https://www.nasa.gov/mission_pages/noaa-n/climate/climate_weather.html. Mark Lynas, Benjamin Z. Houlton, Simon Perry, and Mark Lynas, "Greater Than 99% Consensus on Human Caused Climate Change in the Peer-Reviewed Scientific Literature," in *Environmental Research Letters*, Vol. 16, Number 114005, IOP Publishing Ltd., October 19, 2021, https://iopscience.iop.org/article/10.1088/1748-9326/ac2966 Hiroko Tabuchi, "How One Firm Drove Influence Campaigns Nationwide for Big Oil," November 11, 2020, https://www.nytimes.com/2020/11/11/climate/fti-consulting.html?campaign_id=54&emc=edit_clim_20201118&instance_id=24224&nl=climate-fwd%3A&regi_id=60287200&segment_id=44826&te=1&user_id=410753199cfc813e7dfcccdbf42c624e.
5. IPCC is the Nobel Prize-winning body of the United Nations that synthesizes peer-reviewed research. IPCC, *AR6 Climate Change 2021*: The Physical Science Basis—Summary for Policymakers, 2021, A.1.8, https://www.ipcc.ch/report/ar6/wg1/downloads/report/IPCC_AR6_WGI_SPM_final.pdf.
6. IPCC, *AR6 Climate Change 2021*, A.2.
7. António Guterres, "IPCC Report: 'Code Red' for Human Driven Global Heating, Warns UN Chief," https://news.un.org/en/story/2021/08/1097362.
8. GE.22-03273(E) Conference of the Parties, Report of the Conference of the Parties on its twenty-sixth session, held in Glasgow from October 31 to November 13, 2021, https://unfccc.int/sites/default/files/resource/cp2021_12_add1E.pdf.
9. Inés San Martín, "Outcome of COP26 'Mostly Negative' Says Catholic Climate Activist," *The Tablet,* https://thetablet.org/negative-outcome-cop26-catholic-climate-argentine-tomas-insua/#.
10. Ibid.
11. Tara C. Trapan, "Religious Activity around COP26," November 3, 2021, Yale Forum on Religion and Ecology, https://fore.yale.edu/blogs/entry/1635975885. "US Catholics Petition Biden Administration and Congress for Climate Action," https://catholicclimatecovenant.org/news/us-catholics-petition-biden-administration-and-congress-climate-action. "World Religious Leaders and Scientists Make pre-COP26 Appeal," October 5, 2022, External Statement, https://unfccc.int/news/world-religious-leaders-and-scientists-make-pre-cop26-appeal.

12. *Holy See Statement on COP26*, November 11, 2021, https://press.vatican.va/content/salastampa/en/bollettino/pubblico/2021/11/11/211111e.html.
13. Barbara Fraser, "EarthBeat Weekly: COP26 Results Are Still Too Little, Though Perhaps Not Too Late," November 12, 2021, https://www.ncronline.org/news/earthbeat/earthbeat-weekly-cop26-results-are-still-too-little-though-perhaps-not-too-late.
14. Institute for Advanced Sustainability Studies e.V. (IASS). "Policymakers Underestimate Methane's Climate and Air Quality Impacts," *ScienceDaily*, May 16, 2022, https://www.sciencedaily.com/releases/2022/05/220516124038.htm.
15. Lucy Handley, The Road to COP26, "Pacific Island Minister Films Climate Speech Knee-Deep in the Ocean," November 8, 2021 8:04 AM EST, https://www.cnbc.com/2021/11/08/tuvalu-minister-gives-cop26-speech-knee-deep-in-the-ocean-to-highlight-rising-sea-levels.html. See IPCC, *AR6 Climate Change 2021*, A.3.4. Also, IPCC, *AR6 Climate Change 2021*, B.3.1 and B.3.4.
16. Spencer Weart & American Institute of Physics 2003–22, "The Discovery of Global Warming," April 2022, https://history.aip.org/climate/timeline.htm. National Centers for Environmental Information, National Oceanic and Atmospheric Administration, "Billion-Dollar Weather and Climate Disasters," https://www.ncei.noaa.gov/access/billions/events.
17. Yvonne Su, "UN Ruling on Climate Refugees Could Be Gamechanger for Climate Action," *Climate Home News*, January 29, 2020, 3:36pm https://www.climatechangenews.com/2020/01/29/un-ruling-climate-refugees-gamechanger-climate-action/.
18. Susan Strauss, *The Passionate Fact* (Golden, CO: North American Press, 1996), 9.
19. Arbara Brandt, *Whole Life Economics* (Gabriola Island, BC: New Society, 1995). Economisim prizes money, work, and possessions.
20. *Octogesima Adveniens*, §21, Apostolic Letter of Pope Paul VI, https://www.vatican.va /content/paul-vi/en/apost_letters/documents/hf_p-vi_apl_19710514_octogesima-adveniens.html.
21. Message of His Holiness Paul VI to Mr. Maurice F. Strong, Secretary-General of the Conference on the Environment, https://www.vatican.va/content/paul-vi/en/messages/pont-messages/documents/hf_p-vi_mess_19720605_conferenza-ambiente.html.
22. Catholic Climate Covenant, Climate Change Teachings, https://catholicclimatecovenant.org/teachings.
23. See: https://www.usccb.org/resources/global-climate-change-plea-dialogue-prudence-and-common-good.
24. Philip Pullella, "Vatican Lists 'New Sins,' Including Pollution," *Reuters*, Vatican City, March 10, 2008, https://www.reuters.com/article/us-pope-sins/vatican-lists-new-sins-including-pollution-idUSL109602320080310.

25. Pope John Paul II, General Audience Address, January 17, 2001, https://www.vatican.va/content/john-paul-ii/en/audiences/2001/documents/hf_jp-ii_aud_20010117.html.
26. Philip Pullella, "Pope Commits Vatican to Net Zero Carbon Emissions by 2050," *Reuters,* December 12, 2020, https://www.reuters.com/article/climate-change-un-summit-pope/pope-commits-vatican-to-net-zero-carbon-emissions-by-2050-idUSKBN28M0RP.
27. *LS* § 8 Pope Francis cites Address in Santa Barbara, California (November 8, 1997); cf. John Chryssavgis, *On Earth as in Heaven: Ecological Vision and Initiatives of Ecumenical Patriarch Bartholomew* (Bronx, NY: Fordham University Press, 2012).
28. *LS* § 24.
29. *LS* § 25.
30. *LS* § 25.
31. *LS* §52. See USCCB, *Global Climate Change: A Plea for Dialogue, Prudence and the Common Good* (June 15, 2001). *LS* § 170. See Bolivian Bishops' Conference, Pastoral Letter on the Environment and Human Development in Bolivia El universo, don de Dios para la vida (March 2012), 86.
32. *LS* § 169.
33. *LS* § 172.
34. *LS* § 181.
35. Tom Pyszczynski, "Terror," in *International Encyclopedia of the Social Sciences*, ed. William A. Darity, Jr., 2nd ed., Vol. 8 (Detroit: Macmillan Reference USA, 2008), 326–7, especially 326 *Gale Virtual Reference Library*. http://go.galegroup.com/ps/i.do?id=GALE%7CCX3045302728&v=2.1&u=chic95518&it=r&p=GVRL&sw=w.
36. David Adam, "Scientists Fear Worst on Global Warming," *Guardian*, April 14, 2009, 14, https://www.theguardian.com/environment/2009/apr/14/scientists-global-warming-conference-poll.
37. Alastair McIntosh, *Hell and High Water: Climate Change and the Human Condition* (London: Birlinn, 2008).
38. Shahram Heshmat PhD, "What Is Confirmation Bias?" *Psychology Today*, April 23, 2015, https://www.psychologytoday.com/us/blog/science-choice/201504/what-is-confirmation-bias.
39. Staff, *Psychology Today* "Motivated Reasoning—Confirmation Bias," https://www.psychologytoday.com/us/basics/motivated-reasoning.
40. Bill Lawhorn, "Where the Green Jobs Grow: Green Jobs with the Most Projected Openings 2019–2029," US Department of Labor Blog, April 21, 2021, https://blog.dol.gov/2021/04/21/where-the-green-jobs-grow. US EPA, "Green Jobs in Your Community," March 3, 2022, https://www.epa.gov/G3/green-jobs-your-community.

41. González-Gaudiano and Meira-Cartea, "Climate Change Education and Communication," 28. Garrett Hardin, "The Tragedy of the Commons," *Science* 162 (1968): 1243–8. Stephen M. Gardiner, "A Perfect Moral Storm: Climate Change, Intergenerational Ethics, and the Problem of Corruption," in *Climate Ethics: Essential Readings*, ed. Stephen M. Gardiner, Simon Caney, Dale Jamieson, and Henry Shue (New York: Oxford University Press, 2010), 88–9.
42. Sunita Narain, "A Million Mutinies," *New Internationalist* (January–February 2009): 10–11. Vandana Shiva, *Soil Not Oil: Climate Change, Peak Oil and Food Insecurity* (London: Zed Books, 2008), 9–47.
43. US Environmental Protection Agency, "Environmental Justice," 2022, https://www.epa.gov/environmentaljustice. Robert Bullard, *Dumping in Dixie: Race, Class, and Environmental Quality, Third Edition* (New York: Routledge, 2018). Noel Sturgeon, *Ecofeminist Natures: Race, Gender, Feminist Theory and Political Action* (New York: Routledge, 1997). Melanie Harris, *Ecowomanism: African American Women and Earth-Honoring Faiths* (Maryknoll: Orbis, 2017. US Environmental Protection Agency, "EPA Report Shows Disproportionate Impacts of Climate Change on Socially Vulnerable Populations in the United States," September 2, 2021, https://www.epa.gov/newsreleases/epa-report-shows-disproportionate-impacts-climate-change-socially-vulnerable.
44. McIntosh, *Hell and High Water*, 88.
45. McIntosh, *Hell and High Water*, 208.
46. Jess Worth, "Is the Economic Crisis Going to Be the End of Green?" *New Internationalist* 419 (2009): 1. Maggie Astor, "Do Airline Climate Offsets Really Work? Here's the Good News, and the Bad," May 18, 2022, https://www.nytimes.com/2022/05/18/climate/offset-carbon-footprint-air-travel.html.
47. Edgar González-Gaudiano, Educación Ambiental: Tragectorias, rasgos y escnarios [Environmental Education: Paths, Features, and Settings] (Mexico: Plaza y Valdés-UANL/Instituto de Investigacionses Sociales, 2007). UNESCO and UNEP education treated climate change as "business as usual."
48. Edgar González-Gaudiano and Pablo Meira-Cartea, "Climate Change Education and Communication: A Critical Perspective on Obstacles and Resistances," in *Education and Climate Change: Living in Interesting Times*, ed. Fumiyo Kagawa and David Selby (New York: Routledge, 2010), 14.
49. *Laudato Si'* Chapter Six, Ecological Education and Spirituality [202–46], https://www.vatican.va/content/francesco/en/encyclicals/documents/papa-francesco_20150524_enciclica-laudato-si.html.
50. "AP Announces Sweeping Climate Journalism Initiative," February 15, 2022, https://www.ap.org/press-releases/2022/ap-announces-sweeping-climate-journalism-initiative.

51. *LS* §s 32, 50,109,184, 203, 209, 210, 215, 219, 232.
52. Mike Hulme, "Climates Multiple: Three Baselines, Two Tolerances, One Normal," *Academia Letters*, Article 102, https://doi.org/10.20935/AL102.
53. *LS* §s 91, 117. Also "integral ecology," *LS* §s 10, 11, 62, 124, 137, 159, 225, 230.
54. IPCC, *Scientific Assessment 2001*, 162 http://www.ipcc.ch/publications_and_data/publications_and_data_reports.shtml.
55. *Climate Change 2022—Impacts, Adaptation and Vulnerability—Summary for Policy Makers*, https://www.ipcc.ch/report/ar6/wg2/downloads/report/IPCC_AR6_WGII_SummaryForPolicymakers.pdf.
56. Compare *The OECD Environmental Outlook to 2050, Key Findings on Climate Change*, COP 17, Durban, South Africa, 2011, UN Framework Convention on Climate Change, https://read.oecd-ilibrary.org/environment/oecd-environmental-outlook-to-2050_9789264122246-en#page1.
57. *LS* §s 52 and 170.
58. World Economic Forum, Davos 2022, "17 Ways Technology Could Change the World by 2027," https://www.weforum.org/agenda/2022/05/17-ways-technology-could-change-the-world-by-2027/. "The World Bank Will Help Strengthen the National System for Science, Technology and Innovation to Support Sustainable Development in Peru," February 17, 2022, https://www.worldbank.org/en/news/press-release/2022/02/17/the-world-bank-will-help-strengthen-the-national-system-for-science-technology-and-innovation-to-support-sustainable-dev.
59. "The Coal Mine Next Door How the US Government's Deregulation of Mountaintop Removal Threatens Public Health," December 10, 2018, https://www.hrw.org/report/2018/12/10/coal-mine-next-door/how-us-governments-deregulation-mountaintop-removal-threatens. Nicholas Kusnetz, "Canada's Tar Sands: Destruction So Vast and Deep It Challenges the Existence of Land and People," *Inside Climate News*, November 21, 2021, https://insideclimatenews.org/news/21112021/tar-sands-canada-oil/. Jennifer Bjorhus, "In the Courtroom and the Skies, Tribe Carries on Its Challenge of the Line 3 Pipeline," *Star Tribune*, April 9, 2022, https://www.startribune.com/in-the-courtroom-and-the-skies-tribe-carries-on-its-challenge-of-the-line-3-pipeline/600163677/.
60. Jocelyn Timperley, "Why Fossil Fuel Subsidies Are So Hard to Kill?" *Nature* 598 (2021): 403–5, DOI: https://doi.org/10.1038/d41586-021-02847-2.
61. Mark Lynas, *Six Degrees: Our Future on a Hotter Planet* (London: Fourth Estate, 2007). Jared Diamond, *Collapse: How Societies Choose to Fail or Succeed* (New York: Viking-Penguin, 2005). Morris Berman, *Dark Ages in America: The Final Phase of Empire* (New York: Norton, 2007).

62. Abraham H. Maslow, "A Theory of Human Motivation," *Psychological Review* 50/4 (1943): 370–96, http://psychclassics.yorku.ca/Maslow/motivation.htm. Kelly Dye, S.V. "Abraham Maslow," in *International Encyclopedia of the Social Sciences*, ed. William A. Darity, Jr., Vol. 5, 2nd ed. (Detroit: Macmillan Reference USA, 2008), 11–12.
63. The World Commission on Environment and Development, *Our Common Future* (New York: Oxford University Press, 1987).
64. Ibid., 43.
65. James B. Martin-Schramm and Robert L. Stivers, *Christian Environmental Ethics: A Case Study Method Approach* (Maryknoll: Orbis Books, 2003), 90.
66. Leonardo Boff, *Cry of the Poor* (Maryknoll: Orbis Books, 1997), 66.
67. Ibid., 105, *passim*.
68. WCC, *Accelerated Climate Change: Sign of Peril, Test of Faith* (Geneva: WCC Publications, 1994).
69. *LS* §s 62–100.
70. Sue McGregor, *Consumerism as a Source of Structural Violence*, 2003, https://wwwresearchgate.net/publication/229000866_Consumerism_as_a_Source_of_Structural_Violence.
71. *LS* § 190. Also, *LS* §s 109, 123, 195, 203, 209–10.
72. David Bohm and Mark Edwards, Changing Consciousness Exploring the Hidden Source of Social, Political and Environmental Crisis Facing Our World (San Francisco: Harper, 1991), 17.
73. Diarmuid O'Murchu, *Quantum Theology: Spiritual Implications of the New Physics* (New York: Crossroads, 2004), 139–40.
74. Joanna Macy, "The Greatest Danger: *Apatheia*, the Deadening of Mind and Heart," in *Coming Back to Life: Practices to Reconnect Our Lives, Our World*, ed. Joanna Macy and M. Young Brown (Gabriola Island, BC: New Society, 1998), 26. Greek, *apatheia*, means the refusal to experience pain.
75. Ibid., 23–38.
76. *LS* §s 202 and 217.
77. *LS* §203.
78. *LS* §s 222–5.
79. *LS* § 222.
80. *LS* § 206.
81. *LS* § 231.
82. *LS* § 245.
83. David Selby, "As the Heating Happens: Education for Sustainable Development of Education for Sustainable Contraction," *International Journal of Innovation and Sustainable Development* 2/3/4 (2007): 258.
84. Duane Elgin, *Voluntary Simplicity: Toward a Way of Life That Is Outwardly Simple and Inwardly Rich* (New York: William Morrow, 1981), 40.

85. Saint Francis. "The Testament," in *Francis of Assisi: Early Documents, Volume I—The Saint*, trans. and ed. Regis J. Armstrong, J. A. Wayne Hellmann, and William J. Short (New York: New City Press, 1999), 124.
86. O'Murchu, *Quantum Theology*, 190–3.
87. "The Joint Appeal in Religion and Science: Statement by Religious Leaders at the Summit on Environment," June 3, 1991, https://fore.yale.edu/sites/default/files/files/Joint%20Appeal.pdf.
88. LS §s 1–2, 10–12, 66, 87, 91, 125, 218, 221.
89. Leonardo Boff, *St. Francis: A Model for Human Liberation*, trans. John W. Diercksmeier (New York: The Crossroad Publishing Company, 1982), 131.
90. Ibid., 133.
91. Margaret A. Farley, *Compassionate Respect: A Feminist Approach to Medical Ethics and Other Questions*, Madeleva Lecture in Spirituality (New York: Paulist Press, 2002).
92. "The Life of St. Francis by Thomas of Celano (1228–1229)," Book II, chapter VIII, 109–11 in *Francis of Assisi: Early Documents*, Volume II—*The Founder*, trans. and ed. Regis J. Armstrong, J. A. Wayne Hellmann, and William J. Short (New York: New City Press, 2000), 277–9.
93. Boff, *St. Francis*, 146.
94. Evolutionary sciences show that some species reach their limits and become extinct, while others adapt and exist for many generations.
95. Ernesto Dezza, "John Duns Scotus on Human Beings in the State of Innocence," *Traditio* 75 (2020): 289–310. DOI: https://doi.org/10.1017/tdo.2020.10.
96. Boff, *St. Francis*, 151.
97. Cited in ibid., 153.
98. *Journeying Towards Care for Our Common Home, Five Years after Laudato Si'* (Vatican City: Libreria Editrica Vaticana, 2020), https://www.skeparchy.org/wordpress/libreria-editrica-vaticana-journeying-towards-care-for-our-common-home-five-years-after-laudato-si/.
99. Ibid., 15.
100. Ibid., 17.
101. Pavel Chalupnicek, "*Laudato Si'* and Economics: A Survey of Responses," *Journal of Catholic Social Thought* 18/2 (2021): 283–306.
102. The Economy of Francesco, November 21, 2020, https://francescoeconomy.org/final-statement-and-common-commitment/.
103. Website: Economy of Francesco: https://francescoeconomy.org/.
104. *Global Climate Change a Plea for Dialogue Prudence and the Common Good*, a Statement of the United States Conference of Catholic Bishops, June 15, 2001, https://www.usccb.org/resources/global-climate-change-plea-dialogue-prudence-and-common-good.

8

Wholly of Water—Water and a Sacramental Universe

Introduction: Morally Significant Facts

Imagine at the end of a long day you have dinner at your favorite restaurant. You order 4 oz. glass of wine; 8 oz. beef steak; 6 oz. white rice; 8 oz. lettuce salad. When you pay the check, you will not see a charge for the 969 gallons of water needed to produce the food you consumed.[1] Considering the global cost of water, however, you soon realize the level of sheer opulence your meal represents. But why is this an issue?

Health experts recommend adults drink eight 8-ounce glasses of water a day.[2] The minimum daily requirement per person for water (drinking, cooking, bathing, and sanitation) is 13 US gallons. Each American averages 82 gallons of water a day at home![3] The average African uses 12 gallons at home each day.[4]

Globally, Water.Org reports: 771 million people—1 in 10—lack access to safe water. According to the World Economic Forum in January 2021 the water crisis is the fifth greatest global risk in terms of impact to society. Internationally, 46 percent of people do not have access to safely managed sanitation. Six percent of the global population defecate in the open. Every 2 minutes a child dies from a water-related disease. Women and girls spend 200 million hours every day collecting water. Access to improved sanitation leads to a reduction in assault and violence on women and girls. The lifetime income of a girl can increase by 15–25 percent for every year she stays in school.[5]

Today the Earth has the same amount of water that it had 2,000 years ago.[6] Then the world population was about 200 million. Currently, some

7.95 billion people share that same finite water supply.[7] Between 1900 and 2000, global water consumption rose sevenfold—more than double the population growth rate![8] The western United States, northern China, northern and western India, and north and west Africa continue to pump out groundwater faster than aquifers can be replenished. One-third of US rivers, one-half of US estuaries, and more than one-half of US lakes are unfit for fishing and swimming.[9] Two billion people depend on international cooperation to ensure an adequate water supply.

The human newborn is 91 percent water; the human adult is about 75 percent water, while the human brain alone is 75 percent water. A drop in body-water of a mere 2 percent brings fuzzy, short-term memory, trouble doing basic math, or difficulty focusing on a computer screen. As the Pontifical Justice and Peace Council asserted in its 2003 statement, "[w]ater is an essential element for life."[10]

The Hydrologic Cycle: Basic Facts

People have lost track of the interrelatedness of our entire world, especially the world's water supply. The tides, currents, and weather patterns that sustain the water supply in any one part of the globe are intimately connected to all others. We cannot excise the quality of the air or the soils from the quality of the water. For example, the coal-generating power plants of Chicago spew mercury into the air.[11] The mercury filters down into Lake Michigan and enters the food supply of small fish and the plants eaten by humans and other fishes. The toxic effect of mercury bio-accumulates with other toxins, and eventually the plants in the lake can no longer filter out the biological waste contained in the run-off flowing into the lake from rivers, streams, and agricultural lands. The contaminated waters make fishing, swimming, and drinking this water hazardous to humans and all living beings. The hydrologic system is tremendously complex and interconnected with every other earth system. Basically, the hydrologic system has six interrelated processes that keep water falling and flowing in any part of the earth—all the genius of the God of Creation—and not of human making![12]

So what's the problem? Simply put, water is (often wastefully and carelessly) being consumed and retained faster than the hydrologic cycle can process it in a world where the human population now poised to exceed 8 billion—thus, the crisis exists.

The Global Water Crisis: An Exposé

The water the dinosaurs drank millions of years ago is the same recycled water that falls as rain today! If all of Earth's water (liquid, ice, freshwater, saline) was put into a sphere it would be about 860 miles (about 1,385 kilometers) in diameter (about the distance from Salt Lake City, Utah, to Topeka, Kansas, USA). In volume that amounts to a mind-boggling 1,338,000,000 km^3 or 321,000,000 mi^3.[13]

Nearly 70 percent of the world's freshwater is locked in ice.[14] Most of Earth's remaining water is locked in aquifers that we're draining faster than it can be replenished. Two-thirds of our water is used to grow food. With an annual global population increase of approximately 83 million more people each year, we must act with urgency to halt water waste of God's most precious gift. Three interconnected water issues that require our attention are access to safe drinking water, pollution and climate change, and scarcity and depletion of water sources.[15]

Access to Water: For Whom?

A lack of adequate and affordable technologies, institutional will, and political obstacles to financing reservoirs, treatment systems, or delivery systems for ever growing needs prohibit water access.[16] The UN Sustainable Development Goal target 6.1 calls for universal and equitable access to safe and affordable drinking water.[17] In 2020, 2 billion people were without safely managed services available 30 minutes away or with limited or no protections for water purity. Sharp geographic, sociocultural, and economic inequalities persist as well.[18] Even with generous loans or donations of the structures or technologies, maintenance costs remain prohibitive.

Globally progress has been made toward assisting people with a variety of low-cost technologies such as rainwater harvesting systems.[19] Creative water purification techniques are available such as the "Purifier of Water," a powder developed by Pur and distributed by Population Services International.[20] The Swiss-pioneered solar disinfection process (SODIS) has been used in Nairobi's Kibera Slum.[21] The ultraviolet radiation kills bacteria, viruses, and parasites making the water potable.[22] Several creative finance mechanisms partner public and private resources for building adequate water supply systems.[23]

Pollution—Can the Polluter Pay?

Even when otherwise adequate delivery and storage facilities exist in numerous locales, safe drinking water is unavailable due to pollution from industrial chemicals, toxins, microbes, and bacteria from untreated sewage and agricultural sources. Corruption, collusion, absence of enforcement of environmental regulations, and lack of political will are key to the insufficient potable water supply. Such situations are normally accompanied by extreme poverty, and the poorest suffer even though technological remedies exist.[24]

Even when political will and enforcement regulations exist, the greatest problems involve "non-point source pollution," which includes organic and chemical run-off from artificially fertilized fields and animal operations, or exhaust from industrial sites spewing toxins into the air with impunity. It is difficult, if not impossible to pin down the cause-and-effect relationship of non-point source polluters. Offering loans or tax breaks for emitters who voluntarily reduce pollution may be helpful. Yet it would still be possible for any one polluter to "catch a free ride" off the efforts of others.[25]

Water Scarcity

Water scarcity "refers to a situation when the water supply is inadequate in relation to the water demand for basic human and ecological necessities, including the production of food and other economic goods. … One-third of the developing world will confront severe water shortages in this century due to increasing population size and changing climate conditions."[26] Increased numbers and duration of long-term droughts and increasing demands can render even the best designed water supply systems useless. Early sample cases include the drought suffered by Atlanta, Georgia, 2006–2011; the Colorado River watershed 1999–2007, Lake Mead and Lake Powell 50 percent water level drop in 2011 (and further by 2022) and Arizona and Texas severe wildfires in 2011.[27] Similar conditions have continued into 2022.

There is one solution to water scarcity that is "market driven": treating water as a "rare commodity." If such strategies are attempted, they are best done with price caps in place and within only local and carefully limited sectors. But, while these limits may help the overall local systemic water conservation efforts, other difficulties arise, e.g., farmers needing to compete with other farmers whose water use is unrestricted.

Water consumption in urban centers breaks down at 70 percent industrial, 20 percent institutional, and 6–10 percent domestic. Large corporate users notoriously evade the cost of their water altogether.[28] Yet most of the discussions about water pricing are around individual water use. Thus, water pricing will likely not have much of an impact. On a global scale, water pricing, combined with privatization, sealed water's fate as a commodity under the terms of international trade agreements supported by the World Trade Organization (WTO) and the North American Free Trade Agreement (NAFTA). Both groups considered water to be a tradable good, subject to the same rules as any other good.[29]

Water Politics, Environmental Justice, and Virtual Water

Likely US citizens don't spend much effort thinking about the global water supply. But droughts in North India; China's Yellow; Long Island, New York; and Ethiopia with a three-hour walk by women and children for the day's water supply are all too real.[30] The US and other "water-rich nations" have basked in luxurious oblivion concerning the fact that the world's climate is not exclusively a local thing. The hydrological cycle is affected by atmospheric conditions that are formed across the globe. Indeed, "the climate is a direct bridge between local rainfall or water availability and global processes."[31]

Further evidence of the interconnectedness of the world's water supply is seen when considering phenomena such as the El Niño Southern Oscillation that causes concurrent and persistent droughts in large areas of the world.[32] In wealthy nations the possibilities for water storage and technological prowess that allow for evermore innovative access to water supplies from greater depths and distances have masked the realities of increased water depletion—especially from water wastefulness. The wealthy have relied on ever greater amounts of grain—crops that demand high water—for food and have been able to import foods from across the globe, making up for low local water supplies. However, in the global equation, importation of foods from across the globe, making up for inadequate water supplies, is limited. This "virtual transfer of water" is multiplied in spades when we consider the impact of importing other products—all requiring vast amounts of water in their production, transport, and arrival in our homes.

Thomas M. Kostigan noted, there is an "embedded water footprint of everything from boxers to bikinis." Two-thirds of the world's freshwater is used to grow food.[33] While the import/export of "virtual water" via food supplies seems like a possible solution to water crisis, it bears the constant threat of "price shocks"—the risk of soaring food prices, should there be crop failure or some other disruption in the patterns people depend on. Using corn for biofuel (ethanol) was an early example of such a disruption.[34] Further, currently ethanol is being scrutinized for its ineffectiveness in lowering of carbon emissions, and another disruption will likely occur.

Kostigen helpfully illustrates the global interdependence of the hydrologic system with these scenarios:

> The snow falling on New York City might once have been water at the bottom of Lake Superior, or rain runoff from someone's driveway in San Diego. Via evaporation, transpiration, and precipitation, among other processes, water moves about. But when we use more here, it means less there. There are increasingly more people on the planet, and the things we do require water.[35]

From the Writings of St. Francis

***A Mirror of Perfection of the Status of a Lesser Brother* (The Sabatier Edition, 1928)**

"The Exceptional Love He had for Water, Stones, Wood, and Flowers," Chapter 11, 118[36]

Next to the fire he had a singular love for water through which holy penance and tribulation is symbolized and by which the filth of the soul is washed clean and because of which the first cleansing of the soul takes place through the waters of baptism.

Because of this, when he washed his hands, he chose a place where the water that fell to the ground would not be trampled underfoot.

Reflection and Application

A Culture of Water: What Is It?

Aware of the true value of water as God's precious gift, a "culture of water" requires us to live within the limits of the hydrological cycle.[37] Like St. Francis, we need to understand the singular vitality of water in our very existence from the moment of our conception and our nine-month swim within our mother's womb; its vital role in sustaining our health in every moment of our existence; through to its role in receiving and recycling our bodies into the earth upon our death. A water culture requires that we care for all places where water is held, as well as for the catchment forests, flowers, and fauna that must be healthy to play their role in recharging the gift of water. Water that flows freely is truly living water that provides vitality for all. But this is not true for water confined to unlimited paved surfaces or restricted by dams, making it impossible for it to soak into the soil.

There are things we cannot do and actions we must do if we desire to live in a water culture. We must limit our water use to what is necessary, rather than what we might desire. We must conceive of our existence as sisters and brothers of all plant, animal, and microbial life, each having a right to its share of water. Water follows the economies of ecosystems, the smaller scale, the local elements that form the web of life—human and otherkind.[38] Even with a global population of 7.96 billion people, if we live with respect for water, we can all have the water we need.[39]

Illusions of Safety: Bottled Water and Water Privatization

The Case of Bottled Water

Individual efforts to conserve water are useful and necessary. But, in recent decades, the corporate commodification and privatization of water raised a dangerous global specter. Rather than treating water as a human right and common good, increasingly water is considered a commodity for profit on the global market.

The historical facts tell the story. We cannot buy our way out of the hydrologic cycle. In the 1970s greater attention to health and fitness exposed the unhealthy nature of soft drinks. Sales peaked for companies such as Coca-Cola, Nestle, Pepsi, or Suez.[40] Perrier and Evian filled the gap offering healthy "crystalline waters" as a luxury to European elites. "By the late 1990s, a fetish commodity had come of age in the industrial world."[41]

Water companies set out to manufacture a need for their product, playing on people's fears concerning the safety of local water supplies—tap water. Bottled water was claimed the remedy against unsafe, local, 50–100-year-old, improperly maintained water infrastructure. At best, such appeals were half-truths. The bottled water industry was unregulated.[42] There was no guaranteed purity of bottled water either! Independent, random testing found trace of carcinogens and bacteria in those bottles, and up to 40 percent of the bottled water sold was local tap water.[43] Nor did they mention the annual environmental cost of 1.5 million pounds of nonbiodegradable plastic bottles or the fuel and global shipping costs.[44]

Some turned to water filters as a remedy. But exposure to the most harm happens when people breath air polluted with volatile chemicals, pesticides, and solvents as impure water is released, or toilets flushed. Filters are thus ineffective and must be changed and disposed of every three-six months. From "the trash," chemicals leach back into the soil or, when incinerated, pollute the air. Either way the hydrological cycle will be harmed! It is wiser to address the pollution at its source, maintain all water delivery systems, enforce regulations, and require transparent accountability to citizens.

Bottled water sales of have-not dropped. Market size value in 2022 was projected to be USD 303.9 billion with a revenue forecast in 2030 of USD 509.2 billion.[45] Water bottlers now engage in "greenwashing," touting their wares as "carbon negative" enterprises.[46] We still confront the larger issues of other forms of privatization of access to water and water delivery systems.

Privatization of Drinking Water

The aging water systems in the United States are in urgent need of repair and updating, yet they get attention only in emergencies.[47] Rising populations and strong citizen tax resistance for funding the common good and make it increasingly difficult for cities to maintain water infrastructures.[48] Already in 2005, the Leadership Conference of Women Religious—Global Concerns Committee said such thinking smacks of moral and spiritual deficiency—a clear violation of Christian ethics! They noted: "The private sector, especially a handful of transnational corporations, has recognized that water is the 'blue gold' of the 21st century."[49] Water is thus treated exclusively as a commodity and with impunity.

Over the decades six major approaches to water privatization have developed, each with their commercial advantages and ethical challenges:[50] municipal services;[51] contractually own water in whole territories or bioregions; companies divert water for exclusive industrial or agribusiness use; use by private parties for mining, oil drilling, etc.; state-subsidized transnational private companies;[52] and companies monopolize technologies to extract and purify water.[53]

Privatization has always been with us in some form, but on a vastly smaller scale and size. But at the 2000 Stockholm Water Symposium it was announced that by 2025, two-thirds of the world's population would suffer water shortages or absolute water scarcity. In a globalized economy everything has its price, and nothing is "off limits" including water![54]

Recent trade agreements left doors wide open for water to be marketed and managed—like any other economic resource—as a commodity. As Barlow puts it, "Huge corporate factories are moving up the rivers of the Third World, sucking them dry as they go."[55] Barlow cites numerous examples. Companies claim they provide socially beneficial services. But Mr. During of Suez Lyonnaise des Eaux was clear, "We are here to make money. Sooner or later the company that invests recoups its investment, which means the customer has to pay for it."[56] The top priority in commercial water management is to more consumption, thus more profit.

Privatization severely limits or eliminates citizens' control, and the transparency of the water systems management. The World Bank has minimal disclosure requirements.[57]

With water privatization, public health and safety is understood differently. In Ontario, Canada, high risk for *E. coli* contamination in rural wells was common knowledge. Thus, the government Drinking Water Surveillance Program (DWSP) had trained personnel who regularly tested those waters. After Ontario privatized its water system, the DWSP was cut from the budget. In June 2000, fourteen people, including a baby, died from drinking water in Walkerton, Ontario.

> The town had subcontracted to a branch-plant of a private testing company from Tennessee. A&L Laboratories discovered E. coli in the water, but failed to report the contamination to provincial authorities, an *option* it had under the new "common sense" rules.[5] In true corporate-speak, a lab spokesman said that the test results were "confidential intellectual property." As such, they belonged only to the "client"—the public officials of Walkerton who were not trained to deal with the tests.[58]

Commercial pricing of water is most often a bad idea. For poor people, it exacerbates the existing global inequality of access to water—only the rich can pay.[59] Basic fairness dictates that the burden of proof must be on those who use water most and the benefits in the form of profits be removed. Business has no right to deprive anyone of their inalienable human rights; if that is the price of profit, the price is too high. And beyond that, if left unchecked, the "chickens will come home to roost" when the very ecosystems that create and sustain the hydrological cycle, but are not included in the corporate equation, lie in ruin. Simply put, if we lose public control of our water systems, there may be no one left with the ability to claim water—this life-giving source for *all*.

Toward a Way Forward

We must first believe that water belongs to the Earth and all species, and thus it is sacred to all life on the planet. All decisions about water must be based on genuinely sustainable ecosystem and watershed-based management. Second, the basic human right to water must be sustained and incorporated into the normative codes of law with meaningful enforcement. Third, such codes must hold water as a public trust to be guarded at all levels of government. No one has the right to appropriate it at another's expense or for profit. Water must not be privatized, traded, or exported for commercial gain. Above all, we, as human beings, must change our behaviors to preserve God's precious gift of water.

Water: A Human Right with Challenges for Implementation

On July 28, 2010, the UN General Assembly passed *Resolution 64/292 the Human Right to Water and Sanitation*.[60] Bolivia's Permanent UN Representative Pablo Solon introduced the measure.[61] One hundred twenty-two members voted in support, but 41 nations including the United States abstained.[62] The significant portion of the resolution was contained in the last three points of the document.[63]

1. *Recognizes* the right to safe and clean drinking water and sanitation as a human right that is essential for the full enjoyment of life and all human rights;
2. *Calls upon* states and international organizations to provide financial resources, capacity-building, and technology transfer through international assistance and cooperation;
3. *Welcomes* the decision by the Human Rights Council to request that the independent expert on human rights obligations related to access

to safe drinking water and sanitation submit an annual report to the General Assembly, and encourages her to continue working on all aspects of her mandate.

In September 2010 the UN Human Rights Council affirmed the human right to clean water and sanitation is "inextricably related to the right to the highest attainable standard of physical and mental health as well as to the right to life and human dignity."[64] This is a significant moral mandate for incorporating the right to water and sanitation with equal weight with the *1948 Universal Declaration of Human Rights*.[65] Thus, the language used in the resolution was highly intentional. Proponents rejected the phrase "*access* to water" in favor of "the human *right* to water and sanitation." Use of the terms "access to water" could indicate availability at a price not affordable for the poor and thus render the "right" mute. The Special Rapporteur carries out thematic research, undertakes country missions, collects good practices, and works with development practitioners on the implementation of the rights to water and sanitation.[66]

Subsequent developments include legal attempts to reserve rights to water (itself) on a noneconomic basis. *The Declaration of the Rights of Mother Earth* by the Peoples Conference in Bolivia in 2010 upheld that "Mother Earth and the beings of which she is composed" have "the right to water as a source of life."[67] In 2017, Aotearoa/New Zealand gave the status of a legal person to the Whanganui River, according to the Maori understanding.[68] More broadly, legal work on the concept of *ecocide*, a concept that includes degradation of water, is in process worldwide.[69]

A View from Christian Ethics

Water is the most frequently named earth element in the Bible. The primary meaning of water comes from the physical reality that without water, all living things die. Water has a capacity for healing, purification, and biological life-giving, and it is physically and spiritually necessary for all people. Some familiar references can serve to remind us—in Psalm 51:4 or John 13:5, or again, in John 3:5.

The earliest Christians, often in the minority in their communities, frequently adopted the governance of the locales where they lived. While no explicit guidance from the Bible fits today's water questions, values can be drawn from the biblical material. Consistently, water is viewed as a free gift from the Creator, and thus, it is idolatrous for anyone to presume *absolute* ownership. Fundamental human dignity is breached when no legal recourse is available for obtaining the basic survival needs of water and sanitation.

Water in the Hebrew Testament links creation, stewardship, and hospitality (Gen. 2—caring for the garden). These themes are extended to the Christian Testament. Related to the Bible, ethical arguments developed, showing basic access and use of water is a matter of justice.

How justice for the poor was fulfilled was the ultimate test of morality. Indeed, the ultimate test of the fulfillment of justice was how needs for a life of dignity were fulfilled for the poor and the vulnerable.

Today that test of justice holds that the poor cannot be deprived of the access and use of water to meet their basic needs, through privatization of water by treatment, delivery, or diversion of sources.[70] Humans are called to fulfill an "ecological vocation," sharing nature's gifts compelled by love of God and neighbor. Today we must consider water, as well as our human companions, as our neighbor.[71]

Today in our market economy, optimal conservation of water is imperative. In most instances conservation implies some form of water pricing. Some people must bear the just costs of extraction, treatment, storage, transportation, and recycling of water in a closed loop system—particularly in the urban areas where most of the world's people live.[72]

Gudorf helpfully suggests several pricing models that render justice for the poor and provide incentives for conservation, practical mechanisms for financial requirements, and provisions for legal recourse if violations against basic human water rights occur. In Saudi Arabia, until 1994 water was provided to all for free. But thereafter near full pricing was introduced by the government "to acquaint its citizens with the cost of providing water services."[73]

Thirty liters of water per person per day is a generous measure of water sufficient to meet the basic thirst of each person. Thus, the Iranian system provides that amount free to all domestic customers in urban areas. The full cost is then charged for additional liters while commercial customers pay the full cost for all water used. Ecologically, everyone benefits: water is sufficient, conserved, included in a separate sewer system, and proper maintenance occurs.[74]

In Dhaka, Bangladesh, a local NGO, DSK, and the international NGO WaterAid worked with the Dhaka Water Supply and Sewage Authority (DWSSA) to meet the moral right to water at a fair price for slum dwellers.

DSK was the initial guarantor of the cost for installing the water faucets. The slum dwellers formed committees to maintain the faucets and ensure everyone paid their bills. Eventually the DWSSA turned over control to the slum dwellers and DSK was no longer needed; everyone benefited.[75]

These models pool the resources of the community at the local level and ultimately reduce costs. Without intentionally organized community water supplies, poor people normally pay more than the full price municipalities charge for water to meet their needs. Street venders and truckers usually charge 75–100 percent or more above the municipal full cost.[76]

It is possible to control privatization, obtain justice for the poor, and conserve God's precious gift without sacrificing either sustainability or just access and use of water to meet fundamental human needs. The Catholic Rural Life Conference of the United States recommends twelve excellent guiding principles that provide moral guidance for water resource management, decisions about resource distribution, and implementation across the globe.[77]

Considerations for Decision-Making

Water management and resource distribution must be guided by considerations for the common good of the people of the world and the natural systems of the planet itself. As people of faith in the resurrected Christ, the one who is the Living Water of Life, we can analyze the problem and act to make a difference.

Water and Catholic Social Teaching

John Paul II set out a clear direction for our faith-filled choice to ensure that all have enough water to sustain life and health. "Water by its very nature cannot be treated as a mere commodity among other commodities. Catholic social thought has always stressed that the defense and preservation of certain common goods such as the natural and human environments cannot be safeguarded simply by market forces, since they touch on fundamental human needs which *escape market logic.*"[78] This signals how CST understands water.

The history behind defining water as an economic commodity to be owned or as a human right continues to influence how world powers deal with water. At the 1992 UN Conference on Environment and Development Dublin, the World Water Council, comprised of multinational corporations, insisted that "[w]ater has an economic value in all its competing uses and should be recognized as an economic good." As a result of that value "it is vital to recognize first the basic right of all human beings to have access to clean water and sanitation at an affordable price."[79] Non-corporate activists and representatives of nongovernmental organizations objected to that language because it opens the possibility to enshrine the "right" based on the ability to pay, thus threatening poor people. The World Water Council continues to valorized water as a commodity, insisting on market remedies to the world's water problems.

The Pontifical Justice and Peace Council has presented several memoranda to the World Water Forum meetings since 2003.[80] These outline CST concerning water and our mandate for water justice for all and our planet: *Water: An Essential Element for Life* (2003) and *Water: An Essential Element for Life: An Update* (2006).[81] The teachings in these documents were reaffirmed and elaborated by John Paul II, Benedict XVI, and especially Pope Francis in *Laudato Si'—On Care for Our Common Home* (2015), and the Dicastery for Promoting Integral Human Development, *Aqua fons vitae Orientations on Water: Symbol of the Cry of the Poor and the Cry of the Earth* (2020).[82]

Today the principal problem concerning water is not one of absolute scarcity, but rather of distribution and resources. In recent years Catholic leaders have made strong arguments that the right to sufficient, free, and safe water is intimately linked to respect for the life and dignity of each human person. Indeed, the foundational principle determining all Catholic morality, including the use of safe and sufficient water, is the invaluable worth and dignity of each person.

Beyond this, given what the ecological sciences teach us about the interconnection of the web of life, we usually cannot have maximum human well-being without environmental integrity.[83] Therefore, the Pontifical Justice and Peace Commission (PJPC) teaches: "The first priority of every country and the international community for sustainable water policy should be to provide access to safe water to those who are deprived of such access at present."[84]

The PJPC stresses a third pertinent principle: "the *universal destination of the goods of creation* [which] confirms that people and countries, including future generations, have the *right* to fundamental access to those goods that are necessary for their development. Water is the primary common good of humankind."[85] This principle grounds giving priority to poverty-stricken living with water scarcity. It also provides the basis for prohibitions against the powerful managing water supplies through policies that allow them to foul, waste, or manipulate water with impunity. The Pontifical Council for Justice and Peace states, in this regard, governments are obligated to respect, protect, and fulfill the human right to safe, drinkable water.[86]

Even with the July 28, 2010, passage of the UN General Assembly *Resolution 64/292*, at present there is no single global organization mandated to coordinate and deal with water and its related issues among the community of nations. However, various international treaties and declarations legally support those claims.[87]

The PJPC asserts that *"people must become the 'active subjects'* of safe water policies." Both women and men should be involved, have equal voice in managing water resources, and equitably share the benefits from sustainable water use.

The PJPC calls us to attend to "solidarity [which] is a firm and persevering determination to commit oneself to the common good, to the good of all, and of each individual. It presupposes the effort for a more just social order and requires a preferential attention to the situation of the poor."[88] Both individuals and nations have the same duty of solidarity; advanced nations have the weightiest obligation to help the developing people.

Knowledge of local water supplies and their ecological functions and histories is normally best known by local people. Considering that it is not only good common sense but also good moral practice to evoke the Catholic moral principle of "subsidiarity" when shaping policies pertaining to the human right to water.[89] It is important that the considerable wisdom about water be utilized through grassroots engagement of local peoples throughout any water program.

The PJPC also teaches that "while vital to humanity, water has a strong social content."[90] Its role is critical in establishing (1) agriculture and food security, (2) health and sanitation, (3) peace and conflict resolution, and (4) control of global warming and natural disasters.

Globally, agriculture is a key sector in all economies, but it cannot be sustained without sufficient water. Worldwide, agriculture accounts for 80 percent of the use of water and will continue to be necessary for food security.

Special training in water conservation techniques is needed to assist people in maximizing and conserving their precious water supplies. Also, the traditional forms of knowledge of indigenous people should be esteemed, and it can be vital and decisive in addressing and solving the question of water.[91]

In a world threatened by both water scarcity and food insecurity, it is vital that such lands and water sources be reclaimed. "Policies must encourage harnessing the wider potential of rain-fed farming, incorporating water management for gardens and foods from common property resources."[92] There is an intimate relationship between human health and the use of sufficient and safe water. So policymakers need to be concerned with issues of quantity, and the safe quality of water keeping it free from waterborne diseases.[93]

As the PJPC concludes, "Whether it relates to quantity, quality, or disease, the trend away from centralized government agencies and toward empowering local governments and local communities to manage water must be emphasized. This necessitates building community capacities, especially concerning personnel and the allocation of resources to the local level."[94]

Access to safe and sufficient water "is a strategic factor for the establishment and maintenance of peace in the world. Water is a dimension of what is referred to today as resource security."[95] Global warming and climate change are exacerbating this development. Two glaring examples are in the Horn of Africa and the Middle East. "Water scarcity can present a clear danger to the internal stability of countries" in entire regions.[96] There is also a long, and in many ways stronger, history of water-related cooperation of a hydro-solidarity among countries and communities.[97]

The effects of global warming and climate change pose substantial additional threats to areas of the globe that are already impoverished and poor in water. The IPCC indicates that the wet places in the world will get wetter and dry places will become drier. Justice and solidarity now demand that we not only plan to assist people in the usual disasters but also make realistic strategic plans and provide life's necessities for climate refugees, who need to relocate and seek new livelihoods because of vast climatic shifts. The PJPC could not be clearer: A new "culture of water" is needed. "Water is central to life. However all too often water is not perceived as the luxury it really is but is paradoxically wasted. This action of wasting water is morally unsustainable."[98]

In facing the hard challenge posed by the water issue, there are many signs of hope, including the UN International Decade for Action on Water for Sustainable Development, 2018–2028.[99] The issue of access to safe water and sanitation has become one of the top priorities of the international system. As Pope Paul VI declared years ago, "This hope in the Author of nature and of the human spirit, rightly understood, is capable of giving new and serene energy to all of us."¹⁰⁰ Solutions for access to safe water and sanitation should express preferential love and justice for the poor. The water issue is truly a right-to-life issue.

Wholly of Water and Holy Water in a Sacramental Universe

For Catholics, baptism in "Holy Water" is the starting point for the life of faith. Through the waters of baptism, we take on a new life in Christ, and we are empowered by the Holy Spirit to live by God's grace and with hope. But this empowerment comes with responsibilities and calls for commitment "to follow in the in the footprints of Jesus." The waters of baptism must remain "living waters" in our lives. We need to pass on the life Christ the Spirit offers, by our practical actions of justice and mercy, in relationship with our fellow creatures, and Earth itself.

Reflecting on *Laudato Si'—On Care for Our Common Home*, Peter McGrail challenges Catholics especially to consider the sacramental and practical meaning of water amid our "Climate Emergency."¹⁰¹ He questions whether we can retain authentic membership among the baptized (and anointed with consecrated oil) "without recognizing that those same natural elements, can speak *also* of the poisoning of the natural world, of unequal access to healthy drinking water, and the social impact of consumption." Can we lead our life of faith with integrity today, having failed to explore these questions? Can we ignore sacramental ecology?"¹⁰² We need to attend to Pope Francis' focus on the Sacraments and the sacramental value of Creation in *LS* §s 233–7, especially § 235. It is this capacity of nature to communicate realities that extend beyond the realm of the senses that forms the experiential bedrock of the sacramental system at the heart of the liturgy.

In *Laudato Si'* Pope Francis' primary concern is access to fresh drinking water, which is "a basic and universal human right, since it is essential to human survival and, as such, is a condition for the exercise of other human rights. Our world has a grave social debt towards the poor, who lack access to drinking water because they are denied the right to a life consistent to their unalienable dignity" (*LS* § 30).

This reality of exclusion contrasts with the lavish exuberance celebrating the gift of water in the Easter Vigil. There we hear the invitation, "Let everyone who thirsts, come to the waters" (Isa. 55:1). The Vigil closes with the comparison, of the vital effect of God's Word, on the life-giving winter rain and snow (Isa. 55:10–11). Water is portrayed as a free gift from the heavens, which satisfies a thirsty humanity and brings fruitfulness to creation. Water is so lavish and fruitful that it serves as an image for God's word and God's very will.[103]

In the light of *Laudato Si'*, we must ask what it means "to proclaim those words in a location of desertification, or to hear them as a member of a community with little or no access to clean drinking water. The words may, indeed, express profound hope in such contexts, but they do so precisely because they also tie into anxieties, evoke painful memories, and reflect present realities."[104] Here water becomes an ambiguous symbol, "soiled by human activity," interacting "subversively, with the biblical proclamation."[105]

And further, "the tensions thus set up have the potential to generate dissonance on the lips of assemblies, in more affluent parts of the world. They respond to that reading: 'Surely, God is my salvation … with joy you will draw water from the wells of salvation'" (Isaiah 12:2–6).[106] That message is to be proclaimed to all nations, to all peoples, throughout the earth. "But as Pope Francis reminds us, in many parts of the earth, it will instead receive a response that is 'the cry of the poor.'"[107]

Thus, if we are open to conversion, "one of the most joyous sections of the Easter Vigil, can plunge us into a discomforting recognition" of the challenging "meanings that our core symbol of baptism holds in tension. What, then, does this say to us of baptism itself?"[108]

According to *Sacrosanctum Concilium*, 6 Baptism is a plunging into Christ's paschal mystery by which women and men "die with him, are buried with him, and rise with him."[109] When we celebrate Baptism, we are also acknowledging the reality that "the material world is caught up in systems of death, but are also proclaiming and celebrating union with Christ in his transforming death and resurrection."[110] For Catholics (also potentially all people of good will) this reality contains a mandate to bring about a new culture of water.

Indeed, as Jesus tells us: "… and whoever gives even a cup of cold water to one of these little ones in the name of a disciple—truly I tell you, none of these will lose their reward" (Mt. 10:42). The Christian life is attuned to gratitude and praise for God's gifts of creation—for Sister Water—and a reverence that mandates careful use (never abuse) of such treasures. It is from a stance of gratitude that we most deeply appreciate God's generous love for the whole world, indeed, a world that is wholly dependent on water for life! But true worship is made credible through congruent actions. This necessity calls us to intentional lives of prayer and reflection with an attitude of ongoing discernment about what God is inviting and requiring us to be and do. For many of us this will involve individual lifestyle changes. But the whole Christian community also needs to mobilize and act collaboratively through the justice and peace ministries of the churches in concerted efforts for water justice.

Making these changes is not impossible! A key to success is to decide to gradually add a new action every week—perhaps during Advent or Lent. All of this is possible. Each time you act, be conscious of the sacredness of God's gift of water. Pray with St. Francis of Assisi, the patron of ecology: "Praised be You, my Lord, through Sister Water, who is useful, and humble, precious and chaste."[111]

Questions for Reflection and Discussion

1. Do you know the source of the water piped into your home?
2. If you or your friends use commercial bottled water, what is the major reason for doing so?
3. What is the meaning of "common good" and "subsidiarity" in Catholic Social Teaching as it pertains to water?
4. Research the supply of water in your bioregion. How secure is the water supply in your area?
5. What are the major factors for the impending global water crisis?

Suggestions for Action

1. Inquire of your water utility what the source of your tap water is. Legally they must tell you.
2. Eliminate bottled water from your lifestyle.
3. Learn 100 ways to conserve water: http://www.projectwater.info/100-ways-to-conserve-water.html.
4. Use phosphate-free soaps and detergents, and eliminate chemical cleaners, fertilizers, and pesticides that require vast water use in their manufacture and pollute waterways.

5 Ask the US Ambassador to the UN, the White House, and your Representative about what the United States is doing to comply with its commitment the UN Sustainable Development Goals.

Sources for Further Study

Catholic Rural Life Conference. *Pure Water: A Sacramental Commons*. https://catholicrurallife.org/water-a-sacramental-commons-for-all/.

Chamberlain, Gary L. *Because Water Is Life*. Winona, MN: Anselm Academic, 2018.

Dicastery for Promoting Integral Human Development. *Aqua Fons Vitae: Orientations on Water—Symbol of the Cry of the Poor and the Cry of the Earth*. Vatican City: March 2020, https://www.humandevelopment.va/content/dam/sviluppoumano/documenti/Aqua%20fons%20vitae%20_%2003%202020.pdf

Dicastery for Promoting Integral Human Development. *A Collection of Statements, Tools and Initiatives from the Holy See and the Catholic Church Related to Aqua Fons Vitae*. https://www.humandevelopment.va/content/dam/sviluppoumano/documenti/ACQUA-FONS-VITAE-Catholic-toolbox-2020.pdf. Vatican City: March 2020.

McGrail, Peter. "Initiation and Ecology: Becoming a Christian in the Light of *Laudato Si'*." *Liturgy* 31, no. 2 (2016): 55–62. DOI: 10.1080/0458063X.2016.1123951.

Notes

1. "It Took 969 Gallons of Water to Produce This Meal," *Los Angeles Times*, April 6, 2015, https://www.latimes.com/visuals/graphics/la-me-g-how-much-water-to-produce-food-20150406-htmlstory.html.
2. "How Much Water Should You Drink per Day?" https://www.healthline.com/nutrition/how-much-water-should-you-drink-per-day.
3. US EPA, https://www.epa.gov/watersense/statistics-and-facts.
4. UN, *Water for Life Decade: 2005–2015* (New York: United Nations Department of Public Information, 2005). https://www.un.org/waterforlifedecade/. "Key Water.org Facts," https://water.org/.
5. "World Health Organization—Drinking-Water," March 21, 2022, https://apps.who.int/iris/bitstream/handle/10665/254637/9789241549950-eng.pdf;jsessionid=F77106FE760286A15B0317B52256CCE0?sequence=1.

6. *National Geographic,* A Special Issue: Water—Our Thirsty World (April 2010): 112–13 and passim.
7. UN World Population Fund, "World Population Dashboard," https://www.unfpa.org/data/world-population-dashboard.
8. UNESCO, *The United Nations World Water Development Report 2022,* "Groundwater: Making the Invisible Visible," Facts & Figures, https://www.unwater.org/publications/un-world-water-development-report–2022/. The increase is approximately 1 percent per year and fits the current population growth rate.
9. "Ogallala Aquifer Depletion: Situation to Manage, Not Problem to Solve—Courage, Experimentation, Voices Needed to Drive Change," March 19, 2021, https://agrilifetoday.tamu.edu/2021/03/19/ogallala-aquifer-situation-to-manage-not-problem-to-solve/. Kase Wilbanks, "2022 Measurements Show Groundwater Level Declines in High Plains Water District," March 31, 2022, https://www.kcbd.com/2022/04/01/2022-measurements-show-groundwater-level-declines-high-plains-water-district/.
10. Pontifical Council for Justice and Peace, *Water: An Essential Element for Life* 2003, http://www.vatican.va/roman_curia/pontifical_councils/justpeace/documents/rc_pc_justpeace_doc_20030322_kyoto-water_en.html. Hereafter, PCJP, 2003.
11. Environment Illinois, "Clean Up Dirty Power Plants," https://www.csu.edu/cerc/documents/IllinoisDirtyPowerPlantsFactSheet.pdf.
12. Frank B. Golley, *A Primer for Environmental Literacy* (New Haven: Yale University Press, 1998), especially chapters 4–13. "The Water Cycle for Adults and Advanced Students," *Water Science School,* November 6, 2019, https://www.usgs.gov/special-topics/water-science-school/science/water-cycle-adults-and-advanced-students.
13. Peter H. Gleick, ed., *Water in Crisis: A Guide to the World's Fresh Water Resources* (New York: Oxford University Press, 1993), 13.
14. US Geological Survey, "How Much Water Is There On, In, and Above the Earth?" https://www.usgs.gov/special-topics/water-science-school/science/how-much-water-there-earth. UN Department of Economic and Social Affairs, "World Population Projected to Reach 9.8 Billion in 2050, and 11.2 Billion in 2100," https://www.un.org/en/desa/world-population-projected-reach-98-billion-2050-and-112-billion–2100.
15. Upmanu Lall and others, "Water in the 21st Century: Defining Elements of Global Crisis and Potential Solutions," *Journal of International Affairs* 61/2 (Spring/Summer 2008): 1–17.
16. Ibid., 2. Peter H. Gleick, "The Millennium Goals for Water: Crucial Objectives, Inadequate Commitments," in The *World's Water 2004–2005,* ed. Peter H. Gleick (Washington, DC: Island Press, 2004), 1–15.

17. World Health Organization—Drinking-Water, March 21, 2022, https://www.who.int/news-room/fact-sheets/detail/drinking-water.
18. Ibid.
19. Lall and others, "Water in the 21st Century," 1–17.
20. *National Geographic,* 112–13. Centers for Disease Control (CDC), Global Water, Sanitation, & Hygiene (WASH), Flocculant/Disinfectant Powder, https://www.cdc.gov/healthywater/global/household-water-treatment/flocculant-filtration.html.
21. CDC, Solar Disinfection, https://www.cdc.gov/healthywater/global/household-water-treatment/solardisinfection.html.
22. *National Geographic,* 36.
23. World Health Organization, *International Scheme to Evaluate Household Water Treatment Technologies,* Tools and Toolkits, https://www.who.int/tools/international-scheme-to-evaluate-household-water-treatment-technologies.
24. Lall and others cite: "David Malakoff, Death by Suffocation in the Gulf of Mexico," *Science* 281/5374 (1998): 190–2; Cavel Brown et al., "Re-evaluation of the Relationship between Pfiesteria and Estuarine Fish Kills," *Ecosystems* 6/1(2003): 1–10; David Dudgeon, "Large Scale Hydrological Changes in Tropical Asis: Prospects for Ravine Biodiversity," *BioScience* 50/9 (2000): 793–806.
25. Consider this: Imagine a lake surrounded by ten factories. Each wants to discharge wastewater containing 1,500 ppm of a toxin. Suppose the lake could absorb one factory's worth of discharge; they will each argue that their discharge is not a risk and they are providing necessary jobs for the local economy. If they convince the relevant legislators, then all ten will be discharging toxins into the lake and the lake will be seriously poisoned. Once it is noticed that the fish and frogs are dying off and it's not safe to swim or boat on the lake anymore, the arguments will continue fast and furiously about how to solve the problem—which factories will be shut down? Who will pay for the costs of cleaning the discharge before it goes into the lake? While the arguments continue, the toxins will continue to build up and may even enter the groundwater supply, spreading the toxins far beyond the shores of the lake into the drinking water of many more people.
26. Lall and others, "Water in the 21st Century," 6. American Geophysical Union. "Water Scarcity Predicted to Worsen in More Than 80% of Croplands Globally This Century," *ScienceDaily,* www.sciencedaily.com/releases/2022/05/220505143802.htm.
27. Michael Grunwald, "Did Georgia Bring the Drought on Itself?" *Time Magazine,* November 19, 2007. Andrew E. Knaak, Timothy K. Pojunas, and Michael F. Peck, "Extreme Drought to Extreme Floods: Summary

of Hydrologic Conditions in Georgia, 2009," *Proceedings of the 2011 Georgia Water Resources Conference*, held April 11–13, 2011, University of Georgia, https://smartech.gatech.edu/bitstream/handle/1853/46000/2.6.1_Knaak_15.pdf?sequence=1&isAllowed=y. Michael Elizabeth Sakas, "Colorado River States Need to Drastically Cut Down Their Water Usage ASAP," Colorado Public Radio, June 17, 2022, https://www.cpr.org/2022/06/17/colorado-river-states-need-to-reduce-water-use/. Christopher Weber, Mark Thiessen, Jim Anderson, and Susan Montoya Bryan, "Western Wildfires Force Evacuations in Arizona, California," *Nation*, June 13, 2022, https://www.pbs.org/newshour/nation/western-wildfires-force-evacuations-in-arizona-california.

28. Maude Barlow, "Water as Commodity—the Wrong Prescription," *Backgrounder* 7/3 (Summer 2001), https://archive.foodfirst.org/publication/water-as-commodity-the-wrong-prescription/.
29. Shiney Varghese, "NAFTA and the Challenge for Water Justice," October 5, 2017, https://www.iatp.org/blog/201901/nafta-and-challenge-water-justice.
30. Lall and others, "Water in the 21st Century," 8. Water.org, "India's Water and Sanitation Crisis," https://water.org/our-impact/where-we-work/india/. W. Baosheng, W. Zhaoyin, and L. Changzhi, "Yellow River Basin Management and Current Issues," *Journal of Geographical Sciences* 14 (2004): 29–37. https://doi.org/10.1007/BF02841104. New York Water Science Center, "Groundwater Sustainability of the Long Island Aquifer System," March 1, 2018, https://www.usgs.gov/centers/new-york-water-science-center/science/groundwater-sustainability-long-island-aquifer-system.
31. Lall and others, "Water in the 21st Century," 8.
32. National Weather Service, "What Is El Niño-Southern Oscillation (ENSO)?" https://www.weather.gov/mhx/ensowhat.
33. "Understanding Virtual Water to Conserve Water," Commentary, Section 1, 21, *Chicago Tribune*, March 25, 2010. Water Footprint Network, *Glossary*, https://waterfootprint.org/en/water-footprint/glossary/. *National Geographic*, 52.
34. Jason Hill, "The Sobering Truth about Corn Ethanol," *Proceedings of the National Academy of Sciences of the United States of America* 119/11 (e2200997119, March 9, 2022), https://doi.org/10.1073/pnas.2200997119.
35. "Understanding Virtual Water to Conserve Water," 21.
36. *Francis of Assisi: Early Documents*, Volume III—*The Prophet*, trans. and ed. Regis J. Armstrong, J. A. Wayne Hellmann, William J. Short (New York: New City Press, 2001), 366.
37. Pontifical Council for Justice and Peace, *Water: An Essential Element for Life: An Update,* VI. A Culture of Water, https://www.vatican.va/roman_curia/pontifical_councils/justpeace/documents/rc_pc_justpeace_

doc_20060322_mexico-water_en.html. Hereafter PCJP, 2006. Andy Opel, "From Water Crisis to Water Culture: Dr. Vandana Shiva, an Interview by Andy Opel," *Cultural Studies* 22/3-4 (May-July 2008): 498-509.
38. Hurricane Katrina (2005) in New Orleans, LA, was the result of engineering strategies based on "Knowledge Based World View" models. R. Eugene Turner, "Doubt and the Values of an Ignorance Based World View for Restoration: Coastal Louisiana Wetlands," *Estuaries and Coasts* 32 (2009): 1054-68. Harry Shearer, Director, and Writer, "The Big Uneasy" documentary, DVD video: NTSC color broadcast system, FilmBuff, 2010. See https://harryshearer.com/projects/the-big-uneasy/.
39. Opulent water waste is global. *National Geographic,* 30; A twenty-acre swimming hole at Chili's San Alfonso del Mar resort cost $3.5 million. See *National Geographic,* 150: Annually Florida uses 3,000 gallons to water grass for each golf game played. US swimming pools lose 150 billion gallons to evaporation.
40. Annie Leonard, "The Story of Bottled Water: Fear, Manufactured Demand and a $10,000 Sandwich," Greenpeace USA, December 6, 2017, https://www.huffpost.com/entry/the-story-of-bottled-wate_b_507942.
41. Christiana Zenner, *Just Water: Theology, Ethics, and Fresh Water Crisis,* Revised ed. (Maryknoll: Orbis Books, 2018), 52.
42. US Food and Drug Administration, "Bottled Water Everywhere: Keeping It Safe," https://www.fda.gov/consumers/consumer-updates/bottled-water-everywhere-keeping-it-safe. Federal bottled water quality standards were first adopted in 1973.
43. Cameron Woodworth, "A Clean Drink of Water," *PCC Sound Consumer,* August 2004, 4.
44. Zenner, *Just Water,* 53.
45. Grand View Research, "Bottled Water Market Size, Share & Trends Analysis Report by Product, by Distribution Channel, by Region, and Segment Forecasts, 2022-2030," https://www.grandviewresearch.com/industry-analysis/bottled-water-market.
46. Zenner, *Just Water,* 55. Peter Gleick, *Bottled and Sold: The Story behind Our Obsession with Bottled Water* (Washington, DC: Island Press 2010), 170.
47. David Sedlak, "How Development of America's Water Infrastructure Has Lurched through History," *PEW Trend Magazine,* March 3, 2019, https://www.pewtrusts.org/en/trend/archive/spring-2019/how-development-of-americas-water-infrastructure-has-lurched-through-history.
48. Charles Duhigg, "Saving US Water and Sewer Systems Would Be Costly," Toxic Waters Series, *New York Times,* March 14, 2010, https://www.nytimes.com/2010/03/15/us/15water.html.
49. Suzanne Golas, "Privatization of Water," *Resolutions to Action* 14/3 (June 2005): 1-2. S. Tully, "Water, Water, Everywhere," *Fortune Magazine* 141/10 (May 2000): 342-54.

50. Christine E. Gudorf, "Water Privatization in Christianity and Islam," *Journal of the Society of Christian Ethics* 30/2 (2010): 20–1.
51. Ibid., 20.
52. Ibid., 21. Gudorf cites Costa Rica's attempt to levy an export tax on such activities. Mara Flores-Estrada, "CAFTA Threatens to Turn Water into Merchandise," Latinamerica Press 20 (October 31, 2007): 6.
53. Bill McKibben, "Water, Water, Everywhere," *Sojourners Magazine*, June 2010, 14. *Gale Academic OneFile,* https://link.gale.com/apps/doc/A228995458/AONE?u=mlin_m_bostcoll&sid=bookmark-AONE&xid=256b0f36.
54. Barlow, "Water as Commodity—the Wrong Prescription."
55. Ibid.
56. Ibid.
57. Ibid.
58. Ibid.
59. *Worldatlas,* "Highest Usage of Freshwater by Country," https://www.worldatlas.com/articles/highest-use-of-freshwater-by-country.html.
60. See https://www.un.org/waterforlifedecade/human_right_to_water.shtml. Download full text at https://digitallibrary.un.org/record/687002?ln=en.
61. Terrance McGoldrick, "A Theological Argument for Water as a Human Right: The Bolivian Pachamama/Mother Earth Encounter with Catholic Thought," *Journal of Catholic Social Thought* 15/1 (2018): 109–37.
62. UN Department of Public Information, News and Media Division, New York, https://www.un.org/press/en/2010/ga10967.doc.htm.
63. Full text https://digitallibrary.un.org/record/687002?ln=en.
64. Maude Barlow, "Our Right to Water: A People's Guide to Implementing the United Nations' Recognition of the Right to Water and Sanitation," *Council of the Canadians*, June 2011, https://conseildescanadiens.org/sites/default/files/publications/report-rtw-5yr-1115.pdf.

    See "History of the Rights to Water and Sanitation at the United Nations," https://www.ohchr.org/en/special-procedures/sr-water-and-sanitation/about-mandate.
65. Full text of *The Universal Declaration of Human Rights*, 1948 at http://www.un.org/en/documents/udhr/.
66. "About the Mandate: Special Rapporteur on the Human Rights to Safe Drinking Water and Sanitation," https://www.ohchr.org/en/special-procedures/sr-water-and-sanitation/about-mandate.
67. See https://pwccc.wordpress.com/support/.
68. European Wilderness Society, "A River in New Zealand Legally Becomes a Person," https://wilderness-society.org/a-river-in-new-zealand-legally-becomes-a-person/.
69. Ecocide Law, "Legal Definition and Commentary 2021," https://ecocidelaw.com/.

70. Gudorf, "Water Privatization in Christianity and Islam," 19–38.
71. Elizabeth A. Johnson, *Ask of the Beasts: Darwin and the God of Love* (London: Bloomsbury, 2014), 281 and 305. She cites John Paul II, "Peace with God the Creator, Peace with All Creation," §16: "respect for life and the dignity of the human person extends beyond the human species also to the rest of creation."
72. Gudorf, "Water Privatization in Christianity and Islam," 29.
73. Ibid., 30.
74. Ibid.
75. Ibid., 34.
76. Ibid., 35.
77. Catholic Rural Life Conference, Pure Water: A Sacramental Commons, *Considerations for Decision-Making,* https://catholicrurallife.org/water-a-sacramental-commons-for-all/.
78. John Paul II, *Centesimus Annus,* http://www.vatican.va/holy_father/john_paul_ii/encyclicals/documents/hf_jp-ii_enc_01051991_centesimus-annus_en.html.
79. The International Conference on Water and the Environment (IGWE), "The Dublin Statement," January 26–31, 1992, https://wedocs.unep.org/handle/20.500.11822/30961.
80. This section utilizes the structure of two documents, PCJP, 2003, PCJP, 2006. It is built from excerpts and paraphrases from those and subsequent revisions in Dicastery for Promoting Integral Human Development, *Aqua fons vitae Orientations on Water: Symbol of the Cry of the Poor and the Cry of the Earth* (2020), https://www.humandevelopment.va/content/dam/sviluppoumano/documenti/Aqua%20fons%20vitae%20_%2003%202020.pdf, hereafter DPIHD, 2020.
81. PCJP, 2003. Also, PCJP, 2006.
82. Pope Francis, *Laudato Si'—On Care for Our Common Home,* https://www.vatican.va/content/francesco/en/encyclicals/documents/papa-francesco_20150524_enciclica-laudato-si.html. Hereafter, *LS* § followed by paragraph number (s).
83. Ibid., and DPIHD, 2020, § 5, 8, 29, 48, 55, 59, 75 106, 109.
84. PCJP, 2003.
85. PCJP, 2003, and DPIHD, 2020, § 6–8, 15, 30, 32, 50, 55, 75, 109.
86. PCJP, 2006 and DPIHD, 2020, § 9, 12 18, 32, 35, 40, 89.
87. UN Committee on Economic, Social, and Cultural Rights, Supervisory Body of the Covenant on Economic, Social and Cultural Rights, General Comment in 2002, https://digitallibrary.un.org/record/486454?ln=en. Also, International Covenant on Economic, Social, and Cultural Rights, Article 2, §1. For additional treaties and declarations see DPIHD, 2020 page 21, note 65. PCJP, 2006. PCJP, 2003 and DPIHD, 2020, § 8, 15, 32, 55, 56, 77, 86, 95, 102, 109.

88. PCJP, 2003 and DPIHD, 2020, § 3, 8, 15, 26, 55, 60, 63, 73, 75, 94, 104, 105, 109.
89. Ibid.
90. Ibid. Also Jeremy J. Schmidt and Christiana Z. Peppard, "Water Ethics on a Human-Dominated Planet: Rationality, Context, and Values in Global Governance," WIREs, Water 2014, 1: 533–47. DOI: 10. 1002/wat2. 1043.
91. PCJP, 2003 and DPIHD, 2020, § 3, 8, 15, 26, 55, 60, 63, 73, 75.
92. PCJP, 2003.
93. Ibid., and DPIHD, 2020, § 35, 41, 44–5, 66. PCJP, 2003.
94. Ibid.
95. PCJP, 2006.
96. Ibid., and DPIHD, 2020, § 54, 67, 84.
97. Ibid., and DPIHD, 2020, § 27, 37, 82.
98. PCJP, 2006.
99. See http://www.un.org/waterforlifedecade/. December 2017 the UN General Assembly resolution 71/222 on an International Decade for Action on "Water for Sustainable Development" 2018–2028. See: https://www.unwater.org/un-2023-water-conference/.
100. Paul VI, "Speech to the Members of the Pontifical Academy of Sciences," April 19, 1975, https://www.vatican.va/content/paul-vi/fr/speeches/1975/documents/hf_p-vi_spe_19750419_accademia-scienze.html.
101. Peter McGrail, "Initiation and Ecology: Becoming a Christian in the Light of Laudato Si'," *Liturgy* 31/2 (2016): 55–62. This section utilizes the structure of McGrail's article and is built from quotations and paraphrases of that work.
102. Ibid., 56.
103. Ibid., 59.
104. Ibid.
105. Ibid.
106. Ibid.
107. Ibid.
108. Ibid.
109. Constitution on the Sacred Liturgy *Sacrosanctum Concilium* Solemnly Promulgated by His Holiness Pope Paul VI on December 4, 1963, https://www.vatican.va/archive/hist_councils/ii_vatican_council/documents/vat-ii_const_19631204_sacrosanctum-concilium_en.html.
110. McGrail, *Initiation and Ecology*, 60.
111. Armstrong, Hellmann, Short, trans. and eds, *FAED*, I—*The Saint*, 114.

9

Eating Is a Moral Act—Access to Food and Food Security

Introduction

Select one item from your last meal. Where was that item grown? Who were the workers who labored to raise; harvest; clean; butcher; process and package; transport; and shelve the item, prepare it, and serve it on your plate? Most Americans live far removed from agriculture and are illiterate concerning the land, farming, or ranching; waters for fishing; or food processing. The land is merely property, and the waters are simply playgrounds. We go to the supermarket, rarely thinking about our food sources or the people who brought it to us. Our worry is the price of groceries, rarely the environmental or human costs.

Many are oblivious to the dangers of salts, sugars, and fats in processed foods.[1] Obesity is our national scourge. In 2022, of fifty US states, Colorado had the lowest prevalence of obesity at the rate of 23.8 percent of its population; Mississippi had the highest rate at 40.8 percent. Thirty-five states had a higher than 30 percent rate and twelve states had 35 percent or higher.[2] In 2020, 6.1 million children lived with adults in food-insecure households. Also 23.5 million Americans live in food deserts, and more than half of those (13.5 million) are low-income persons.[3] Globally, over 828 million people were afflicted by hunger, not because the world failed to produce plenty of food but because food is not proportionately distributed and affordable.[4]

This chapter addresses the *good news* that we can *relearn* what truly constitutes a sustainable food system, and then *act*, changing our lifestyles so everyone can be well fed. St. Francis and St. Clare show us the meaning of feasting and fasting. Like them, we are called to a morally conscious relationship with food, land, and waters, following in the footprints of Jesus, who is the "Bread of Life."

First, we briefly review the global industrial food system, its life-threatening characteristics, and the US involvement in it. Then we examine the biblical moral vision concerning care for the land and food along with Catholic Social Teaching, especially *Laudato Si'—On Care for Our Common Home*.[5] In Leviticus 25:23, the Creator summarily exhorts, "Land must not be sold in perpetuity, for the land belongs to me. And to me you are only strangers and guests."[6] It is the Creator's intent that food from the Earth is shared equitably and generously. Yet domestically and globally we have acted on far different premises! Taking food for granted rendered us unconscious of a burgeoning globalized industrialized food system that benefits an elite group of agra-businesses, while leaving billions malnourished or starving. The first step toward making a change is to learn how we got into this mess in the first place.

Understanding Food Security

Most people in the United States fail to appreciate their privileged status as individuals who have never worried about having enough to eat. Few Americans need to spend a lifetime *necessarily* consumed with finding enough food and water simply to survive another day. The United Nations Food and Agriculture Organization (FAO) states, "[F]ood security exists when all people, at all times, have physical and economic access to sufficient, safe, and nutritious food that meets their dietary needs and food preferences for an active and healthy life."[7] Food security has four main dimensions: (1) the physical ability to produce, stock, and trade for food; (2) economic and physical ability to access food; (3) food utilization, i.e., sufficient calorie and nutrient intake, and good biological utilization of food consumed; and (4) stability of the other three dimensions over time. All four of these objectives need to be fulfilled simultaneously to have food security. Additional gradations of hunger are utilized to specify the severity of a person's food needs.[8] Scientifically classified, "hunger" is the sensation that is caused by insufficient food-energy consumption, and it is more accurately called *food deprivation*. The current globalized industrialized food system fails to adequately meet these needs for millions and increasingly threatens the food secure nations, the United States included.

Background: The 2008 Access to Food Crisis

Despite the 1960s "Green Revolution" and technological advances within the first decade of the twenty-first century, the world entered another food crisis.[9] Several factors converged to cause the crisis.[10] Most of those causes still do harm today. But hope is found in potential global correctives initiated by the September 2021 UN Food Systems Summit.[11] Those proposals show promise for greater alignment of global food ways with biblical wisdom, Catholic Social Teachings, and particularly Pope Francis', *Laudato Si'—On the Care for Our Common Home*.[12]

Key Contributing Factors—The 2008 Access to Food Crisis and Beyond

Shifting from food-farming methods—where farmers sustained a long-term mutual nurturing relationship with the natural cycles of the soil—to industrial manipulation of vast fertilized acreages for monocrops, tilled with tractors for profit, initially seemed to be good for the world. But the lethal downside to industrial farming was the nearly exclusive priority of profit-making.[13]

A Global Perspective—Factors Present in 2008 and Persisting to the Present

Global *agriculture liberalization* began with the 1980s debt crisis. Global south governments were forced to sign loan agreements eliminating all "barriers to trade" before getting loans from the International Monetary Fund, World Bank, and other international sources.[14] Lowered tariffs allowed imported cheaper foods to flood markets of borrowing nations. Food-deficit Africa became unable to produce or afford to import enough food to feed its population.[15]

Major international financial institutions cut back their agricultural aid, a 54 percent reduction from 1980 to 2005 ($8 to $3.4 billion). In 2008 they gave less than 4 percent of their aid to agriculture, even less to small farmers. Simultaneously, by 2000 reserves of corn and rice stock were halved, making nations more vulnerable to crop failures and price fluctuations.

*Three major changes in land **use*** accompanied agriculture liberalization. Small farmers lost their land and livelihoods, fewer acres were committed to growing food crops, while urbanization increased leaving less land for farming. Industrial scale mono-cropping on huge expanses of land, e.g., for agrofuels (biofuels) primarily for export, thrived.[16] From 2000 to 2008 cereals grown for food and animal feed increased by only 4–7 percent, while cereals for industrial purposes grew by 25 percent. Third, raising crops exclusively for feeding massive animal herds for meat surged.

A larger middle class in China and India doubled the dietary demand for meat in 2008, posing two dangers. First, general food production efficiency was lost with 100 million tons of grain diverted to biofuel (in 2008), and over seven times more used to feed animals.[17] Secondly, animal waste produced large amounts of methane gas—a most lethal greenhouse gas (GHG).[18]

In Summer 2008 *climate change* caused Earth's dry regions to become drier—longer droughts, frequent and destructive fires, and wetter places to become wetter—flooding causing crop loss.[19] Record-setting flooding hit the US "breadbasket" states, fires raged in California, and drought in Australia's wheat belt sent grain prices upward.[20] GHG-laden fossil fuels power the entire global industrialized food system: tractors; fossil fuel-based fertilizers; pesticides; treated seed for monocrops, and huge fossil fuel expenditures for transport.

Oil and food commodities were sold in US dollars. With *a weak US dollar*, oil exporters needed to drive up the price of oil per barrel to keep their purchase power against other stronger currencies. The global effect was also to raise food prices.

During the 2008 food crisis, *more than forty countries banned exports of food to keep their food at home.* This left a huge dent in the globalized industrialized food system, causing global food shortages.[21]

A *small number of agribusinesses raked in profits at unprecedented rates.* Cargill, the largest grain trader, gained 86 percent in profits in the first quarter of 2008 from commodity trading; Bunge, a food trader, had a 77 percent profit increase the last quarter of 2007; Monsanto, the largest seed company, gained 108 percent December 2007–February 2008; Archer Daniel Midlands gained 42 percent; and Mosaic, a top fertilizer company, gained profits of 1,134 percent in the first quarter of 2008.

Years of under investment in agriculture productivity ravaged poor and small farmers. Agriculture expert Tim Mahoney explained, "There has been an underinvestment in smallholder agriculture for the last two to three decades. Now that agriculture production is down, the ability of small farmers to meet increased demands is not there. They just don't have the capacity."²² The 1960s "Green Revolution" investments favored farmers with secure access to land, water, and markets. Now, with depleted soils and water scarcity, higher levels of technological knowledge to produce food were unavailable to poor farmers.

A most insidious cause of the 2008 food crisis resulted from a dramatic increase during the prior 3–4 years in *financial speculation in the commodities futures markets*, which artificially drove up prices of wheat, corn, soybeans, oil, gas, metals, and minerals. The Reagan Administration's Commodity Futures Trading Commission revised commodities laws, allowing outside parties to invest unlimited amounts in commodities.²³ An example of the resulting effect is that, in 2004, the total value of futures contracts in twenty-five principal commodities was only $180 billion. But in the first 55 days of 2008, speculators placed $55 billion into these markets. These long-term effects are still felt today.²⁴

Agriculture in the United States and the 2008 Global Food Crisis²⁵

In 1930 there were 7 million farms in the United States.²⁶ By 2001, there were only an estimated 2.16 million US farms, and 10 percent of those farms account for nearly 70 percent of all agriculture production.²⁷ By 2012 farms numbered about 2 million, with only 565,000 being small family operations. It is estimated that the United States loses 330 farms every week.²⁸

Concentration and Vertical Integration

US food production became concentrated and vertically integrated. In 1997, the top five food retailers held 24 percent of the US market; by 2000 that share increased to 42 percent of retail food sales.²⁹ Today, only four giant firms process the majority of beef, pork, and broilers.³⁰ In 2021, the three largest processors controlled the wheat and soybean market.³¹ In 2009, 93 percent of soybeans and 80 percent of corn grown in the United States were grown from genetically engineered seeds patented by one company, Monsanto.³² As the corporate concentration of farming inputs and distribution developed, farmers had fewer overall options. Egregious hybridization and technological manipulation of seeds destroy biodiversity and remove ancient characteristics that have allowed food plants to thrive in local soils and climatic conditions.³³ Corporate pressures on governments for deregulations, favoring profit-making, increased exponentially. For example, in 2010, agribusiness spent $121,335,788 on lobbying the US federal government.[34]

Several significant factors emerge from this data. Overall, food production increased due to massive use of advanced technologies in agriculture. Globally, a few huge and powerful agribusiness enterprises consolidated concentration of farming and ranching and still retain controlled. Corporate executives make decisions that affect people unseen and unknown to them. Traditional sustainable farming and ranching for food production have nearly been lost to an elite few, maximizing production for profits. Industrial agriculture wreaked havoc on natural plant diversity, vital to sustainable production, contributing to food insecurity.

2008 Efforts toward Correction of the Food Crisis

Attempts at resolution of the 2008 food crisis included the G-8 and G-20 July 8–10, 2009, meeting in L'Aquilla, Abruzzo, Italy. The G-8 nations failed to garner the political will to alleviate the global food crisis targeted by the UN Millennium Development Goals for 2015.[35] The G-20 nations signed the L'Aquila commitments but were slow to finance agreed pledges, failed to establish regulatory policies governing over-the-counter derivatives and commodity futures, or establish agricultural risk management tools and social safety nets.

Hope from the 2009 Rome World Food Summit

In Rome, November 16–18, 2009, sixty heads of state met with the UNFAO. They faced projections indicating that by 2050 Earth will be home for 9.1 billion people. Seventy percent more food will need to be raised in extreme and unpredictable weather.[36] There will be 1 billion hungry people, that is, 105 million more than in 2008.[37]

The Rome *Declaration of the World Summit on Food Security—November 2009* pledged a substantial increase of aid to agriculture in developing nations, so the world's hungry could become more self-sufficient.[38] They also pledged to meet the UN Millennium Development Goal #2 but failed to fund the annual $44 million agricultural aid the UNFAO deemed necessary for coming decades.[39] The *Declaration*'s Five Rome Principles for Sustainable Global Food Security were the basis of the agreement.[40]

From Millennial Development Goals to Sustainable Development Goals

The Millennium Development Goals Report 2015 enumerated the major successes. It affirmed the goal: "with targeted interventions, sound strategies, adequate resources and political will, even the poorest can make progress."[41]

The successor, Sustainable Development Goals, included *Goal 2: End hunger, achieve food security and improved nutrition and promote sustainable agriculture.*[42] By 2021, some progress was made on *Goal 2*, but the massive, unyielding, industrialized food system continued to thwart advances. Conflict, climate change and extremes, and economic issues continued to be the major drivers slowing progress. The Covid-19 pandemic made the pathway towards SDG2 steeper.[43]

Movement toward Food Crisis 2022

In 2019, *Lancet* called for a food revolution to solve the world's climate and nutrition problems. The "EAT-*Lancet*" study concluded that "to stabilize climate and get people healthy, the world needs to overhaul its diet and agriculture systems."[44] "EAT-*Lancet*" raised compelling evidence that, necessarily, agricultural and health policies must be linked to meet the Paris climate targets of 1.5°C. Globally people must consume less meat.

EAT-*Lancet* proposed scientific targets for diet and food production to improve human health and simultaneously achieve planetary sustainability. Government food policies must require major reduction of industrial farming practices. Model National Dietary Guidelines of Denmark, Germany, and the United Kingdom explicitly advise citizens to cut meat consumption, but the United States has no such mandate.[45] The quinquennial US Dietary Guidelines Advisory Committee's guideline renewal process is controlled by "Big Food." It has continually blocked advice to cut back on meat consumption.[46]

US agriculture and agricultural policy currently support commodity crops (e.g., soy, corn), which provide little direct nutrition. Agriculture has narrowly focused on a few staples—maize, rice, wheat—rarely on "mostly of vegetables, fruits, whole grains, legumes, nuts, and unsaturated oils, including a low to moderate amount of seafood and poultry, and no or a low quantity of red meat, processed meat, added sugar, refined grains, and starchy vegetables."[47]

The *Lancet's Commission on Obesity* recognized "The Global Syndemic." Obesity, malnutrition, and climate change are interrelated and drive one another. They claim "'food production shocks' linked to climate change have been rising globally, putting food security at risk."[48] The current industrial land-based food system with heavy livestock production is highly vulnerable to droughts.[49]

Hope for change is rising. People are connecting the need for plant-based diets, healthy eating, conquering obesity, and cutting GHG with industrial farming, meat production causing global warming. Recently, eighty investor groups with $6.5 trillion in assets challenged six top fast-food companies to target cutting GHG emissions from their meat and dairy supply chains.[50]

Toward a World Food Systems Summit 2021

By 2021 the Sustainable Development Goals for food and nutrition were unmet, and the situation was worsening with the Covid-19 pandemic and intensified impacts of climate change. The UN World Food Program estimates showed acute hunger victims doubled to 265 million by 2020.[51] The UNFAO scheduled a summit for September 2021 seeking "healthier, more sustainable and equitable food systems."[52] A "pre-summit," met on July 26–28, in Rome and virtually on five themes: universal access to safe and nutritious food, sustainable consumption, "nature-positive" production, equitable livelihoods, and resilience.[53]

Pope Francis urged prioritizing small farmers, farm families, and traditional knowledge about environmentally sound food production. The Vatican's Cardinal Peter Turkson stressed drawing on the knowledge of Indigenous and traditional peoples calling the industrial-scale use of chemical pesticides and fertilizers "ecocidal practices."[54]

Sadly, corporations dominated the pre-summit because most ordinary people could not travel, access technology, or use English for the virtual sessions. Norman Wirzba stressed, "you have to appreciate that their [corporations] main interest is not the nutrition of eaters, it's not the health of eaters — their main interest is profit margin."[55] CIDSE, a Catholic consortium of humanitarian and development agencies, sponsored a "People's Counter-Mobilization to Transform Corporate Food Systems," highlighting the right to sufficient nutritious food and agroecological solutions to the food crisis.[56] Michael Fakhri, UN Special Rapporteur on the Right to Food, gave the same critique as CDISE and sought corrections for the September 2021 Summit.[57]

The September 2021 UN Food Systems Summit

The UN Food Systems Summit convened online on September 23, 2021. Over 51,000 people—civil society leaders, farmers, youth, Indigenous peoples—from 193 countries made nearly 300 commitments to accelerate action and to transform food systems.[58] Their focus was relief of post-Covid conditions where "up to 811 million people in the world faced hunger in 2020—a 20% increase in just one year. Over 41 million were on the doorstep of starvation."[59]

Reaching the UN Sustainable Development Goals for 2030 became increasingly unlikely. However, "sustainable food production systems should be recognized as an essential solution to these existing challenges. It is possible to feed a growing global population while protecting our planet."[60]

The summit committed to five action objectives for building the resilience of food systems to respond to shocks and vulnerabilities, pandemics, and climate disruption.[61] The UNFAO's "State of Food and Agriculture 2021" report addressed nations' ability to respond to stresses and offered guidance to governments on improving resilience.[62] Annually, the world's complex agri-food systems produce 11 billion tons of food, employing billions of people. Yet about 3 billion people cannot afford a healthy diet, and 1 billion would be unable to access healthy food if their incomes declined by one-third due to a shock.[63]

Key to resilience against shocks are diverse pathways for absorbing shocks. High resilience requires having a mix of food and nonfood products and selling to a wide range of domestic and international markets. Sustaining small- and medium-agri-food enterprises and cooperatives helps maintain diversity in domestic food markets. Diverse transport options are also needed. All countries need to devise network systems that can quickly overcome disruptions by shifting sources of supply, transport, marketing, and labor. Resiliency ultimately requires better health and education services, gender equality, and women's participation in all facets of the agroecological system and recognition of agroecology's role in stewardship of the natural environment. The UNFAO concluded the report by committing to take concrete action on all of these areas "leaving none behind."[64]

2022—A Year of Unprecedented Hunger

The major causes of hunger and famine are conflict, climate shocks, pandemics, and economic costs of reaching people in need. On February 24, 2022, Russia invaded Ukraine, upending the potential for achieving the 2021 Summit objectives. Those two nations are major global exporters of wheat, maize, and sunflower oil. A global food crisis that threatened to be even more devastating, deadly, and longer lasting than the food crisis of 2007–2008, or the Covid-19 pandemic, loomed. According to the UNFAO inflation-adjusted figures, food commodity prices rose 23.1 percent in 2021.[65] February 2022 prices were the highest since 1961 tracking prices for meat, dairy, cereals, oils, and sugar.

An April 2022 study of thirteen countries, by the NGO, ActionAid provided a global snapshot of the Russia-Ukraine war's effects on Africa, Asia, Latin America, and the Middle East—locales disproportionately affected by the warring between Russia and Ukraine.[66] The World Food Programme predicted that up to 323 million people would face acute food insecurity (in 2022) if the war continued.[67] Rising fuel costs, due to sanctions placed on Russia's major exports of oil and gas, exacerbated the food scarcity. Fertilizer prices soared because production of synthetic nitrogen fertilizers necessary for industrial farming requires large amounts of fossil fuel. This situation provided a perfect example of what the 2021 Food Systems Summit commitments seek to prevent by reorganizing and creating a global resilient eco-agricultural system.

ActionAid offered four types of recommendations to governments to alleviate the crisis.[68] First, governments must provide universal social protection and public services.[69] Locally free meals, cash transfers, food transfers, and more must assist people in bridging the crisis. Wealthier nations need to assist with debt relief, refrain from imposing austerity conditions, and provide basic health care and education for all.

Second, without access to fertilizers, drops in agricultural production levels will result. Swift and thorough training in sustainable agroecological farming practices need to be made available.[70] Those practices will further the progress toward reduction of reliance of GHG-inducing use of fertilizers, promote soil-enhancing practices, more efficient use of water, and care for biodiversity.[71]

Third, ActionAid recommended building up food reserves. Nations need to set up food reserves that can be distributed in emergency situations. Transparent processes for gathering and distributing food should be created and implemented with the equitable participation of all parts of society, especially for the most vulnerable.

Finally, public and private financing must be shifted to investments in renewable energy and agroecology. Current harmful agricultural subsidies should be immediately withdrawn in favor of agroecological mechanisms.[72]

Considering these difficult and heart-rending realities, what is an ordinary person to do? To answer this query we turn first to Scripture, Catholic Social Teaching, and then to some insights from St. Francis and current spiritual writers. Finally, we highlight some effective actions that are changing the unjust food system and suggest practical steps we can take.

Theology of the Land and the Moral Vision of Leviticus 25

The Theme of '*Eretz*: "Land" and "Earth"

The Hebrew word 'eretz or ha'aretz occurs 2,504 times in the Hebrew Testament, signaling the importance of the land for the Israelites and for us.[73] The land holds profound meaning as a source of wealth, a conditional grant from God, lots distributed to families, God's inheritance, regulated by Sabbath laws, and a host country for immigrants.[74]

Biblical scholar Walter Brueggemann studied the social, political, and moral significance of how the term 'eretz is translated throughout the Hebrew Testament.[75] The Earth is God's gift to humankind and a creature intended for establishing fruitfulness and well-being. The term 'eretz is properly translated as "earth" when it refers to the overall sovereignty of God that serves to relativize all other claims to ownership of the "land" (Ezek. 29–30). If the "earth" is the Lord's, great power and freedom accompany the promises and interventions of God in the concrete lives of humankind. Then Exodus becomes a narrative of defiance and withdrawal from an oppressive "land" system (Gen. 47) and is the start of the grand experiment at play in Leviticus.

Throughout its history, two ideologies about the "land" functioned in Israel. First, the *royal ideology* sought to keep the land without heeding the *Torah*, resulting in loss of land and enslavement for Israel. But the *prophetic* stance held that those who were dispossessed would receive land from God (I Sam. 2:6-7). Israel's identity included the "land" and the belief that God provided the land for *all* people who live in holiness. Without land, there is no food, livelihood, or accompanying social power to benefit from it, and people cannot be fully human. Considering this, we now examine Leviticus 25.

Leviticus 25 and Its Context

Leviticus (*wayyiqr´*) means "and he called." God called Moses to receive the revelation given in this book. This call was to holiness, understood as wholeness, a complete response to the mystery of God: "Be holy, for I, the Lord your God am holy" (11:44-45; 19:2; 20:7, 26). People must order their lives, reflecting the perfect wholeness of the God who calls them.[76] The Holiness Code (Lev. 17-27) provides instructions for attaining holiness by observing the Sabbath, Sabbatical Year, and the Jubilee year.

God, Creator and Liberator, spoke through Moses from Mount Sinai (vv. 1; 38, 42, 55). God's first words in Leviticus 25 command rest—for *people*, but *also* the *land* (v. 2)![77] Every seventh year the land is to rest (not just being left fallow or doing crop rotation). Why? "for the Lord" (vv. 2-4)! This is an act of worship, not a utilitarian agricultural strategy. Holy people honor God by giving intrinsic value to the land and allowing it to rest. This sets the tone for a lifestyle bearing abundant ecological responsibility and care for the land. Indeed, the land itself is an integral part of the Covenant and thus part of the redemption people seek.[78] High priority is given to *rest* for the land; it must occur every seventh year.

In the fiftieth year (following 7 × 7 Sabbatical years) a grand celebration of Jubilee occurred. The Jubilee Year is observed by all classes of people.

In the fallow years, it is *God's* providence—not human effort—that supplies sufficient goods and produce to fill the needs of humans and animals. No hoarding is necessary (or allowed) and all share equally according to their needs.

Renewal of the land is connected to renewal of the human person; indeed, humans are inseparable from the land. Jubilee restores all imbalances of debts, ownership, and enslavement.

Further, the Jubilee Year reveals God's care *for the poor* who cannot thrive because they are disconnected from the land. All humans without distinction must rely on the land and a community for their sustenance. At the time of the conquest, the land was proportionately distributed among Israel's tribes according to the size of clans and families, indicating a concern for equity, fairness, and significantly, acknowledging the unalienable character of the land. There is no hint of an *absolute right* to private property or legitimating huge land grabs! Restoration of property is clearly a *gift* given by God!

Holiness also required just and fair pricing in exchange for goods and the land (vv. 15-17). The wealthy and powerful were held to a standard of *justice*, not merely to generosity. Throughout the Holiness Code, there are various mechanisms that protect the poor from exploitation and becoming landless, on the one hand, while limiting the accumulation of exorbitant wealth on the other.[79] The fear of the Lord is the singular reason for practicing justice (v. 17). Peace and security are the reward for living justly (v. 18). The fruitfulness of the land is a sign of the blessing of peace (v. 19), especially during the year prior to the Sabbatical Year (vv. 21-22).

In this broader context we read Leviticus 25:23: "Land must not be sold in perpetuity, for the land belongs to me. And, to me you are only strangers and guests" (Jerusalem Bible). Here is the pivotal relativizing statement in Lev 25. Thus, *if* God is the sole owner, *then* the only possible relationship of the people to the land is that of a steward/farmer.[80] The steward must dispose of or use the land in fulfillment of the owner's instructions. The farmer must nurture, care for, and tend to the needs of the land to sustain its fertility and fecundity.

There are many ways people can become poor—illness, drought, etc.[81] However, three pathways for the redemption of land and property are as follows: one buys back the land with the help of a relative (v. 25); one saves money and buys back their land (vv. 26-27); or one awaits the Jubilee Year when debts are reprieved, and land is returned (v. 28).

Throughout the Jubilee Year mandates, especially considering Leviticus 25:23, we see that the ecological well-being of the land is intimately tied to the spiritual and material well-being of the people of Israel. The God who owns the land is attentive to the needs of the poor and the need of the land for rest. The laws of holiness, when heeded, bring wholeness to human persons and all of creation.

The Jubilee Year is doubly referenced in Luke 4: 18-19 where Jesus reads Isaiah 61:1-2 in the temple and then refers to Isaiah 58:6. Here Jesus outlines his mission, and subsequently, he teaches his followers to participate in bringing about the Kingdom of God. Such language harkens back to the great prophetic promises and talk of the New Covenant (Jer. 31:31-34), the Resurrection (Ezek. 37:1-4), and the New Creation (Isa. 65:17-25).

Critique of US and Global Land Use and the Food Crisis Considering Leviticus 25

Today the moral vision of Leviticus 25 is as relevant as ever. The moral obligations it reveals still compel us to worship God and to live in loving and just relationship to self, neighbor, all creatures, and the land.[82] Those norms stand against the greed and abuses of power which destroy the vitality of both humans and land, ultimately causing the poor across the globe to starve.

Considering Leviticus 25, the data presented in our present work indicts our current global industrial food system with its harmful policies and food production practices perpetrated by gigantic globalized industrialized mono-crop operations. Those strategies are rooted in economic theories that presume scarcity (real or created) rather than an abundance of God's providence. Such operations have failed to serve the common good. Instead, they exhaust the land, trying to maximize production, using petrochemicals and exorbitant amounts water, ultimately threatening the world's potable water supply, exacerbating our "Climate Emergency," while still failing to feed the hungry. Farm laborers suffer from the demands to maximize productivity without just wages, worker's health and safety, and integrity of the land. The God of Sabbath, Sabbatical, or Jubilee rest is absent from this scenario!

In stark contrast, as an agricultural system, the Jubilee Year requires and promotes "the caring for what has been entrusted to us … an economics of care, or an economics of enough."[83] Such a system requires and enables a modest lifestyle, gives prime time to adequate rest, relationships with God, neighbors, and the land, maintaining health and wholeness. Today the poor are often left as the "collateral damage" of the "invisible hand" of the "free market" that industrializes and commodifies the land—farms, farmers, food, and food-processing workers. Often only when the poor masses threaten violence (e.g., food riots of 2007), or when shortages hit home (e.g., the 2022 baby formula shortage) is change or land reform or systemic change offered out of fear, as pacification, or motivated by self-interest, rather than as just action protect the exercise of an intrinsic right to proper nutrition.[84] Today the vision of sacred Scripture and Catholic Social Teaching points to another way.

Catholic Social Teaching

Pope John Paul II, "Homily, at Living History Farms"[85]

"Disturbing changes in rural America" motivated the US Midwest Heartland Catholic Bishops to engage farming communities in dialogue. Pope John Paul II joined their efforts, offering Mass on October 4, 1979, in the Diocese of Des Moines, Iowa.

At Living History Farms, the Pope addressed farmers:

> The land is God's gift entrusted to humanity from the very beginning ….it is also man's responsibility … The land must be conserved with care since it is intended to be fruitful for generation upon generation … You are stewards of some of the most important resources that God has entrusted to humanity. Therefore, conserve the land well, so that your children's children and generations after them will inherit an even richer land than was entrusted to you.[86]

Here is the foundation for a Catholic land ethic. Several principles include the following:

- ✓ Land is a *trust* that requires a caring relationship.
- ✓ Land ownership and management are the human's role and *responsibility*.

✓ Land as an inheritance from God is an *intergenerational responsibility* and a subject with intrinsic value, not a mere object manipulated with cold calculation for profit.
✓ Humans are obligated to *conserve* the land and its goods.
✓ Farming is a vocation to *cooperate* with God in creative action and Earth's rhythms fruitfulness.

Strangers and Guests: Toward Community in the Heartland[87]

On May 1, 1980, seventy-two bishops from twelve US states promulgated the pastoral letter, *Strangers and Guests: Toward Community in the Heartland*. Stressing key principles from John Paul II's 1979 homily, they held that all too frequently earth "is being subjected to harmful farming, mining and development practices" (1). The bishops called for "the social reforms that are necessary to preserve our land, ... and promote justice for our people" (8). The primary focus in *Strangers and Guests* is protecting and promoting the owner-operated family farm.

Reflecting on Leviticus 25, the bishops proposed ten "Principles of Land Stewardship" (§50) as a theological basis for care for God's creation. These echo their principles of a Catholic land ethic and consciousness of the impacts of land use practices on land owners and laborers. The bishops applied each principle to the various forms of land abuse and other related moral violations.

Voices and Choices—Forty-One Catholic Bishops of the US South[88]

As US farming operations shifted to industrial mega-farms, the mass production of poultry, hogs, cattle, and factory farms followed. Rapid growth in gigantic meat-processing plants ensued, hiring unskilled laborers— usually people of color and/or new immigrants. US poultry and food processors were notorious for their egregious labor practices and dangerous working conditions.

With over twenty years of personal experiences, on November 15, 2000, forty-one Catholic Bishops of the southern United States issued a pastoral letter entitled *Voices and Choices*. They detailed the high "price" poultry workers paid so that US consumers have plentiful, inexpensive poultry. That "price" included serious injuries, disabling repetitive-motion trauma, disrespectful treatment, and inadequate pay, lack of adequate health care, and deportation threats. According to a 1997 US Department of Labor study, 60 percent of poultry companies surveyed were found in violation of the Fair Labor Standards Act.[89] In 2000, the United Food and Commercial Workers International Union (UFCW) found that poultry workers were mostly African American and female with Latinos rapidly filling the workforce.[90]

The bishops addressed moral questions concerning the poor illegal immigrants entering the United States without other means to feed their families.[91] They taught: "While the laws regarding immigration and immigrants must be respected, everything must be done to aid and protect this most vulnerable and exploitable group of brothers and sisters."[92] They emphasized the essential priority of shared responsibility and decision-making—the "voices and choices"—in the workplace, noting that the poultry workers' right to just employment is grounded in the reality of the *imago Dei*.[93]

The bishops cited the National Catholic Rural Life Conference, "The ramifications of 'factory farming' impact prices, wages, natural resources, and the future of family farming, placing enormous power in the boardrooms of a few companies."[94] They called for legal and structural changes to address the intricate and interconnected web of environmental, technological, political, financial, and international issues involved. Finally, they challenged the Catholic Community to live out the Six Basic Principles of Catholic Social Teaching.[95]

USCCB, Catholic Reflection on Food, Farmers, and Farmworkers[96]

In 2003 the USCCB revisited the status of land use and agriculture in the United States and the interrelated issues of poverty and food scarcity. The problems cited in 1980 had deepened. Their November 18, 2003, document considered the imperative of the Last Judgment to care for people in need (Mt. 25:35) and the call of Leviticus 25:4-6.[97] They set six criteria against which policies concerning land use and agriculture must be measured:

1 Overcoming Hunger and Poverty
2 Providing a Safe, Affordable, and Sustainable Food Supply
3 Ensuring a Decent Life for Farmers and Farmworkers
4 Sustaining and Strengthening Rural Communities
5 Protecting God's Creation
6 Expanding Participation

The document concluded with a "Catholic Agenda for Action: Pursuing a More Just Agricultural System." Concerning "US Farmers and Farm Policies," they challenged, "the continuing concentration in the ownership of land and resource and in the marketing and distribution of food [that] leaves control in the hands of too few and diminishes effective participation."[98]

The most extensive set of actions called for addressing various issues of "US Agricultural Workers." They called for just and living wages for workers; required worker participation in work and community-related decisions; and stressed adequate protection for hazardous work.

The section on "International Trade, Aid, and Development" addressed the needs of small farmers and farm workers in the United States and abroad. There must be strong vigilance over free trade agreements effecting small farmers' market access, and they must provide flexibility, just opportunities for poor and desperate nations, stable and accessible food prices, and just health and safety standards.[99]

"Emerging Technologies" that contribute opportunities for the world's poorest moving out of poverty and into food security were encouraged, such as increased public support for ongoing research to develop food crops that can grow in more arid and less fertile regions of the world. But bishops raised strong cautions concerning genetically modified organisms, especially for food (GMOs).[100] GMOs present two fundamental moral questions: "Who will decide about the use and availability of these new technologies? And who will benefit from them?"[101]

"Stewardship of Creation" must be the goal of agricultural policies. Concluding, the bishops firmly asserted that conservation and improvement of soils, water quality, wildlife, and biodiversity are important. They urged protections for farmworkers from pesticides and chemicals and minimal use of those toxins. They seriously questioned huge monocrop and animal factory farms.

Pope Benedict XVI, "Address to the World Food Summit"[102]

On November 16, 2009, Pope Benedict XVI became the first pontiff to address the UNFAO at its Rome headquarters, opening a World Food Summit. He warned against the greed of speculators in cereal markets and criticized aid that gravely damages the agricultural sector. Citing *Caritas in Veritate* (*CV*), §27, he noted that food insecurity was a problem of providing access to food.[103]

Benedict stressed that any adequate system providing access to food must work to fully integrate poor countries into the world's economic system. Citing *CV* §s 27 and 47 the Pope insisted that integral human development requires that subsidiarity and solidarity be key criterion for the global food system.[104] Benedict insisted that the food insecurity of Lesser Developed Nations not merely be written off by wealthy nations:

> It is not so, and it must never be so! To fight and conquer hunger it is essential to start redefining the concepts and principles that have hitherto governed international relations, in such a way as to answer the question: What can direct the attention and the consequent conduct of States towards the needs of the poorest? ... only in the name of common membership of the worldwide human family can every people, and therefore every country, be asked to practice solidarity, that is, to shoulder the burden of concrete responsibilities in meeting the needs of others, so as to favor the genuine sharing of goods, founded on love.[105]

The Pope continued, making significant distinctions between love, justice, the moral and the juridical obligations of Christians (*CV*§ 59).[106]

Pope Benedict insisted that food production primarily for profit-making is a huge error. Sufficient, healthy, and nutritious food and safe and sufficient water is a human right. Thus, all analysis and actions for development and increased food security must safeguard the environment as a shared good. This also requires all people to change their habits of consumption and their perceptions of what is truly needed. He concluded:

> Hunger is the most cruel and concrete sign of poverty. Opulence and waste are no longer acceptable when the tragedy of hunger is assuming ever greater proportions ... the Catholic Church ... is committed to support, by word and deed, the action taken in solidarity—planned, responsible and regulated ... yet it must not exclude the religious dimension, with all the spiritual energy that it brings, and its promotion of the human person. Acknowledgment of

the transcendental worth of every man and every woman is still the first step towards the conversion of heart that underpins the commitment to eradicate deprivation, hunger, and poverty in all their forms.[107]

Laudato Si'—On Care for Our Common Home[108]

In *Laudato Si'* § 15, Pope Francis formalized earlier environmental ethical teaching of the Church's Magisterium as "now added to the body of the Church's social teaching." Wholesome earthly living always requires food that is safe, sufficiently nutritious, accessible, and affordable. Food is a common human need and a God-given human right.

In Chapter One, Francis warns that the "throw away culture" is at the root of the harmful consumption that is destructive of human sensibilities and sensitivities to the cycles of the natural world (*LS* § 20). He promotes moderate consumption of the earth's goods, and learning to maximize the efficiency of things, reusing and recycling them when possible (*LS* § 22). Not only land-based agriculture is threatened, but also acidification of oceans and water sources threatens the marine food chain (*LS* § 24). Scarcity of water will lead to the scarcity of food (*LS* § 31). Deforestation threatens biodiversity necessary to sustain the food chain (*LS* § 32-40). He summarizes, "[W]e know that approximately a third of all food produced is discarded, and 'whenever food is thrown out it is as if it were stolen from the table of the poor'" (*LS* § 50).[109]

In Chapter Three, Francis favors productive diversity of an economy with traditional small-scale farming (*LS* §s 124-128). He states:

> For example, there is a great variety of small-scale food production systems which feed the greater part of the world's peoples, using modest amount of land and producing less waste, be it in small agricultural parcels, in orchards and gardens, hunting and wild harvesting or local fishing. Economies of scale, especially in the agricultural sector, end up forcing smallholders to sell their land or to abandon their traditional crops. Their attempts to move to other, more diversified, means of production prove fruitless because of the difficulty of linkage with regional and global markets, or because the infrastructure for sales and transport is geared to larger businesses. Civil authorities have the right and duty to adopt clear and firm measures in support of small producers and differentiated production.
>
> (*LS* § 129)

Francis holds that restraints need to be imposed occasionally to balance out greater resources and financial power. He sees the calls by the powerful for economic freedom to be dangerous, when reigning conditions bar many people from actual access to it. Francis is not anti-business, but he is "pro-fair play." Overall, technology must serve the common good.

In Chapter Five, Pope Francis seeks a global consensus that would lead to planning a sustainable diversified agriculture, developing renewable less polluting forms of energy. Fossil fuels need to be replaced without delay—including the use of petrochemicals in agriculture (*LS* § 165). He proposes dialogue as a primary strategy for resolving the climate emergency that is imposing on the entire Earth for environment in the international community; for new national and local policies; for transparency in decision-making; with politics and economy in dialogue for human fulfillment; and for religions in dialogue with science.

Chapter Six addresses environmental education and spirituality. Many things need to change to achieve a sustainable world—but mostly it is the humans that need to change. We need to recall our common origins in the heart of the Creator. People need to move out of themselves toward each other. We need to set limits on ourselves for the sake of others having what is needed. Our task is to be attentive to the impact of each action in relation to others and the earth. Our lifestyle must change, engaging moderation and a "less is more" attitude (*LS* § 222).

From the Writings of St. Francis

A Mirror of Perfection, Rule, Profession, Life and True Calling of a Lesser Brother, 24[110]

Blessed Francis used to say: "My brothers, I say that each of you must consider his own constitution, because although one of you may be sustained with less food than another, I nevertheless want one who needs more food not to try imitating him on this. Rather, considering his constitution, he should provide his body with what it needs. Just as we must be aware of overindulgence in eating, which harms the body and soul, so we must be aware of excessive abstinence even more, because the 'Lord *desires mercy and not sacrifice*' [Hos.6:6]."

Reflection and Application

Catholic Social Teaching principles clearly frame an ethics of eating. These principles originate in the Scriptures and in the texts we have examined. The National Catholic Rural Life Conference provided a concise list of these *Principles for Ethical Eaters*.[111]

Eating as a Moral Act: What's Your "Foodprint"?

A 2007 Cornell University study by Chris Peters and others compared forty-two diets with the same number of calories and a core of grains, fruits, vegetables, and dairy products, but with varying amounts of meat (from 0 to 13.4 ounces daily) and fat (from 20 to 45 percent of calories) to determine each diet's "agricultural land foodprint" (footprint).[112] They found a fivefold difference between the two extremes. What is significant for conserving land and other resources with our diets is limiting the amount of meat we eat and for farmers to rely more on grazing and forages to feed their livestock. Consumers must realize that foods differ not only in their nutrient content but in the number and kind of resources required to produce, process, package, and transport them.

Changes in lifestyle require work. But as the Cornell study showed, one can still enjoy some of life's pleasures while eating with a moral conscience.[113] Food needs to be grown in ways that nurture the earth, i.e., little or no use of chemical fertilizers, pesticides, or herbicides and keeping the soils fertile, the waters pure, and the air clean.[114] We need to consume foods that are environmentally good to grow. The health and safety of all who handle the food from seed to table must be secured. God's animal creatures are not mere objects for our consumption but sensate beings that require our respect and careful treatment. These principles rule out eating foods produced on most factory farms.[115]

Our origin and development of habits, values, and virtues around food are usually formed at home with family. L. Shannon Jung suggests, at regularly shared meals children develop mutual relationships that are critical for life and ecological living.[116] Family meals offer early occasions for sharing the concerns of each member's daily life. Children can learn othercenteredness through helping cook the meal, shopping, or working in the garden. Such accompaniment is needed to reverse the value of "Mcfood" culture that demands the mass production of animals and monocrops.

Eating lower on the food chain will positively impact our health, land use, water quality, and soil conservation. This requires reaching for whole foods and cooking from scratch. It is highly significant that whole foods require less energy to be produced and processed. The Cornell study showed chicken and wild-caught fish are among the most efficient when adding meat to the diet. Recipes from the 1950s or earlier and cuisine of Latinx, Middle Eastern, and Asian cultures offer up tasty whole foods and meatless meals.

Organically grown foods are the best because they use up to 35 percent less energy to produce while being good to the earth.[117] "Community Supported Agriculture" is a earth-friendly system by which people buy a share in local farm production. While expenses for local food vary, the key value saving advantage is the local food is sustainably produced.[118]

Feasting and Fasting in the Footprints of Jesus

Conversion: Feasting and Fasting

As a youth, Giovanni di Pietro di Bernardone (Francis of Assisi) was known for his carousing, opulence, and feasting.[119] Yet his joy in such festivities was ultimately found wanting—never satisfying his deepest desires. It was when he embraced a simplified life, desiring to walk in the footprints of Jesus that he finally saw the Giver of All Good Gifts and the radical incarnational relatedness of everything and everyone.

In the Rule of 1221, Francis directed the Order to fast from the Feast of All Saints to Christmas and from Epiphany to Easter, as well as every Friday.[120] As a spiritual practice, he rarely ate cooked food, diluted it with cold water, or spread ashes on it.[121] Yet, when invited to feasts or fine dinners, he would eat some of what was placed before him (Jesus' mandate, Lk.10:8). Following in the footprints of Jesus meant living at the margins with the poor, being content with having food and clothing (I Tim. 6:8). Material possessions lost their attraction, for he knew from his past how empty of lasting value those are. Instead, he prized the Giver of the Gift of food and the relationships it symbolized.

Food was the occasion for realizing life's interdependency and contingency—we do not create our own food and we must continually replenish it—lest we die. Indeed, everyone depends on the Earth itself and God's providence, and this dependency is also an opportunity for brothers and sisters to realize and respect the diversity among them. Not all of St. Francis' brothers had the physical constitution for fasting. But even St. Francis gave in to the needs of the hungry brothers as a gesture of hospitality.

St. Francis' feasting and fasting seem extreme to our sensibilities. Yet, if as a spiritual practice we reflect on our efforts at fasting, we can learn much about the ethics of eating and seeking justice. Many religious, including Muslims and Catholics, are called to fast on various occasions—Ramadan, Fridays, or Lent. By feeling the real bodily stress of "hunger" we can become clear about what it is like for millions who go hungry each day. We can grow in empathy and genuine compassion—that compels us to action, not pity. Isaiah reminded, "The kind of fast I want is that you remove the chains of oppression and the yoke of injustice and let the oppressed go free, share your food with the hungry and open your homes to the poor" (Isa. 58:6-7).

Fasting can awaken a realization of the effects of our eating habits on our personal health. Genuine ethical earth care requires we take seriously how money, time, and energy spent on excess food could be more justly spent on whole foods, projects of NGOs providing food to the poor, or changing the industrial food system. Fasting can teach us that "less is more." We can then nurture our real needs for love, intimate conversations, acceptance, and healthy self-confidence. Fasting from food can demonstrate that we *can* "live without" with *much* less. A wise rabbi once said, "God ignores fasting that does not result in greater compassion"—and I would add—and just action.

The Eucharistic Feast

For Christians the finest meal is the Eucharist. At each Eucharist the fruits of the earth and the work of human hands join together giving us but a foretaste of the eternal banquet. Pope Francis reminds us: "The Sacraments are a privileged way in which nature is taken up by God to become a means of mediating supernatural life. Through our worship of God, we are invited to embrace the world on a different plane" (*LS* § 235).

Peter McGrail expands on the marvelous cosmic meaning Pope Francis draws from the relatedness of cosmos, Incarnation, and Eucharist:

> The very event of the incarnation sets in motion the transformation of the entire material cosmos. Pope Francis draws out the sacramental import of this relationship between the incarnate Christ and the cosmos by examining the Eucharist, opening with an affirmation of the materiality of the incarnation. "The Lord in the culmination of the mystery of the Incarnation, chose to reach our intimate depths through a fragment of matter. He comes not from above, but from within, he comes that we might find him in this world of ours" (LS § 236). From there, the Pope moves to stating that the Eucharist is "an act of cosmic love … [that] joins heaven and earth and … penetrates the whole of creation" (LS §236).
>
> Each celebration of the Eucharist, no matter how humble the circumstances in which it takes place, impacts the entire created order: "The world which came forth from God's hands returns to him in blessed and undivided adoration" (LS § 236). Borrowing the words of Pope Benedict XVI, the letter sets out the significance of all this in terms of the destiny of the whole material order: "In the bread of the Eucharist, 'creation is projected towards divinization, towards the holy wedding feast, towards unification with the Creator himself'" (LS § 236). Pope Francis then directs his readers from contemplation to action. If the Eucharist is the point at which the full meaning and end of the cosmos is manifested, then participation in it necessarily carries consequences for the manner in which we approach the material world. The sacrament is "a source of light and motivation for our concerns for the environment, directing us to be stewards of all creation" (LS § 236). Theologically, this is breathtaking …[122]
>
> [Our] … reception of Holy Communion is also a commissioning. The very materiality of the sacrament implies—one might say calls for—a conversion of mind and heart with regard to the material world. The Amen spoken by the communicant includes a Yes to environmental stewardship—and a consequent refusal to close one's eyes to the injustices that Pope Francis identifies as implicated in ecological abuse.[123]

We leave the Eucharistic table empowered to become "Eucharist," an occasion of thanksgiving for our world. This Eucharist makes it impossible for us to ignore the cries of the earth and the hungry. It compels us to make the "right to food" a reality in our world. As long as there is one hungry person in the world, we are in danger of celebrating the Eucharist to our determent (I Cor. 11: 21-29). As Monika Hellwig concluded, the Eucharist should prompt Christians to support organizations that feed the hungry. This activity "is to become oneself in some measure bread for the life of the world … in tune with the life and spirit of Jesus."[124]

Toward a Just Food System: A Hope-Filled Path Forward

In this chapter we have explored the numerous intertwining and complex factors that make food insecurity and hunger a crisis in our world. Our faith offers us a hope-filled vision, a set of values and principles, the example of St. Francis, as well as numerous church and faith-related agencies that can assist us in creating a new and sustainable prosperity for all of our sisters and brothers across the globe. As St. Francis said, "I have done what is mine to do, may Christ teach you what is yours to do!"[125]

Questions for Reflection and Discussion

1. What feelings come to you when reading of millions of hungry people in the world?
2. What do you know about working conditions of farmers, ranchers, and food-processing workers?
3. Are labor, health, and safety laws and standards enforced for farmworkers and food-processing workers? Would you be willing to work under such conditions?
4. Which of the top four or five globalized agribusinesses produce your favorite foods? What do you know about their agricultural and employment practices?
5. What do you know about commodity futures? Visit the Interfaith Center for Corporate Responsibility at https://www.iccr.org/iccrs-issues/food-safety-and-sustainability.

Suggestions for Action

1. Make hunger tangible by religious fasting and prayer for food justice.
2. Purchase foods grown or produced within 100 miles of home.
3. Advocate for Community Supported Agriculture initiatives.
4. Learn about fair trade practices that ensure farmers and laborers receive fair wages.

5 Watch "Meet Benin's Zero Waste Farmer," https://www.cnn.com/2020/06/24/africa/zero-waste-farming-godfrey-nzamujo-benin-spc-intl/index.html and "Songhaï: A 'Zero Waste' Agricultural System in Africa," https://www.bbc.com/news/av/world-africa-58930317.

Sources for Further Study

Hellwig, Monika K. *Eucharist and the Humger of the World*. Kansas City: Sheed and Ward, 1992.

McGann, Mary E. *The Meal That Reconnects*. Collegeville, MN: Liturgical Press, 2020.

National Catholic Rural Life Conference. *Food Security & Economic Justice: A Faith Based Study Guide on Poverty and Hunger*. https://catholicrurallife.org/resources/education-and-action/food-justice/study-guide/.

Steck, S. J. Christopher. *All God's Animals: A Catholic Theological Framework for Animal Ethics*. Moral Traditions Series (Washington, DC: Georgetown University Press, 2019.

Wirzba, Norman. *Food and Faith: A Theology of Eating*. New York: Cambridge University Press, 2011.

Notes

1. World Population Review, "Obesity Rate by State 2022," https://worlpopulationreview.com/state-rankings/obesity-rate-by-state.
2. Ibid.
3. The Annie E. Casey Foundation, "Food Deserts in the United States," February 13, 2021, https://www.aecf.org/blog/exploring-americas-food-deserts. Economic Research Service, US Department of Agriculture, Food Security in the US, Key Statistics & Graphics, https://www.ers.usda.gov/topics/food-n.
4. UN Food and Agriculture Organization, "UN Report: Global Hunger Numbers Rose to as Many as 828 Million in 2021," https://www.fao.org/newsroom/detail/un-report-global-hunger-SOFI-2022-FAO/en.
5. See https://www.vatican.va/content/francesco/en/encyclicals/documents/papa-francesco_20150524_enciclica-laudato-si.pdf.
6. Translation is mine.
7. The EC—FAO Food Security Programme, "An Introduction to the Basic Concepts of Food Security," FAO 2008, https://www.fao.org/3/al936e/al936e.pdf. Food Security was defined in the 1996 World Food Summit,

"Rome Declaration on World Food Security," https://www.fao.org/3/w3613e/w3613e00.htm.
8. "An Introduction to the Basic Concepts of Food Security," https://www.fao.org/3/al936e/al936e.pdf.
9. New World Encyclopedia Contributors, "History of Agriculture," *New World Encyclopedia*, https://www.newworldencyclopedia.org/entry/History_of_agriculture. Elizabeth Shelburn, "The Great Disruption," *The Atlantic* (September 2008): 28–9. The Secretary General's High Level Task Force on Global Food and Nutrition Security (HLTF) https://www.un.org/en/issues/food/taskforce/establishing.shtml.
10. Derek Headey and Shenggen Fan, *Reflections on the Global Food Crisis—How Did It Happen? How Has It Hurt? And How Can We Prevent the Next One?* Research Monograph 165 (Washington, DC: International Food Policy Research Institute, 2010), "Lessons for the Future: Does the Global Food System Need Fixing," 92–101.
11. Dr. Agnes Kalibata, "UN Secretary-General's Special Envoy to the 2021 Food Systems Summit, the Food Systems Summit—a New Deal for People, Planet and Prosperity, 21 September 2021 | New York," https://www.un.org/en/food-systems-summit/news/food-systems-summit-new-deal-people-planet-and-prosperity.
12. Pope Francis, "Encyclical Letter *Laudato Si'—On the Care for Our Common Home*, https://www.vatican.va/content/francesco/en/encyclicals/documents/papa-francesco_20150524_enciclica-laudato-si.html.
13. New World Encyclopedia Contributors, "History of Agriculture," *New World Encyclopedia*, https://www.newworldencyclopedia.org/entry/History_of_agriculture. Wenonah Hunter, *Foodopoly: The Battle over the Future of Food in America* (New York: The New Press, 2012).
14. Headey and Fan, *Reflections on the Global Food Crisis.* Maryknoll Office for Global Concerns, "Food Crisis," *NewsNotes* 33/4 (July–August 2008): 14–15. Maryknoll Office for Global Concerns, "UN: Invest in Food Systems Resilience," *NewsNotes*, January–February 2022, https://maryknollogc.org/resources/newsnotes/un-invest-food-systems-resilience.
15. United States Conference of Catholic Bishops (USCCB), *Catholic Reflections on Food, Farmers and Farmworkers,* November 18, 2003, https://www.usccb.org/resources/i-was-hungry-you-gave-me-food-november-2003 and its *Data Boxes* https://www.usccb.org/issues-and-action/human-life-and-dignity/agriculture-nutrition-rural-issues/for-i-was-hungry-data-boxes. For technical data substantiating the USCCB's statement see the *Data Boxes* appended to the USCCB, *Catholic Reflections* document. USCCB, *Data Boxes,* cites FAO, *Gender and Food Security*. In sub-Saharan Africa, women produce up to 80 percent of basic food products. USCCB, *Data Boxes*, cites International Fund for Agricultural Development (IFAD), *Drylands: A Call to Action* (1998), 6.

16. Maryknoll, "Food Crisis," 15. Joshua Boak and Mike Haughlett, "Corn Bonanza Won't Cut Food Prices: A Fortunate Mix of Sunshine and Rain Is Helping Produce a Bumper Crop, but Much of the Grain Will Be Used to Make Ethanol," *Chicago Tribune,* August 13, 2008, section 3, page 3–4.
17. Maryknoll, "Food Crisis," 15.
18. Ibid.
19. Wulf Killmann and the Interdepartmental Working Group on Climate Change, *Climate Change and Food Security Framework Document—2008,* https://www.fao.org/3/au035e/au035e.pdf.
20. Julie Ingwersen, "Farmers Scramble to Finish Harvest from Hell," *Reuters,* November 13, 2009, https://www.reuters.com/article/us-usa-crops-harvest/farmers-scramble-to-finish-harvest-from-hell-idUSTRE5AC3BS20091113.
21. Maryknoll, "Food Crisis," 15.
22. Tim Mahoney, "Understanding the Global Food Price Crisis," *Oxfam Exchange* 9/3 (Fall 2009): 6.
23. Maryknoll Office for Global Concerns, "Speculation and World Food Prices," *NewsNotes* 33/4 (July–August 2008): 17. Stephen Suppan, "Commodities Market Speculation: The Risk to Food Security and Agriculture" (Minneapolis: Institute for Agriculture and Trade Policy, 2008), pdf download, https://www.iatp.org/documents/commodities-market-speculation-the-risk-to-food-security-and-agriculture.
24. Suppan, "Commodities Market Speculation."
25. USCCB, *Catholic Reflections on Food, Farmers and Farmworkers* November 18, 2003, https://www.usccb.org/resources/i-was-hungry-you-gave-me-food-november-2003.
26. "US Agriculture in the Twentieth Century," Economic History Association, https://eh.net/encyclopedia/u-s-agriculture-in-the-twentieth-century/.
27. USCCB, *Data Boxes,* cites National Agriculture Statistics Service (NASS) (2002), 23. USCCB, *Data Boxes,* cites US Department of Agriculture, *Food and Agricultural Policy: Taking Stock of the New Century* (September 2001), Appendix 1, Table A-1.
28. Economic Research Service, USDA, "Farming and Farm Income," https://www.ers.usda.gov/data-products/ag-and-food-statistics-charting-the-essentials/farming-and-farm-income/. Roberto A. Ferdman, "The Decline of the Small American Family Farm in One Chart," September 16, 2014, https://www.washingtonpost.com/news/wonk/wp/2014/09/16/the-decline-of-the-small-american-family-farm-in-one-chart/.
29. USCCB, *Data Boxes,* cites Mary Hendrickson, William Heffernan, Philip Howard, and Judith Heffernan, Executive Summary, Report to National Farmers Union, *Consolidation in Food Retailing and Dairy: Implications for Farmers and Consumers in a Global Food System.* In 2021 see "Who Are the Top 10 Grocers in the United States?" https://www.foodindustry.

com/articles/top-10-grocers-in-the-united-states-2019/. USCCB, *Data Boxes*, William Heffernan, *Multi-National Concentrated Food Processing and Marketing Systems and the Farm Crisis, 7*. A paper given at AAAS conference, February 14–19, 2002. In 2002, four top beef firms processed 81 percent of all the cattle; the four largest pork firms processed 59 percent of pork; and four chicken firms processed 50 percent of all broilers.

30. Nicole Goodkind, "Meet the 4 Meat Empires Biden Says Are Unreasonably Jacking Up Prices for Americans," Politics Big Meat, FORTUNE, January 6, 2022, 2:45 PM CST, https://fortune.com/2022/01/06/meat-prices-biden-inflation-tyson-cargill-jbs/.
31. USCCB, *Data Boxes*, cites *Multi-National Concentrated Food Processing, 7*. The four largest wheat processors had 61 percent of the market; the four largest soybean processors have 80 percent of the market. Archer-Daniels-Midland, Bunge Limited, Cargill, Incorporated were the top producers in 2022, IBIS World, https://www.ibisworld.com/united-states/market-research-reports/soybean-processing-industry/.
32. Food & Water Watch, "Food System," https://www.foodandwaterwatch.org/issues/food-system/.
33. Veranda Shiva, *Who Really Feeds the World? The Failures of Agribusiness and the Promise of Agroecology* (Berkeley, CA: New Atlantic Books, 2016), 67–83. Clare Hope Cummings, *Uncertain Peril: Genetic Engineering and the Future of Seeds* (Boston: Beacon Press), 7–10. Jeffery M. Smith, *Seeds of Deception: Exposing Industry and Government Lies about Safety of Genetically Engineered Foods You're Eating* (Fairfield, IA: Yes! Books, 2003). And Jeffery M. Smith, *Genetic Roulette* (Fairfield, IA: Yes! Books, 2007).
34. Compare *Open Secrets*, "Interest Groups—Agrabusiness: Money to Congress—Top 20 Recipients," https://www.opensecrets.org/industries/summary.php?ind=A&recipdetail=M&sortorder=U&mem=Y&cycle=2022.
35. The year 2008 marked the halfway point in reaching Millennium Development Goals set by the UN General Assembly in September 2000. "The Millennium Development Goals Report 2015," https://www.undp.org/publications/millennium-development-goals-report-2015. "L'Aquila" Joint Statement on Global Food Security, L'Aquila Food Security Initiative (AFSI) http://www.g7.utoronto.ca/summit/2009laquila/2009-food.pdf. See "Letter from National Conferences of Catholic Bishops to the Leaders of the G8 Nations, June 22, 2009," https://www.usccb.org/resources/letter-g8-leaders-bishops-conferences-global-poverty-and-climate-change-june-22-2009. See *Letter of His Holiness Benedict XVI to Hon. Mr. Silvio Berlusconi, Prime Minister of Italy, on the Occasion of the G8 Summit*

(*L'Aquila, 8–10 July 2009*)," https://www.vatican.va/content/benedict-xvi/en/letters/2009/documents/hf_ben-xvi_let_20090701_berlusconi-g8.html. *ActionAid, Two Years On: Is the G8 Delivering on Its L'Aquila Hunger Pledge?* https://actionaid.org/publications/2011/two-years-g8-delivering-its-laquila-hunger-pledge. Also, *2022 Action Aid*, https://actionaid.org/sites/default/files/publications/Doubly%20Devastating%20-%20ActionAid%202.pdf. Save the Children—UK, "G8 & G20: Two Summits to Tackle the Hidden Malnutrition Crisis," https://resourcecentre.savethechildren.net/pdf/6007.pdf/.

36. "UN: Climate Change Deal Key to Fighting Hunger," http://www.voanews.com/english/news/a-13-2009-11-16-voa16-70423912.html.
37. Ibid.
38. *Declaration of the World Summit on Food Security*, http://www.fao.org/fileadmin/templates/wsfs/Summit/Docs/Final_Declaration/WSFS09_Declaration.pdf.
39. "UN Millennial Development Goals," http://www.un.org/millenniumgoals/. "Sustainable Development goal #2," https://www.un.org/sustainabledevelopment/hunger/.
40. See *Declaration of the World Summit on Food Security*, 2–7.
41. United Nations Development Programme, *The Millennium Development Goals Report 2015*, April 17, 2017, https://www.undp.org/publications/millennium-development-goals-report-2015.
42. UNFAO, "Sustainable Development Goals," https://www.fao.org/sustainable-development-goals/goals/goal-2/en/.
43. UNFAO, "The State of Food Security and Nutrition in the World 2021: The World Is at a Critical Juncture," https://www.fao.org/state-of-food-security-nutrition.
44. Tamara Lucas and Richard Horton, The EAT–Lancet Commission, "The 21st-Century Great Food Transformation," January 16, 2019. https://doi.org/10.1016/S0140-6736(18)33179-9, https://www.thelancet.com/pdfs/journals/lancet/PIIS0140-6736(18)33179-9.pdf?utm_campaign=tleat19&utm_source=HubPage.
45. Georgina Gustin, "Wealthy Nations Are Eating Their Way Past the Paris Agreement's Climate Targets," https://insideclimatenews.org/news/15072020/paris-agreement-food-agriculture-wealthy-nations.
46. Ibid.
47. Ibid. Tamara Lucas and Richard Horton, The EAT–Lancet Commission.
48. R. S. Cottrell, K. L. Nash, B. S. Halpern et al., "Food Production Shocks across Land and Sea," *Nature Sustainability* 2 (2019): 130–7, https://doi.org/10.1038/s41893-018-0210-1.
49. Georgina Gustin, "Investors Join Calls for a Food Revolution to Fight Climate Change," *Inside Climate News*, January 29, 2019, https://

insideclimatenews.org/news/29012019/global-food-system-shocks-climate-change-mcdonalds-obesity-malnutrition-investors-lancet-scientists/.
50. Ceres, "Global Investors Turn up Heat on Fast Food Companies to Tackle Climate and Water Risks," https://www.ceres.org/news-center/press-releases/global-investors-turn-heat-fast-food-companies-tackle-climate-and-water.
51. UN World Food Programme, "COVID-19 Will Double Number of People Facing Food Crises Unless Swift Action Is Taken," April 21, 2020, https://www.wfp.org/news/covid-19-will-double-number-people-facing-food-crises-unless-swift-action-taken.
52. The concept of *food systems* refers to everything involved in getting food from the field to the table—farming, food processing, and distribution.
53. "The Pre-summit of the UN Food Systems Summit," https://www.un.org/en/food-systems-summit/pre-summit.
54. Card. Peter K. A. Turkson, Prefect of the Dicastery, July 27, 2021, "Indigenous Food Systems: Game-Changing Solutions," https://www.humandevelopment.va/en/eventi/2021/food-for-all-an-event-at-the-pre-summit-of-the-un-food-systems-s.html.
55. A Duke University theology professor of food ethics authored *Food and Faith: A Theology of Eating* (New York: Cambridge University Press, 2019). Online publication, June 2012, https://doi.org/10.1017/CBO9780511978982.
56. Elizabeth Mpofu and Edgardo Garcia, "Here Is Why We Are Boycotting the UN Food Systems Summit," *Aljazeera*, July 25, 2021, https://www.aljazeera.com/opinions/2021/7/25/here-is-why-we-are-boycotting-the-un-food-systems-summit. "Civil Society and Indigenous Peoples' Organizations," https://www.csm4cfs.org/hundreds-of-grassroots-organizations-to-oppose-the-un-food-systems-summit/.
57. The Special Rapporteur, "Policy Brief: Last Chance to Make the Food Systems Summit Truly a 'People's Summit,'" August 19, 2021, https://www.ohchr.org/sites/default/files/Documents/Issues/Food/Policy_brief_20210819.pdf.
58. Food Systems Summit 2021, "Nearly 300 Commitments," https://www.un.org/en/food-systems-summit/news/nearly-300-commitments-highlights-summit%E2%80%99s-inclusive-process.
59. "Secretary-General's Chair Summary and Statement of Action on the UN Food Systems Summit," September 23, 2021, https://www.un.org/en/food-systems-summit/news/making-food-systems-work-people-planet-and-prosperity.
60. Ibid.

61. Ibid.
62. UNFAO, "State of Food and Agriculture 2021," https://www.fao.org/publications/sofa/sofa-2021/en/.
63. Ibid.
64. Ibid.
65. Christian Bogmans, Jeff Kearns, Andrea Pescatori and Ervin Prifti, "Chart of the Week War-Fueled Surge in Food Prices to Hit Poorer Nations Hardest," March 16, 2022, https://blogs.imf.org/2022/03/16/war-fueled-surge-in-food-prices-to-hit-poorer-nations-hardest/.
66. ActionAid, "Doubly Devastating: Local Communities Disproportionately Affected by Food, Fuel and Fertilizer Price Rises," https://www.actionaidusa.org/publications/doubly-devastating-local-communities-disproportionately-affected-by-food-fuel-and-fertilizer-price-rises/.
67. World Food Programme, "Projected Increase in Acute Food Insecurity Due to War in Ukraine," April 6, 2022, https://www.wfp.org/publications/projected-increase-acute-food-insecurity-due-war-ukraine?&utm_source=twitter&utm_medium=organicpost&utm_campaign=projectedincreaseinacutefoodinsecurityduetowarinukraine&utm_content=squarevideo.
68. ActionAid, "Doubly Devastating," https://www.actionaidusa.org/publications/doubly-devastating-local-communities-disproportionately-affected-by-food-fuel-and-fertilizer-price-rises/.
69. ActionAid, "Avoiding the Climate Poverty Spiral: Social Protection to Avoid Climate-Induced Loss & Damage," January 29, 2021, https://actionaid.org/publications/2021/avoiding-climate-poverty-spiral-social-protection-avoid-climate-induced-loss. UN Deputy Secretary-General Amina Mohammed, "World Facing Unprecedented Hunger Crisis, Deputy Secretary-General Warns Economic and Social Council, Urging Governments to Support Resilience at Scale," June 20, 2022, https://press.un.org/en/2022/dsgsm1752.doc.htm.
70. ActionAid, "Principles for a Just Transition in Agriculture," January 7, 2020, https://actionaid.org/publications/2019/principles-just-transition-agriculture.
71. IPCC, "Special Report: Climate Change and Land," https://www.ipcc.ch/srccl/.
72. United Nations Environment Programme, "UN Report Calls for Repurposing of USD 470 Billion of Agricultural Support That Distorts Prices, Environment and Social Goals," September 14, 2021, https://www.unep.org/news-and-stories/press-release/un-report-calls-repurposing-usd-470-billion-agricultural-suppor.
73. Kathleen Anne Farmer, "Land," in *The Westminster Theological Wordbook of the Bible*, ed. Donald E. Gowan (Louisville: Westminster John Knox Press, 2003), 281–4.

74. Ibid., 284. Farmer cites Norman C. Hable, *The Land Is Mine* (Minneapolis: Fortress Press, 1995).
75. Walter Brueggemann, "The Earth Is the Lord's: A Theology of Earth and Land," *Sojourners* 15 (October 1986): 28–32.
76. Thomas Hieke, "Leviticus," in *The Jerome Biblical Commentary for the Twenty-First Century*, ed. John J. Collins, Gina Hens-Piazza, Barbara E. Reid, OP, and Donald Senior, CP, First Fully Revised ed. (London: Bloomsbury, 2022), 281–2.
77. Cf. Exod. 23:10-11; Deut. 15:1-2
78. C. René Padilla, "The Relevance of the Jubilee in Today's World (Leviticus 25)," *Mission Studies* XIII/1&2 (1996): 14.
79. Cf. Isa. 5:8; Ezek. 46: 18. Hieke, "Leviticus," 305–6.
80. Rabbi Lord Jonathan Sachs, "The Stewardship Paradigm," in *An Ecological Commentary on Genesis and Exodus*, ed. Yonatan Neril and Leo Dee, Eco Bible, Vol. 1 (Jerusalem: Interfaith Center for Sustainable Development, 2020), 11–12.
81. The *Torah* provides restorative mechanisms to deal with these events even beyond the Sabbatical and Jubilee years, thus enabling everyone to have some access to their sustenance from the land, e.g., gleaning (Lev. 19:9; Deut. 24-19-22), storage and distribution of the triennial tithe (Deut. 14:22-27; 26:12ff).
82. James Gustafson, "The Place of Scriptures in Christian Ethics: A Methodological Study," in *Theology and Christian Ethics* (Philadelphia: United Church Press, 1974), 121–45. The values revealed in Lev. 25 fit his category of "general norms of revealed morality."
83. Padilla, "The Relevance of the Jubilee," 15. Padillia cites Goudzwaard and Lange.
84. David Leonhardt, "The Baby Formula Crisis," *New York Times*, May 13, 2022, https://www.nytimes.com/2022/05/13/briefing/baby-formula-shortage-us-economy.html.
85. "Apostolic Journey to the United States of America, Holy Mass at the Living History Farms, *Homily of His Holiness John Paul II*," https://www.vatican.va/content/john-paul-ii/en/homilies/1979/documents/hf_jp-ii_hom_19791004_usa-des-moines.html.
86. Ibid., 1.
87. Signed by seventy-one diocesan bishops from Colorado, Iowa, Illinois, Indiana, Kansas, Minnesota, Missouri Nebraska, North Dakota, South Dakota, Wisconsin, and Wyoming. Full text: https://iowacatholicconference.org/strangers-and-guests-toward-community-in-the-heartland/. Numbers in ( ) indicate paragraph numbers.
88. Full text: "Voices and Choices: A Pastoral Letter from the Catholic Bishops of the South," November 15, 2000 in the Catholic Committee of the South, *Voices and Choices* (Cincinnati, OH: St. Anthony Press, 2000).

89. All data included with these scenarios is found in *Voices and Choices: A Pastoral Letter*. Also, Susan Stevenot Sullivan, ed., "Voices and Choices: Workplace Justice and the Poultry Industry," *Southern Changes: The Journal of the Southern Regional Council, 1978–2003* 23/1 (2001): 3–7, https://southernchanges.digitalscholarship.emory.edu/sc23-1_001/sc23-1_002/.
90. Ibid.
91. See "Justice for Migrants: We Are One Family under God—Catholic Social Teaching," https://justiceforimmigrants.org/home/about-us/catholic-social-teaching/. Also "Catholic Social Teaching on Immigration and the Movement of Peoples," https://www.usccb.org/issues-and-action/human-life-and-dignity/immigration/catholic-teaching-on-immigration-and-the-movement-of-peoples.
92. "Voices and Choices, a Pastoral Letter from the Catholic Bishops of the South," November 15, 2000.
93. Ibid.
94. Ibid.
95. Ibid. Six principles are: protect human dignity (the right to food); the social nature of the human person (call to family, community, and participation); option for the poor and the vulnerable; dignity of work and the right and duties of worker and owners; solidarity; and respect for creation.
96. Full text: https://www.usccb.org/resources/i-was-hungry-you-gave-me-food-november-2003.
97. USCCB, *Catholic Reflections on Food*, 6.
98. Ibid., 17.
99. Ibid., 21.
100. Ibid., 22. Archbishop Renato R. Martino, Address at the Ministerial Conference on Science and Technology in Agriculture, Sacramento, California, June 23–25, 2003, http://www.vatican.va/roman_curia/secretariat_state/2003/documents/rc_seg-st_20030625_gmo-martino_en.html.
101. USCCB, *Catholic Reflections on Food*, 22.
102. Address of His Holiness Benedict XVI to FAO on the Occasion of the World Summit on Food Security, FAO Headquarter, Rome Monday, November 16, 2009, http://www.vatican.va/holy_father/benedict_xvi/speeches/2009/november/documents/hf_ben-xvi_spe_20091116_fao_en.html.
103. Encyclical Letter *Caritas in Veritate* of the Supreme Pontiff Benedict XVI, https://www.vatican.va/content/benedict-xvi/en/encyclicals/documents/hf_ben-xvi_enc_20090629_caritas-in-veritate.html.
104. Benedict XVI, Address to the World Food Summit.

105. Ibid.
106. Ibid.
107. Ibid.
108. Pope Francis, Encyclical Letter *Laudato Si'*. In this section all references to *Laudato Si'* will be made in text, using parentheses and the paragraph number.
109. Francis cited: Catechesis (June 5, 2013): Insegnamenti 1/1 (2013): 280.
110. *Francis of Assisi: Early Documents*, Volume III—*The Prophet*, trans. and ed. Regis J. Armstrong, J. A. Wayne Hellmann, and William J. Short (New York: New City Press, 2001), 234.
111. Jim Ennis, "Eating Is a Moral Act: Revisiting the Ethics of Eating," National Catholic Rural Life Conference, https://catholicrurallife.org/eating-is-a-moral-act-revisiting-the-ethics-of-eating-by-jim-ennis/.
112. Susan Lang, "Diet for Small Planet May Be Most Efficient If It Includes Dairy and a Little Meat, Researchers Report," *Chronicle On-Line*, October 4, 2007, https://news.cornell.edu/stories/2007/10/diet-little-meat-more-efficient-many-vegetarian-diets. Zach Conrad, Nicole Tichenor Blackstone, and Eric D. Roy, "Healthy Diets Can Create Environmental Trade-Offs, Depending on How Diet Quality Is Measured," *Nutrition Journal* 19 (2020): 117, https://doi.org/10.1186/s12937-020-00629-6,.
113. Numerous resources exist, e.g., *FoodPrint*, "Eating Sustainably," https://foodprint.org/eating-sustainably/.
114. Wes Jackson, "Farming in Nature's Image: Natural Systems of Agriculture," in *Andrew Kimball, Fatal Harvest* (Washington, DC: Island Press, 2003), 68.
115. Christopher Steck, S. J., *All God's Animals: A Catholic Theological Framework for Animal Ethics* Moral Traditions Series (Washington, DC: Georgetown University Press, 2019). Jesse Ramirez, "Faith Seeking Food: Animals, Factory Farms, and Catholic Social Teaching," A paper presented on May 25, 2005, Santa Clara University Student Research Ethics Conference, http://www.scu.edu/ethics/publications/submitted/Ramirez/FaithSeekingFood.html. *The Catechism of the Catholic Church*, 2416–2418 on the treatment of animals, https://www.vatican.va/archive/ENG0015/__P8B.HTM.
116. L. Shannon Jung, *Sharing Food: Christian Practices for Enjoyment* (Minneapolis: Fortress, 2006), 6.
117. US Department of Agriculture, "USDA Organic," https://www.usda.gov/topics/organic.
118. Julie Hanlon Rubio, "Toward a Just Way of Eating," in *Green Discipleship: Catholic Theological Ethics and the Environment*, ed. Tobais Winright (Winona, MN: Anselm Academic, Christian Brothers Publications, 2011), 360–78.

119. "The Life of Saint Francis by Thomas of Celano (1228–1229)," Book I, Chapter I, in FA:ED, Volume I—*The Saint*, 183–4.
120. "Earlier Rule [Rule without the Papal Seal] (1209/10-1221)," Chapter III, in FA:ED, Volume I—*The Saint*, 65.
121. "The Life of Saint Francis by Thomas of Celano (1228–1229)," First Book, Chapter XIX, 51, in FA:ED, Volume I—*The Saint*, 227.
122. Peter McGrail, "Initiation and Ecology: Becoming a Christian in the Light of Laudato Si," *Liturgy* 31/2 (2016): 55–62 DOI: 10.1080/0458063X.2016.1123951.
123. Ibid., 58.
124. Monika K. Hellwig, *The Eucharist and the Hunger of the World* (New York: Paulist Press, 1976), 39.
125. "The Remembrance of the Desire of a Soul by Thomas of Celano (1245–47)," Book II, CLXII, 214, "How in the End He Encouraged and Blessed the Brothers," in *Francis of Assisi: Early Documents*, Volume II—*The Founder*, trans. and ed. Regis J. Armstrong, J. A. Wayne Hellmann, and William J. Short (New York: New City Press, 2000), 386.

10

Freedom from Fossil Fuels—Financing Family

Introduction: Hoodoos and Oil Sands

In 2008 I first experienced the grandeur of the Canadian Rockies in Alberta, Canada. From plains of bright green tall grass, jagged light-gray mountain peaks thrust skyward, exposing melting snowcaps against an azure blue sky dotted with cotton-ball-puffed clouds. Hiking along, I was treated to magnificent, ice-cold ribbons of water cascading hundreds of meters downward, forming whirlpools in the streams below.

But later, when driving toward St. Paul, returning to Calgary, the scenery shifted to moonscapes of ecological destruction that were simply shattering! My eyes burned from airborne chemicals, as I viewed huge tracts of land with the "overburden" of water, soil, and ancient boreal forests—muskeg, peat, and sand—ripped away, roots and all—and cast aside in heaps to expose the "tar sands," the new "black gold!" My heart cried out at this Baconian disaster in progress, this region's ecological health lost for generations to come, and adding tons of CO_2 to global warming.[1]

Imperial Ecology versus Kinship of Creation

Mining the "tar sands" champions Francis Bacon's stance that humans are the lords and masters over nature.[2] Indeed, humans have become *like* gods. We *have* gained "control" over the Earth. We *do know* the fundamental workings of Earth's major systems. Yet we are like adolescents who seek "the good life" but, lacking moral wisdom, ignore the harms our pillaging inflicts. In the depths of our beings, we know—"*We are responsible*"—and this often drives us to ever more vicious cycles of denial and false hope.

This chapter examines the global energy situation with particular attention to US involvement. We briefly review early Catholic Social Teachings by the USCCB, the Bishops of Appalachia, and by Luc Bouchard, Bishop of the Diocese of St. Paul in Alberta, Canada.[3] We reference Chapter 10 of *Compendium of Social Doctrine of the Church*, and Pope Francis' *Laudato Si'—On Care for Our Common Home*.[4]

Next, we present ethical criteria for morally responsible energy use. We measure current and alternative energy options against those ethical criteria. Finally, because the "Climate Emergency" is evermore imminent, we note the USCCB *Socially Responsible Investment Guidelines 2021* as well as the July 2022 *Policy of the Investment Committee of the Holy See*. Both focus on moral actions of divesting from fossil fuels and investing in renewable energy sources as moral actions.

Fossil Fuels and Early Catholic Social Teaching (CST)

Twenty-four US Catholic Bishops of Appalachia published *This Land Is Home to Me* (1975), one of the first US magisterial statements on ecological justice. In *At Home in the Web of Life* (1990) they addressed many of the same ecological issues, but with greater urgency. In both pastorals, exploitative "mountaintop removal" coal mining was the most pressing reality underlying ongoing ethical and ecological issues the bishops addressed. "Mountaintop removal" not only harms coalminers but as an energy source, coal endangers consumers, whole ecosystems, and contributes to global warming.[5]

This Land Is Home to Me emphasized the capricious wasteful consumption and pollution of the coal industry. *At Home in the Web of Life* also stressed the consumer society that generates human and ecological waste and the need to build sustainable communities by linking those issues to a central concern for the poor. Both pastorals echo Pope John Paul II's call to choose life by creating sustainable communities that nurture future generations, regenerating families and their relationships with nature. Solar energy and organic gardening, agriculture, and forestry are stressed.

Early US bishops' teaching did not specifically address fossil fuels but applied time-tested broader tenets of social justice and human dignity to the issue. Thus, CST from all magisterial levels undergird two major USCCB pastorals *Renewing the Earth* (1991) and *Global Climate Change* (2001).[6]

In *Renewing the Earth*, Section III, the US bishops outline seven themes that frame "distinctive perspectives on environmental ethics": a God-centered and sacramental view of the universe; respect for human life; global interdependence and the common good; an ethics of solidarity; the universal purpose of created things; an option for the poor; and authentic development.[7]

The bishops apply explicit criteria concerning the relationship of consumption and population growth to environmental problems. In public discussions, two areas require greater care and judgment from people: *consumption of resources* and *growth in world population*.[8] The bishops do not see environmental issues apart from their relationship to other concerns within a web of life.[9]

In *Global Climate Change*, the bishops explicitly accept the scientific consensus that global warming is real and dangerous and that fossil-fuel use is its major cause. The Christian virtue of prudence necessitates immediate action to reverse global warming.[10]

The bishops underscore four dimensions of the universal common good criteria that are found in Catholic Social Teaching, namely Stewardship of God's Creation and the Right to Economic Initiative and Private Property, Protecting the Environment for Future Generations, Population and Authentic Development, and Caring for the Poor and Issues of Equity.[11]

A Pastoral Letter: The Integrity of Creation and the Athabasca Oil Sands[12]

In January 2009, Bishop Luc Bouchard published his landmark pastoral concerning the Athabasca Oil Sands, the second largest deposit of oil in the world located in the St. Paul Diocese.[13] Buchard warned against the development of the tar sands and TransCanada's Keystone XL pipeline to carry Canadian crude oil 1,700 miles across the US heartland to refineries on the US Gulf Coast.[14]

The Athabasca Oil Sands held about 1 trillion barrels of oil, with, theoretically, 315 billion barrels extractable.[15] The bishop's analysis focused on tar sands mining operations near Fort McMurray.[16] He explained why safeguarding the natural environment is a religious obligation; described effects of oil sands development on the air, land, and water in northeastern Alberta; drew religious and moral conclusions from the analysis and recommended actions that must be considered, if the integrity of the environment is to be respected; and suggested political and personal responses to this moral challenge.

Bishop Bouchard applied the seven major environmental ethical themes from Catholic Social Teaching on the environment to the tar sands situation. He then summarized the impacts of the oil sands extraction and stated his analysis of their moral implications. Though the pastoral letter deserves lengthy citation, space allows only a summary of the text.

The Environmental Impact of Oil Sands Development

Surface mining of oil sands is a multi-phased, complex operation: large tracts of boreal forest are prepared for mining by draining off ground water; removing the trees and topsoil; and removing the "overburden" of muskeg, peat, sand, etc., in order to expose the underlying oil sands. To produce a barrel of oil requires excavating two tons of earth and muskeg (22).[17] The oil sands, which have firm sandstone like density, are then surface mined and crushed into a granular state, which is then mixed with water and solvents and piped to an onsite processing plant (23–4).

Destruction of the Boreal Forest Ecosystem

All of the oil sands leases slated for development are in terrain classified as boreal forest. This type of ecological site is environmentally valuable because it has the unique ability to store large amounts of carbon in its bogs, peat, soil, and trees. The destruction of boreal forest reduces the earth's capacity to store carbon and releases greenhouse gases into the atmosphere as it is destroyed (25).

Potential Damage to the Athabasca Water Shed

In total 2–4.5 barrels of water are required to produce a barrel of oil from oil sands (27). This water is used to create the slurry of bitumen and oil that is heated and processed. Despite impressive recycling efforts and improvements, for every barrel of oil produced approximately one barrel of water is contaminated in the process and deposited into a tailings pond (30). "Over the long term, the Athabasca River may not have sufficient flows to meet the needs of all the planned mining operations and maintain adequate instream flows" (31). This possible shortage threatens fish, wildlife, downstream communities, and transportation in the Mackenzie delta (32).

The Release of Greenhouse Gases

Very large amounts of natural gas are required to heat water in order to process bitumen. By 2011, it is estimated that the then existing oil sands plants will burn enough natural gas to annually release 80 million tons of CO_2 into the atmosphere. This is far more than all the CO_2 released annually by all of Canada's passenger cars (34).

Heavy Consumption of Natural Gas

To produce a barrel of oil processed from oil sands requires approximately one thousand cubic feet of natural gas per barrel. It is estimated that as proposed, future oil sands projects come on stream, and 20 percent of Canada's total natural gas production will be burned in order to extract bitumen (35).

The Creation of Toxic Tailings Ponds

The "middlings" (water, suspended clay, and bitumen) that are deposited into tailings ponds settle over time into a layer termed "mature fine tailings," which compact into a stable suspension that cannot, at present, be further recycled. This suspension is very toxic, containing naphthenic acids, phenolic compounds, ammonia-ammonium with traces of copper, zinc, and iron as well as residual bitumen and naphtha (36). Despite a great deal of research and effort, no fully effective means of neutralizing the toxicity of these tailings ponds has to date been devised, although some slow progress is being recorded (37).

The bishop concluded:

> I am forced to conclude that the integrity of creation in the Athabasca Oil Sands is clearly being sacrificed for economic gain. The proposed future development of the oil sands constitutes a serious moral problem. Environmentalists and members of First Nations and Metis communities who are challenging government and industry to adequately safeguard the air, water, and boreal

forest eco-systems of the Athabasca oil sands region present a very strong moral argument, which I support. The present pace and scale of development in the Athabasca oil sands cannot be morally justified. Active steps to alleviate this environmental damage must be undertaken.[18]

In the last section of the pastoral, "An Action Plan to Safeguard Creation," Bishop Bouchard proposed ten ways the moral concerns need to be addressed (40–9).

The US bishops published no statement on the tar sands or XL Keystone Pipeline. But the Catholic Coalition on Climate Change to which the USCCB subscribed, Catholic college and university students, religious orders, and the Franciscan Action Network cited Catholic Social Teachings when strongly opposing the pipeline.[19] Catholics, persons of other faiths and good will, still see the pipeline as a symbol of the critical crossroads concerning energy ethics, global warming, and especially the US energy future.[20]

An Ethical Framework for Assessing Energy Sources

Our "Climate Emergency," with its related health and safety hazards, demands careful analysis of the benefits and burdens of current and alternative energy sources using religious ethics norms, including humanitarian standards, like the Fifth Directive of the Global Ethic.[21] Given the limits of this book, here we only utilize Christian ethics and Catholic Social Teaching. Ethical criteria and guiding principles for discerning energy policies were developed by World Council of Churches (WCC), the Presbyterian Church in the Unites States (PCUSA), the Evangelical Lutheran Church in America (ELCA), and the United States Conference of Catholic Bishops (USCCB).[22] Christians widely agree upon principles clearly rooted in the Bible and the essential criteria: sustainability, sufficiency, participation, and solidarity.

Ecojustice

Ecojustice indicates an inclusive planetary value for the mutual sustainable thriving of humans and otherkind, their habitats, and global ecosystems. The Hebrew Testament is grounded in God's covenant love for *all* of creation. God is loving and just; thus those characteristics distinguish God's actions. The Hebrew Testament creation texts, the prophets, and the Christian Scriptures about Jesus' life and ministry show God's character in action, sensitizing and impassioning people to seek justice—especially for the poor and vulnerable. Justice is the work of love brought to the social, public, and planetary realms, meeting needs sufficiently for the common good.[23]

Sustainability

Christians understand sustainability as rooted in God's generosity and goodness—there is enough for all.[24] Martin-Schramm defines sustainability as "the long-range supply of sufficient resources to meet basic human needs and the preservation of intact natural communities. It expresses a concern for future generations and the planet as a whole and emphasizes that an acceptable quality of life for present generations, must not jeopardize the prospects for future generations."[25] Humans must nurture creation, mindful that the God-given intrinsic value of each element prohibits humans doing harm to others. The Psalms and God's numerous covenants with humans, creatures, and the earth itself seal this value and God's pledge to sustain everything.[26]

Sufficiency

Sufficiency addresses the entitlement of each creature to an adequate share in the goods of creation. This norm prohibits unlimited consumption and wastefulness and supports frugality, humility, and generosity. Leviticus 25 shows how God provided "enough" for Israel and conveys our ideal attitude toward creation. Human dignity requires having genuine needs met: care for the poor, rest, and resources for renewal. Also, God's generosity imparts a sense of fullness, abundance, gratitude, and appreciation. Acquisition of wealth must be gained justly but also shared.

Throughout Christian history, some believers have lived in "voluntary poverty," as exemplified Saints Francis and Clare. They serve as a reminder of the necessity to live in relationship to God among the poor and with sensitivity to our other-than-human sisters and brothers.

Participation

God modeled the norm of participation from the moment of creation by creating in partnership with otherkind and humans (Gen. 1: 11-13, 20, 24, 26). God invited Adam to participate in the act of naming all creatures, signaling the ecological vocation of humans as the guardians of creation (Gen. 2:16-17). Jesus renewed this nurturing engagement as a characteristic of the Kingdom of God (Mk 1:14-15).

Formation of thriving genuine relationships requires limits on the size and scale of communities. Jesus taught the Reign of God, deals in small things empowered by God's providence, and/or close human bonds (Mk 4:30-32; Mt. 13:31-32; Lk. 13:18-19). Personal relationships allow people to be more openly share their gifts with others. When determining energy sources and technologies, those most affected must have a voice in deciding what is best for them and the common good of the planet through open and democratic means. Participation includes creative means, like use of environmental impact studies, to "hear" the "voices" of the nonhuman environment.[27]

Solidarity

As St. Bonaventure shows, the Trinitarian God models participation and solidarity. As equal persons in one divine being, God is one. Our radically relational God created a world that is relational to its core. Humans and the entire planet exist in reciprocal and mutual relationship with one another.[28] People are created for community (Gen. 2:15) and when one suffers all suffer (I Cor. 12:26). As the *imago Dei*, humans thrive when they extend to all creation overflowing goodness and mercy, serving others as Jesus did (Rom. 8; Mt. 19:3; Phil. 2:6-7). Indeed, our salvation depends on fulfilling the call to solidarity (Mt. 25:31-45).[29]

Energy Policy Guidelines

In environmental ethical policies Christians share wide agreement concerning the application and incorporation of the four norms (above). The four foundational principles provide starting points for discerning the morality of using various energy options, in that affect today's "Climate Emergency." The key facts about energy sources can be surfaced. Then utilizing the four criteria we can determine how various energy source meet each criterion. By comparison, we can indicate which energy sources are genuinely sustainable and those that are not. Together, the four norms provide important moral indicators for energy policy amid our "Climate Emergency."

Moral Problems and Fossil Fuels

According to the US Energy Information Administration (EIA), the United States uses and produces diverse energy sources, including fossil fuels (petroleum, natural gas, and coal), nuclear energy, and renewable sources of energy.[30] In 2021, total US primary energy consumption was equal to about 97 quadrillion Btu. Production exceeded consumption in 2020 and in 2021. Fossil fuels accounted for about 79 percent of total US primary energy production in 2021.

The percentage shares and amounts (in quads) of total US primary energy production by major sources in 2021 were as follows: natural gas—36 percent; petroleum (crude oil and natural gas plant liquids)—31 percent; coal—12 percent; renewable energy—13 percent; nuclear electric power—8 percent.[31] Fossil fuels have dominated the US energy mix for more than 100 years, but the mix has changed over time.[32] We will briefly review the major US energy sources and apply the four criteria of the energy policy guidelines to each.

Coal

US coal production was forecast to increase by 21 million short tons (MMst) to 599 MMst in 2022 and to 601 MMst in 2023. The EIA expected coal consumption to be slightly lower in 2022 at 541 MMst, relative to 546 MMst in 2021. That decline resulted from constraints on coal generation, mine shutdowns, and coal transportation limitations. Coal plants continue to shut down. Coal consumption is expected to decline by 9 percent to 493 MMst in 2023. However, coal exports increased from 85 MMst in 2021 to 87 MMst in 2022 and to 98 MMst in 2023.[33] Americans are now more aware of the health hazards of coal and its contribution to GHG emissions.[34]

Positively, coal is a reliable domestic energy source, thus not risking armed conflict. Large numbers are employed by the industry in extraction, transportation, and utility businesses and it is affordable. Coal can also be processed into liquid fuels and synthetic natural gas.

Negatively, coal is not renewable and carbon intensive. In 2020 coal accounted for 54 percent of CO_2 emissions from the energy sector, but it represented only 20 percent of the electricity generated in the United States.[35] Coal's toxic impact disproportionately affects multiple generations, harming especially people of color, pregnant women, and children through mercury pollution, acid rain; fly ash disposal, and ecological destruction like mountaintop removal, violations of sustainability and solidarity.[36]

Coal companies attempted to develop "clean coal" technologies such as "carbon capture sequestration" (CCS) but with little success.[37] The CO_2 will eventually escape and cause further global warming. Deep ocean storage would acidify the water and damage the ecosystems of the ocean floor. CCS technology has been proven costly and risky.[38]

The norms of sustainability and solidarity require that a moratorium be placed on coal-fired power plant construction. Investment in renewable energy innovations and reducing demands for electricity through conservation is more ethical and financially sound.

Oil

Crude oil or petroleum is a liquid fossil fuel made up mostly of hydrocarbons. Oil is found underground, under oceans, and accessed by drilling or strip-mining. It is refined into many forms: gasoline, propane, kerosene, and jet fuel, and used in plastics and paint. Petroleum supplies about 35 percent of US energy needs with the transportation sector consuming the most. In 2021, the United States consumed roughly 13.3 million barrels of petroleum per day (19.8 million barrels per day including petroleum products).[39] Overall, petroleum use in the United States grew between 1990 and 2021.[40]

Between 2020 and 2022 during the Covid-19 pandemic, demand for oil plummeted but returned to its highest point since 2019. This return was partly due to the volatile global market amid Russia's invasion of Ukraine. US consumption of petroleum products is forecast to decrease, at least through 2038, due to critically stronger fuel efficiency standards. US shale oil and natural gas extraction has increased production growth due fracking.[41]

Oil violates all four of the norms of ecojustice. Our need to stop using it points to huge economic challenges.[42] Notably, all US administrations since Truman have engaged in war over oil![43] Oil is non-renewable and unsustainable. Oil violates solidarity with all living beings causing GHG accumulation and threatening their health. Oil is inefficient—thus breaching the sufficiency criteria. US oil trade partners and governments have questionable human rights records—thus contravening the participation criteria. Therefore, moral reason requires stopping our use of oil as immediately as possible, while developing alternatives.

Natural Gas

Positively, natural gas is about 50 percent less carbon intensive than either coal or oil. It can be utilized efficiently in the production of electricity. Gas-fired power plants are less expensive to build, and production permits are easier to acquire.

Negatively, increased use of natural gas for electricity generation has forced a rise in prices for home heating, commercial, industrial, and agricultural uses. The extraction technology known as "fracking" is problematic.[44] Fracking uses huge amounts of water and chemicals to extract natural gas from coal shale beds. The 2005 Energy Policy Act exempted hydraulic fracturing, thus placing potable water supplies at risk.[45] Cave-ins, earthquakes, and the fouling of drinking water have occurred near these extraction sites.[46]

Positively, natural gas is a flexible and efficient fuel resource that supplies about 1/3 of the US energy from domestic sources. It poses somewhat fewer risks to health, safety, and peace and its extraction does less aesthetic damage than oil or coal.

Natural gas is an emitter of the GHG methane, the second largest near-term cause of global warming.[47] Reducing methane emissions is critical to avoid the worst effects of climate change. Natural gas is not renewable with the global supply peaking by 2050. Prices fell in 2016 but were expected to spike, raising the potential for global conflict originating with the Middle East and Russia.[48]

Martin-Schramm holds that the norms of sufficiency, sustainability, and solidarity require that we utilize natural gas wisely as a "bridge" to a future of only sustainable energy. Prudence requires consumers being highly vigilant against a false sense of security, denying its dangers and global warming. Use of natural gas is an evil, so prudence must govern it. The driving imperative and priority is for making a considerable investment in renewable energy and a transition possible.[49]

Nuclear Power

Arguably nuclear power is a clean energy source, a low emitter of GHGs. Yet the Union of Concerned Scientists and environmental groups oppose scaling up nuclear energy for at least seven reasons.[50] Nuclear power remains controversial with its history of hazards and meltdowns.[51] With Russia's capture of nuclear plants in Ukraine, the hazardous radiation potential of nuclear energy resurfaced.[52] On average it takes 14–12 years to build a nuclear plant—from planning to operation (wind and solar construction 2–5 years). Thus, potential human health hazards from "dirty" emissions are bound to be far greater while awaiting nuclear power startups.[53]

Cost overruns are common. The Levelized Cost of Energy for a new nuclear plant based on Lazard is $151 (112–89) MWh. This does not include annual waste storage fees of some $500 million.[54] (Cost for onshore wind $43 (29 to 56)/MWh and $41 (36 to 46)/MWh for utility-scale solar PV from the same source.)

Waste storage presents and security and safety issues, and thus violates the norm of solidarity with current and future generations.[55] Usually consumed fuel rods are stored at plant sites. Those hundreds of radioactive sites need to be secured for 200,000 years away from water supplies, crops, animals, and humans.

Weapons proliferation is a risk. Countries can harvest plutonium from fuel rods and enrich uranium to weapons grade. Uranium miners are at high risk for lung cancer because of their exposure to radon gas whose decay products are carcinogenic, thus violating equity criteria. The low GHG emissions of nuclear power partially meet the norm of sustainability and adequacy guidelines. Nuclear energy may be tolerated as a "bridge" solution while firmly resolved to develop sustainable solutions.[56] But prudence strongly begs the question: Why—risk all of the hazzards presented by nuclear energy production—when other safer and fully sustainable sources are available?

Solar Energy

The most powerful energy source is the Earth's sun. The European Renewable Energy Council says that sunlight "provides 2,850 times more energy than human communities currently consume."[57] Solar energy is harnessed first by solar thermal technologies and second photovoltaics (PVs) are semiconductors that generate electrical current from sunlight.[58] Only 3 percent of US electricity was generated with solar technologies in 2020.[59] For the first time ever, the United States generated more electricity from renewable sources in 2020 than from coal.[60] The US Department of Energy holds that solar power has the potential to provide 65–75 percent of home heating, hot water, dehumidifying, and cooling needs.[61]

Solar power complies with all the four ecojustice norms. The Biden-Harris Bipartisan Infrastructure Law funding will support solar energy careers in underserved areas and new digital platform will make reliable solar power more accessible.[62] Pairing wind and solar provides consistent clean energy to the grid.[63] To achieve a net zero power sector goal by 2035, solar power and energy storage must become more affordable.[64] The clear advantages and potential for this technology justify and even compel continued and substantial investment in this vital and renewable source.[65]

Wind

Wind energy is generated in two ways: offshore and land based.[66] The US Department of Energy, Office of Energy Efficiency & Renewable Energy, *Off-Shore Wind Market Report 2022* stated: "Falling offshore wind prices, state-level commitments, and an unprecedented expansion into new leasing areas drove the US offshore wind pipeline to grow 13.5% over the previous year, with 40,083 megawatts (MW) now in various stages of development."[67]

According to the Wind Energy Technologies Office, *Land-Based Wind Market Report: 2022 Edition*, August 16, 2022: "the 13,413 megawatts (MW) of new utility-scale wind capacity in 2021, was largely attributed to a significant improvement in the cost and performance of wind power technologies, along with supportive federal and state-level policies. The additions bring the United States' cumulative capacity total to 135,886 MW, enough energy to power 39 million American homes per year."[68]

By April of 2022, the United States generated 20 percent of its energy from wind and solar power, driven by a wind boom in the Great Plains and the Midwest, across states such as Texas, Oklahoma, Kansas, Nebraska, and the Dakotas.[69] Windy areas of the United States are far from high-energy demand areas. Winds blow irregularly, and the windiest times are usually at night when demands normally are lower. New transmission and storage technologies can meet those demands, coupled with solar.

Wind power easily meets the test of all four ecojustice norms and the energy guidelines. The norm of sustainability is met by wind combined with solar or natural gas to maintain steady transmission. Wind power has grown, electrical costs have decreased, while thousands of new jobs were created. Wind turbines are easily installed and lack heavy security risks. The ecojustice norms and energy guidelines support investment in wind energy.

Biomass

Biomass energy has two forms. "Biopower energy," produced from agricultural and forestry residues such as wood, crop residue, and switch grass, is used to generate heat and power. Biofuels are made from plants fermented into transportation fuels.[70] Biofuels can replace coal if power plants are properly retro fitted. Biomass from sewage, landfills, livestock waste, and organic matter emits methane, which can be used as fuel for heat or power.

Food crop residue should never be used for biofuel because that shrinks the global food supply, driving higher prices.[71] Biofuels may require significant increases in cropland and irrigation water use. Most promising for biofuel production is cellulose ethanol made from non-food parts of plants, fast-growing trees, and switch grass.[72] Biofuel production can cost more in GHG emissions than is ever saved in GHGs by using it. However, a recent promising discovery uses algae as a biofuel source.[73] Use of human sewage as a biofuel source is in experimental stages.

Use of corn in ethanol production violates the norms of sufficiency and solidarity. The biofuels industry is heavily dependent on government mandates and incentives, so close monitoring for genuine sustainability is needed. Biomass energy is available domestically and thus meets the sustainability standard of ecojustice norms as well as that of solidarity.[74] It satisfies the norms of sufficiency and participation, as well as the employment, appropriateness, and peace energy guidelines. Biomass energy deserves further development, but great care is needed to balance GHG and methane emissions with any perceived advantages.

Hydropower

Hydropower accounts for about 6.3 percent of the electricity produced in the United States from dams across major rivers.[75] Facilities may be flexible in their capacity to adjust their output of electricity according to demand by changing water flow through the turbines connected to the dam. But climate change is making water level subject to frequent droughts or floods.[76]

Ecologists note damming rivers as highly problematic.[77] Dams disrupt the migration of fishes, other wildlife, and river ecosystems and destroy forests, agricultural and recreational areas. Sediment is retained behind the dam and causes water scouring the stream bed below it. Dams provide questionable net saving in GHG reduction due to production of methane from the rotting vegetation that accumulates behind them.[78] In our "Climate Emergency," dams are most inefficient for saving GHGs. Free-flowing waters help mitigate the climate drawing CO_2 from the atmosphere. Most hydropower projects fail "Hydropower Sustainability Standards."[79] Large dam projects have violated rights of indigenous peoples, displacing them from homelands and livelihoods. Costly overruns and delays in building dams are common though many have been highly subsidized by governments.

Other ecological harms to river life and endangered species make compliance with the norm of sufficiency questionable.[80] Other renewable options are more promising.

Geothermal

The United States holds around 25 percent of the world's installed geothermal energy capacity, and 95 percent of that is in the Western States. California generated the most electricity from geothermal energy.[81] Geothermal energy accounts for 0.4 percent of net electricity generation in the United States.[82] Geothermal resources are reservoirs, mile-or-more-deep wells of hot water that exist deep below the Earth's surface. They can be drilled into to tap steam and hot water for electricity generation, direct use, and heating and cooling.

Geothermal heat pumps (GSHPs) are the primary method for use of geothermal energy. GSHPs use the shallow ground as an energy reservoir because it maintains a nearly constant temperature between 50 and 60° F.[83] GSHPs transfer heat from a building to the ground during the cooling season and from the ground into a building during the heating season.

High drilling costs and the use of large amounts of water in water-stressed areas are problematic. Also, CO_2, mercury, and hydrogen sulfate are released during drilling. Drilling can relieve geological stresses that cause earthquakes.[84] Geothermal pumps can be used relatively risk free anywhere in the United States and are "the most energy efficient, cost effective, and environmentally clean space conditioning technology available."[85]

Geothermal heat pumps satisfy all the ecojustice norms and the guideline criteria. Participation requires that people most affected by any drilling would be consulted in advance of any activity and that the safety of local populations be given the highest consideration. Great care for ecosystems and a safe, adequate accessible water supply are imperative to be addressed prior to drilling.

Marine Energy

Wave, tide, and ocean current–generated energy could readily meet 1 percent of all US electricity demands.[86] Tidal traps capture water at high tide and then release the water back to its source, generating electricity when passing through turbines on its way.[87] This process was tested in New York's East River and in Tacoma, Washington, in Puget Sound.[88]

There is a complex multilevel set of government agencies that have authority over the oceans and waterways and that require permits before any energy development can take place. Ecological concerns include the potential harm of high voltage passing over the ocean floor and the migration of fishes and whales. Current costs are high per kilowatt hour.[89] This kind of power could easily comply with the four norms and the energy guidelines.[90] The difficulty remains that this technology is just in its infancy and further research is needed.

Hydrogen

Hydrogen as a power source seems quite attractive from the moral point of view. However, even though it is the most abundant element on earth, it does not exist in pure form anywhere. It needs to be extracted from water (H_2O), ammonia (NH_3), or other fossil fuels. Such extraction processes require the emission of GHGs, so the question becomes one of economy and the net savings, especially in a "Climate Emergency." Hydrogen is highly flammable, and it easily escapes storage containers. Hydrogen can be used in fuel cells or internal combustion engines, but currently it is very costly to produce.[91] As hydrogen energy is developed its ethical use must be evaluated according to ecojustice norms.

> ### From the Writing of St. Francis
>
> **Thomas of Celano, "The Remembrance of the Desire of the Soul (1245–1247)," CXXIV**[92]
>
> When the brothers are cutting wood
> he forbids them to cut down the whole tree,
> so that it might have hope of sprouting again.

Reflection and Application

From Fossil Fuels to Family—Genuine Hope versus False Hope

In St. Francis' day, wood was central to life as fossil fuels are central to us. Without wood, medieval societies would have collapsed. If we removed all oil-based products from our homes, we would have precious little left. Providentially, St. Francis saw a familial relationship between people and trees that would sustain them both in life and hope! He instructed the brothers to leave a portion of each tree uncut, so it could regenerate.[93] This was a first and necessary step toward sustainable living! Indeed, the medieval ax devastated forests and harmed ecosystems. But our context of "Climate Emergency" knows a size and scale of technological prowess creating a distinct urgency Francis could have never imagined. Yet his call for hope is worth our consideration.

The Bible is awash in symbols of hope. The Hebrew Testament denounces political, economic, and military alliances that bring us false hope (Isa. 31:1-3; 36:4-9; Hos. 10:13). Indeed, genuine hope is identified with God. "God is the hope of Israel" (Jer. 14:8; Ps. 71:5). In Rom. 15:13, St. Paul points to a "God of hope" in whose presence we should "overflow with hope."

Jesus refers to hope in his "Inaugural Address" in Luke 4:18-19. He recalls Leviticus 25: 23: "The land shall not be sold in perpetuity, for the land is *mine*; with me you are but aliens and tenants." Just and sustainable relationship with the land is key to genuine hope. Hope, peace, and joy abound when we care for the land as God cares for us. In selfishness we spiral downward into insensitivity to the needs of others and become fearful and insecure. It is fear and insecurity (not hope) that are classical impediments to sound moral judgment.

St. Bonaventure of Bagnoregio *Imitatio Christi* and Virtue Ethics

St. Bonaventure of Bagnoregio developed what St. Francis of Assisi taught about Christ, creation, creatures, and humans.[94] His love-oriented virtue ethics framework is known as the *Imitatio Christi*.[95]

The *Imitatio Christi* has internal and external dimensions. Humans are embodied and spiritual earth creatures, who seek union with God, while in *this* world, that bursts with the signs of God. We learn how to live morally by studying Jesus' whole life, as the Word incarnate explained in the Gospels and interpreted by St. Francis. We move beyond merely mimicking his actions to *spiritual* transformation. In those two ways God's grace assists us in the moral life.[96] Central to this transformation are the virtues of humility, poverty, obedience, and love.

Humility

Humility is the virtue central to the God-human relationship. God, in the Incarnation, entered our reality, choosing intimate relationship with us *earthcreatures*.[97] We must reclaim our *creaturely* identity, using our considerable, limited scientific and technological ability to care for one another and the planet.[98]

Humility is particularly important when contemplating invasive, massive, and destructive ecosystemic interventions in our common home. As scientist R. Eugene Turner explains:

> Embracing doubt, a signature of strength of science, is an essential core component of an Ignorance Based World View (IBWV) that assumes the areas of certainty are small and relative. The contrasting Knowledge Based World View (KBWV) assumes small and mostly insignificant knowledge gaps exist. When the KBWV is combined with a sense of urgency to "do something," then the intellectual landscape is flattened, the introduction of new ideas is impeded, monitoring and adaptive management is marginalized, risky behaviors continue, and social learning is restricted.[99]

Christian environmental ethics is normatively rooted in values that strongly embrace prudence and the precautionary principle when dealing with questions of great complexity, the unknown, or the unknowable. Thus, an IBWV approach is clearly the preferred methodology for any approach to our interactions with our sisters and brothers—human and otherkind and our life together on Earth.

In a similar vein, the United Nations mandated the 2005 report on *The Precautionary Principle*.[100] The Precautionary Principle deals with the complexities of economic activities that would exploit natural resources using technologies that could result in serious and/or irreversible harm.[101] The objective of the Precautionary Principle is to provide guidance in cases of risk where outcomes and probabilities are not well known.[102]

Poverty

Bonaventure held that material poverty (Christian simplicity) must accompany humility. Often, materially wealthy people know only a false poverty (material), the illusion of never having enough "stuff," but craving something more (spiritual poverty). Today, we must choose to live within what is sufficient for a life of dignity and ecologically sustainable. True poverty is to be confident in God's generosity, ready with open hands and heart, and to give away whatever we can to another in need (Mt. 10:8). This means refraining from supporting or consuming energy from unsustainable sources and developing renewable energy sources.

Obedience

Jesus Christ modeled this virtue by listening to his Father's will, caring for people and nonhuman others.[103] Today, we must address the suffering Earth, become ecologically literate, engage in prayerful discernment, and then act to halt environmental destruction. There is an intimate relationship between the virtues of obedience and prudence.

Prudence is a Christian virtue based on Aristotle's *phronêsis* or practical wisdom.[104] It is elaborated in the *Catechism of the Catholic Church*, Article 7, 1806:

> *Prudence* is the virtue that disposes practical reason to discern our true good in every circumstance and to choose the right means of achieving it ... Prudence is "right reason in action," (Aquinas, *STh* II-II,47, 2). It is not to be confused with timidity or fear, nor with duplicity or dissimulation.[105]

Prudence, when used in environmental ethical analysis, functions to conserve known values, while remaining open to new knowledge.[106]

Love

Recipients of God's love, humans must share it with all of creation (Jn 13:34-35).[107] But humans love imperfectly, so justice and the discipline of law are necessary. Christ is the ultimate norm and negotiator of justice (love).[108] Today we must relate to creation with justice and love as God relates to us. We must establish and enforce policies and laws that keep air, water, and soils pure; disallow the plundering of our warming planet; and restore environmental damage.[109]

Imitatio Christi: Practices of Divesting and Investing

Like St. Francis, Bonaventure held a hope-filled, positive, and radically relational view of God, creation, redemption, and ethical praxis.[110] Each creature responds to God's love in its unique way. The Incarnation unites humans with the whole cosmos, and Jesus Christ incarnate embodies and exemplifies the norm and standard for all ethical relations. Humans can read the signs of the divine in creation and then *act* morally.[111] By following Jesus, humans can participate with Christ and become co-creators and co-redeemers of the cosmos. Today's "Climate Emergency" demands swift and effective action to eliminate fossil fuels from our world so that our common planetary home can thrive and that our family—human and other kind—may fully live. This will require active participation from all, each utilizing our gifts for and with one another.

Questions for Reflection and Discussion

1. Do you know what renewable energy sources your utility company utilizes?
2. In what way are massive projects that damage or destroy Earth's ecosystems idolatrous?
3. What concrete steps will you take to conserve energy and avoid fossil-fuel use?
4. What is most difficult for you when contemplating living with less oil dependency?
5. What factor would persuade you to change your lifestyle to make it more sustainable?

Suggestions for Action

1. Download the *Energy Savers Guide*: https://www.energy.gov/energysaver/articles/energy-saver-guide.

2   Join a car cooperative; group errands together so you make fewer trips in your vehicle.
3   Explore the website of *Interfaith Power and Light* at http://interfaithpowerandlight.org/.
4   Avoid using plastics; purchase products made from recycled and natural materials.
5   Trade in your vehicle for an electric one.

Sources for Further Study

Catholic Association of Diocesan Ecumenical and Interreligious Officers (CADIO), Catholic Climate Covenant, United States Conference of Catholic Bishops. *Ecumenical and Interreligious Guidebook: Care for Our Common Home*. Springfield: CADIO, 2021.

Fiorani, Luca. *Francis. Still Dreams: Five Years after Laudato Si'*. Trans. Cecelia Blackden and Augustine Doronila. Perugia: E.F.I. Edizione Francescane Italiane, 2020.

Interdicasterial Working Group of the Holy See on Integral Ecology. *Journeying Towards Care for Our Common Home: Five Years after Laudato Si'*. Vatican City: Libreria Editrice Vaticana, 2020.

Lester, Richard K. and David M. Hart. *Unlocking Energy Innovation: How America Can Build a Low-Cost, Low-Carbon Energy System*. Cambridge, MA: The MIT Press, 2012.

Martin-Schramm, James B. *Climate Justice: Ethics, Energy and Public Policy*. Minneapolis: Fortress Press, 2010.

Notes

1.   With tar sands fully mined, stabilizing Earth's climate would be implausible with disastrous global impacts. See the IPCC's *Fourth Assessment Report*, https://www.ipcc.ch/working-group/wg3/. Conventional oil and gas alone would take atmospheric CO_2 well above a disastrous 400 ppm. If coal was phased out over the next few decades and if all unconventional fossil fuels were left in the ground, earth's climate could stabilize. Danielle Droitsch, "NASA's James Hansen: Tar Sands Is the 'Dirtiest of Fuels' and 'Game over for the Climate.'" National Resource Defense Council, https://www.nrdc.org/experts/danielle-droitsch/nasas-james-hansen-tar-sands-dirtiest-fuels-and-game-over-climate.

2. David Toolan, *At Home in the Cosmos* (Maryknoll: Orbis Books, 2001), 48–9.
3. USCC, in *Renewing the Earth: An Invitation to Reflection and Action on Environment in Light of Catholic Social Teaching: A Pastoral Statement of the United States Catholic Conference November 14, 1991*, https://www.usccb.org/resources/renewing-earth. USCCB, *Global Climate Change a Plea for Dialogue Prudence and the Common Good, A Statement of the United States Conference of Catholic Bishops, June 15, 2001*, https://www.usccb.org/resources/global-climate-change-plea-dialogue-prudence-and-common-good. *This Land Is Home to Me* (1975) & *At Home in the Web of Life* (1995), https://static1.squarespace.com/static/5e0ebce33d6a6002f3105cc7/t/5e3321856cac3d0b6f059a5a/1580409225664/AppalachianBishopsPastorals.pdf. *A Pastoral Letter on the Integrity of Creation, and the Athabasca Oil Sands* (2009) by Luc Bouchard, Bishop of the Diocese of St. Paul in Alberta, Canada, https://omiusajpic.org/wp-content/uploads/2009/02/2009-January-25-Tar-Sands-Pastoral-Letter.pdf.
4. Pontifical Justice and Peace Council, *Compendium of the Social Doctrine of the Church*, especially chapter 10: "Safeguarding the Environment," https://www.vatican.va/roman_curia/pontifical_councils/justpeace/documents/rc_pc_justpeace_doc_20060526_compendio-dott-soc_en.html#CHAPTER%20TEN. *Laudato Si'—On Care for Our Common Home*, https://www.vatican.va/content/francesco/en/encyclicals/documents/papa-francesco_20150524_enciclica-laudato-si.html.
5. US EPA, "Surface Coal Mining in Appalachia—Basic Information," https://www.epa.gov/sc-mining. Richard Schiffman, "A Troubling Look at the Human Toll of Mountaintop Removal Mining," *Yale Environment 360*, https://e360.yale.edu/features/a-troubling-look-at-the-human-toll-of-mountaintop-removal-mining. Dan Stockman, "Appalachian Coal Country, Where Sisters See Little Change in 40 Years," *National Catholic Reporter*, March 2, 2017, https://www.globalsistersreport.org/news/environment/appalachian-coal-country-where-sisters-see-little-change-40-years-45256.
6. Pontifical Justice and Peace Council, *Compendium of the Social Doctrine of the Church*, especially Chapter 10: "Safeguarding the Environment," https://www.vatican.va/roman_curia/pontifical_councils/justpeace/documents/rc_pc_justpeace_doc_20060526_compendio-dott-soc_en.html.
7. USCCB, *Renewing the Earth*, https://www.usccb.org/resources/renewing-earth.
8. Ibid.
9. Ibid.
10. *Global Climate Change*, https://www.usccb.org/resources/global-climate-change-plea-dialogue-prudence-and-common-good.

11. Ibid.
12. Full text: https://omiusajpic.org/wp-content/uploads/2009/02/2009-January-25-Tar-Sands-Pastoral-Letter.pdf. The author conducted a telephone interview with Bishop Bouchard, January 30, 2012.
    Glen Argan, "Oilsands Pastoral Letter Deserves Attention," *The Shepherd's Trust*, February 25, 2019, https://www.catholicregister.org/opinion/columnists/item/29051-glen-argan-oilsands-pastoral-letter-deserves-attention. Bob Mckeon, "Bouchard Took 'Catholic View' of Oilsands," Journey to Justice Column, Western Catholic Reporter, February 3, 2014, https://www.wcr.ab.ca/Columns/Columns/entryid/5075.
13. Timothy G. Pernini et al., "Estimating Oil Sands Emissions Using Horizontal Path-Integrated Column Measurements," *Atmospheric. Measurement. Techniques* 15 (2022), 225–40, https://doi.org/10.5194/amt-15-225-2022.
14. January 18, 2012, President Obama initially denied permission for the XL Keystone Pipeline construction as proposed. The project remains controversial today.
15. Consider the United States consumed 20.7 million barrels per day. Richard K. Lattanzio, Analyst in Environmental Policy, "Canadian Oil Sands: Life-Cycle Assessments of Greenhouse Gas Emissions," *Congressional Research Service*, March 10, 2014, https://sgp.fas.org/crs/misc/R42537.pdf.
16. In "Bouchard Took 'Catholic View' of Oilsands," Bob McKeon noted Roman Catholic Diocese of Mackenzie-Ft. Smith Bishop Murray Chatlain's April 15, 2009, Pastoral Letter supporting Buchard.
17. Interview, January 30, 2012: Bouchard stressed in footnotes: "We cited the [tar sands] industry's own data to make our point." *A Pastoral Letter* (22): Jennifer Grant, *Fact or Fiction: Oil Sands Reclamation*, Drayton Valley, AB: Pembina Institute, 2008, 6. Pastoral endnote numbers are given in parentheses.
18. Emphasis in original after note 40.
19. Creighton University's Creighton Center for Service and Justice, "Sustainability—Keystone Pipeline Petition," October 5, 2011. Franciscan Action Network, https://franciscanaction.org/.
20. Dennis Sadowski, "Country's Debate over Keystone XL Pipeline Is Far from Over," *US Catholic*, January 27, 2012, https://www.ncronline.org/news/countrys-debate-over-keystone-xl-pipeline-far-over. Nicholas Kusnetz, "Tar Sands Face High Costs, Waning Profits," *InsideClimate News*, July 31, 2020, https://insideclimatenews.org/news/31072020/big-oil-coronavirus-losses.
21. Parliament of the World's Religions, "The Fifth Directive: Commitment to a Culture of Sustainability and Care for the Earth," https://www.youtube.com/watch?v=BWFwJdcBOj4. Also, Parliament of the World's Religions, "What Is the Global Ethic?" https://parliamentofreligions.org/globalethic/

22. James B. Martin-Schramm, *Climate Justice: Ethics, Energy, and Public Policy* (Minneapolis: Fortress Press, 2010), 23–6, 37–44. Christiana Z. Peppard, Julia Watts Besler, Erin Lothes Biviano, and James B. Martin-Schramm, "What Powers Us? A Comparative Religious Ethics of Energy Sources, Power and Privilege," *Journal of the Society of Christian Ethics* 36/1 (2016): 10–15.
23. Key texts: Gen. 9:8-17; Exod. 22:21-24; Mic. 6:8; Amos 2:6, 5:11, 8:4-8; Isa. 10:1-2; Jer. 22:13-17; Mt. 5:1-14; Lk. 4:16-20, 6:20-26; Acts 1-5; and Gal. 3:28.
24. The 1987 UN World Commission on Environment and Development understood "sustainable development" as raising productivity, accumulation of goods, and technological innovations. See their *Our Common Future* (New York: Oxford University Press, 1987) at 8 "meets the needs of the present without compromising the ability of future generations to meet their own needs."
25. Martin-Schramm, *Climate Justice*, 28–9. Also Peppard et al., "What Powers Us?" 11.
26. See Ps. 104, 145; Gen. 1:24; (The Noahic Covenant) Gen. 9; (Sinai Covenant) Deut. 3:16; Exod. 20-24; Lk. 12:42; and Rom. 8: 18-14.
27. Martin-Schramm, *Climate Justice*, 28–9. Peppard et al., "What Powers Us?" 12.
28. Pope John Paul II, *Sollicitudo Rei Socialis*, 39, https://www.vatican.va/content/john-paul-ii/en/encyclicals/documents/hf_jp-ii_enc_30121987_sollicitudo-rei-socialis.html.
29. Peppard et al., "What Powers Us?" 12.
30. US EIA, "Energy Facts Explained," https://www.eia.gov/energyexplained/us-energy-facts. The data that follows here is from this source unless otherwise noted.
31. Ibid.
32. Ibid.
33. US EIA, "Short-Term Energy Outlook August 2022," https://www.eia.gov/outlooks/steo/pdf/steo_text.pdf.
34. EcoAmerica, "American Energy Attitudes: Support Grows for Nuclear Power, Drops for Coal, Remains Strong for Wind & Solar," *American Climate Perspectives* V (2020), https://ecoamerica.org/wp-content/uploads/2020/11/acps-2020-vol.-v-american-energy-attitudes.pdf.
35. US EPA, "Sources of Greenhouse Gas Emissions," https://www.epa.gov/ghgemissions/sources-greenhouse-gas-emissions.
36. Frederica Perera, Dr. P. H., PhD, and Kari Nadeau, MD, PhD, "Climate Change, Fossil-Fuel Pollution, and Children's Health," *New England Journal of Medicine*, June 16, 2022, 386: 2303–14, https://www.nejm.org/doi/full/10.1056/NEJMra2117706.

37. Martin-Schramm, *Climate Justice*, 51. Annie Leonard, "The Story of Cap and Trade," http://www.youtube.com/watch?v=pA6FSy6EKrM. Dr. David M. Kuchta, "What Is Clean Coal Technology? Overview, History, Carbon Emissions," https://www.treehugger.com/what-is-clean-coal-technology-5200812. US GAO, "Federal Government Efforts to Reduce Emissions from Coal-Fired Power Plants," March 10, 2022, https://www.gao.gov/blog/federal-government-efforts-reduce-emissions-coal-fired-power-plants.
38. Julie Wernau, "Ameren Casts Dark Cloud over Cleaner Coal Plant," *Chicago Tribune*, November 29, 2011, http://articles.chicagotribune.com/2011-11-29/business/ct-biz-1129-ameren-20111129_1_futuregen-alliance-futuregen-project-coal-plant.
39. N. Sönnichsen, "Petroleum Consumption in the US 1985–2021," *Stastica*, June 21, 2022, https://www.statista.com/statistics/244423/estimated-petroleum-consumption-in-the-united-states/.
40. N. Sönnichsen, "Petroleum Consumption in the United States in Selected Years from 1990 to 2021, by Sector," April 1, 2022, https://www.statista.com/statistics/244442/us-petroleum-energy-consumption-by-sector/.
41. Mike Soraghan, "Baffled about Fracking? You're Not Alone," Business Day—Energy & Environment, *New York Times*, https://archive.nytimes.com/www.nytimes.com/gwire/2011/05/13/13greenwire-baffled-about-fracking-youre-not-alone-44383.html?ref=earth. Food and Water Watch, Issue Briefs, "Fracking and Earthquakes," May 2015, https://www.foodandwaterwatch.org/2015/05/04/fracking-and-earthquakes/.
42. Alabama Deepwater Horizon Restoration | 2022 Update, https://www.outdooralabama.com/sites/default/files/Deepwater/PDFs/Alabama%20Deepwater%20Horizon%20Oil%20Spill%20Progress%20Report%202022%20Update.pdf
43. Martin-Schramm, *Climate Justice*, 55.
44. Mike Soraghan, "Baffled about Fracking?"
45. US EPA, "Regulation of Hydraulic Fracturing under the Safe Drinking Water Act," http://water.epa.gov/type/groundwater/uic/class2/hydraulicfracturing/wells_hydroreg.cfm.
46. Food and Water Watch, "Fracking," https://www.foodandwaterwatch.org/2015/05/04/fracking-and-earthquakes/.
47. International Energy Agency, "Methane Emissions from Oil and Gas," https://www.iea.org/reports/methane-emissions-from-oil-and-gas. Shanti Menon, "Mission Methane," *Solutions* 51/2 (Spring 2020): 8–11.
48. Martin-Schramm, *Climate Justice*, 61. Peppard et al., "What Powers Us?" 14
49. Peppard et al., "What Powers Us?" 15.
50. Elliott Negin, "With Nuclear Power, 'Advanced' Isn't Always Better," *Catalyst*, Vol. 21 (Spring 2021): 8–11, 21. Mark Z. Jacobson, "7 Reasons

Why Nuclear Energy Is Not the Answer to Solve Climate Change," *One Earth*, June 23, 2022, https://www.oneearth.org/the-7-reasons-why-nuclear-energy-is-not-the-answer-to-solve-climate-change/?gclid=CjwKCAjw0dKXBhBPEiwA2bmObT9gWH-HMETMS-SEr2t7EL-p2QgEJFvPJ6212FG-kJB6kD6iP_X7TxoCeM0QAvD_BwE.

51. USNRC, "Backgrounder on Chernobyl Nuclear Power Plant Accident," https://www.nrc.gov/reading-rm/doc-collections/fact-sheets/chernobyl-bg.html. USNRC, "Backgrounder on the Three Mile Island Accident," http://www.nrc.gov/reading-rm/doc-collections/fact-sheets/3mile-isle.html. World Nuclear Association, "Fukushima Daiichi Accident." https://world-nuclear.org/information-library/safety-and-security/safety-of-plants/fukushima-daiichi-accident.aspx.
52. Reuters, "Putin Agreed to Send IAEA Mission to Ukraine Plant, Macron's Office Says," August 19, 2022, https://www.reuters.com/world/europe/putin-agreed-send-iaea-mission-ukraine-plant-macrons-office-says-2022-08-19/.
53. World Health Organization, "Air Pollution," https://www.who.int/data/gho/data/themes/theme-details/GHO/air-pollution.
54. Jacobson, "7 Reasons."
55. Susan Montoya Bryan, "US Awards $3B Contract to Manage Nuclear Waste Repository," *US News*, July 12, 2022, https://www.usnews.com/news/best-states/new-mexico/articles/2022-07-12/us-awards-3b-contract-to-manage-nuclear-waste-repository.
56. Martin-Schramm, *Climate Justice*, 69.
57. Cited by Martin-Schramm, *Climate Justice*, 83.
58. Vikas Bajaj, "Interested in Solar Panels?" May 26, 2022, https://www.nytimes.com/2022/05/24/business/energy-environment/solar-panel-advice.html.
59. US EIA, *Monthly Energy Review*, April 2021.
60. "3 Charts That Show the Energy Transition in 50 States," May 8, 2021, *Inside Clean Energy*, newsletters@insideclimatenews.org.
61. Martin-Schramm, *Climate Justice*, 83.
62. US DOE, "Biden-Harris Administration Launches New Solar Initiatives to Lower Electricity Bills and Create Clean Energy Jobs," July 27, 2022, https://www.energy.gov/articles/biden-harris-administration-launches-new-solar-initiatives-lower-electricity-bills-and.
63. Dan Gearino, "Pairing Wind + Solar for Cheaper, 24-Hour Renewable Energy," *Inside Climate News*, October 4, 2018, https://insideclimatenews.org/news/04102018/wind-solar-24-hour-renewable-energy-reliability-lower-cost-power-plant/.
64. Carolyn Fortuna, "Just the Facts: The Cost of Solar Has Fallen More Quickly Than Experts Predicted," *CleanTechnica*, June 8, 2022, https://

cleantechnica.com/2022/06/08/just-the-facts-the-cost-of-solar-has-fallen-more-quickly-than-experts-predicted/.
65. Ibid.
66. An excellent primer on offshore wind energy: Wind Energy Technologies Office, "Top 10 Things You Didn't Know about Offshore Wind Energy," August 16, 2022, https://www.energy.gov/eere/wind/articles/top-10-things-you-didnt-know-about-offshore-wind-energy.
67. Access report: https://www.energy.gov/eere/wind/articles/offshore-wind-market-report-2022-edition.
68. Access report: Wind Energy Technologies Office, https://www.energy.gov/eere/wind/articles/land-based-wind-market-report-2022-edition.
69. Electreck, https://electrek.co/2022/05/10/us-hits-a-record-20-of-electricity-from-wind-and-solar-in-april/.
70. Martin-Schramm, *Climate Justice*, 93.
71. Ibid., 95.
72. Anna Austin, "A Study by a Group of Forest Scientists Confirms Forest-Derived Bioenergy Results in No Net Carbon Release," *Biomass Magazine*, January 25, 2012, http://biomassmagazine.com/articles/6122/words-from-the-wise/.
73. "Energy Resources: US Energy Department Backs Plan to Produce Algae Crude Oil," January 16, 2012, https://www.upi.com/Energy-News/2012/01/16/US-Energy-Department-backs-plan-to-produce-algae-crude-oil/61091326752182/.
74. Martin-Schramm, *Climate Justice*, 98–9.
75. US EIA, "Hydropower Explained," https://www.eia.gov/energyexplained/hydropower/.
76. Brooke Hirsheimer, "New Study: US Hydropower Threatened by Increasing Droughts Due to Climate Change," February 24, 2022, https://www.worldwildlife.org/press-releases/new-study-us-hydropower-threatened-by-increasing-droughts-due-to-climate-change.
77. Josh Klemm and Eugene Simonov, "10 Reasons Why Hydropower Dams Are a False Climate Solution," April 6, 2022, https://www.internationalrivers.org/news/10-reasons-why-hydropower-dams-are-a-false-climate-solution/.
78. Field Notes, "Hydropower's Surprising Climate Impacts," *Environmental Defense Fund Solutions* 51/2 (Spring 2020): 4.
79. Klemm and Simonov, "10 Reasons."
80. Martin-Schramm, *Climate Justice*, 100–1.
81. Renewable Energy World, "Western Governors Launch Bid to Spur Geothermal Energy Development," April 8, 2022, https://www.renewableenergyworld.com/baseload/western-governors-launch-bid-to-spur-geothermal-energy-development/.

82. US EIA *Monthly Energy Review*, April 2021.
83. "Geothermal Energy Factsheet," Center for Sustainable Systems, University of Michigan, 2021. Pub. No. CSS10-10, https://css.umich.edu/publications/factsheets/energy/geothermal-energy-factsheet.
84. Lori Dajose, "Producing Clean Energy Can Diminish Earthquake Risk," June 30, 2021, Caltech, https://www.caltech.edu/about/news/producing-clean-energy-can-diminish-earthquake-risk.
85. M. Samotyj, EPRI Project Manager, "Geothermal Heat Pumps Technical Update," Technology and Market Overview, 1016076 Technical Update, December 2008, https://www.epri.com/research/products/1016076.
86. Martin-Schramm, *Climate Justice*, 103.
87. International Energy Agency, *Ocean Power—Tracking Report*, https://www.iea.org/reports/ocean-power. Straits Research, "Wave and Tidal Energy Market Size Is Projected to Reach USD 28.80 Billion by 2030, Growing at a CAGR of 41.92%," https://www.globenewswire.com/en/news-release/2022/08/02/2490663/0/en/Wave-and-Tidal-Energy-Market-Size-is-projected-to-reach-USD-28-80-Billion-by-2030-growing-at-a-CAGR-of-41-92-Straits-Research.html. "Tapping into Wave and Tidal Ocean Power: 15% Water Power by 2030," January 27, 2012, http://energy.gov/articles/tapping-wave-and-tidal-ocean-power-15-water-power-2030.
88. Martin-Schramm, *Climate Justice*, 104.
89. Ibid.
90. Kevin Knodell, "Here's Why the Navy Is Betting on Wave Energy Research in Hawaii," *Honolulu Civil Beat*, August 22, 2021, https://www.civilbeat.org/2021/08/heres-why-the-navy-is-betting-on-wave-energy-research-in-hawaii/.
91. US EIA, "Hydrogen Explained Use of Hydrogen," https://www.eia.gov/energyexplained/hydrogen/use-of-hydrogen.php.
92. Thomas of Celano, "The Remembrance of the Desire of the Soul (1245–1247)," CXXIV, 165 in *Francis of Assisi: Early Documents*, Volume II—*The Founder*, ed. Regis J. Armstrong, J. A. Wayne Hellmann, and William J. Short (New York: New City Press, 2000), 353–4.
93. Ibid., 4.
94. Kenan B. Osborne, ed, *The History of Franciscan Theology* (St. Bonaventure, NY: The Franciscan Institute, 1994), vii–ix. Zachary Hayes, "The Life and the Christological Thought of St. Bonaventure," in *Franciscan Christology: Selected Texts, Translations and Introductory Essays*, ed. Damian McElrath. Franciscan Sources No. 1 (St. Bonaventure, NY: The Franciscan Institute, 1980), 62–4. Timothy Johnson, "Lost in Sacred Space: Textual Hermeneutics, Liturgical Worship, and Celano's *Legenda ad usum chori*," 12. E. R. Daniel, *The Franciscan Concept of Mission in the High Middle Ages* (New York: The Franciscan Institute, 1975), 48.

95. Zachary Hayes, "Christ, Word of God and Exemplar of Humanity," *Cord* 46 (1996): 6.
96. Zachary Hayes, *The Hidden Center: Spirituality and Speculative Christology in St. Bonaventure*, Franciscan Pathways (St. Bonaventure, NY: The Franciscan Institute, 1992), 42.
97. Bonaventure, Sermon on the Nativity (IX, 106), citied by ibid.
98. Leonard J. Bowman, "The Cosmic Exemplarism of Bonaventure," *The Journal of Religion* 55 (1985): 187.
99. R. Eugene Turner, "Doubt and the Values of an Ignorance-Based World View for Restoration: Coastal Louisiana Wetlands," *Estuaries and Coasts* 32 (2009): 1054.
100. *The Precautionary Principle*, https://unesdoc.unesco.org/ark:/48223/pf0000139578. Commission of the Bishops' Conferences of the European Community (COMECE), *A Christian View on Climate Change: The Implications of Climate Change for Lifestyles and EU Policies* (Brussels, Belgium: COMECE, 2008), 17.
101. COMEST and UNESCO, *The Precautionary Principle*, 8. See the 1972 Polluter Pays Principle, which requires that the costs of pollution be borne by those who cause the pollution. See also the 1992 Earth Summit, Agenda 21 as a principle of sustainable development. Today it is a recognized principle of International Environmental Law. Also see *1992 Rio Declaration on Environment and Development*.
102. COMEST and UNESCO, *The Precautionary Principle*, 13.
103. See Heb. 10:7, 9; Jn. 14:31; Jn. 5:30. Hayes, *The Hidden Center*, 37. Bonaventure's commentary on Luke stresses Jesus' obedience to people.
104. T. Gilby, S. V. "Prudence," in *New Catholic Encyclopedia*, Vol. 11, 2nd ed. (Detroit: Gale, 2003), 787–92. Scott Carson, S. V. "Phrronêsis," in *Encyclopedia of Philosophy*, ed. Donald M. Borchert, Vol. 10, 2nd ed. (Detroit: Macmillan Reference USA, 2006), 27–8. Charles J. List, "The Virtues of Wild Leisure," *Environmental Ethics* 27 (Winter 2005): 355–73. Vasileios E. Pantazis, "Reverence ('Ehrfurcht') for the Living World as the Basic Bioethical Principle: Anthropological-Pedagogical Approach," *Ethics, Place and Environment* 12 (June 2009): 255–66, especially at 262.
105. https://www.vatican.va/archive/ENG0015/__P64.HTM.
106. "Scientific Knowledge and the Virtue of Prudence," in NCCB/USCC, *Global Climate Change: A Plea for Dialogue, Prudence, and the Common Good*, June 15, 2001, https://www.usccb.org/resources/global-climate-change-plea-dialogue-prudence-and-common-good.

    Steven Bouma-Prediger, "Why Care for Creation? From Prudence to Piety," *Christian Scholar's Review* 27 (Spring 1998): 277–97.
107. Hayes, *The Hidden Center*, 38–9. In Bonaventure's speculative theology and spirituality, love drives the Christ mystery.

108. Ibid., 202–3. Hayes cites Hex. 1, 31-33 (V, 334); Aristotle, II *Ethics*, c.6; and Hex.1, 34-36 (V, 335).
109. Hayes, *The Hidden Center*, 39: "To perceive the life of Christ as a paradigm, is to accept its fundamental values as normative for human life. The fundamental attitude and values of Christ must be so personalized in one's life, that they truly define one's relationship to reality." The spiritual life in Christ is a journey deeper into the foundational realities of the world. Understanding those realities also shapes Christian ethics.
110. Leonardo Boff, *Cry of the Earth, Cry of the Poor*, trans. Phillip Berryman (Maryknoll: Orbis Books, 1997), 174–86. John Duns Scotus and Chardin make this link even more explicit. See Jn. 1:3, 14; Heb. 1:2; Col. 1:15-20; Eph. 1:3-14; Rev. 1:8 and 21:6. Ilia Delio, *A Franciscan View of Creation: Learning to Live in a Sacramental World*, The Franciscan Heritage Series, Vol. 2 (St. Bonaventure, NY: The Franciscan Institute, 2003), 31: "Bonaventure consistently claims that Christ belongs to the very structure of reality—as the Word, to the reality of God; as the Incarnate Word, to the reality of the universe created by God. It is Christ who reveals to the world its own meaning." Hayes, "Christology—Cosmology," 41–58.
111. Denis Edwards, *Ecology at the Heart of Faith* (Maryknoll: Orbis Books, 2006), 58–60. Duncan Reid, "Enfleshing the Human," in *Earth Revealing-Earth Healing: Ecology and Christian Theology*, ed. Denis Edwards (Collegeville, MN: Liturgical Press, 2000), 69–83. Neils Henrick Gregersen, "The Cross of Christ in an Evolutionary World," *Dialog* 40 (2001): 205.

Afterword: Franciscan Hope amid Ecological Sin and a "Climate Emergency"

We are living in a "Climate Emergency." Scientists, Christians, Jews, and Muslims, numerous religious and spiritual persons, are teaching and living the deep moral values and vision required to support halting the ecocide already in progress and promoting actions to reverse course.[1] The Franciscan charism continues to provide guidance for the necessary corrective endeavors.

We noted the dominant role of fossil fuels as the primary culprit in anthropogenically induced global warming. Sustainable energy sources are now well known, ever more technologically sound and economically accessible. It is now simply unacceptable to treat the fossil-fuel industry like any other. Already in 2001, the USCCB accepted the scientific consensus asserting that reality.

In 2015, Pope Francis clearly contended in *Laudato Si'* – especially §s 23, 26, and 165 that divestment from fossil fuels is imperative for escaping planetary devastation. He called on all people of faith and good will to do just that. Investment in "renewable energy sources" is equally imperative. In June of 2018, he told major oil executives, "Civilization requires energy, but energy must not destroy civilization."[2]

Progress has occurred in the divesting of fossil fuels and investing in renewables, but much more remains to be done. In November 2021 the revised *Socially Responsible Investment Guidelines for the USCCB* named the "the common good and the environment" as a category requiring moral consideration when investing and "shareholder engagement" as a strategy toward achieving corporate change.[3]

On July 19, 2022, the Vatican's Investment Committee of the Holy See released new statutes governing investments. They discouraged "speculative investments" in oil, mining industry, and nuclear energy but encouraged investment in companies working to protect the environment and promote the use of clean energy.[4]

The USCCB and the Vatican strategies are supported by fiscal and scientific wisdom. Numerous studies indicate that over the next three to ten years the energy technology revolution will begin displacing coal, oil, and gas as the pre-eminent fuels for economic activity.[5] Key findings include that a "Carbon Bubble" is anticipated, indicating in-ground fossil fuels are overvalued and overpriced and ultimately worthless. The science case for investing in "Climate-Smart Power Systems" is dramatically illustrated in the Union of Concerned Scientists report, *Killer Heat in the United States: Climate Choices and the Future of Dangerously Hot Days*.[6]

Each of us must do our part to heal our planet. Throughout this book, I have indicated resources for action. *Journey toward Care for Our Common Home* by the Interdicasterial Working Group of the Holy See on Integral Ecology is a good beginning read.[7]

Personal choices concerning divestment and reinvestment require expertise beyond the scope of this work. However, from the ethical standpoint, the Christian practice of moral discernment is an advisable starting point.[8] Two central questions for discernment need attention: "What is God enabling me and requiring me to do?" and "What ought I to do?" The time-tested process of See—Judge—Act is useful here. See—requires collecting knowable facts and predictable outcomes concerning continued use of fossil fuels. Judge—entails one weighing the facts in view of Christian ethics and Catholic Social Teaching. Act—involves deciding the meaning of the prior two steps for the present. Consulting investment experts such as Christian Brothers or Catholic Impact Investing is critical and wise, along with the Bishops Guidelines.[9]

God is active in history. Christians and others of good will can receive a call from God to act. Options facing a person are tested against the global awareness of the self. Metanoia means rethinking one's personal history through new images. Peace, radical satisfaction, and delight are the signs which determine which options harmonize with one's sense of self. Authentic conversion produces a character which bears some resemblance to the character of Jesus in the Gospels.

When at the end of his life, St. Francis, impassioned to serve Christ evermore perfectly, used to say: "Let us begin brothers, to serve God. Let us begin ... And let us make progress, because up to now we have made too little progress."[10] May we be filled with hope—and together resolve our "Climate Emergency."

Notes

1. United Nations Environment Programme and the Parliament of the World's Religions Climate Action Program, *Faith for Earth: A Call for Action*, https://parliamentofreligions.org/climate-action/faith-for-earth-a-call-for-action/.
2. Carol Glatz, "Pope to Oil Execs: 'No Time to Lose' in Switch to Alternative Energy," *Catholic News Service*, https://catholicphilly.com/2018/06/news/world-news/pope-to-oil-execs-no-time-to-lose-in-switch-to-alternative-energy/.
3. *Socially Responsible Investment Guidelines 2021 for the United States Conference of Catholic Bishops*, https://www.usccb.org/resources/socially-responsible-investment-guidelines-2021-united-states-conference-catholic-bishops.
4. Junno Arocho Esteves, "Vatican Investments Must Follow Catholic Social Teaching, New Policy Says," *Catholic News Service*, July 19, 2022, https://www.ncronline.org/news/vatican/vatican-investments-must-follow-catholic-social-teaching-new-policy-says.
5. Larry Coble and Joe Antoun, CFP, "The Fiscal Case for Fossil Fuel Divestment," 350.ORG. Chicago, https://world.350.org/chicago/the-fiscal-case-for-fossil-fuel-divestment/.
6. Download: https://www.ucsusa.org/resources/killer-heat-united-states-0. See especially Chapter 6.
7. Download: https://catholicclimatecovenant.org/resource/journeying-towards-care-our-common-home.
8. Erin Lothes Biviano, Daniel DiLeo, Cristina Richie, Tobias Winright, "Is Fossil Fuel Investment a Sin?" *Health Care Ethics*, Vol. 26. No. 1 (Winter 2018): 1–8. https://www.chausa.org/publications/health-care-ethics-usa/archives/issues/winter-2018/is-fossil-fuel-investment-a-sin
9. Christian Brothers Investment Services, https://cbisonline.com/us/resources/news/. Catholic Impact Investment Collaborative, https://www.catholicimpact.org/.
10. "The Life of St. Francis by Julian of Speyer (1232–1235)," 67, in *FA:ED*, Volume I—*The Saint*, 414.

Bibliography

Books

Bartoli, Marco. *Saint Clare: Beyond the Legend*. Translated by Frances Teresa Downing. Cincinnati, OH: St. Anthony Messenger Press, 2010.
Bergant, Dianne. *Genesis: In the Beginning*. Collegeville: Liturgical Press, 2013.
Bergant, Dianne. *A New Heaven a New Earth: The Bible and Catholicity*. Catholicity in an Evolving Universe Series. Maryknoll: Orbis Books, 2016.
Bodo, Murray. *Francis, The Journey and the Dream*. 40th Anniversary Edition. Cincinnati, OH: St. Anthony Press, 2011.
Boff, Leonardo. *Cry of the Earth, Cry of the Poor*. Maryknoll: Orbis Books, 1997.
Boff, Leonardo. *St. Francis: A Model for Human Liberation*. Translated by John W. Diercksmeier. New York: The Crossroad Publishing Company, 1982.
Boff, Leonardo and Mark Hathaway. *The Tao of Liberation: Exploring the Ecology of Transformation*. Maryknoll: Orbis Books, 2009.
Bohm, David and Mark Edwards. *Changing Consciousness Exploring the Hidden Source of Social, Political and Environmental Crisis Facing Our World*. San Francisco: Harper, 1991.
Bonansea, Bernardino M. and John K. Ryan. *John Duns Scotus 1265–1965*. Paperback Edition. Washington, DC: Catholic University of America Press, 2018.
Bonaventure. *On the Reduction of the Arts to Theology*. Translation with Introduction and Commentary by Zachary Hayes. St. Bonaventure: Franciscan Institute, 1996.
Bourgerol, Guy J. *Introduction to the Works of Bonaventure*. Patterson, NJ: St. Anthony Guild Press, 1964.
Buber, Martin. *Between Man and Man*. Translated by Ronal Gregor Smith. London: Kegan Paul, 1947.
Bullard, Robert. *Dumping in Dixie: Race, Class, and Environmental Quality*. Third Edition. New York: Routledge, 2018.
Carney, Margaret. *The First Franciscan Woman: Clare of Assisi & Her Form of Life*. Quincy, IL: Franciscan Press, 1993.
Castillo, Daniel P. *An Ecological Theology of Liberation: Salvation and Political Ecology*. Maryknoll: Orbis Books, 2019.

Chamberlain, Gary L. *Because Water Is Life*. Winona, MN: Anselm Academic, 2018.
Cocksedge, Simon, Samuel Double and Nicholas Alan Worssam. *Seeing Differently: Franciscans in Creation*. London: Canterbury Press, 2021.
Coloe, Mary L. PBVM. "John 1–10." Vol. 44a, *Wisdom Commentary*, Volume Editor. Mary Ann Beavis, Barbara E. Reid, OP, General Editor. A Michael Glazier Book. Collegeville: The Liturgical Press, 2021.
Cousins, Ewert. *Bonaventure*. The Classics of Western Spirituality. Edited by Richard J. Payne. New York: Paulist Press, 1978.
Cummings, Clare Hope. *Uncertain Peril: Genetic Engineering and the Future of Seeds*. Boston: Beacon Press, 2009.
Dalarun, Jacques. *The Canticle of Brother Sun: Francis of Assisi Reconciled*. Translated by Philippe Yates. Paris: Alma Editeur, 2014.
Darragh, Neil. *At Home in the Earth*. Auckland: Accent Publications, 2000.
Delio, Ilia. *Crucified Love: Bonaventure's Mysticism of the Crucified Christ*. Quincy, IL: Franciscan Press, 1998.
Delio, Ilia. *Simply Bonaventure: An Introduction to His Life, Thought, and Writings*. New York: New City Press, 2001.
Delio, Ilia. *The Emergent Christ: Exploring the Meaning of Catholic in an Evolutionary Universe*. Maryknoll: Orbis Books, 2011.
Delio, Ilia, Keith Douglas Warner, and Pamela Wood. *Care for Creation: A Franciscan Spirituality of the Earth*. Cincinnati, OH: St. Anthony Messenger Press, 2008.
Doyle, Eric. *St. Francis and the Song of Brotherhood and Sisterhood*. [Reprint of *St. Francis and the Song of Brotherhood*, New York: Seabury Press, 1981.] St. Bonaventure, NY: The Franciscan Institute, 1997.
Edwards, Denis. *Ecology at the Heart of Faith*. Maryknoll: Orbis Books, 2006.
Edwards, Denis. *Partaking of God: Trinity, Evolution, and Ecology*. Collegeville: Liturgical Press, 2014.
Elgin, Duane. *Voluntary Simplicity: Toward a Way of Life That Is Outwardly Simple and Inwardly Rich*. New York: William Morrow, 1981.
Farley, Margaret A. *Compassionate Respect: A Feminist Approach to Medical Ethics and Other Questions*. Madeleva Lecture in Spirituality. New York: Paulist Press, 2002.
Fiorani, Luca. *Francis. Still Dreams: Five Years after Laudato Si'*. Perugia: E.F.I. Edizione Francescane Italiane, 2020.
Glacken, Clarence J. *Traces on the Rhodian Shore: Nature and Culture in Western Thought from Ancient Times to the End of the Eighteenth Century*. Berkeley: University of California, 1967.
Gleick, Peter. *Bottled and Sold: The Story behind Our Obsession with Bottled Water*. Washington, DC: Island Press 2010.

Guardini, Ramono. *The End of the Modern World*. Wilmington: Intercollegiate Studies Institute, 1998.

Gudme, Anne Katrine and Ingrid Hjelm, eds. *Myths of Exile: History and Metaphor in the Hebrew Bible*. London: Routledge, 2015.

Guinan, Michael D. *The Franciscan Vision and the Gospel of John*. The Franciscan Heritage Series, Vol. 4. St. Bonaventure, NY: The Franciscan Institute, 2006.

Habel, Norman C. *An Inconvenient Text: Is a Green Reading of the Bible Possible?* Adelaide: AFT Press, 2009.

Habel, Norman C. *Finding Wisdom in Nature: An Eco-Wisdom Reading of the Book of Job*. Sheffield: Sheffield Phoenix Press, 2014.

Haught, John F. *Science and Faith: A New Introduction*. Mahwah, NJ: Paulist Press, 2012.

Hayes, Zachary. *A Window to the Divine: A Study of Christian Creation Theology*. Quincy, IL: Franciscan Press, 1997.

Hayes, Zachary. *The Hidden Center: Spirituality and Speculative Christology in St. Bonaventure*. St. Bonaventure, NY: The Franciscan Institute, 1992.

Hayes, Zachary. *What Manner of Man? Sermons on Christ by Bonaventure*. Chicago: Franciscan Herald Press, 1974.

Headey, Derek and Shenggen Fan. *Reflections on the Global Food Crisis—How Did It Happen? How Has It Hurt? And How Can We Prevent the Next One?* Research Monograph 165. Washington, DC: International Food Policy Research Institute, 2010.

Hellwig, Monika K. *Eucharist and the Humger of the World*. Kansas City: Sheed and Ward, 1992.

Homer-Dixon, Thomas. *Commanding Hope: The Power We Have to Renew a World in Peril*. Toronto: Knopf Canada, 2020.

Horan, Daniel P. *Postmodernity and Univocity a Critical Account of Radical Orthodoxy and John Duns Scotus*. Baltimore, MD: Project Muse, 2014.

Ingham, Mary Beth. *Scotus for Dunces: An Introduction to the Subtle Doctor*. St. Bonaventure, NY: Franciscan Institute Publications, 2003.

Ingham, Mary Beth. *Understanding John Duns Scotus: Of Realty the Rarest-Veined Unraveller*. St. Bonaventure, NY: Franciscan Institute Publications, 2017.

Interdicasterial Working Group of the Holy See on Integral Ecology. *Journeying Towards Care for our Common Home: Five Years after Laudato Si'*. Vatican City: Libreria Editrice Vaticana, 2020.

Johnson, Elizabeth A. *Ask of the Beasts: Darwin and the God of Love*. London: Bloomsbury, 2014.

Johnson, Elizabeth A. *Creation and the Cross: The Mercy of God for a Planet in Peril*. Maryknoll: Orbis Books, 2018.

Johnson, Elizabeth A. *She Who Is: The Mystery of God in Feminist Discourse.* New York: Crossroad, 1992.

Johnson, Elizabeth A. *Woman, Earth, Creator Spirit.* 1993 Madelava Lecture. New York: Paulist Press, 1993.

Lester, Richard K. and David M. Hart. *Unlocking Energy Innovation: How America Can Build a Low-Cost, Low-Carbon Energy System.* Cambridge, MA: MIT Press, 2012.

Macquarie, John. *Christian Hope.* New York: Crossroad, 1978.

Maguire, Daniel C. *The Moral Choice.* San Francisco: Winston/Harper & Row, 1979.

Maguire, Daniel C. *The Moral Core of Judaism and Christianity: Reclaiming the Revolution.* Minneapolis: Fortress Press, 1993.

Martin-Schramm, James B. *Climate Justice: Ethics, Energy and Public Policy.* Minneapolis: Fortress Press, 2010.

Martin-Schramm, James B. and Robert L. Stivers. *Christian Environmental Ethics: A Case Study Method Approach.* Maryknoll: Orbis Books, 2003.

Massynbaerde Ford, Josephine. *Redeemer, Friend, and Mother: Salvation in Antiquity and in the Gospel of John.* Minneapolis: Fortress, 1997.

McGann, Mary E. *The Meal That Reconnects.* Collegeville, MN: Liturgical Press, 2020.

McIntosh, Alastair. *Hell and High Water: Climate Change and the Human Condition.* London: Birlinn, 2008.

Miller, Vincent J., ed. *The Theological and Ecological Vision of Laudato Si'— Everything Is Connected.* New York: Bloomsbury T&T Clark, 2017.

Monti, Dominic V. and Katherine Wrisley Shelby, eds. *Bonaventure Revisited: Companion to the Breviloquium.* St. Bonaventure, NY: Franciscan Institute Publications, 2017.

Mooney, Catherine M. *Clare of Assisi and the Thirteenth-Century Church: Religious Women, Rules, and Resistance.* Philadelphia: University of Pennsylvania Press, 2016.

Moore, Bryan L. *Ecological Literature and the Critique of Anthropocentrism.* Cham: Palgrave Macmillan, 2017.

Nothwehr, Dawn M., ed. *Franciscan Theology of the Environment: An Introductory Reader.* Quincy, IL: The Franciscan Press, 2002.

Nothwehr, Dawn M. *Mutuality a Formal Norm for Christian Social Ethics.* [(San Francisco: Catholic Scholars Press, 1998) Reprinted Eugene, OR: Wipf & Stock Publishers, 2005].

Nothwehr, Dawn M. *The Franciscan View of the Human Person: Some Central Elements.* The Franciscan Heritage Series, Volume Three. CFIT/ESC-OFM. St. Bonaventure, NY: The Franciscan Institute, 2005.

O'Brien, Kevin J. *An Ethics of Biodiversity: Christianity, Ecology, and the Variety of Life.* Washington, DC: Georgetown University Press, 2010.

O'Hara, Dennis, Matthew Eaton, and Michael T. Ross, eds. *Integral Ecology for a More Sustainable World: Dialogues with Laudato Si'*. Lanham: Lexington Books, 2020.

O'Leary, Don. *Roman Catholicism and Modern Science: A History*. New York: The Continuum Publishing Group, Inc., 2006.

O'Murchu, Diarmuid. *Quantum Theology: Spiritual Implications of the New Physics*. New York: Crossroads, 2004.

Peterson, Ingrid J. *Clare of Assisi: A Bibliographical Study*. Quincy, IL: Franciscan Press, 1993.

Pontifical Justice and Peace Council. *Compendium of the Social Doctrine of the Church*. https://www.vatican.va/roman_curia/pontifical_councils/justpeace/documents/rc_pc_justpeace_doc_20060526_compendio-dott-soc_en.html#CHAPTER%20TEN.

Rasmussen, Larry L. *Earth Community Earth Ethics*. Maryknoll: Orbis Books, 1996.

Ruether, Rosemary Radford. *Gaia and God: An Ecofeminist Theology of Earth and Healing*. San Francisco: Harper, 1992.

Schaefer, Jame, ed. *Confronting the Climate Crisis: Catholic Theological Perspectives*. Milwaukee, WI: Marquette University Press, 2011.

Schreiter, Robert J., ed. *Plural Spiritualities—North American Experiences*. Cultural Heritage and Contemporary Change Series VIII. Christian Philosophical Studies, Vol. 14. Washington, DC: The Council for Research in Values and Philosophy, 2015.

Schüssler Fiorenza, Francis. "Systematic Theology: Task and Method." In *Systematic Theology: Roman Catholic Perspectives*, edited by Francis Schüssler Fiorenza and John P. Galvin, 1–78. Minneapolis: Fortress Press, 2011.

Scotus, John Duns. *John Duns Scotus: God and Creatures, The Quodlibital Questions*. Translated by Felix Alluntis and Allan B. Wolter. Paperback Edition. Washington, DC: Catholic University of America Press, 1981.

Shannon, Thomas A. *The Ethical Theory of John Duns Scotus: A Dialogue with Medieval and Modern Thought*. Quincy, IL: Franciscan Press, 1995.

Shiva, Vandana. *Soil Not Oil: Climate Change, Peak Oil and Food Insecurity*. London: Zed Books, 2008.

Shiva, Vandana. *Who Really Feeds the World? The Failures of Agribusiness and the Promise of Agroecology*. Berkeley, CA: New Atlantic Books, 2016.

Smith, Jeffery M. *Genetic Roulette*. Fairfield, IA: Yes! Books, 2007.

Smith, Jeffery M. *Seeds of Deception: Exposing Industry and Government Lies about Safety of Genetically Engineered Foods You're Eating*. Fairfield, IA: Yes! Books, 2003.

Sorrell, Roger D. *St. Francis of Assisi and Nature: Tradition and Innovation in Western Christian Attitudes toward the Environment*. New York: Oxford University Press, 1988.

Steck, SJ, Christopher. *All God's Animals: A Catholic Theological Framework for Animal Ethics*. Moral Traditions Series. Washington, DC: Georgetown University Press, 2019.
Suppan, Stephen. *Commodities Market Speculation: The Risk to Food Security and Agriculture*. Minneapolis: Institute for Agriculture and Trade Policy, 2008. https://www.iatp.org/documents/commodities-market-speculation-the-risk-to-food-security-and-agriculture.
The World Commission on Environment and Development. *Our Common Future*. New York: Oxford University Press, 1987.
Toolan, David. *At Home in the Cosmos*. Maryknoll: Orbis Books, 2001.
Tracy, David. *Blessed Rage for Order: New Pluralism in Theology*. Chicago: University of Chicago Press, 1995.
Tracy, David. *The Analogical Imagination: Christian Theology and the Culture of Pluralism*. New York: Crossroad Publishing, 1998.
UNEP and Parliament of the World's Religions. *Faith for Earth: A Call for Action*. Nairobi: United Nations Environment Programme, 2020.
von Rad, Gerhard. *Old Testament Theology*. Edinburgh: Oliver and Boyd, 1962.
Westermann, Claus. *Genesis 1-11: A Commentary*. Translated by John J. Scullion. Minneapolis: Augsburg Publishing House, 1974.
Wiesel, Elie. *Night*. New York: Bantam Books, 1982.
Wirzba, Norman. *Food and Faith: A Theology of Eating*. New York: Cambridge University Press, 2011.
Wolter, Allan B. *Duns Scotus on the Will and Morality*. Washington, DC: Catholic University of America Press, 1986.
Zenner, Christiana. *Just Water: Theology, Ethics, and Fresh Water Crisis*. Revised Edition. Maryknoll: Orbis Books, 2018.

Chapters in Books

Bowe, Barbara. "Soundings in the New Testament Understandings of Creation." In *Earth, Wind & Fire: Biblical and Theological Perspectives on Creation*, edited by Carol J. Dempsey and Mary Margaret Pazdan, 57–66. Collegeville: The Liturgical Press, 2004.
Carney, Margaret. "Franciscan Women and the Theological Enterprise." In *The History of Franciscan Theology*, edited by Kenan B. Osborne. St. Bonaventure, NY: The Franciscan Institute, 1994.
Clifford, Anne M. "Foundations for a Catholic Ecotheology of God." In *And God Saw It Was Good: Catholic Theology and the Environment*, edited by Drew Christiansen and Walter Grazer, 19–46. Washington, DC: United States Conference of Catholic Bishops, Inc., 1996.

Dreyer, Elizabeth A. "'[God] Whose Beauty the Sun and the Moon Admire': Clare and Ecology." In *Franciscan Theology of the Environment*, edited by Dawn M. Nothwehr, 129–41. Quincy, IL: Franciscan Press, 2002.

Fretheim, Terrence E. "Issues of Interdependence in Matters of Creation: An Old Testament Perspective." In *Eco-Reformation: Grace and Hope for a Planet in Peril*, edited by Lisa E. Dahill and James B. Martin-Schramm, 12–139. Eugene, Or: Wipf & Stock Publishers, 2016.

González-Gaudiano, Edgar and Pablo Meira-Cartea. "Climate Change Education and Communication: A Critical Perspective on Obstacles and Resistances." In *Education and Climate Change: Living in Interesting Times*, edited by Fumiyo Kagawa and David Selby, New York: Routledge, 2010.

Hayes, Zachary. "Bonaventure: Mystery of the Triune God." In *The History of Franciscan Theology*, edited by Kenan B. Osborne, 39–125. St. Bonaventure, NY: Franciscan Institute, 1994.

Hayes, Zachary. "The Cosmos: A Symbol of the Divine." In *Franciscan Theology of the Environment: An Introductory Reader*, edited by Dawn M. Nothwehr, 249–67. Quincy, IL: Franciscan Press, 2002.

Hayes, Zachary. "The Life and the Christological Thought of St. Bonaventure." In *Franciscan Christology: Selected Texts, Translations and Introductory Essays*. Franciscan Sources No.1, edited by Damian McElrath, 59–88. St. Bonaventure, NY: The Franciscan Institute, 1980.

Hieke, Thomas. "Leviticus." In *The Jerome Biblical Commentary for the Twenty-First Century*. First Fully Revised Edition, edited by John J. Collins, Gina Hens-Piazza, Barbara E. Reid, OP, and Donald Senior, CP, 281–2. London: Bloomsbury, 2022.

Ingham, Mary Elizabeth. "Integrated Vision." In *The History of Franciscan Theology*, edited by Kenan B. Osborne, 185–230. St. Bonaventure, NY: The Franciscan Institute, 1994.

Karris, Robert J. "Colossians 1: 15-20—Jesus Christ as Cosmic Lord and Peacemaker." In *Franciscan Theology of the Environment*, edited by Dawn M. Nothwehr, 67–96. *Franciscan Theology of the Environment: An Introductory Reader*. Quincy, IL: The Franciscan Press, 2002.

Kittredge, Cynthia Briggs and Claire Miller Colombo. "Colossians." In *Philippians, Colossians, Philemon*, edited by Mary Ann Beavis, 123–200. *Wisdom Commentary*, volume 51. Collegeville, MN: Liturgical Press, 2017.

Macy, Joanna. "The Greatest Danger: *Apatheia*, the Deadening of Mind and Heart." In *Coming Back to Life: Practices to Reconnect Our Lives, Our World*, edited by Joanna Macy and M. Young Brown, 26. Gabriola Island, BC: New Society, 1998.

McGinn, Bernard. *The Foundations of Mysticism*. Vol. 1. *The Presence of God: A History of Western Christian Mysticism*. New York: Crossroad, 1991.

McGoldrick, Terrance. "A Theological Argument for Water as a Human Right: The Bolivian Pachamama/Mother Earth Encounter with Catholic Thought." *Journal of Catholic Social Thought* 15, no. 1 (2018): 109–37.

Meany, Mary Walsh and Felicity Dorsett, eds. "Her Bright Merits." In *Spirit and Life, Essays on Contemporary Franciscanism*, Vol. 17. Essays Honoring Ingrid Peterson, OSF. St. Bonaventure, NY: Franciscan Institute Publications, 2012.

Mulholland, Séamus. "Christ: The *Haecceitas* of God—The Spirituality of John Duns Scotus's Doctrine of *Haecceitas* and the Primacy of Christ." In *Franciscan Theology of the Environment: An Introductory Reader*, edited by Dawn M. Nothwehr, 305–12. Quincy, IL: Franciscan Press, 2002.

Osborne, Kenan B. "Incarnation, Individuality, and Diversity." In *Franciscan Theology of the Environment: An Introductory Reader*, edited by Dawn M. Nothwehr, 295–303. Quincy, IL: Franciscan Press, 2002.

Nothwehr, Dawn M. "The Brown Thread in *Laudato Si'*: Grounding Ecological Conversion and Theological Ethics Praxis." In *Integral Ecology for a More Sustainable World: Dialogues with Laudato Si'*, edited by Dennis O'Hara, Matthew Eaton, and Michael T. Ross, 111–26. Lanham, MD: Lexington Books, 2020.

Nothwehr, Dawn M. "The Quest for Interconnectedness: Cosmic Mutuality." In *Plural Spiritualities—North American Experiences*, Christian Philosophical Studies, XIV, edited by Robert J. Schreiter, 11–33. Washington, DC: The Council for Research in Values and Philosophy, 2015.

Peterson, Ingrid. "Franciscan Spirituality: The Footprints of Jesus in the Classroom and the Marketplace." In *As Leaven to the World: Catholic Perspectives on Faith, Vocation, and the Intellectual Life*, edited by Thomas M. Landy. Franklin, WI: Sheed & Ward, 2001.

Reid, Duncan. "Enfleshing the Human: An Earth-Revealing, Earth-Healing Christology." In *Earth Revealing Earth Healing: Ecology and Christian Theology*, edited by Denis Edwards, 69–83. Collegeville: Liturgical Press, 2001.

Rubio, Julie Hanlon. "Toward a Just Way of Eating." In *Green Discipleship: Catholic Theological Ethics and the Environment*, edited by Tobais Winright, 360–78. Winona, MN: Anselm Academic, Christian Brothers Publications, 2011.

Sacks, Rabbi Lord Jonathan. "The Stewardship Paradigm." In *Eco Bible*, Vol. 1: *An Ecological Commentary on Genesis and Exodus*, edited by Rabbi Yonatan Neril and Rabbi Leo Dee, 11–13. Jerusalem: Interfaith Center for Sustainable Development, 2020.

Short, William. "Pied Beauty: Gerard Manley Hopkins and the Scotistic View of Nature." In *Franciscan Theology of the Environment, An Introductory Reader*, edited by Dawn M. Nothwehr, 313–23. Quincy, IL: Franciscan Press, 2002.

Wolter, Allan B. "John Duns Scotus on the Primacy and Personality of Christ." In *Franciscan Christology: Selected Texts, Translations and Essays*, Franciscan Sources No. 1, edited by Damian McElrath, 147–55. St. Bonaventure, NY: Franciscan Institute Publications, 1980.

Journal Articles

Aranda, Antonio. "La Cuestión Teológica de la Encarnatión del Verbo: Relectura de Tres Posiciones Características." *Scripta Theologica* 25 (1993): 49–94.

Armstrong, Regis J. "Francis of Assisi and the Prisms of Theologizing." *Greyfriars Review* 10, no. 2 (1996): 179–206.

Bahmani, Fatemeh, Mitra Amini, Seyed Ziaeddin Tabei, Mohamad Bagher Abbasi. "The Concepts of Hope and Fear in the Islamic Thought: Implications for Spiritual Health." *Religion and Health* 57 (2018): 57–71. DOI: 10.1007/s10943-016-0336-2.

Barlow, Maude. "Our Right to Water: A People's Guide to Implementing the United Nations' Recognition of the Right to Water and Sanitation." *Council of the Canadians*. June 2011. https://conseildescanadiens.org/sites/default/files/publications/report-rtw-5yr-1115.pdf

Barlow, Maude. "Water as Commodity—The Wrong Prescription." *Backgrounder* 7, no. 3 (Summer 2001). https://archive.foodfirst.org/publication/water-as-commodity-the-wrong-prescription/.

Brueggemann, Walter. "The Earth Is the Lord's: A Theology of Earth and Land." *Sojourners* 15 (October 1986): 28–32.

Chalupnicek, Pavel. "*Laudato Si*' and Economics: A Survey of Responses." *Journal of Catholic Social Thought* 18, no. 2 (2021): 283–306.

Dezza, Ernesto. "John Duns Scotus on Human Beings in the State of Innocence." *Traditio* 75 (2020): 289–310. DOI: https://doi.org/10.1017/tdo.2020.10.

Einhorn, Catrin. "A 'Crossroads' for Humanity: Earth's Biodiversity Is Still Collapsing." *New York Times*. September 15, 2020. https://www.nytimes.com/2020/09/15/climate/biodiversity-united-nations-report.html?smid=em-share.

Enns, Peter. "When Was Genesis Written and Why Does It Matter?" *The BioLogos Foundation*. 2019. https://wp.biologos.org/wp-content/uploads/2019/02/enns_scholarly_essay3.pdf.

Esteves, Junno Arocho. "Vatican Investments Must Follow Catholic Social Teaching, New Policy Says." *Catholic News Service*. July 19, 2022. https://www.ncronline.org/news/vatican/vatican-investments-must-follow-catholic-social-teaching-new-policy-says.

Fraser, Barbara. "COP26 Results Are Still Too Little, Though Perhaps Not Too Late." *EarthBeat Weekly*. November 12, 2021. https://www.ncronline.org/news/earthbeat/earthbeat-weekly-cop26-results-are-still-too-little-though-perhaps-not-too-late.

Glatz, Carol. "Pope to Oil Execs: 'No Time to Lose' in Switch to Alternative Energy." *Catholic News Service*. https://catholicphilly.com/2018/06/news/world-news/pope-to-oil-execs-no-time-to-lose-in-switch-to-alternative-energy/.

Gregersen, Niels Heinrich. "The Cross of Christ in an Evolutionary World." *Dialog: A Journal of Theology* 40 (2001): 192–207.

Guardian. "Pope Francis Declares 'Climate Emergency' and Urges Action." June 14, 2019. https://www.theguardian.com/environment/2019/jun/14/pope-francis-declares-climate-emergency-and-urges-action.

Gudorf, Christine E. "Water Privatization in Christianity and Islam." *Journal of the Society of Christian Ethics* 30, no. 2 (2010): 19–38.

Hardin, Garrett. "The Tragedy of the Commons." *Science* 162 (1968): 1243–8.

Hayes, Zachary. "New Cosmology for a New Millennium." *New Theology Review* 12, no. 3 (1999): 29–39.

Heshmat, Shahram. "What Is Confirmation Bias?" *Psychology Today*. April 23, 2015. https://www.psychologytoday.com/us/blog/science-choice/201504/what-is-confirmation-bias.

Hill, Jason. "The Sobering Truth about Corn Ethanol." *Proceedings of the National Academy of Sciences of the United States of America* 119, no. 11 (2022): e2200997119. https://doi.org/10.1073/pnas.2200997119.

Iammerrone, Giovanni. "Franciscan Theology Today: Its Possibility, Necessity, and Values." *Greyfriars Review* 8, no. 1 (1994): 103–26.

Ingham, Mary Beth. "Presence, Poise, and Praxis: The Three-Fold Challenge for Reconcilers Today." *The Cord* 53, no. 6 (2003): 303–14.

Ingham, Mary Beth. "The Testimony of Two Witnesses: A Response to Ask the Beasts." *Theological Studies* 77, no. 2 (2016): 473.

Khorchide, M. and U. Topkara. "A Contribution to Comparative Theology: Probing the Depth of Islamic Thought." *Religions* 4, no. 1 (2013): 67–76.

Lucas, Tamara and Richard Horton. The EAT–Lancet Commission. "The 21st-Century Great Food Transformation." January 16, 2019. https://doi.org/10.1016/S0140-6736(18)33, 179–9. https://www.thelancet.com/pdfs/journals/lancet/PIIS0140-6736(18)33179-9.pdf?utm_campaign=tleat19&utm_source=HubPage.

Lynas, Mark, Benjamin Z. Houlton, Simon Perry, and Mark Lynas. "Greater Than 99% Consensus on Human Caused Climate Change in the Peer-Reviewed Scientific Literature." *Environmental Research Letters* 16, no. 114005, IOP Publishing Ltd. October 19, 2021. https://iopscience.iop.org/article/10.1088/1748-9326/ac2966.

McGrail, Peter. "Initiation and Ecology: Becoming a Christian in the Light of *Laudato Si'*." *Liturgy* 31, no. 2 (2016): 55–62. https://doi.org/10.1080/0458063X.2016.1123951.

Negin, Elliott. "With Nuclear Power, 'Advanced' Isn't Always Better." *Catalyst* 21 (Spring 2021): 8–11, 21.

Nothwehr, Dawn M. "Called to Ecological Conversion." *New Theology Review* 22, no. 1 (February 2009): 84–7.

Nothwehr, Dawn M. "For the Salvation of the Cosmos: The Church's Mission of Ecojustice." *International Bulletin of Mission Research* 43, no. 1 (2019): 68–81.

Padilla, C. René. "The Relevance of the Jubilee in Today's World (Leviticus 25)." *Mission Studies* 13, no. 1&2 (1996): 12–30.

Peppard, Christiana Z., Julia Watts Besler, Erin Lothes Biviano, and James B. Martin-Schramm. "What Powers Us? A Comparative Religious Ethics of Energy Sources, Power and Privilege." *Journal of the Society of Christian Ethics* 36, no. 1 (Spring/Summer 2016): 3–25.

Perera, Dr. P. H., PhD, Frederica and Kari Nadeau, M. D., PhD. "Climate Change, Fossil-Fuel Pollution, and Children's Health." *New England Journal of Medicine* 386 (June 16, 2022): 2303–14. https://www.nejm.org/doi/full/10.1056/NEJMra2117706.

Plumer, Brad. "Humans Are Speeding Extinction and Altering the Natural World at an 'Unprecedented' Pace." *New York Times*. May 6, 2019. https://www.nytimes.com/2019/05/06/climate/humans-are-speeding-extinction-and-altering-the-natural-world-at-an-unprecedented-pace.html.

Quinn, John F. "Chronology of St. Bonaventure (1217–1274)." *Franciscan Studies* 32 (1972): 168–86.

Ripple, William J., Christopher Wolf, Thomas M. Newsome, Phoebe Barnard, and William R. Moomaw. "World Scientists' Warning of a Climate Emergency." *BioScience* 70, no. 1 (January 2020): 8–12. https://doi.org/10.1093/biosci/biz088.

Schiffman, Richard. "A Troubling Look at the Human Toll of Mountaintop Removal Mining." *Yale Environment 360*. https://e360.yale.edu/features/a-troubling-look-at-the-human-toll-of-mountaintop-removal-mining.

Schneiders, Sandra. "God So Loved the World ... Ministerial Religious Life in 2009." (Talk on vowed religious life given to the IHM Congregation, June 14, 2009): 22–4. https://scholarcommons.scu.edu/cgi/viewcontent.cgi?article=1153&context=jst.

Selby, David. "As the Heating Happens: Education for Sustainable Development of Education for Sustainable Contraction." *International Journal of Innovation and Sustainable Development* 2, no. 3/4 (2007): 258.

Shirvani, S. M. H. "'Raising Hope' in Quran and Psychology," *HTS Teologiese Studies/Theological Studies* 74, no. 1 (2018): 2. https://doi.org/10.4102/hts.v74i1.4828.

Turner, R. Eugene. "Doubt and the Values of an Ignorance-Based World View for Restoration: Coastal Louisiana Wetlands." *Estuaries and Coasts* 32 (2009): 1054.

World Commission on the Ethics of Scientific Knowledge and Technology. *The Precautionary Principle*. https://unesdoc.unesco.org/ark:/48223/pf0000139578.

Roman Catholic and Roman Catholic Magisterial Documents

Catechism of the Catholic Church. Part Three: Life in Christ, Section One— Man's Vocation Life in the Spirit, Chapter One: The Dignity of the Human Person. Article 8, Sin. https://www.vatican.va/archive/ENG0015/__P69.HTM.

Catholic Bishops of the South. "*Voices and Choices: A Pastoral Letter from the Catholic Bishops of the South*." November 15, 2000. In The Catholic Committee of the South, *Voices and Choices*. Cincinnati, OH: St. Anthony Press, 2000.

Common Declaration of Pope Francis and the Ecumenical Patriarch Bartholomew I. https://www.vatican.va/content/francesco/en/speeches/2014/may/documents/papa-francesco_20140525_terra-santa-dichiarazione-congiunta.html.

Dicastery for Promoting Integral Human Development. *Aqua Fons Vitae: Orientations on Water—Symbol of the Cry of the Poor and the Cry of the Earth*. Vatican City. March 2020. https://www.humandevelopment.va/content/dam/sviluppoumano/documenti/Aqua%20fons%20vitae%20_%2003%202020.pdf.

Heartland Bishops. *Strangers and Guests: Toward Community in the Heartland*. May 1, 1980. https://iowacatholicconference.org/strangers-and-guests-toward-community-in-the-heartland/.

Interdicasterial Working Group of the Holy See on Integral Ecology. *Journeying towards Care for Our Common Home, Five Years after Laudato Si'*. Vatican City: Libreria Editrica Vaticana, 2020.

Ioannes Paulus Pp. II. *Litterae Apostolicae, Inter Sanctoss, Franciscus Assisiensis Caelestis Patronus Oecologiae Cultorum Eligitur.* https://www.vatican.va/content/john-paul-ii/la/apost_letters/1979/documents/hf_jp-ii_apl_19791129_inter-sanctos.html.

Luc Bouchard. Bishop of the Diocese of St. Paul in Alberta, Canada. *A Pastoral Letter on the Integrity of Creation, and the Athabasca Oil Sands.* 2009. https://omiusajpic.org/wp-content/uploads/2009/02/2009-January-25-Tar-Sands-Pastoral-Letter.pdf.

Pope Francis. *Encyclical Letter Laudato Si' of the Holy Father Francis on Care for Our Common Home.* https://www.vatican.va/content/francesco/en/encyclicals/documents/papa-francesco_20150524_enciclica-laudato-si.html.

Pope John Paul II. *Letter of His Holiness John Paul II to Reverend George V. Coyne, S.J. Director of the Vatican Observator.* http://www.vatican.va/content/john-paul-ii/en/letters/1988/documents/hf_jp-ii_let_19880601_padre-coyne.html.

Pope Leo XIII. *Aeterni Patris*, Encyclical of Pope Leo XIII on the Restoration of Christian Philosophy, 1879, §14. https://www.vatican.va/content/leo-xiii/en/encyclicals/documents/hf_l-xiii_enc_04081879_aeterni-patris.html.

Pope Paul VI. *Octogesima Adveniens*, Apostolic Letter of Pope Paul VI. https://www.vatican.va/content/paul-vi/en/apost_letters/documents/hf_p-vi_apl_19710514_octogesima-adveniens.html.

Pope Pius XII. *Divino Afflante Spiritu.* https://www.vatican.va/content/pius-xii/en/encyclicals/documents/hf_p-xii_enc_30091943_divino-afflante-spiritu.html.

Synod of Bishops Special Assembly for the Pan-Amazonian Region. *The Amazon: New Paths for The Church and for an Integral Ecology—Final Document.* Vatican. October 26, 2019. http://www.vatican.va/roman_curia/synod/documents/rc_synod_doc_20191026_sinodo-amazzonia_en.html.

The Pontifical Council for Justice and Peace. "Towards Reforming the International Finance and Monetary Systems in the Context of Global and Public Authority." https://www.vatican.va/roman_curia/pontifical_councils/justpeace/documents/rc_pc_justpeace_doc_20111024_nota_en.html.

United States Conference of Catholic Bishops. *Catholic Reflections on Food, Farmers and Farmworkers*, November 18, 2003. https://www.usccb.org/resources/i-was-hungry-you-gave-me-food-november-2003.

United States Conference of Catholic Bishops. *Global Climate Change a Plea for Dialogue Prudence and the Common Good.* June 15, 2001. https://www.usccb.org/resources/global-climate-change-plea-dialogue-prudence-and-common-good.

United States Conference of Catholic Bishops. *Socially Responsible Investment Guidelines 2021 for the United States Conference of Catholic Bishops*. https://www.usccb.org/resources/socially-responsible-investment-guidelines-2021-united-states-conference-catholic-bishops.

Vatican Council II. *Dei Verbum*. https://www.vatican.va/archive/hist_councils/ii_vatican_council/documents/vat-ii_const_19651118_dei-verbum_en.html.

Ecumenical and Interreligious Documents

National Religious Partnership for the Environment. "The Joint Appeal in Religion and Science: Statement by Religious Leaders at the Summit on Environment." New York City. June 3, 1991. https://fore.yale.edu/sites/default/files/files/Joint%20Appeal.pdf.

Suckling, Elena, Zach Christensen, and Dan Walton. *Poverty Trends: Global, Regional and National*. https://devinit.org/resources/poverty-trends-global-regional-and-national/.

United Nations Agency Data and Reports

AR6 Climate Change 2021: The Physical Science Basis. https://www.ipcc.ch/report/ar6/wg1/.

Guterres, António. "IPCC report: 'Code Red' for Human Driven Global Heating, Warns UN Chief." https://news.un.org/en/story/2021/08/1097362.

IPCC. *AR6 Climate Change 2021*. The Physical Science Basis—Summary for Policymakers. 2021, A.1.8. https://www.ipcc.ch/report/ar6/wg1/downloads/report/IPCC_AR6_WGI_SPM_final.pdf.

The EC—FAO Food Security Programme. "An Introduction to the Basic Concepts of Food Security." FAO, 2008. https://www.fao.org/3/al936e/al936e.pdf.

UN Food and Agriculture Organization. "UN Report: Global Hunger Numbers Rose to as Many as 828 Million in 2021." https://www.fao.org/newsroom/detail/un-report-global-hunger-SOFI-2022-FAO/en.

UN General Assembly. *Resolution 64/292 The Human Right to Water and Sanitation.* July 28, 2010. https://www.un.org/waterforlifedecade/human_right_to_water.shtml.

UNFAO. State of Food and Agriculture 2021, https://www.fao.org/publications/sofa/sofa-2021/en/.

World Health Organization—Drinking-Water. March 21, 2022. https://www.who.int/news-room/fact-sheets/detail/drinking-water.

United States Government Agency Data and Reports

Economic Research Service, US Department of Agriculture, Food Security in the US, Key Statistics & Graphics. https://www.ers.usda.gov/topics/food-n.

National Aeronautics and Space Administration. Goddard Space Flight Center. https://ozonewatch.gsfc.nasa.gov/facts/SH.html.

US Environmental Protection Agency. "Environmental Justice." 2022. https://www.epa.gov/environmentaljustice.

US Environmental Protection Agency. Climate Change Science. "Basics of Climate Change." https://www.epa.gov/climatechange-science/basics-climate-change.

US Environmental Protection Agency. "EPA Report Shows Disproportionate Impacts of Climate Change on Socially Vulnerable Populations in the United States." September 2, 2021. https://www.epa.gov/newsreleases/epa-report-shows-disproportionate-impacts-climate-change-socially-vulnerable.

US Food and Drug Administration. "Bottled Water Everywhere: Keeping It Safe." https://www.fda.gov/consumers/consumer-updates/bottled-water-everywhere-keeping-it-safe.

Encyclopedias, Dictionaries, Reference Works

Greenberg, Moshe Shmuel Safrai, and Aaron Rothkoff. "Sabbatical Year and Jubilee." In David L. Lieber, *Encyclopedia Judaica*, edited by Michael Berenbaum and Fred Skolnik, Vol. 17. Second Edition, 623–30. Detroit: Macmillan Reference USA, 2007.

Index

Locators followed by "n." indicate endnotes

Abrahamic religions 4, 13–14, 16–17
acceptatio 148, 155 n.44
ActionAid 223–4
agribusiness 194, 217, 219
agriculture 201, 219, 221
    agricultural land foodprint (footprint) 235
    industrial 219
    land use and 230
    liberalization 216–17
    petrochemicals 234
    production 217–18
    sustainable 220, 234
    in the United States 218
agroecological system 222–3
Aletti, Jean-Noël 123
Alexander of Hales 115
al-Ghazālī, A. H. 10
Amal 8
American Dream (Global Nightmare) 173
Apostolic Penitentiary, ecological offences 57, 162
Aqua fons vitae Orientations on Water: Symbol of the Cry of the Poor and the Cry of the Earth 200, 212 n.80
Aquinas, Thomas 6–7, 24, 51, 144–5
    Summa Theologica 14, 18 n.13
Archer Daniel Midlands 217
Aristotle 131 n.13
    entelechy principle 53, 63 n.39
    phronêsis 269
Ark (Genesis 6:16) 42 n.47
Armstrong, Regis J. 75–7, 156 n.55

Assisi Compilation 72
astute hope 6, 13–14
Athabasca Oil Sands 253–6
    Athabasca water shed, damage 254–5
    boreal forest ecosystem, destruction 254
    environmental impact 254
    greenhouse gases 255
    natural gas, heavy consumption 255
    toxic tailings ponds 255–6
At Home in the Web of Life 252
St. Augustine 24, 120

Babe of Bethlehem xi
Babylon 26–7, 31, 37
Bacon, Francis 101–2, 251
Baconian disaster 251
Barlow, Maude 195
Barr, James 29
Benedict XVI, Pope 200, 232–3, 238
Berezovsky, Sholom 26
Bergoglio, Jorge Mario. *See* Francis, Pope
Bernadone, Pietro 73
biblical hope 3–5
    cosmological 5–6
    epistemological 7
    ideological 7–8
biblical texts 3–4, 23, 39–40 n.19, 47, 198
    analogical sense 39 n.10
    interpretation 24–34, 39 nn.9–10, 40 n.19
    literal sense 39 n.9
    and science 24–34

Biden-Harris Bipartisan Infrastructure
    Law 263
Big Bang Theory 51–3
"Big Food" 220
biomass energy 264
Boff, Leonardo 52, 70, 72, 74, 85–6,
    174–6
Bohm, David 171
St. Bonaventure of Bagnoregio xiii–xiv,
    xvii, 24, 51, 53, 63 n.44, 65 n.69,
    73–6, 115, 137, 170, 258
  Christ-centered theology 116, 119,
    121
  circumincessio 54, 63 n.44
  contemplation and right action
    127–8
  creation and God 119
  fontalis plenitude 116
  imagination and metaphysics 116–18,
    131 n.13
  Imitatio Christi 267–8, 270
  The Journey of the Soul into God 126
  macrocosm 117–19
  material poverty 269
  Perpetual Vows 115
  philosophy and theology 127
  Quaest. Disp. de Myst. Trinitatis 128
  *On the Reduction of the Arts to
    Theology* 116, 131 n.12
  science and theology 127
  Seraphic Doctor 115–16, 118
  theology of Trinity xiv, 115, 121
  thought 116–19
bottled water case 193–4
Bouchard, Luc 252–4, 256
Bowe, Barbara 45, 49–50
  ktizō and *kosmos* 45–6, 61 n.7
  "Prologue" of the Gospel 49–50
Brady, Ignatius C. 156 n.55
Brueggemann, Walter 224
Brundtland Commission xv, 171
  Our Common Future 170
Bunge 217

Callicott, J. Baird 127
Camus, Albert 80
Canticle of the Creatures (St. Francis of
    Assisi) xiv, 31, 56, 72, 79–81, 83,
    176
  cosmic elements and human person
    83
  implications for praxis 84–6
  microcosm 83
  moral imagination 83–4
  relativizing function 84
Carbon Bubble 282
carbon capture sequestration (CCS) 260
Cargill 217
Caritas in Veritate (*CV*) 232, 248 n.103
Catechism of the Catholic Church 57, 64
    n.53, 170, 269
"Catholic Agenda for Action: Pursuing
    a More Just Agricultural System"
    231
Catholic Coalition on Climate Change
    256
*Catholic Reflections on Food, Farmers and
    Farmworkers* (USCCB) 230–1,
    241 n.15
Catholic Rural Life Conference of the
    United States 199, 230
Catholics xiii, 4, 24, 57, 69, 160, 172, 204,
    237, 256
  natural law 59
  subsidiarity 201
Catholic Social Teaching (CST) 40 n.23,
    150, 170, 224, 228, 252, 254, 256
  "Address to the World Food Summit"
    232–3
  *Catholic Reflections on Food, Farmers
    and Farmworkers* 230–1, 241 n.15
  Christian ethics and 256, 282
  ethics of eating 235–6
  food crisis 216
  fossil fuels and 252–3
  "Homily, at Living History Farms"
    (Paul II) 228–9

Laudato Si' 215–16, 233–4
oil sands extraction 254
Six Basic Principles of Catholic Social Teaching 230, 248 n.95
Strangers and Guests: Toward Community in the Heartland 229
Voices and Choices (Catholic Bishops of the US south) 229–30
water and 199–203
Chardin, Teilhard de 134 n.50
Christianity/Christians 3, 5, 12, 25, 76, 95, 98–9, 103, 124, 127–8, 143, 147, 159, 232, 238, 281. *See also* Jesus Christ
biodiversity 141
care 160–2
cosmic generosity 17
Creator God of Genesis 45
for decision-making 199
environmental ethics 258, 268
ethics and CST 197–9, 256, 282
hope 5, 8, 12–13
Irenaeus and Athanasius 124
Scriptures 4, 7, 22, 34–5, 45–7, 52, 256
simplicity 162, 172–3, 269
sustainability 14, 171, 257
virtue ethics 110 n.50, 253, 269
christification process 142
Christogenesis 121, 134 n.50
Christology (Bonaventure) xvii
cosmic dimensions 121–2
creation and Incarnation 120–1
Deep Incarnation 124–5
Franciscan theological tradition 119–20
Romans 8:18-27 125–6
Wisdom Sophia 122–4
Church's Social Teachings 162, 233
CIDSE 222
citizenship 166
St. Clare of Assisi xvii, 23–5, 34, 53, 78, 93, 101, 137, 214, 257
Abbess 94–6, 100

The Acts of the Process of Canonization (1254) 97, 101
climate emergency 96–101
community-minded living 94
community of footwashers 96
cosmic mutuality 104–5
courtesy and civility 96–7
engaging heart 95
example of humility 94
Form of Life (1253) 94, 96, 100, 104
humans 97–8
imperial ecology 101–2
The Legend of Saint Clare (1254–55) 96
Letters to Agnes of Prague 94–5, 99, 104
mutuality defined 103–4
poverty 99
power and kinds 102–3
reverence and respect 94
Rule 94, 98, 100
sacredness of creation 95
Second Letter to Blessed Agnes of Prague 22
The Testament (1247–53) 94–7, 104
classics 79–80
Clayton, Philip 52
Clifford, Anne M. 125
climate change xvii, 11–12, 16–17, 161–3, 202, 217, 221, 261, 264. *See also* denial, climate change
climate crisis xv–xvi
Climate Emergency xiii–xiv, xvi–xvii, 3–4, 11–12, 15–16, 22, 36–7, 44, 53, 56, 70, 72, 82–3, 93, 95, 102, 116, 119, 120, 128, 137, 149–51, 159–61, 164, 166–7, 174, 203, 227, 252, 256, 258, 265–7, 270, 281, 283
awareness 172
Clare's intervention 96–101
desperate responses 11
power-with 103, 105

Scotistic ethics 146–7
and sustainable living 122
Climate Refugee 161
Climate-Smart Power Systems 282
climate-sustainable economy 164
"Code Red" moment (IPCC) 55, 59, 160
cognitive-affective map (CAM) 12, 15–16
Coloe, Mary L., PBVM 124–5
Colombo, Claire Miller 122
Colossians 1:15–20 122–3
commanding hope 3, 11–14, 16–17
    astute hope 13–14
    honest hope 13, 15
    powerful hope 13–14
    social and complexity sciences 11
    tempered intelligence's pessimism 14
    will's optimism 14
Commodity Futures Trading Commission (Reagan Administration) 218
"Community Supported Agriculture" 236
Compendium of Social Doctrine of the Church 252
complexity science 3, 11–12, 15–17, 17 n.1
COP26 160, 170
Cornell University study 235–6
Cosmic Christ xii, 122–3
cosmic mutuality 103–5, 128
Covid-19 pandemic 85, 220–1, 223, 260
creation/redemption 4, 36, 45, 51, 59, 72, 116, 121, 126–7, 138–40, 144, 151, 172, 176, 257–8, 269
    beyond Genesis 30
    covenant 25, 28–9
    divine dynamism 54, 238, 270
    Sts. Francis, Clare, and biblical stories 22–3
    in Genesis 1–11 26–9
    Hebrew Testament texts, gleanings 33–4, 198, 256
    humans' dominion over nature 28–9
    and Incarnation 78–9, 120–1
    Neoplatonic cause of 53
    Prophets (Hosea and Jeremiah) 30–1
    Psalms 31–2
    Romans 8:18-27 125–6
    sacrament and ecological conversion x–xii, 72, 203
    second book of revelation 24
    Second Isaiah 30
    theology and virtue ethics xiii–xiv
    unity of the stories 25–6
    Wisdom literature 32–3
Crucified Jesus 72
crystalline waters 193
culture of care 172

Darragh, Neil 124
The Declaration of the Rights of Mother Earth 197
deification 142
Deism, god of 101
Dei Verbum (Vatican Council II) 4, 24, 39 n.19
Delio, Ilia 53–4
    circumincession 54, 63 n.44
    Emergent Christ 63 n.34
dēmiourgeō 45
denial, climate change 164
    climate complexity poses 167–9
    confirmation bias 164
    human-induced global warming 162–3
    human limitations and education (problem solving) 166
    individualism, consumerism, and "technocratic paradigm" 167, 171, 177
    media, role 166
    motivated reasoning and 164
    personal psychosocial dynamics of 164
    psychological and cognitive limits 164–5

sociopolitical and economic
    dynamics 165-6
writ large and inaction 165
Descartes, René 101-2
Dhaka Water Supply and Sewage
    Authority (DWSSA) 198-9
di Bernardone, Giovanni Francesco. *See*
    St. Francis of Assisi
Dicastery for Promoting Integral Human
    Development 200
disaster events (United States) 161
Divine 25, 28, 49, 52-4, 56, 81, 126, 133
    n.48, 138, 270
  dynamism 54, 63 n.44
  exemplarity 117, 127
  hope 17
  human and, relationship 145-6
  and human realms 50
  image 70, 85, 99
  revelation 37, 77, 121, 138-9, 141,
    145
double-think syndrome 165
Douglas-Klotz, Neil 52
Doyle, Eric 81
  heart sight 98
Drinking Water Surveillance Program
    (DWSP) 195

eco-agricultural system 223
Eco Bible (Neril & Dee) 41 n.29, 42 n.47
ecocidal practices 165, 221
ecocide 58-9, 65 n.66, 159, 163, 165, 171,
    197, 281
ecojustice xv, 170, 256-7, 260, 263-6,
    252
ecology (ecological) 143
  conversion x-xii, 60, 119, 162, 172
  crisis xii, 31, 172
  destruction 58, 163, 251
  Ecological Footprint xiv
  economics 178
  emergency 51, 58, 71, 85
  and environmental ethics 141

sin xiv, xvi-xvii, 57, 65 n.60
vocation 83, 100, 159, 163, 172, 198,
    258
economics xv, 149, 177-8, 227-8
The Economy of Francesco 177
economy of God xv
ecosystems xiv-xv, 58, 72, 102, 104, 124,
    160, 162, 169-70, 193, 195-6, 252,
    254, 260, 265, 267
ecotheology xvii, 74, 77, 117, 137
  Incarnation deified creation 78
  relationship with Christ, authentic
    humanness 78-9
  Scotistic theology and 151
  world is good 77
Edwards, Denis 63 n.44, 123-4
egalitarian relationships 27
Elgin, Duane 173
Elimate Emergency xv
El Niño Southern Oscillation (ENSO)
    191
emergence theory 53
encyclical 4, 24, 36, 39 n.18, 40 n.23,
    58, 69, 162, 177. *See also specific
    encyclical*
Energy Policy Act (2005) 261
energy sources 252, 256, 259. *See also*
    fossil fuels
  ecojustice 256-7
  energy policy guidelines 258
  participation 257-8
  solidarity 258
  sufficiency 257
  sustainability xvii, 257, 281
The Enuma Elish (Babylonian creation
    myth) 27
environmental ecology 85
environmental education 166, 172-3, 234
environmental literacy 166
'eretz 224-5
Eros 174-5
escape market logic 199
Esser, Kajetan 62 n.14

Eucharist/Eucharistic feast 76, 237–8
European Green Deal strategy 160
European Renewable Energy Council 262
Evangelical Lutheran Church in America (ELCA) 256
evolutionary sciences 186 n.94
evolutionary worldview 6, 51–2, 121

Fair Labor Standards Act 230
Fakhri, Michael 222
fate (cosmological setting) 5–6
fear 7, 9–10, 14, 16–17, 82, 176, 193, 226, 228
Ferris, Timothy 127
The Final Document of the Amazonian Synod xvi, 57–8
food
    deprivation 215
    Eucharistic feast 237–8
    feasting and fasting 236–7
    hope-filled vision 239
    insecurity 167, 202, 219, 223, 232, 239
    security 201, 215, 221, 231–2
    systems 239, 245 n.52
food crisis (2008 & 2022)
    access to 216–19
    agriculture in the United States 218
    commodities 218
    concentration and vertical integration 218–19
    Declaration of the World Summit on Food Security-November 2009 (Rome) 219–20
    EAT-*Lancet* 220
    efforts toward correction of 219–20
    food production efficiency 217
    Leviticus 25 227–8
    Model National Dietary Guidelines 220
    movement toward 220–3
    Sustainable Development Goals 220–2
    UN Food Systems Summit (2021) 222–3
    UN Millennium Development Goals 219–20
    World Food Systems Summit (2021) 221–2
food-deficit Africa 216
Ford, John T., *St. Mary's Glossary* 65 n.67
fossil fuels xii, 69, 160, 165, 173, 217, 223, 234, 281–2
    biomass 264
    coal 259–60
    consumption 167
    and early CST 252–3
    genuine *vs.* false hope 267
    geothermal 265
    hydrogen 266
    hydropower 264–5
    marine energy 266
    natural gas 261
    nuclear power 261–2
    oil 260
    solar energy 262–3
    wind 263
fracking 260–1
Franciscan Action Network 256
St. Francis of Assisi x–xi, xvii, 22, 24–5, 27, 34, 44, 53–4, 62 n.14, 69, 93, 115–16, 120, 132 n.35, 137, 149, 156 n.55, 159, 170, 173, 174, 214, 224, 236, 239, 257, 267–8, 282
    The Admonitions VII 35
    Canticle of the Creatures (*see* Canticle of the Creatures (St. Francis of Assisi))
    Christocentric teaching 70
    death acceptance 174–6
    "*Deus meus et omnia*" ("My God and my all") 74
    The Earlier Rule 77
    ecotheology 74
    feasting and fasting 236–7
    Fifth Admonition 72
    footprints of Jesus xi–xiv, 22, 36, 53, 59, 78, 151, 236
    God with nature 73–4

joy and mercy of God 175
mentor and model 56–7
A Mirror of Perfection of the Status of a Lesser Brother 192
A Mirror of Perfection, Rule, Profession, Life and True Calling of a Lesser Brother, 24 234
moral formation 174–5
mutual deference 97
nature mystic 70
ontological poet 70
perception of the world 76–7
poetry 72–4, 81
prayer 74
radical poverty 74, 79
Regula Bulata 156 n.55
rules 23
sacrament of baptism 71
sacredness of creation 86, 95
Salutation to the Virtues 73, 97
Second Admonition 76
"Sister Death" 82
Source of Life, identification 176–7
spiritual conversion 69, 71, 81
spirituality 116
stigmata 80
sympathy and synergy 79
Testament 23, 75, 173
theological reflection process (*see* theological reflection process)
as vernacular theologian 120
Francis, Pope xvi, xix n.22, 25, 37, 57, 65 n.65, 69, 72, 100, 166–9, 171–2, 174, 177, 221, 238
    integral ecology 84
    Laudato Si'—On the Care for Our Common Home (*LS*) xii–xiii, xvi–xvii, 36, 40 n.23, 54, 57–8, 69–71, 84, 86, 101, 128, 150, 162–3, 170, 172, 177–8, 200, 203–4, 215–16, 233–4, 252, 281
    "less is more" (biblical mantra) 172
    and *Querida Amazonia* 57–8
    sustainable diversified agriculture 234

Friars 23, 81, 178
    Minor 81, 136
    montes pietatis 178

Gale Virtual Reference Library Dictionary 109 n.30
genetically modified organisms (GMOs) 231
genuine hope 13, 267
geothermal energy 265
geothermal heat pumps (GSHPs) 265
Glasgow COP26 160
Global Biodiversity Outlook 5 report 84
Global Climate Change (2001) 162, 252–3
Global Concerns Committee 194
global industrial food system 215, 217, 227
The Globalization of the Technocratic Paradigm 71
Global Methane Pledge (COP26) 160
global warming 16, 150–1, 160, 162, 168, 170–1, 202, 221, 251–3, 256, 260–1, 281
    aggregate effect 167
    human-induced 163, 167
    personal psychosocial dynamics of denial 164
    psychological and cognitive limits 164–5
global water crisis 187
    access to water 189
    pollution 190
    water politics, environmental justice, and virtual water 191–2
    water scarcity 190–1
God xiv, xvii, 5–6, 17, 25, 31, 34, 48, 51, 71, 81, 144, 175, 224, 237, 257, 268, 282
    creation (*see* creation/redemption)
    economy of xv
    faithful love 118
    of Israel 5, 25–7, 30–1, 227
    joy and mercy 174–5
    as Lord (*Rabb*) 9

Pharaoh rule 6
predominates, ways 123–4
reality and relationships 147–9
self-revelation 118, 121, 126, 137, 141
way of naming 77
"God So Loved the World" movement 44
Gospel of John 45, 59, 62 n.14, 124
"Bread of Life" discourse 50
Jesus as Wisdom of God 48–50
Prologue 48–50, 124
greenhouse gas (GHG) emissions xv, 69, 150, 164–5, 167–70, 173–4, 217, 221, 254–5, 259, 261–2, 264, 266
Green Revolution 216, 218
Gregersen, Niels Henrik 53
deep incarnation 125
Guardini, Romano xii
The End of the Modern World 101
Guinan, Michael D. 49
Guterres, António xiii, 160

haecceitas
principle 140–2
spirituality 143–5
Haeckel, Ernest 34, 85
Harrison, Wildung 102
Hathaway, Mark 52
Hayes, Zachary 26, 51, 117–19, 121, 127
Hebrew Testament 4, 22, 25, 30, 198, 224
gleanings from 33–4
God 26–7, 29, 45, 48–9, 124, 256, 267
"subdue" (*kābās*) 29
Wisdom Woman of 34
Hellenistic Judaism 45
Hellwig, Monika 238
Hoebing, Phil 117, 127
Holy Communion 238
Holy Qur'an 8–9, 19 n.27. *See also* qur'anic hope
Holy Spirit 74, 76, 100, 203
Holy Water 203–5
Homer-Dixon, Thomas 11, 15, 20 n.62
cognitive-affective mapping tool 12
commanding hope 11–14, 16–17

Commanding Hope: The Power We Have to Renew a World in Peril 11, 17 n.1
defining hope 12
fear 14
home systems (ecosystems) xv. *See also* ecosystems
honest hope 13, 15
wisdom and imagination 15
hoodoos and oil sands 251–2
hope 3, 32, 36–7, 126, 202–4, 216, 283
biblical (*see* biblical hope)
food system 239
genuine *vs.* false 267
harmonizing 16–17
imagination and possibilities 14–16
qur'anic (*see* qur'anic hope)
World Food Summit (Rome, 2009) 219–20
Hopkins, Gerard Manley 144
Hosea (prophet) 30–1, 125
human-nature relationships 28–9, 121, 126
human will
and affections 146–7
and freedom of choice 147–8
humility 94, 106, 268
hunger 214–15, 222–4, 232, 237, 239
Hurricane Katrina 210 n.38
hydrogen 266
hydropower 264–5
Hydropower Sustainability Standards 265

Ignorance Based World View (IBWV) 268
imago Dei 6, 70, 94, 121, 142, 230, 258
Imitatio Christi (St. Bonaventure) 267
practices of divesting and investing 270
and virtue ethics 267–8
imperial ecology 101–2
vs. kinship of creation 251–2
"Man the Maker" (*homo faber*) 102

impunity 69, 162
Incarnation xi–xii, xv, 45, 50, 59, 70, 72, 94, 105, 117, 121, 126, 154 n.15, 238, 270
    Bonaventure's Christology 120–1, 124–5
    deifies creation 78
    as God's Masterpiece 141–3
Industrial Revolution 160, 167
Ingham, Mary Beth 140, 142, 146, 151
    faculty psychology 155 n.39
    Scotus for Dunces 155 n.45
integral ecology xii, 58, 84, 104, 177
Interdicasterial Working Group of the Holy See on Integral Ecology (Vatican) xiii, 177, 282
Intergovernmental Panel on Climate Change (IPCC) xv, 6, 55, 168, 202
    AR Six Report 168
    Climate Change 2021: The Physical Science Basis Scientists 55
    Fourth Assessment Report 271 n.1
    Scientific Assessment 168
    Sixth Assessment Report 84, 160
International Association of Penal Law (Rome) 57, 65 n.65
"International Trade, Aid, and Development" 231
International Union for Conservation of Nature (IUCN) 84
Iranian system 198
Isaiah (prophet) 28, 46–7, 227, 237
Islam (Muslims) 3–4, 8, 12, 17, 237, 281
    cosmic generosity 17
    qur'anic hope (*see* qur'anic hope)

Jeremiah (prophet) 30–1, 125
    mournful dirge 31
Jesus Christ xi–xii, 7, 22, 35–6, 45, 52–3, 59, 99, 121–3, 143, 151, 227, 258, 269, 280 n.109
    disciples 46, 48, 50, 204
    haecceitas of God 142

"Inaugural Address" 46–7, 267
Incarnation xii, 22–3, 59, 70, 93, 96, 98, 119, 122, 141–2, 172, 270
    Wisdom of God in Gospel of John 34, 48–50
Jews 4, 12, 34, 281
    cosmic generosity 17
    hope 5, 8, 13
Johnson, Elizabeth A. 47
Journeying towards Care for Our Common Home (*JCTOCH*) xiii, 177, 282
Jubilee Year 46–7, 225–7
Judaism 3, 5, 8, 12, 17, 34, 45
Jung, L. Shannon 235

Karo, Isaac 41 n.39
Karris, Robert J. 122–3
Kay, Jeanne 34
Killer Heat in the United States: Climate Choices and the Future of Dangerously Hot Days 282
Kittredge, Cynthia Briggs 122
Knowledge Based World View (KBWV) 210 n.38, 268
Kofe, Simon 160
kosmos 45–6, 61 n.7
Kostigan, Thomas M. 191–2

Lady Chiara di Favarone di Offreducio. *See* St. Clare of Assisi
Lady Ortulana 93, 96
Lady Wisdom 33, 48, 122
Lancet's Commission on Obesity 221
Land-Based Wind Market Report: 2022 Edition 263
Leadership Conference of Women Religious 194
Lectura 156 n.46
Leibush, Meir 42 n.47
lepers 72, 75, 78, 159, 170, 173
LePlace, Pierre Simon 102
Lesser Brothers 96–7
Levelized Cost of Energy 262

Leviticus 25 46–7, 215, 225–7, 230, 257, 267
    ecological well-being of land 226
    'eretz 224–5
    holiness 225–6
    "land" system 225
    land use and food crisis 227–8
    "Principles of Land Stewardship" 229
    royal ideology 225
living souls/creatures 26
Lombard, Peter, *Sentences* 136
love xi, 34, 36, 46, 50, 54, 59, 71–2, 81–2, 95–6, 99, 103, 105, 117–18, 122, 126, 137–9, 144, 147–8, 151, 232, 256–7, 269
Luke (Synoptic Gospel) 46, 227, 267

Macquarrie, John 5
Macy, Joanna 171
Magdalene, Mary 50
magnanimity 7, 17
Maguire, Daniel C. 4–8
    ideology, defining 7
    The New English Bible 18 n.7
Mahoney, Tim 217
malkuta 52
Māori 197
Marcel, Gabriel 176
Marduk (god) 27
marine energy 266
Marks, Gil 42 n.39
Martin-Schramm, James B. 257, 261
Maslow, Abraham, hierarchy of needs 170
Massynbaerde Ford, Josephine 49–50
material poverty 76, 269
Matthew (Synoptic Gospel) 48, 99
Mcfood culture 236
McGrail, Peter 203, 238
McGregor, Sue 171
mental ecology 85
Merton, Thomas 77
Midrash 42 n.47
mono-cropping 217, 227
Monsanto 217–18

Mosaic 217
Mulholland, Séamus 143–4
Murtagh, Thomas 71
mutuality 74, 98, 100, 102–5, 128, 142, 148, 151

Nairn, Thomas A., moral imagination 83–4
Nairobi's Kibera Slum (SODIS) 189
National Catholic Rural Life Conference 230, 235
natural law 59, 65 n.67, 145–6, 177
Nebuchadnezzar 31
Neoplatonic philosophy 98
Neo-Platonism 109 n.37, 117
New Covenant 47, 227
New Creation 30–1, 34, 59, 227. *See also* creation/redemption
    evolutionary worldview 51–2
    immense 51
    interrelated 51
    Jesus' "Inaugural Address" 46–7
    Lady Wisdom and Jesus 48–50
    original creation and 47
    planet Earth, unique 51–2
    Reign of God 47, 52–4, 75, 99, 146, 176, 258
    rich heritage 45–6
    Synoptic Gospels 47–8
    unfinished 51
"New Forms of Social Sin" 57, 162
"New Jerusalem" 102
New Testament 34, 45, 48, 70, 74, 122
Newton, Isaac 51, 102
Noahic covenant 28–31, 37, 42 n.47, 81, 100
non-point source pollution 190
North American Free Trade Agreement (NAFTA) 191

obedience 73, 97, 115, 269
obesity 214, 221
Off-Shore Wind Market Report (2022) 263
oikos xv, 84, 170–1
oikumēnē xiv–xv

O'Murchu, Diarmuid 171, 174
opulent water waste 210 n.39
Osborne, Kenan B. 140

Pablo Solon 196
"Paths of Pastoral Conversion" 58
Patriarch Bartholomew, Ecumenical xvi, 57, 100, 162
St. Paul 35, 48, 70, 125, 251–3, 267
Paul II, Pope John 69, 132 n.35, 162, 199–200, 252
   "Homily, at Living History Farms" 228–9
Pauline community 123
Paul VI, Pope 162, 202
Peoples Conference in Bolivia (2010) 197
Peters, Chris 235
Peterson, Ingrid J. x, xiii
philosophy 83, 98, 109 n.37, 117, 127, 131 n.16, 137, 149, 151
Pius XII, Pope, *Divino Afflante Spiritu* 4, 24
planning 7
Plato 109 n.37, 117
Plotinus 109 n.37
   emanation doctrine 53
Policy of the Investment Committee of the Holy See 252, 282
Pontifical Justice and Peace Commission (PJPC) 150, 156 n.57, 188, 200–2
Poor Christ 71, 93, 105
Poor Ladies of San Damiano (Poor Clares) 22–3, 93–6, 98, 104
Population Services International 189
potentia absoluta 139
potentia ordinata 139
poverty xii, xv, 9, 72–6, 79, 82, 85–6, 98–100, 119, 169–70, 190, 230–2, 257, 269
powerful hope 13–14
The Precautionary Principle 268, 279 nn.100–1
Presbyterian Church in the Unites States (PCUSA) 256

pricing, water 191, 195, 198
Primacy and Predestination of Christ 142–3
Principles for Ethical Eaters 235
privatization, water 194–6, 198
Privilege of Poverty 97
prudence 147, 253, 261–2, 268–9
Psalms 31–2, 197, 257
   Psalm 146 32, 47
   Psalm 104 (Franciscan Psalm) 31–2
Pseudo-Dionysius, goodness 116–17, 120
public health crisis 159
Pur 189
Purifier of Water 189

qur'anic hope 3, 8–9
   fear (*khawf*) 9–10
   hope and fear 10, 17
   hope (*rajā*) 10
   Infagh 9
   monotheism 8
   prophecy 8
   resurrection day 8
   zekr 8

rainwater harvesting systems 189
raja 8–10
Rasmussen, Larry xv
Regent Master of the Franciscan School 115
Reid, Duncan 124
renewable energy sources 224, 234, 252, 259–63, 269, 281. *See also* energy sources
Resolution 64/292 the Human Right to Water and Sanitation 196, 201
Resurrection 47, 227
Richard of St. Victor 117, 120
Roman Catholicism 40 n.19, 40 n.23
Romans 8:18-27 125–6
Rome Statute, crimes 58–9
rûah (Spirit of God) 27, 32, 34, 159

Index

Sacks, Lord Jonathan 41 n.29
Sacred Scriptures xi, 22–4, 35–6, 228
    analogical sense 39 n.10
    literal sense 39 n.9
Sacrosanctum Concilium 204, 213 n.109
scarcity, water 190–1, 195, 200, 202, 218, 233
Schneiders, Sandra 46
Scotus, John Duns xvii, 24, 128, 156 n.46
    contingency 138
    De Primo Principio (A Treatise on God as First Principle) 143, 147
    essential order, principle 145–6
    ethics and Climate Emergency 146–7
    First Principle, God as 137–9
    fundamental considerations 150
    God's power 139–40
    haecceitas 140–1, 143–5
    Incarnation as God's masterpiece 141–3
    loving creator, God 139
    metaphysical wing of St. Francis 136–7
    metaphysician 137
    Ordinatio I 156 n.46
    Ordinatio III 154 n.15, 156 n.51
    Quodlibetal Questions 148
    reality and relationships 147–9
    Reportatio 154 n.15
    subsidiarity and solidarity 150
    Subtle Doctor 136, 140, 142
    sustainable economic life 148–9
    theology and philosophy for ecotheology 151
    univocity of being, theory of 144
"Second Isaiah" 30
Selby, David, education for contraction 172
Short, William 70, 144
sin xvi, 8, 10, 26, 28–9, 31, 34, 36, 45, 57–8, 64 n.53, 75–6, 86, 121, 123, 125, 142, 162, 176. *See also* ecology (ecological), sin

Smerilli, Alessandra, Sr. 177
social ecology 85
social justice xv, 170, 252
Socially Responsible Investment Guidelines (2021, USCCB) 252, 281
solar energy 252, 262–3
special revelation, theory 24
Spirit of God. *See rûah* (Spirit of God)
spiritual malaise 82, 122, 174
Stainer, John, *The Crucifixion* 44
"The State of the Planet" report xiii
state space 15–16
Stockdale, James 11
Stockholm Water Symposium (2000) 195
The Stop Ecocide Foundation 59
suicidal option (cosmological setting) 5–6
sustainability xiv–xv, 34, 98, 199, 220, 257, 260, 262–4
    intoxication to 170–1
    sustainable development/living xv, 37, 122, 160, 170, 274 n.24, 279 n.101
    sustainable energy 69
Swiss-pioneered solar disinfection process (SODIS) 189
Synoptic Gospels 46–8

Tamanna 8
Ten Commandments 146
theological reflection process 51, 70, 74, 86, 127
    penance 75
    poverty 75–6
    prayer 76–7
This Land Is Home to Me 252
Thomas of Celano 71, 73, 78
    "The Life of St. Francis," XXIX, 81 55
    "The Remembrance of the Desire of the Soul (1245–1247)" 266
threshold effects 168
Toolan, David, imperial ecology 101
Torah 29, 49, 225, 247 n.81
toxins, discharging 190, 208 n.25

Tracy, David 15
  The Analogical Imagination 79–80
tragedy (cosmological setting) 5–6
Trinity xii, xiv, 54, 116, 128, 156 n.46
  ad intra and extra 147–8
  as divine exemplarity 117
  mutuality 148
truth 7, 13, 16, 55, 116, 118, 137
Turkson, Peter 221
Turner, R. Eugene 268

Umbrian economy 94
uncertainty 168–9
UN Conference on Environment and Development Dublin 200
UN Convention on Biological Diversity 84
UN Food Systems Summit (2021) 216, 221–3
UN High Commission on Refugees 161
UN Human Rights Council 196–7
UN International Decade for Action on Water for Sustainable Development 202
United Food and Commercial Workers International Union (UFCW) 230
United Nations Development Program 85
United Nations Food and Agriculture Organization (UNFAO) 215, 219–23
United States Conference of Catholic Bishops (USCCB) 230–1, 241 n.15, 252, 256, 281–2
  Catholic Reflections on Food, Farmers and Farmworkers 230–1, 241 n.15
  Global Climate Change 252–3
  Renewing the Earth 252–3
Universal Declaration of Human Rights (1948) 197
UN Millennium Development Goals 219–20, 243 n.35

UN Sustainable Development Goal 189, 220–2
UN World Food Program 221, 223
US Energy Information Administration (EIA) 259
US Gulf Coast 253

vernacular theology xvii, 120
virtual water 191–2
von Rad, Gerhardt 32

water xvi–xvii, 71, 224, 232–3. *See also* global water crisis
  of baptism 203–4
  bottled water 193–4
  Christian ethics 197–9
  conservation techniques 201
  consumption 188
  and CST 199–203
  culture of 192–3, 202
  decision-making considerations 199
  and Holy Water 203–5
  human right with challenges 196–7
  hydrologic cycle 188, 193
  privatization of drinking water 194–6
WaterAid 198
Water: An Essential Element for Life (2003) 200
Water: An Essential Element for Life: An Update (2006) 200
Water.Org reports 187
Wiesel, Elie 6
wind energy 263
Wirzba, Norman 221
wisdom (*Hôkmah/Sophia*) 32–3, 48, 122–4
Wisdom Woman 34, 49
Wolter, Allan B. 155 n.40
Word of God 22, 50, 70, 73, 99
world xv, 27, 46, 70–1, 77–8, 83, 93, 117–19, 138–9, 142–3, 151, 172, 199, 258
  and continues sustaining 45–6

economic systems 139, 232
future consummation 124
natural xiv, xvi, 23–5, 27, 31, 47–8, 57, 59, 81, 85, 100, 162, 203, 233
as *oikumēnē* xiv
as second book of revelation 24
worldviews 15–16, 20 n.70, 51–2, 95, 105, 115, 121, 164

World Council of Churches (WCC) 256
World Economic Forum 169, 187
World Trade Organization (WTO) 191
World Water Council 200
World Water Forum 200
Worster, David 101
Worth, Jess 165

www.ingramcontent.com/pod-product-compliance
Lightning Source LLC
Chambersburg PA
CBHW051628230426
43669CB00013B/2221